INCENTIVES, ORGANIZATION, AND PUBLI(

The Editors wish to thank Cornell University and the Society for Economic Analysis Limited for the generous financial support they have provided to assist this project.

Incentives, Organization, and Public Economics

Papers in Honour of Sir James Mirrlees

Edited by
PETER J. HAMMOND
GARETH D. MYLES

OXFORD
UNIVERSITY PRESS

OXFORD
UNIVERSITY PRESS

Great Clarendon Street, Oxford OX2 6DP
Oxford University Press is a department of the University of Oxford.
It furthers the University's objective of excellence in research, scholarship,
and education by publishing worldwide in

Oxford New York

Athens Auckland Bangkok Bogotá Buenos Aires Calcutta
Cape Town Chennai Dar es Salaam Delhi Florence Hong Kong Istanbul
Karachi Kuala Lumpur Madrid Melbourne Mexico City Mumbai
Nairobi Paris São Paulo Shanghai Singapore Taipei Tokyo Toronto Warsaw

and associated companies in Berlin Ibadan

Oxford is a registered trade mark of Oxford University Press
in the UK and certain other countries

Published in the United States
by Oxford University Press Inc., New York

British Library Cataloguing in Publication Data
Data available

Library of Congress Cataloging in Publication Data
Incentives, organization, and public economics : papers in honour of Sir James Mirrlees /
    edited by Peter J. Hammond, Gareth D. Myles.
        p. cm.
    Includes bibliographical references and index.
    1. Microeconomics. 2. Mirrlees, James A. I. Hammond, Peter J. II. Myles, Gareth D.
III. Mirrlees, James A.
    HB172.I57 2000   330—dc21   00–060686

ISBN 0-19-924229-1

10 9 8 7 6 5 4 3 2 1

Typeset by Graphicraft Limited, Hong Kong
Printed in Great Britain
on acid-free paper by
Biddles Ltd., Guildford & King's Lynn

CONTENTS

Part I

PERSPECTIVE

1 Introduction

PETER J. HAMMOND AND GARETH D. MYLES

Professor Sir James Mirrlees was born in Minnigaff, Scotland in 1936. His university education was at Edinburgh University from 1954–7, then at Trinity College, Cambridge from 1957–63. He was awarded the Nobel Prize in Economics in 1996 in recognition of his work on optimal income taxation and its extension to information and incentive problems in general. He was subsequently awarded a knighthood in the first Honours List of the new Labour Government, in 1997.

During his career at Trinity College, Cambridge, up to 1968, then at Nuffield College, Oxford, from 1968 to 1995, and subsequently back at Trinity, he has undertaken the supervision of many students and engaged in several fruitful research collaborations. This volume, due to be published shortly before his 65th birthday, is the opportunity for a small sample of those students and co-authors to express their admiration for what Jim has contributed to economics as author, colleague, and teacher.

Jim attended school in Newton Stewart, near his birthplace in the south-west corner of Scotland. There he developed an early interest in mathematics under the guidance of a particularly helpful teacher. This interest and his rapid progress eventually led to him being admitted directly into the second year of the mathematics degree at Edinburgh University, thus shortening the programme from its standard four years to just three. He had intended to sit the Cambridge scholarship examination earlier but sudden illness prevented this. In his final year at Edinburgh he finally was able to sit the scholarship examination, and was duly awarded a grant to complete a second undergraduate degree at Cambridge. He arrived in Trinity College, Cambridge in 1957 to enter Part II of the Cambridge Mathematics Tripos.

Parts I and II of the tripos are sufficient to earn a degree from Cambridge, whereas Part III represents preparation for research. Jim obtained a first-class result in Part II and consequently became a 'wrangler'. He also completed Part III with distinction, which made him eligible to be admitted for research in mathematics. But by this time his interests were beginning to move towards the social sciences. Like many other economists, his motivation to pursue the subject arose from observing social problems which he believed that economics should be able to solve. In Jim's case, it seems to have been a concern for the poverty he saw reported in less developed countries that encouraged him to apply his mathematical skills in the service of economic science.

A grant from the Department of Scientific and Industrial Research provided Jim with three years of funding to undertake his Ph.D. The first year of this was spent following the Diploma in Economics, a special qualification designed to help students trained in other subjects convert to economics, and make them eligible to begin a Ph.D. This provided the opportunity to attend the lectures of several eminent Cambridge economists of the time. Having passed the Diploma, Jim was assigned as a research student to Richard Stone who involved him in the newly launched Programme for Growth. As a consequence Jim was introduced to Ramsey's work on optimal saving, about which Stone (1955) himself had written a few years earlier, before other mathematical economists began applying the new techniques of control theory to the problem.

It was in growth theory that Jim made his first significant contributions to economics. Initially, his particular concern was with technical progress. Kaldor (1957, 1961) had earlier developed growth models in which the usual production function relating output to capital was replaced by a 'technical progress function' relating the growth rate of output to the growth rate of capital. In Kaldor's work, such technical progress would apply throughout the economy, regardless of whether a firm was using old or new capital. Following the 'putty–clay' or vintage capital model devised by Johansen (1959) and Salter (1960), the new paper by Kaldor and Mirrlees (1962) assumed that technical progress could only be embodied in new investment. More specifically, there was a new technical progress function making the growth rate of productivity per worker operating on new machines an increasing concave function of the growth rate of investment per worker. The paper was published as the second article in the June 1962 issue of the *Review of Economic Studies*, in a symposium on production functions and economic growth that began with Arrow's (1962) famous paper on learning by doing. In many ways, along with Arrow's paper, it was an early precursor of what has since become known as 'endogenous growth theory', with inherent externalities between different firms' investment decisions.

Technical progress played an important role in two other major early works by Jim. The problem of optimal growth in an economy subject to deterministic technical change was extensively discussed in Mirrlees (1967). An early version of the paper had been presented to the Econometric Society meeting in Zurich, 1964. It was another contribution to a *Review of Economic Studies* symposium, this time on 'Problems in the Theory of Optimal Accumulation'. Not content with treating just deterministic technical change, Jim also tackled the much harder problem when technical change was governed by a stochastic diffusion process in continuous time. This was truly pioneering work. A fundamental insight was the observation that increased uncertainty would often lead to more saving, not less. The results emerged in his Ph.D. dissertation, 'Optimal Accumulation under Uncertainty'. Sadly, the dissertation remained mostly unpublished, but papers from it such as Mirrlees (1965) still had an impact, judging from the citations they received in connection with the early development of stochastic continuous-time finance. Merton (1990), for example, makes his feeling of indebtedness to Jim's work quite evident. Some flavour of the analysis can be inferred from Mirrlees (1974*a*).

Research on the dissertation was interrupted for a year while Jim visited MIT and then travelled to New Delhi to join the India Project. It was at this time that the enormously fruitful collaboration with Peter Diamond began. There is no doubt that the time in India provided the impetus for the later work on cost–benefit analysis. In particular, experience of how public investment decisions were actually made contributed to the focus on developing practical methods for applying the theory of project appraisal.

Returning to Cambridge, Jim took up the teaching Fellowship at Trinity College which had been offered prior to leaving for India.

In 1968 Jim made the move from Cambridge to take up the Edgeworth Professorship of Economics at Nuffield College, Oxford. He was to remain there until returning to Cambridge in 1995. As a college without undergraduates, Nuffield afforded Jim the opportunity to concentrate all his teaching efforts upon graduate students from all over Oxford University. For many years a few of the best graduate students taking the Oxford M.Phil degree (or its precursor, the B.Phil.) would follow Jim's Mathematical Economics course. Following a tradition he had started in the Economics tripos in Cambridge, the course culminated in an exam containing open-ended questions that required candidates to show their ability at analysing or even developing entirely new theoretical models, rather than merely solving standard problems. Several significant papers are believed to have emerged from candidates who continued to develop their solutions after this examination.

During his time in Cambridge, Jim had begun to supervise a steady flow of Ph.D. students. After moving to Oxford, this flow turned into something of a flood. College records show the number of students he supervised to have reached the one hundred mark by the time of Jim's return to Cambridge—an average just fractionally short of four per year. These students now hold professorships throughout the world, in many of its leading academic institutions. In the UK, the number of Mirrlees students is particularly marked. Through this channel, Jim has had a considerable influence upon the academic economic environment in the UK. No doubt, it has been all the better for it.

There are many anecdotes that can be told of Jim's long years in Oxford. Perhaps it is just an urban myth, but the story is often told of the new graduate student or visitor to Nuffield who spent his first few months trying to figure out why someone who was clearly above average height should be described as 'Little-Mirrlees'. (Of course, had they read Robin Hood and so encountered Little John, they may not have questioned the name.) Others thought Little-Mirrlees was some lesser known paper as opposed to Big Mirrlees of 1971 and 1975. These mistaken epithets were neatly overturned some years later when Nuffield was home to both James Poterba and James Mirrlees—Little Jim and Big Jim respectively. Another anecdote concerns Jim's aversion to white boards, and especially to erasing anything written on such a board. So, during one seminar Jim gave at the University of Essex, those in the audience who knew of his aversion remained in suspense as the fairly extensive white board space gradually filled with equations. Would somebody have to volunteer to erase some material? Jim, however, managed the constraints of time and board space perfectly so that both were exhausted simultaneously, at what seemed an entirely natural conclusion to the seminar. What generations of nervous young Ph.D. students remember best, however, is ascending the staircase to Jim's office on the top floor past the watchful, and rather forbidding, portraits of Edgeworth and Nassau Senior (the latter having been the first Drummond Professor of Political Economy at Oxford). This created the effect of an unbroken timeline leading to the door of the incumbent and a sense of one's lowly place among the shadows beneath these giants of the discipline.

One can attain some appreciation of how much Jim's research has advanced economics by reviewing the achievements cited by the Nobel Prize committee. The papers on income taxation and moral hazard introduced the tools that have proved fundamental for tackling problems involving contract design in the presence of asymmetric information. That so much can be traced back to the work of a single author is quite remarkable. That it was all contained in such a small number of papers is even more so, at least for those who may not be aware of Jim's reluctance to publish anything other than superlative work. We shall begin by discussing the analysis of income taxation but, as will be seen, this is just one application of the greater whole that has emerged from Jim's work on information and incentives.

'An Exploration in the Theory of Optimum Income Taxation' was published in the *Review of Economic Studies* in April 1971, the final version having been received in October 1970. Hence, the publication of this volume coincides with the article's 30th anniversary. The stated intentions of the paper were to establish 'what principles should govern an optimum income tax; what such a tax schedule would look like; and what degree of inequality would remain once it was established' (ibid 175). Apart from a brief discussion in the last section of a remarkably prescient paper by Vickrey (1945), the prior literature on income taxation had failed to capture fully all the issues that are relevant in determining an optimum tax. As Jim so rightly observed, any proper normative analysis has to involve a motive to redistribute income because of endogenously generated inequality. Also, the tax had to create a disincentive affecting the supply of labour. In addition, the system had to be closed through the attainment of equilibrium. Most important, the model had to provide a reason for using an income tax rather than a system of first-best lump-sum taxes and subsidies. It was this latter requirement, and the issues of information transmission it raised, that proved to be so fundamental.

It is a measure of the model's success that it managed to capture all this and yet still remained tractable. After all, Vickrey (ibid. 331) had reached what he called 'a completely unwieldy expression' and ended his rather cursory mathematical analysis by observing that 'even in this simplified form the problem resists any facile solution.' Thanks to Jim's analytical powers, however, the optimum tax could be characterized, theoretical results proven, and numerical methods applied. This is not to say the characterization was in any sense facile; in fact, it required analytical innovations that proved to be at least as important as the results of the income tax model themselves. We return to this theme later. Even now, thirty years later, no better model of income taxation has been proposed. Instead, new results are still being discovered within the original framework and its specializations—see, for example Diamond (1998), Saez (1998), and Myles (2000).

The analytical results of the paper demonstrated that an optimum income tax had to lead to an allocation in which pre-tax income was increasing with ability, and that the marginal tax rate was between zero and one. Furthermore, unemployment was possible at the optimum and, when it occurred, would be of the lowest ability workers. To these results have since been added the facts that when ability is bounded the marginal tax rate is zero for the highest ability worker, and that at the other extreme, the marginal tax rate is zero for the lowest ability person if there is no bunching. The analytical results were supplemented by an extensive numerical analysis of the model. It was this that provided some of the most surprising findings. The first of these was that the optimal marginal rates of tax were low—at least compared to the highest rates applied in the UK and many other countries at the time the paper was written. These optimal rates were in the 30–50 per cent range, and the degree of redistribution implied by them was limited despite the concern for equity that had been built into the social welfare function. Furthermore, the marginal tax rates were fairly constant, so the tax function was close to being linear. These results motivated the observation (1971: 207) that 'I had expected the rigorous analysis of income-taxation in the utilitarian manner to provide an argument for high tax rates. It has not done so.' Indeed, one wonders whether the calculations may have offered support to those who argued that cutting the highest rates of income tax would enhance work effort to such an extent that all consumers would benefit.

Fundamental to the income tax problem is an understanding of the decision problem facing the government. It must offer consumers a budget constraint, possibly non-linear, along which each chooses their optimal location. This leads to the government's choice of the tax function (or equivalently the consumption function) to be one of maximization subject to maximization—the government maximizes social welfare subject to consumers' actions being determined by utility maximization. In models with linear budget constraints and strictly convex preferences, such as the analysis of commodity taxation in Diamond and Mirrlees (1971*a*, *b*), this does not cause any difficulties: consumers' choices are expressible by demand functions that encapsulate all information about their maximization. In the income tax model, with the possibility of a non-linear budget constraint and so multiple optimal choices for the consumers, such demand functions cannot be constructed.

The masterstroke of the paper was to show how these difficulties could be circumvented. To understand this, it is best to think about the problem in a different way. The government can be viewed as selecting an allocation (a consumption–income plan) for each consumer. If the consumers choose the plan allocated to them, then the optimum is achieved. The difficulty facing the government is to ensure that this happens and that no consumer chooses a plan intended for someone else. This is the notion of incentive compatibility: a consumer of ability s must find that the allocation designed for someone of this ability gives at least as much utility as the allocation designed for any other ability s'. The government then conducts its optimization over the set of incentive-compatible allocations. The imposition of incentive compatibility reduces the set of feasible contracts and is responsible for the second-best nature of the optimum tax.

In a model with a finite number of consumers it is straightforward to state the incentive compatibility constraints for each consumer explicitly. However, they will only be practical to manage if consumers' preferences over consumption–income allocations evolve in an orderly way as ability is varied. The restriction upon preferences that was introduced in the income tax paper to ensure this has since become known as the single-crossing condition. Graphically, it implies that at every point in income–consumption space the indifference curve of a high ability worker is flatter than that of a low ability worker. Almost immediately from this observation it can be appreciated that incentive compatibility will require high ability consumers to earn higher incomes and enjoy higher levels of consumption. The single-crossing condition has since found countless applications in problems involving the design of contracts for populations with agents of differing characteristics.

In the original formulation of the income tax model with a continuum of consumers, it is not practical to state the incentive-compatibility constraints directly since there is an uncountable infinity of constraints for each consumer. In the income tax paper, Jim surmounted this problem in a simple but ingenious way. He showed that the incentive-compatibility constraint is equivalent to the fact that each worker's choice of labour supply maximizes utility given the imposed tax function. The first-order condition for this optimization can then be used to generate a differential equation that determines the evolution of utility as a function of ability. This is exactly the form of constraint that can be employed in a calculus of variations analysis. This technique has since become known as the first-order approach to maximization subject to maximization.

There remains an additional wrinkle that was noted in the income tax paper. The differential equation represents the first-order condition for the contract to be optimal. As such, it is necessary but not sufficient. This raises the possibility that the tax function arising from the optimization analysis may violate the monotonicity properties that it should possess. A direct solution to this problem is to incorporate the second-order condition into the optimization—see Ebert (1992). The 1971 income tax paper, however, was the first to appreciate these subtle issues, as well as developing machinery for handling them successfully. The limitations of the first-order approach remained an issue that was addressed further in Jim's later work on the principal–agent problem.

The income tax paper also contained the germ of another important concept. Recall that the optimum involves monotonicity: those with higher skills earn and consume more. As a result, although the government cannot directly observe skill, in equilibrium it can infer skill from income. Thus, given the optimum tax function, the announcement by a consumer of their income is just a proxy for the direct announcement of their level of skill. As the revelation principle of Myerson (1979) and of Dasgupta *et al.* (1979) shows, this makes it possible to replace the income tax with an equivalent direct mechanism in which each consumer announces a skill level and, furthermore, announcing the true skill level is a dominant strategy. 'Equivalent' here means that the same equilibrium allocation of resources will emerge. This idea was not developed in the income tax paper, but it lay there like a gem waiting to be discovered.

Having discussed the income tax paper at some length, we now turn to Jim's work on the general principal–agent problem. A principal–agent relationship arises when one party wishes another to undertake an act on their behalf. If the act undertaken cannot be observed directly and its consequences can only be observed with some random error, then moral hazard can enter the relationship between the principal and agent. That is, the agent can attempt to hide behind the randomness to take an action that is less costly to them personally, but which yields a lower expected return to the principal. As noted in Mirrlees (1974*b*, 1975/1999), such relationships potentially arise in any economic relationship based on contingent contracts. For example, they arise between the owners and the managers of firms, and also between insurance companies and their insurees. Although the precise details differ between applications, the underlying principles remain essentially the same.

The problem for the principal is to structure a contract that gives incentives to the agent to take the action that yields the highest possible expected pay-off to the principal, conditional on the realization of some event that is unobservable to the principal but observable to the agent. There are considerable analytical similarities between the design of this contract and the optimum income tax problem. These similarities arise because the principal is choosing the contract to maximize expected pay-off subject to the agent choosing an action to maximize their pay-off. So again, the issue of maximization subject to maximization arises.

In the case where there are a finite number of possible actions for the agent, the incentive-compatibility constraints ensuring the correct choice of action can be employed directly. This is again impractical for the continuous case where there would be an uncountable infinity of constraints. Consequently, it again becomes necessary to use the first-order conditions for the agent's choice problem as a constraint on the optimization of the principal. There remain limitations with this approach. It had been used in work prior to Jim's analysis of the principal–agent problem, such as Zeckhauser (1970). But it had not been noticed that the approach might not lead to an optimum. This possibility was made very clear in Mirrlees (1975/1999), which provided an example where the first-order approach failed to give the optimum. The paper then proceeded to discuss how the problem could be overcome. The method proposed identified the possible maxima and incorporated them as constraints into the optimization. Although this works, it has proved unwieldy in practice, so most analyses rely on the first-order approach despite its known weaknesses. These issues were explored even further in Mirrlees (1986) and in Mirrlees and Roberts (1980).

An additional question that arises in principal–agent relationships is the formulation of conditions which guarantee that the reward from the contract is monotonic— that is, payment to the agent increases as observed output increases. If there are only two possible output levels, then monotonicity arises naturally. With three possible output levels, monotonicity can easily fail—see Grossman and Hart (1983). Mirrlees (1976) introduced the monotone likelihood ratio condition, which is sufficient for monotonicity. This requires that actions which are more costly for the agent to undertake make more profitable outcomes relatively more likely. Although weaker conditions are available (Jewitt 1988), the monotone likelihood ratio condition has become a fundamental component of the economic theorist's toolkit. It is, of course, closely related to the single-crossing property that plays such an important role in the optimal income tax paper.

Taken together, incentive compatibility, the extension of the first-order approach, and the monotone likelihood ratio condition provide the tools necessary to solve a broad class of principal–agent problems. Their application has formed the foundation of many, many later research papers. There has not been a single area of economics in which they have not found use in the characterization of optimal contracts in the presence of asymmetric information. Indeed, the *Review of Economic Studies* has recently devoted an entire issue to the theory of contracts (January 1999), showing that these issues are as alive as ever. The focus may have moved towards the questions raised by the observation of so many incomplete contracts, but the fundamental tools remain the same.

There can be no doubt that these ideas alone make up an outstanding contribution to economics. But there is so much more that Jim has had to offer. We cannot describe it all within the confines of this introduction, but we do wish to look briefly at just a small sample of this additional material.

In a two-part paper published in the *American Economic Review*, Diamond and Mirrlees (1971*a*, *b*) rewrote the extant theory of commodity taxation. This paper contains many pearls of analysis. By using a general equilibrium framework, they clarify the separation between consumer and producer prices, and so the interpretation of the untaxed commodity. Contrary to the earlier literature, the choice of untaxed commodity was shown just to be a normalization—not a consequence of leisure being untaxable. The latter, which was mistakenly given much focus in studies before Diamond and Mirrlees, was shown to play no role in the determination of optimal tax rules. The paper is also notable for its use of the duality methods which were emerging at that time but not yet widely known. The value of using the indirect utility function was that it allowed the problem to be phrased in terms of its natural choice variables: the after-tax consumer prices.

There are two fundamental results in the commodity taxation papers. The first of these is the interpretation of the tax rules. Through a number of innovative substitutions, these are shown to imply the simple rule of thumb that optimality requires an equal proportionate reduction in compensated demand for all commodities. This conclusion emphasizes that the real effect of the tax system is on consumers' demands, while its effect on prices is only of secondary importance. It can also be shown that the optimal tax rules are direct generalizations of the inverse elasticity rule derived from partial equilibrium analysis.

The second result is even more surprising and of great practical value for policy. The argument used to prove it is so simple and appealing that it is worth working through as a way of introducing the result. Assume that: *either* (i) there is a good such that if its price fell, then all consumers would be no worse off, and some would be strictly better off; *or* (ii) that there is a good supplied by consumers such that if its price rose, then all consumers would be no worse off, and some would be strictly better off. Also assume that the government maximizes a social welfare function that is increasing in all consumers' utilities. Under these assumptions, the optimal commodity taxes must lead to an equilibrium on the frontier of the production set.

The proof of this striking result comes from considering any allocation for which the aggregate net demand vector is interior to the production set. But then in case (i), a small enough reduction in the price of the identified commodity is feasible and must increase social welfare. Alternatively, in case (ii), a small enough increase in the price of the good is feasible and must increase social welfare. So no interior allocation can be optimal. This proves the result that has since become known as the Production Efficiency Lemma. There are some restrictions to this result, most notably the consequences of non-constant returns to scale, which imply that achieving efficiency may require some firms to be shut down, thus adversely affecting their owners' incomes. Such restrictions are clarified in Mirrlees (1972).

The practical value of the Production Efficiency Lemma follows from observing that, because any equilibrium has the economy's aggregate net output vector on the frontier of the production set, it must be efficient. Yet efficiency is only possible if there are no distortions in the input prices faced by producers. Hence, input taxes should not be a feature of the optimal set of commodity taxes or, put more simply, intermediate goods should not be taxed. The policy implications of this result are immediate and significant for the design of tax structures. In particular, they help justify value-added taxation, with tax rebates available for producers who purchase intermediate goods. They also suggest that capital held by firms should not be subject to taxation, though dividends paid to consumers can and probably should be, along with their realized capital gains.

At the analytical level, the Production Efficiency Lemma is especially surprising when contrasted with the conclusions of Lipsey and Lancaster's (1956) celebrated second-best theory. After all, Lipsey and Lancaster's central message was that a distortion in any one sector of the economy should generally be offset by introducing distortions in all other sectors. This finding had achieved great prominence at the time when the Diamond–Mirrlees article was published. By contrast, their Production Efficiency Lemma states that, even when distortionary taxes and subsidies are being introduced into consumer decisions in order to redistribute real income or to finance public goods, this is no reason to distort producer decisions. This is a finding completely counter to the general message of Lipsey and Lancaster.

We have already noted that it was his concern for poverty in the developing nations that first led Jim to study economics. It is therefore no surprise that this eventually bore fruit in the form of the immensely influential Little and Mirrlees (1968, 1974) handbook of project appraisal (commonly known as 'the manual'). Of course, this fulfilled the promise of the title as a practical guide to the use of cost–benefit analysis, but it also provided much more. By showing how better decisions could be taken, the manual was designed to contribute to improvements in the economic conditions of developing countries, thus fulfilling Jim's wish that economic science should serve humanity, especially the poor.

The manual took as its starting point the theory of cost–benefit analysis and, in particular, the use of shadow prices to value all inputs and outputs, regardless of whether they are marketable or non-marketable. On this foundation it set out to elucidate how shadow prices should be determined in every possible circumstance. Most notably, it emphasized the use of border prices to value inputs and outputs when the project was located in a small country. When goods were not traded, it provided methods for valuing them based on the prices of traded goods. A second important point made in the manual was to treat investment finance as scarce because of the government's budget or borrowing constraint. This implied that social profits were to be discounted at the internal rate of return for the marginal investment project.

Generally, the manual was very careful in its consideration of constraints upon policy choices and of the implications that these constraints had for the prices used to calculate the costs and benefits of any project. Indeed, it was also stressed that any government decision must involve value judgements and that these value judgements should be evaluated in monetary terms. The manual also set forward a vision of project appraisal being thoroughly integrated into the policy-making structure.

If used correctly this is a simple but powerful methodology. The original recommendations have been subjected to much theoretical scrutiny, which has generally confirmed their validity. This is a tribute to the two authors' intuitive sense of what is right in economics, especially since their proposals were not themselves derived from an extensive formal analysis.

The practical impact of this Little–Mirrlees approach can be judged from the number of donor agencies that adopted it to guide their decisions. Foremost amongst these was the World Bank, where cost–benefit analysis was the dominant decision-making method throughout the 1970s. However, its use has steadily declined since. Little and Mirrlees (1994) themselves attribute this decline to several factors, amongst them being the changing nature of lending and the internal institutional structure of the World Bank. They note this with apparent sadness—despite their best efforts, inefficient and incorrect choices are still needlessly made to the detriment of those they most wish to help.

This short survey has touched only upon a small fraction of James Mirrlees' research. It has not discussed much of his extensive work on growth theory, or that on the dynamic non-substitution theorem, or on the economics of social insurance. Nor that on the basis of welfare comparisons, or on family size, or on efficiency wages. In all of these contributions can be found fundamental results and penetrating insights. The importance of maximization subject to maximization and the tools used to solve such problems, especially the first-order approach and its limitations, the single-crossing property, incentive compatibility and the monotone likelihood ratio condition; these are the most important of Jim's gifts to economics that stem from his solo publications. All are standard tools and our discipline would be so much poorer without them.

We encourage readers of this volume, however, to contemplate another of Jim's gifts to economics, whose quality we are particularly badly placed to assess. This is the influence on the subject that Jim has exerted through his research students. All of us have benefited enormously from his deep interest in our work and from his sympathetic, encouraging, and conscientious advice—accompanied by just enough criticism to stop us straying further than necessary from the very high standards which we could see he imposed on his own work above all. His criticism, by the way, was often very tactful—serious mistakes in a manuscript offered to Jim for his comments were often met with a mild request that the point be explained more carefully.

Jim, we all offer you our sincere thanks, and hope that the contributions which follow—modest as they may be (with one obvious exception)—serve, as intended, not only to express our admiration and warm appreciation, but also to enhance your well-deserved high reputation as an adviser, colleague, and co-author.

References

Arrow, K. J. (1962) 'The Economic Implications of Learning by Doing', *Review of Economic Studies* 29: 155–73.

Dasgupta, P., P. J. Hammond, and E. Maskin (1979) 'The Implementation of Social Choice Rules: Some General Results on Incentive Compatibility', *Review of Economic Studies* 46: 185–216.

Diamond, P. A. (1998) 'Optimal Income Taxation: An Example with a U-Shaped Pattern of Optimal Marginal Tax Rates', *American Economic Review* 88: 83–95.

—— and J. A. Mirrlees (1971*a*) 'Optimal Taxation and Public Production I: Production Efficiency', *American Economic Review* 61: 8–27.

—— —— (1971*b*) 'Optimal Taxation and Public Production II: Tax Rules', *American Economic Review* 61: 261–78.

Ebert, U. (1992) 'A Reexamination of the Optimal Nonlinear Income Tax', *Journal of Public Economics* 49: 47–73.

Grossman, S. J., and O. D. Hart (1983) 'An Analysis of the Principal–Agent Problem', *Econometrica* 51: 7–45.

Jewitt, I. (1988) 'Justifying the First-Order Approach to Principal–Agent Problems', *Econometrica* 56: 1177–90.

Johansen, L. (1959) 'Substitution versus Fixed Production Coefficients in the Theory of Economic Growth: A Synthesis', *Econometrica* 27: 157–76.

Kaldor, N. (1957) 'A Model of Economic Growth', *Economic Journal* 67: 591–264.

—— (1961) 'Capital Accumulation and Economic Growth', in F. A. Lutz and D. C. Hague (eds.), *The Theory of Capital* (London: Macmillan): 177–220.

—— and J. A. Mirrlees (1962) 'A New Model of Economic Growth', *Review of Economic Studies* 29: 174–90.

Lipsey, R. G., and K. J. Lancaster (1956) 'The General Theory of Second Best', *Review of Economic Studies* 24: 11–32.

Little, I. M. D., and J. A. Mirrlees (1968) *Manual of Industrial Project Analysis in Developing Countries, ii: Social Cost–Benefit Analysis* (Paris: OECD).

—— —— (1974) *Project Appraisal and Planning for Developing Countries* (London: Heinemann).

—— —— (1994) 'The Costs and Benefits of Analysis: Project Appraisal and Planning Twenty Years On', in R. Layard and S. Glaister (eds.), *Cost–Benefit Analysis* (Cambridge: Cambridge University Press).

Merton, R. C. (1990) *Continuous-Time Finance* (Oxford: Blackwell).

Mirrlees, J. A. (1965) 'Optimal Capital Accumulation under Uncertainty' (unpublished).

—— (1967) 'Optimum Growth when Technology is Changing', *Review of Economic Studies* 34: 95–124.

—— (1971) 'An Exploration in the Theory of Optimum Income Taxation', *Review of Economic Studies* 38: 175–208.

—— (1972) 'On Producer Taxation', *Review of Economic Studies* 39: 105–11.

—— (1974*a*) 'Optimal Allocation under Uncertainty', in J. Dreze (ed.), *Allocation Under Uncertainty* (London: Macmillan).

—— (1974*b*) 'Notes on Welfare Economics, Information and Uncertainty', in M. Balch, D. McFadden, and S. Wu (eds.), *Essays in Equilibrium Behavior under Uncertainty* (Amsterdam: North-Holland).

—— (1975/1999) 'The Theory of Moral Hazard and Unobservable Behaviour, Part I', (mimeo, Nuffield College, Oxford), published in the *Review of Economic Studies* 66: 3–21.

Mirrlees, J. A. (1976) 'The Optimal Structure of Incentives and Authority within an Organization', *Bell Journal of Economics* 7: 105–31.

—— (1986) 'The Theory of Optimal Taxation', in K. J. Arrow and M. D. Intrilligator (eds.), *Handbook of Mathematical Economics* (Amsterdam: North-Holland).

—— and K. W. S. Roberts (1980) 'Functions with Multiple Maxima' (mimeo, Nuffield College, Oxford).

Myerson, R. B. (1979) 'Incentive Compatibility and the Bargaining Problem', *Econometrica* 47: 61–73.

Myles, G. D. (2000) 'On the Optimal Marginal Rate of Income Tax', *Economics Letters* 66: 113–19.

Saez, E. (1999) 'Using Elasticities to Derive Optimal Income Tax Rules' (mimeo, MIT).

Salter, W. E. G. (1960) *Productivity and Technical Change* (Cambridge: Cambridge University Press).

Stone, J. R. N. (1955) 'Misery and Bliss', *Economia Internazionale* 8: 72–93.

Vickrey, W. S. (1945) 'Measuring Marginal Utility by Reactions to Risk', *Econometrica* 13: 319–33.

Zeckhauser, R. (1970) 'Medical Insurance: A Case Study of the Trade-off between Risk Spreading and Appropriate Incentives', *Journal of Economic Theory* 2: 10–26.

Part II

INFORMATION

2 Corporate Diversification and Agency

BENJAMIN E. HERMALIN AND MICHAEL L. KATZ

1. Introduction

A frequently stated motive for joint ventures, conglomerate mergers, and investments in new lines of business is a desire to diversify the firm and reduce the riskiness of its returns. According to this view, joint ventures spread the risk of major projects, while conglomerate diversification creates portfolio benefits by pooling uncorrelated returns. A similar logic may drive a corporate decision to pursue simultaneously a variety of different R&D strategies aimed at a common goal.[1] A standard argument, however, suggests that with perfect capital markets there is no financial value to within-firm diversification because investors could instead diversify their own portfolios (Alberts 1966; Levy and Sarnat 1970). Indeed, it may be worse to have the firms themselves diversify because this reduces the number of pure securities that are traded.[2]

Why, then, do firms undertake activities to diversify risk? Many analysts have suggested diversification is the result of the agency relationship that exists between managers and outside investors.[3] The building blocks for an agency-based explanation of diversification are these: risk-averse owners are motivated to hold diversified portfolios and thus (to a first-order approximation) behave in a risk-neutral fashion with respect to the firm's investment decisions.[4] Risk-averse managers would also like to diversify away the risks associated with their firms, but to ensure that a manager has incentives to serve the owners' interests, her current income stream may be tied in an undiversified way to the performance of the firm that employs her. Moreover, through the effects on her reputation, a manager's future income may depend on the returns of the one firm that she currently manages. Lacking the opportunity to diversify in other ways (e.g. part-time managerial positions with multiple firms), managers may value within-firm diversification. Intuitively, even diversified shareholders benefit from a reduction in the riskiness of the firm's profit stream when the reduction lowers the compensation level needed to attract and retain (risk-averse) managers, or reduces the distortions in managers' investment decisions.

This material is based on work supported by the Berkeley Program in Finance, the Olin Foundation, and the National Science Foundation (the latter under Award SES-9112076).

[1] Of course, the firm also could be driven to pursue a variety of positive net present-value projects where the extensive margin is greater than the intensive margin.

[2] Porter (1987) also makes this point from the perspective of corporate strategy. In recent years, several firms have unbundled their securities, either by outright divestiture of operations or by creating separate classes of tracking stocks, each of whose returns are tied to the performance of a specific divisions within the firm.

[3] We briefly discuss alternative explanations in the concluding section.

[4] We do not explore the possibility that the firm is controlled by a 'large shareholder' who is undiversified. See Zhang (1998) for an analysis of investment choice in the presence of such an owner.

In analysing the effects of agency on diversification incentives, however, it is essential to recognize that the relationship between the riskiness of a firm's returns and its manager's well-being is largely endogenous: the relationship is driven by the firm's choice of managerial compensation scheme.[5] As is well known, a risk-neutral principal has incentives to insure a risk-averse agent, but in the presence of a moral hazard the principal must trade off the provision of insurance against the provision of incentives. As is also well known, the terms of this trade-off depend on the degree to which the principal is informed about the agent's actions.[6] One of our central concerns in the present paper is whether riskiness matters as well.

Several earlier authors have (indirectly) addressed the issues of how diversification affects information and riskiness, and whether riskiness matters. Diamond and Verrecchia (1982) present a model in which they fully characterize the optimal managerial compensation scheme and examine the effects of risk reduction on shareholder welfare. They interpret their results as showing that risk reduction benefits shareholders by reducing agency costs. Unfortunately, the parameter in their model that measures riskiness also measures the informativeness of the firm's returns as a signal of the agent's effort. We will argue that changes in informativeness, not risk, are what drive Diamond and Verrecchia's findings.

Marshall *et al.* (1984) argue that diversification can ameliorate agency problems by improving the informativeness of the firm's returns as a signal of the agent's effort and by reducing the risk borne by the agent for any given contract. Marshall *et al.* however, characterize informativeness in an informal and, to some extent, inaccurate manner. Moreover, their discussion of risk reduction is incomplete and potentially misleading in that it fails to account for changes in the optimal compensation scheme in response to changes in risk.

Aron (1988) also argues that diversification is valuable because of the potential benefits of improved information that reduces the cost of agency contracting. She examines a specific model in which diversification into additional lines of business generates new signals whose noise is independent of the other signals and which has no effect on the distribution of the other signals. For this independent-returns case, she shows that diversification reduces the cost incurred by the principal to induce the agent to undertake effort. Aron does not formalize the concept of increased informativeness, however. Indeed, in her comparison of diversification and the use of relative performance schemes, she focuses her answer on the correlation of returns across projects which is not directly related to informativeness.[7]

The effects of corporate diversification on the agency relationship are an example of a more general problem. Changes in the structure of the corporation or the agent's tasks more generally can change the statistical relationship between the agent's ability

---

[5] Indeed, with limited liability, golden parachutes, and stock options, management compensation schemes may be convex functions of firm performance and, thus, induce risk-loving.

[6] See Holmstrom (1979) and Shavell (1979).

[7] As Holmstrom (1979) has shown, informativeness is related to statistical sufficiency, which is different than correlation. Consider, for example, two random variables s_1 and s_2. As long as there exists a function, $t(\cdot)$, such that $t(s_1) = s_2$, s_1 is a sufficient statistic for s_2 regardless of their correlation.

and effort and the resulting returns.[8] Financial instruments, such as insurance contracts and foreign exchange options, similarly change the relationship between the firm's
returns and the management's characteristics and actions. When executive compensation contracts depend on measures of firm performance, such as the level of sales or
profits, the value of the measure is of interest not only as a signal of the agent's effort
or ability, but also because it represents the financial returns to ownership. In evaluating corporate investments, the owners of the firm may care about: (i) the expected
level of returns; (ii) the riskiness of the returns; and (iii) the informativeness of the
returns as a signal of managerial effort or ability.

An important question is how to disentangle these different effects. It is well known
that a firm may be willing to trade off expected returns for improved information.
A more difficult question is how a firm is willing to trade improvements in informativeness against increases in risk, or whether risk even matters.[9] We examine the effects
of diversification in a model of optimal agency contracting that is general enough to
distinguish between changes in riskiness and changes in informativeness. The next section presents a standard agency model in which we show that using the conventional
Blackwell conception of informativeness, an improvement in information (holding
the mean return constant) implies a reduction in risk. Thus, this approach is not well
suited to examining these issues. Moreover, we join Gjesdal (1981) and Kim (1995)
in arguing that Blackwell's definition of informativeness is unduly restrictive for agency
purposes. We develop alternative measures of informativeness to demonstrate that,
when the concepts do not coincide, information—not risk—is what matters in the agency
setting. We demonstrate through examples that shareholders may prefer a returns structure that entails a high degree of risk, but is highly informative, to one that is low-
risk, but uninformative.

In Section 3, we examine the effects of corporate diversification on informativeness. While in Aron's model diversification always improves the information structure
and the costs of diversification derive entirely from the effects of reassigning capital,
we allow for the possibility that spreading effort itself affects the pattern of returns.
In contrast to Aron, we argue that there are plausible cases in which diversification
or risk-spreading activities actually reduce informativeness. We also examine the use
of hedging and insurance contracts and suggest that agency does not provide a good
explanation of the use of these contracts.

In Section 4, we examine what happens when the diversification choice is not verifiable
in court and thus the managerial compensation scheme cannot be made dependent on
it. While in many situations (e.g. mergers and acquisitions) the reasonable assumption

---

[8] See Mirrlees (1976) for an early and insightful analysis of the relationship between agency and firm
structure.

[9] In a model of hidden information, rather than the hidden-action case examined in the present paper,
Hermalin (1993) shows that a manager whose future income is tied to the labour market's posterior estimate of her abilities could rationally prefer that her firm's returns be as risky as possible in order to *reduce*
the informativeness of these returns as signals of her underlying ability. The risk to the manager's reputation is diminished, even though the riskiness of the firm's return is increased. DeMarzo and Duffie (1995)
examine a similar model and find that certain risk-reducing actions may reduce informativeness, to the manager's advantage.

is that the information structure is verifiable, there are diversification decisions (e.g. the number of paths to pursue in new product development or marketing) that the manager makes with little direct oversight. While in principle the principal might be able to obtain such information and verify it in court, it strikes us as very unlikely that shareholders have anything like this level of detailed knowledge in practice.[10] More-over, even in the case of an acquisition, shareholders may delegate the decision to the agent because they lack the information needed to discern whether the transaction is valuable to the firm when evaluated solely in terms of its expected pay-off. Thus, it is worth investigating what happens when the manager controls the diversification deci-sion after the principal has set the compensation scheme.[11] We derive conditions under which the lack of verifiability does not affect the principal because the agent will choose the principal's preferred information structure. We show by example, however, that there are other cases in which the lack of verifiability with respect to the agent's diversi-fication decision is costly to the principal.

2. The Value of Information and Risk Reduction in an Agency Model

2.1. The model

Consider a standard principal–agent model similar to Grossman and Hart's (1983). A risk-neutral owner hires a risk-averse manager by offering her an incentive contract on a take-it-or-leave-it basis. The manager accepts if her expected utility under the contract is at least as great as her reservation utility, which we normalize to zero. The manager's utility is $V(y) - K(a)$, where y is her monetary compensation and a is her action chosen from the finite set $\mathbf{A}$. $K(\cdot)$, the disutility-of-action function, is increasing; $V(\cdot)$, the utility of money function, is strictly increasing, strictly concave, and has an unbounded range. The owner's utility is $x - y$, where x is total revenue generated.

A *returns structure* is a set of densities over revenue levels, denoted by Π^i, where i indexes different returns structures. The vector $\mathbf{x} \equiv (x_1, x_2, \ldots, x_N)'$ represents the set of possible revenue levels.[12] Returns are indexed so that $m < n$ implies $x_m < x_n$. An element of Π^i is $\pi_n^i(a)$, the probability that revenues are x_n under the ith returns structure conditional on action a having been taken. The density over revenue levels conditional on action a is $\pi^i(a) = (\pi_1^i(a), \ldots, \pi_N^i(a))'$. For convenience, we define the index set $\mathbf{N} \equiv \{1, 2, \ldots, N\}$.

---

[10] There is a sizeable—and inconclusive—empirical literature that examines whether managers pursue acquisitions, conglomerate and otherwise, at shareholders' expense. For example, Amihud and Lev (1981), Amihud *et al.* (1986), and Lewellen *et al.* (1989) focus on risk-reduction motives, while Morck *et al.* (1990) and the references cited therein consider acquisitions driven by managerial interests more generally.

[11] We do not examine the (to us) less plausible case where the structure is not verifiable and is controlled by the principal.

[12] The prime (′) denotes vector or matrix transpose.

As is well known, the returns in this agency problem play two roles. First, they are the source of income for the principal and agent. In this capacity, we are interested in the *riskiness* of the returns, and second-degree stochastic dominance is the standard measure of riskiness. For the discrete setting under examination here, $\pi^2(a)$ is riskier than $\pi^1(a)$ if and only if

$$\sum_{i=1}^{n-1}\left(\sum_{j=1}^{i}[\pi_j^1(a) - \pi_j^2(a)]\right)(x_{i+1} - x_i) \leq 0 \ \forall n \in \{2, \ldots, N\} \tag{1}$$

and

$$\pi^2(a)'\mathbf{x} = \pi^1(a)'\mathbf{x}.$$

Second, the level of returns can serve as a signal to the principal of the action taken by the agent. In this role, we are interested in the *informativeness* of the returns.

2.2. Blackwell informativeness and risk in agency settings

The notion of Blackwell informativeness provides a starting point for our analysis. This is the notion that, given the choice between two observation strategies—observe the outcome of an experiment or observe the outcome with noise—a rational experimenter would prefer the former to the latter. Hence, if one information structure is a noisy transformation of a second, then the second is more informative in a Blackwell sense.

Consider two standard agency problems that are identical except for the stochastic relation between revenues and actions. If, for *all* possible a, $\pi^2(a) = \mathbf{Q}\pi^1(a)$, where $\mathbf{Q}$ is a constant stochastic transformation matrix (i.e. a matrix with non-negative elements in which each column sums to one and at least one column has two positive elements), then returns are a more (Blackwell) informative signal of the action under structure 1 than under structure 2. One can think of $\mathbf{Q}$ as 'garbling' the signal that would have obtained in the first agency problem.

Grossman and Hart (1983: Proposition 13) show how the incentive-insurance trade-off in the design of the agent's compensation scheme is affected by an improvement in information in the Blackwell sense. They establish that, if there exists a stochastic transformation matrix $\mathbf{Q}$ such that $\pi^2(a) = \mathbf{Q}\pi^1(a)$ for all actions a, then the principal's expected cost of implementing a given action in the first agency problem is no greater than the expected cost of implementing that action in the second agency problem.

While distinct concepts, Blackwell informativeness and riskiness are closely related, and this relationship can make it difficult to determine which property drives agency costs. We want to examine the risk properties of diversification, and thus want to hold the mean level of returns constant to facilitate comparison. Hence, we examine informativeness in settings in which one returns structure is more informative than another but the expected revenues depend only on the action taken and not on the returns structure. This leads us to restrict attention to *mean-preserving garblings*: stochastic transformation matrices, $\mathbf{Q}$, such that $\mathbf{Q}'\mathbf{x} = \mathbf{x}$. Hence, if $\pi^2(a) = \mathbf{Q}\pi^1(a)$ for all $a \in \mathbf{A}$, then $\pi^2(a)'\mathbf{x} = \pi^1(a)'\mathbf{x}$ for all $a \in \mathbf{A}$.[13] Economically, one can interpret a mean-preserving garbling as follows. Under returns structure Π^1, the pay-off if the nth state occurs is x_n. Under returns structure Π^2, a lottery over revenues is held if the nth state occurs, where the lottery's probabilities are given by the nth column of $\mathbf{Q}$, $\mathbf{q}_{\cdot n}$. Each of these lotteries is mean-preserving (i.e. the nth lottery has mean x_n for all n) because $\mathbf{q}_{\cdot n}'\mathbf{x} = x_n$ by construction.

It is no surprise that, when $\pi^2(a) = \mathbf{Q}\pi^1(a)$ for all $a \in \mathbf{A}$ and $\mathbf{Q}$ is a mean-preserving garbling, the densities in Π^1 are less risky than the densities in Π^2 in the sense of second-degree stochastic dominance—by construction $\pi^2(a)$ is a mean-preserving spread of $\pi^1(a)$.

Proposition 1. *Consider two returns structures, Π^1 and Π^2, for which the stochastic transformation matrix between the first and second returns structures is a mean-preserving garbling. Then:*

   (i) *Π^1 is more informative than Π^2.*
   (ii) *For all $a \in \mathbf{A}$, $\pi^1(a)$ is less risky than $\pi^2(a)$ in the sense of second-degree stochastic dominance.*

Proposition 1(ii) is a straightforward corollary of the following theorem of Blackwell.[14]

Theorem (Blackwell). *Consider two densities, π^1 and π^2, with support $\mathbf{x}$. The first density is less risky than the second, in the sense of second-degree stochastic dominance, if and only if there exists a mean-preserving garbling, $\mathbf{Q}$, such that $\pi^2 = \mathbf{Q}\pi^1$.*

One might suspect that the converse of Proposition 1 is also a corollary of this Theorem. It is not. The theorem holds for a pair of *densities* and not a pair of returns structures. Although the Theorem does not imply the converse of Proposition 1, it does imply the following.[15]

Proposition 2. *Let Π^1 and Π^2 be two returns structures, where: (i) Π^2 is of full rank; (ii) the expected returns conditional on the action taken are the same under the two returns structures; and (iii) for some action $\tilde{a} \in \mathbf{A}$, $\pi^1(\tilde{a})$ is strictly less risky than $\pi^2(\tilde{a})$ in the sense of second-degree stochastic dominance. Then Π^2 is not more informative than Π^1 in the Blackwell sense.*

While the first two results make distinctions between informativeness and riskiness difficult, the following observation helps distinguish between the two concepts:

Remark. *Let Π^1 and Π^2 be two returns structures, where: (i) Π^2 is of full rank and (ii) the expected returns conditional on the action taken are the same under the two returns*

---

[13] If Π^1 has less than full rank, then there may exist stochastic transformation matrices such that $\pi^2(a) = \mathbf{Q}\pi^1(a)$ for all $a \in \mathbf{A}$ and $\pi^2(a)'\mathbf{x} = \pi^1(a)'\mathbf{x}$ for all $a \in \mathbf{A}$, but $\mathbf{Q}'\mathbf{x} \neq \mathbf{x}$. That is, $\mathbf{Q}'\mathbf{x} = \mathbf{x}$ is a necessary condition only if Π^1 has full rank. Because little use can be made (by us) of the additional flexibility that arises if Π^1 has less than full rank, we have chosen not to divide the analysis according to the rank of Π^1.

[14] Marshall and Olkin (1979: 417).

[15] Proofs not in the text may be found in the Appendix.

structures. Π^1 and Π^2 are equally informative in the Blackwell sense if and only if there exists a permutation matrix $\mathbf{M}$, such that $\pi^2(a) = \mathbf{M}\pi^1(a)$ for all actions a.

This remark strongly suggests that riskiness is irrelevant: when two returns structures are equally informative, the cost of implementing any given action is the same under both structures, yet the riskiness of the two returns structures could be vastly different.

2.3. Intuitive informativeness and risk in agency settings

Like Gjesdal (1981) and Kim (1995), we believe that Blackwell's definition of informativeness is unduly restrictive for agency purposes and thus often fails to provide a ranking in situations in which one information structure is in fact superior to the other. Very loosely speaking, the principal cares only about whether he can distinguish between the agent's taking a single desired action and all other actions, and Blackwell informativeness does not make use of this fact.

It is well known that, if the support of the returns varies with the agent's action in the right way, then the principal can completely solve the incentive problem while providing full insurance to an agent who takes the action desired by the principal.[16] The following example exploits this fact to show that the principal may well prefer a returns structure that gives rise to a high level of risk (and information) to one that does not.

Example 1. Suppose $\mathbf{x} = (1, 2, 3)'$; $A = \{0, 1\}$; and

$$\pi^1(0) = \begin{pmatrix} \frac{1}{3} \\ \frac{1}{3} \\ \frac{1}{3} \end{pmatrix}, \ \pi^2(0) = \begin{pmatrix} \frac{1}{6} \\ \frac{2}{3} \\ \frac{1}{6} \end{pmatrix}, \ \pi^1(1) = \begin{pmatrix} \frac{1}{4} \\ 0 \\ \frac{3}{4} \end{pmatrix}, \text{ and } \pi^2(1) = \begin{pmatrix} \frac{1}{6} \\ \frac{1}{6} \\ \frac{2}{3} \end{pmatrix}.$$

It is straightforward to verify that, for both a, $\pi^2(a)$ is less risky than $\pi^1(a)$.[17] Under returns structure 2, the cost of implementing $a = 1$ exceeds the full-information level because the optimal contract that induces the agent to take this action entails her bearing some of the risk. Under returns structure 1, however, obtaining a revenue of 2 is proof that the manager took action $a = 0$, and the owners can thus implement $a = 1$ at the full-information cost. Therefore, the owner prefers the riskier returns structure 1.

Example 1 illustrates the fact that Blackwell informativeness is an imperfect measure of informativeness in an agency problem—while the two returns structures could not be ranked according to the Blackwell criterion, the second structure clearly is more informative in an intuitive sense. Our next result shows that this point is not dependent on the existence of a shifting support.

---

[16] For a subtle and elegant generalization of the so-called 'shifting support' result, see Mirrlees (1999).

[17] Note that there is no *common* stochastic transformation matrix such that $\pi^1(a) = \mathbf{Q}\pi^2(a)$. Because $\pi_2^1(1) = 0$, the middle row of $\mathbf{Q}$ would necessarily consist entirely of zeros, which would be inconsistent with $\pi_2^1(0) = 1/3$. Thus, the returns structures cannot be ranked by the criterion of Blackwell informativeness.

This result builds on the following notion of informativeness. Suppose that the principal wants to induce the agent to choose action $\hat{a}$. Intuitively, the principal's ability to discern whether the agent has indeed chosen this action will depend on how dissimilar are the densities over profits associated with other actions. Thus, we will interpret returns structure 1 as being more informative than returns structure 2 about whether action $\hat{a}$ was taken if for all $a \in A \backslash \{\hat{a}\}$, $\pi^1(a)$ is 'farther' from $\pi^1(\hat{a})$ than $\pi^2(a)$ is from $\pi^2(\hat{a})$.

Proposition 3. *If two returns structures, Π^1 and Π^2, are such that:*

(i) for each $n \in N$ *either*

$$\pi_n^1(a) - \pi_n^1(\hat{a}) > \pi_n^2(a) - \pi_n^2(\hat{a}) \geqslant 0 \quad \forall a \in A \backslash \{\hat{a}\}$$

or

$$\pi_n^1(a) - \pi_n^1(\hat{a}) < \pi_n^2(a) - \pi_n^2(\hat{a}) \leqslant 0 \quad \forall a \in A \backslash \{\hat{a}\};$$

and

(ii) for all $a \in A \backslash \{\hat{a}\}$

$$\min_{n \in N} \frac{\pi_n^2(\hat{a})}{\pi_n^1(\hat{a})} > \max_{m \in N} \frac{\pi_m^2(a) - \pi_m^2(\hat{a})}{\pi_m^1(a) - \pi_m^1(\hat{a})},$$

then the cost of implementing $\hat{a}$ under returns structure Π^1 is less than or equal to the cost under Π^2. If $\hat{a}$ is not a least-cost action (i.e. if $K(\hat{a}) > K(a)$ for some $a \in A$), then the inequality is strict.

It is well known within agency theory that what is important for solving an agency problem are the likelihood ratios,

$$h_n^i(a, \hat{a}) \equiv \frac{\pi_n^i(a) - \pi_n^i(\hat{a})}{\pi_n^i(\hat{a})},$$

because compensation in state n is an increasing function of

$$\mu^i - \sum_{a \in A \backslash \{\hat{a}\}} \lambda^i(a) h_n^i(a, \hat{a}), \tag{2}$$

where μ^i and $\lambda^i(a)$ are positive constants. Proposition 3's two conditions are conditions on the way the $h_n^i(a, \hat{a})$ are distributed under the two information systems. As such, Proposition 3 is related to Kim's (1995) work, which shows that, if the distribution of the likelihood ratios under information structure 1 is a mean-preserving spread of the distribution under information structure 2, then 1 is more informative (leads to a better solution of the agency problem) than 2. Our conditions, although closely related to Kim's, are different. It is possible to show by example that information structures can satisfy our conditions without their likelihood ratios being ordered by second-degree stochastic dominance as required by Kim.[18]

The important point to note is that $\pi^1(\hat{a})$ and $\pi^2(\hat{a})$ may satisfy our conditions even though $\pi^1(\hat{a})$ is riskier than $\pi^2(\hat{a})$, as Example 1 above illustrates. This point can be seen more generally by comparing these two conditions with the definition of second-degree stochastic dominance, inequality (1) above. The following example further illustrates this point.

Example 2. Suppose that $\mathbf{x} = (0, 100, 200)'$,

$$\pi^1(a_1) = \pi^2(a_1) = (0.395, 0.48, 0.125)',$$
$$\pi^1(a_2) = \pi^2(a_2) = (0.32, 0.48, 0.2)',$$
$$\pi^1(a_3) = (0.48, 0.04, 0.48)',$$

and

$$\pi^2(a_3) = (0.46, 0.08, 0.46)'.$$

Moreover, suppose that $3K(a_1) = 2K(a_2) = K(a_3) = \theta > 0$.

The expected returns conditional on actions a_1, a_2, and a_3 are 73, 88, and 100, respectively. Thus, for θ sufficiently low, the principal will choose a contract that induces the agent to take action a_3. By Proposition 3, it costs less to implement a_3 under the first information structure than under the second one. But $\pi^1(a_3)$ is a mean-preserving spread of $\pi^2(a_3)$—the principal chooses the riskier returns structure.

We gain additional insight into Proposition 3 by holding the probability density associated with $\hat{a}$ invariant across the returns structures being compared while varying the densities associated with other actions. By doing this, riskiness is held constant across the two returns structures but informativeness may vary. The following corollary establishes that given the choice between two returns structures with equal riskiness, the principal chooses the one that is more informative as measured by the distance between densities.

Corollary. *If two returns structures, Π^1 and Π^2, are such that*

   (i) $\pi^1(\hat{a}) = \pi^2(\hat{a}) \equiv \hat{\pi}$,

and

   (ii) for each $n \in N$ either $\pi_n^1(a) > \pi_n^2(a) \geqslant \hat{\pi}_n$ $\forall a \in A \backslash \{\hat{a}\}$ or $\pi_n^1(a) < \pi_n^2(a) \leqslant \hat{\pi}_n$
   $\forall a \in A \backslash \{\hat{a}\}$,

then the cost of implementing $\hat{a}$ is less under returns structure Π^1 than under Π^2.[19]

---

[18] An example can be constructed when there are two states and two actions, a and $\hat{a}$, such that $\pi_1^1(a) = 0.7$, $\pi_1^1(\hat{a}) = 0.3$, $\pi_1^2(a) = 0.7$, and $\pi_1^2(\hat{a}) = 0.35$. Details available upon request. Stochastic dominance is not a necessary condition because, although the principal's costs are convex in (2), the weights μ^i and $\lambda^i(a)$ also depend on the information.

[19] The corollary also follows from Kim's (1995) main proposition suitably modified for a discrete state space.

The corollary underscores again that when risk and informativeness are not related, informativeness matters and risk does not.

3. Risk and Information Effects of Diversification and Hedging

3.1. Diversification

Having looked at returns structures in the abstract, we now ask how they relate to diversification. We do so in the context of a simple illustrative example. There are one or two projects, depending on the case under consideration. The agent chooses whether to apply 0, 1, or 2 units of effort to each available project. A project succeeds with probability $\gamma\alpha$, where $\gamma \in (0, \frac{1}{2})$ and α is the effort allocated to *that* project; otherwise it fails. The projects' successes are statistically independent. The agent's cost of effort depends solely on the *total* effort, a, not the allocation between projects. $K(a)$ is finite if $a \in \{0, 1, 2\}$ and is infinite otherwise. The owner's gross benefit is $x_S > 0$ from a project that succeeds. We normalize the pay-off of failure as 0. If two projects succeed, the owner's gross benefit is $2x_S$. Notice that the expected gross benefit for a given level of total effort, $\gamma a x_S$, is independent of how that effort is allocated across projects. Because our focus is on the informational and risk impacts of diversification in a hidden-action problem, we want the expected revenue (conditional on a given level of total effort) to be invariant with respect to the extent of diversification.[20]

Because the projects are *ex ante* identical and independent, there is no loss in generality from assuming that if the manager conducts only one project, she conducts the first. When both projects are available, the manager chooses actions from the set $\{(0, 0), (1, 0), (2, 0), (1, 1)\} \equiv A_2$, where a pair represents effort allocated to the first and second project, respectively. Observe that the manager's choice set when only one project is available, A_1, is equivalent to the subset consisting of the first three elements of A_2.

Because A_1 and A_2 are of different sizes, the resulting information structures cannot be directly compared using Blackwell informativeness or the methods of Proposition 3. However, the problem can be analysed by other means.

Lemma 1. *Suppose* $K(\cdot)$ *is affine (or concave) on* $\{0, 1, 2\}$. *The cost of inducing* $(2, 0)$ *when the agent's action set is* A_1 *is equal to the cost of inducing* $(2, 0)$ *when the action set is* $\{(0, 0), (2, 0)\}$.

Proof. Let $\mathbf{v} \equiv (v_0, v_1) \equiv [V(y_0), V(y_1)]$ denote a contract stated in terms of the agent's utility. Then the incentive compatibility (IC) constraint for the agent to choose $(2, 0)$ instead of $(0, 0)$ is

---

[20] We are not allowing the firm to expand by simply adding more projects of equal size. As Samuelson (1963) (cited in Diamond 1984) showed, adding statistically independent projects in this manner might not reduce the manager's aversion to the risk of any one project. Moreover, managers might be unable to control a larger number of projects if they had to undertake them all without either hiring additional managers or taking on joint venture partners.

$$2\gamma v_1 + (1 - 2\gamma)v_0 - K(2) \geqslant v_0 - K(0),$$

which is equivalent to

$$\gamma(v_1 - v_0) \geqslant [K(2) - K(0)]/2. \tag{3}$$

Using the fact that $[K(2) - K(0)]/2 \geqslant K(2) - K(1)$, inequality (3) implies

$$2\gamma v_1 + (1 - 2\gamma)v_0 - K(2) \geqslant \gamma v_1 + (1 - \gamma)v_0 - K(1),$$

which is the IC constraint for the choice of $(2, 0)$ instead of $(1, 1)$. QED

Proposition 4. *Suppose* $K(\cdot)$ *is affine (or concave) on* $\{0, 1, 2\}$. *The cost of implementing* a = 2 *is independent of whether diversification is feasible.*

Proof. Suppose the choice sets are $\{(0, 0), (2, 0)\}$ and $\{(0, 0), (1, 1)\}$. The following stochastic matrix is a garbling that maps the former returns structure into the latter:

$$\begin{pmatrix} 1 & \frac{\gamma}{2} & 0 \\ 0 & 1 - \gamma & 0 \\ 0 & \frac{\gamma}{2} & 1 \end{pmatrix}.$$

Because adding new possible actions cannot reduce the principal's cost of inducing an existing action, it follows that the cost of inducing a = 2 under $\mathbf{A}_2$ is no less than the minimum of the cost when the choice set is $\{(0, 0), (1, 1)\}$ and the cost when the choice set is $\{(0, 0), (2, 0)\}$. By the first part of this proof, this minimum is no less than the cost when the choice set is $\{(0, 0), (2, 0)\}$. Thus, by Lemma 1, the cost of inducing a = 2 under $\mathbf{A}_2$ is no less than the cost under $\mathbf{A}_1$. On the other hand, because there is a shifting support when the agent chooses $(1, 1)$—this is the only way she could get two successes—the principal can costlessly force the agent *not* to take $(1, 1)$. Therefore, the cost of inducing $(2, 0)$ under $\mathbf{A}_2$ equals the cost of inducing it under $\mathbf{A}_1$. QED

We have shown that there is no advantage to making diversification feasible, but— because the principal can costlessly block it—there is no disadvantage either. It is nonetheless informative to consider the contrived case where the principal must choose between diversification and non-diversification; that is between the action sets $\mathbf{A}_d \equiv \{(0, 0), (1, 0), (1, 1)\}$ and $\mathbf{A}_1$, respectively. When $K(\cdot)$ is affine or concave, the existence of the non-trivial garbling that maps $\{(0, 0), (2, 0)\}$ into $\{(0, 0), (1, 1)\}$ implies that the principal would be strictly worse off given the latter two-element action set than the former because the agent is strictly risk-averse and a = 2 is not a least-cost action for the agent. As Lemma 1 showed, the cost of implementing a = 2 given the former two-element action set is the same as the cost under the larger set $\mathbf{A}_1$. Because adding undesired actions cannot reduce the principal's cost, the cost of implementing a = 2 in the latter two-element action set is no greater than under the larger set $\mathbf{A}_d$. By transitivity, implementing a = 2 without diversification (i.e. implementing $(2, 0)$ under $\mathbf{A}_1$) costs strictly less than implementing a = 2 with diversification (i.e. implementing $(1, 1)$ under $\mathbf{A}_d$).

Now suppose K convex. An argument similar to that used to prove Lemma 1 establishes:

Lemma 2: *Suppose* $K(\cdot)$ *is convex on* $\{0, 1, 2\}$. *The cost of inducing* $(2, 0)$ *when the agent's action set is* A_1 *is equal to the cost of inducing* $(2, 0)$ *when the action set is* $\{(1, 0), (2, 0)\}$.

We can show by example that it can be cheaper to induce $a = 2$ when the choice set is $\{(1, 0), (2, 0)\}$ than when it's $\{(1, 0), (1, 1)\}$.[21] By Lemma 2, the cost under A_1 is equal to the cost under the first action set. Because adding undesired actions cannot reduce the principal's cost of inducing an existing desired action, the cost of inducing $(1, 1)$ under A_d is no less than the cost when the choice set is $\{(1, 0), (1, 1)\}$. Therefore, this example demonstrates that it can be strictly cheaper to induce $a = 2$ without diversification (i.e. under A_1) than by diversifying (i.e. under A_d) regardless of whether $K(\cdot)$ is affine, concave, or convex.

In the situations identified above, *conditional* on $a = 2$, diversification is actually riskier than focusing on a single project.[22] Moreover, diversification reduces informativeness. By splitting effort, the probability of being successful falls for any given project. And success serves as a signal of high effort. Thus, although now there are two projects to observe, the cumulative effects of the decrease in the informativeness of each project outweighs the information gained by having two projects.

This conclusion may appear at odds with Aron's (1988) findings. Her article appears to show that diversification helps ameliorate the incentive problem. The difference lies in our assumptions about whether diversifying lessens the impact of the agent's action on a given project or not. We assume that the *cost* of diversification is that it reduces the probability that any given project will succeed; that is, by splitting a given level of total effort among multiple projects, the probability that any one project succeeds will fall. In contrast, Aron essentially assumes that the probability of success is not diminished, but the reward associated with success is.[23]

When diversification leaves the probability of success unaffected and simply lowers the pay-off from success, diversification increases informativeness. This is not surprising: the sample size doubles without any degradation of the signal. On the other hand, this type of diversification strikes us as more likely to be the exception than the rule. In many situations, we would expect that division of effort among multiple projects (e.g. different R&D directions) would reduce the probability that any given project would succeed. In that case, diversification can decrease informativeness. When diversification changes the quality of the performance signals, the impact of diversification

---

[21] By numerical simulation, it can be shown that if $V(y) = \ln(y)$, $\gamma \in (1/20, 9/20)$, $K(0) = 0$, $K(2) = 2$, and $K(1) = \theta$, $\theta \in (1/10, 9/10)$, then it's cheaper to induce $a = 2$ in the first case than it is in the second.

[22] It is readily shown that this result is not the consequence of having assumed independence between the projects.

[23] In our setting, this approach would correspond to having the probability of success of each project being γa, where a is the agent's total effort. The pay-offs from a project's success would be $x_S/2$ if two projects are chosen and x_S if only one project is undertaken.

on informativeness—and thus the impact on the principal's equilibrium pay-offs—is ambiguous.

3.2. Hedging

Many corporations use financial instruments, such as insurance and foreign exchange futures contracts to hedge risk. As with corporate diversification, economists have pointed to agency as an explanation of why firms with risk-neutral owners would engage in such behaviour.[24] Let $p_i(\omega)$ denote the return from holding one unit of hedging security i when the state is ω, and let $p(\omega)$ denote the corresponding vector of pay-offs for all hedging securities. ω comprises the verifiable variables on which the pay-offs of the financial contracts depend, and $p(\cdot)$ maps these variables into pay-offs. Let $\mathbf{m}$ denote the firm's holdings of hedging securities. Then, the firm's pay-off is $z = x + \mathbf{m}'p(\omega)$, where as before x is the firm's revenue. Note that if the elements of $p(\omega)$ are independent of the agent's action, a, then there can be no benefit to contracting on z instead of x—x is a sufficient statistic for a.[25] Indeed, if $p(\omega)$ is noisy, then z is less informative than x and the firm's owner is worse off contracting on z instead of x.

There is no need to take non-zero positions in these securities even when the distribution of $p(\omega)$ depends on a, and thus the realization of $p(\omega)$ might serve as an informative signal of the agent's action. Because ω is verifiable, the owner can condition the agent's compensation on z *without purchasing any securities*. In fact, because there is little reason to expect that the optimal contract would be a function of the *sum* of x and $\mathbf{m}'p(\omega)$, contracting on z is very likely worse than contracting directly on x and ω. Thus, in our model, if he has the information needed to do so, the owner should forbid the purchase of any hedging securities that offer negative expected returns (e.g. insurance contracts). If, however, the agent has better information about the expected returns, then it may be inefficient for the owner to control $\mathbf{m}$ directly. In such settings, hedging could be a factor in agency problems. We explore issues of who controls the information structure in the next section.

4. Who Controls the Information Structure?

So far, we have assumed that the owner decides whether the firm should diversify or not. In many situations, this is a reasonable assumption: a merger or acquisition often requires shareholder approval, for example, and is of sufficient importance that it can pay owners to become informed about the transaction. On the other hand, there are diversification decisions (e.g. the number of paths to pursue in developing a new product) that managers make with little direct oversight. For there to be a meaningfully distinction between situations in which the principal chooses the information

---

[24] For analyses of incentives to reduce risk through financial contracts, see Smith and Stulz (1985) and DeMarzo and Duffie (1995).
[25] See Holmstrom (1979).

structure and those in which the agent chooses, the principal must not be able to make the agent's compensation contingent on the choice of information structure in the latter case. While this inability may be implausible when the choice entails new lines of business, it is much more likely when the choice is with regard to the number of R&D or marketing projects to pursue.

We can embed the choice of returns structure in a standard agency problem in which the agent chooses an action pair consisting of a productive action, a, and an 'information-structure' action, i. We call the principal–agent problem in which the owner can specify the returns structure in the contract (i.e. the diversification choice is verifiable) the *direct-choice problem*. We call the principal–agent problem in which the agency contract depends solely on the firm's realized returns the *indirect-choice problem* because the owner indirectly chooses the returns structure through the incentive scheme he offers to his manager.[26]

Obviously, the owner's expected profit in the indirect-choice problem is no greater than his expected profit in the direct-choice problem. The first question we ask is: when is his expected profit no less? Because of the congruence of Blackwell informativeness and riskiness, we know that the manager will choose the more informative returns structure if there is a mean-preserving garbling between the two returns structures and the manager is risk-averse with respect to the firm's profits (i.e. the composition of the agent's compensation scheme and her utility function is concave). Recall $v_i \equiv V(y_i)$, where y_i is the agent's monetary compensation contingent on the firm's returns being x_i.

Corollary to Proposition 1. *Consider two returns structures, Π^1 and Π^2, such that the second returns structure is a mean-preserving garbling of the first, and suppose that the composition of the agent's compensation scheme and utility function is concave:*

$$\frac{v_{n+1} - v_n}{x_{n+1} - x_n} < \frac{v_n - v_{n-1}}{x_n - x_{n-1}} \quad \forall n \in \mathbf{N} \setminus \{1, N\}. \tag{4}$$

Then the manager prefers the first returns structure to the second.

For each action, the density in Π^2 is a riskier distribution over revenues than the corresponding density in Π^1. It follows that, for any action she might choose, the manager expects to do better under the first returns structure than the second.

Condition (4) is unsatisfactory, in that it is an assumption about endogenous variables. The next proposition builds on an earlier result of Grossman and Hart (1983) to state its assumptions in terms of exogenous conditions.

Proposition 5. *Consider two returns structures, Π^1 and Π^2, where the second is a mean-preserving garbling of the first. Suppose that the following conditions are satisfied:*

---

[26] The indirect-choice model is an example of a multi-task principal–agent model. For more on multi-task principal–agent problems see Holmstrom and Milgrom (1991).

A1 (No Shifting Support): $\pi_n^i(a) > 0$ *for all* $a \in A$, $n \in N$, *and* $i \in \{1, 2\}$.

A2 (Monotone Likelihood Ratio Property): *For all* a *and* â *in* A, $K(a) < K(â)$ *implies that* $\pi_n^i(a)/\pi_n^i(â)$ *is non-increasing and convex in* n *and* $i \in \{1, 2\}$.

A3 (Concavity of Distribution Function Property): $K(a) = \gamma K(â) + (1 - \gamma)K(ã)$ $(\gamma \in [0, 1])$ *implies* $\mathbf{P}^i(a) \leq \gamma \mathbf{P}^i(â) + (1 - \gamma)\mathbf{P}^i(ã)$, *where* $\mathbf{P}^i(a)$ *is the cumulative distribution function vector over revenues induced by action* a (i.e. $\mathbf{P}^i(a) = (\pi_1^i(a), \pi_1^i(a) + \pi_2^i(a), \ldots, \pi_1^i(a) + \ldots + \pi_N^i(a))'$), $i \in \{1, 2\}$.

A4 (Income Effects on Attitudes toward Risk): $1/V'(y)$ *is concave in* y.

A5 (Convex Revenues): $x_n - x_{n-1}$ *is non-decreasing in* n.

Then the optimal contract for the direct-choice problem is also an optimal contract for the indirect-choice problem. Moreover, this contract induces the manager to choose the more informative returns structure and yields the owner an expected profit equal to what he would receive in the direct-choice problem.

Assumptions 2–5 strike us as restrictive, and there exist plausible settings in which the optimal contract entails the manager's utility being a non-concave function of returns. In such cases, the manager prefers the less informative returns structure and the owner's expected profit is strictly less in the indirect-choice problem. It is useful to explore why. In particular, profits could be lower because fewer actions are implementable in the indirect-choice problem or because those actions that are implementable cost more to implement.

We first compare the set of implementable actions in the two problems. To this end, we define the following property.

Definition (Convexity of Disutility Property). *Action* a *satisfies* convexity of disutility *if* $\pi(a)'\mathbf{x} = \sum_{j \in J} \lambda_j \pi(a_j)'\mathbf{x}$ *implies that* $K(a) \leq \sum_{j \in J} \lambda_j K(a_j)$, *where* $\{\lambda_j\}$ *is a set of non-negative weights summing to one and* J *is an index set for actions other than* a.[27]

This property implies that any mixed strategy over actions that yields the same expected revenue as action *a* must yield the manager a greater expected disutility of effort than *a*.

Proposition 6. *Consider two returns structures,* Π^1 *and* Π^2, *where the second is a mean-preserving garbling of the first. Suppose that action* â *satisfies the convexity of disutility property in the direct-choice problem (i.e. under the first returns structure). Then there exists a contract in the indirect-choice problem that implements* â *and induces the manager to choose the more informative returns structure.*

The convexity of disutility property is a more stringent property than implementability in the direct-choice problem.[28]

---

[27] This property is related to the Concavity of Distribution Function Property above. It differs in that it applies to any convex combination of actions and is based on expected values rather than first-degree stochastic dominance.

[28] Implementability of *a* in the direct-choice problem requires only that there exists *some* vector **v** such that, if $\pi(a)'\mathbf{v} = \sum_{j \in J} \lambda_j \pi(a_j)'\mathbf{v}$, then $K(a) \leq \sum_{j \in J} \lambda_j K(a_j)$, where $\{\lambda_j\}$ is a set of non-negative weights summing to one.

Of course being able to implement an action pair does not imply that the owner would want to implement it. Indeed, it is possible in the indirect-choice problem that the owner would prefer to implement the *less* informative returns structure. We illustrate this with an example.

Example 3. Suppose $V(y) = \ln(y)$, $A = \{0, 1\}$, $K(0) = 0$, $K(1) = 1$, $\pi^1(0) = (0.5, 0.25, 0.25)'$, $\pi^1(1) = (0.4, 0.05, 0.55)'$, and $x = (0, 12, 24)'$. Intuitively, this example represents the following situation. By working hard ($a = 1$), the manager does not greatly reduce the chance that the project will be a complete failure ($x = 0$). But the manager's effort does affect whether a successful project will do all right or extremely well. Now, consider returns structure $\Pi^2 = Q\Pi^1$, where Q is the mean-preserving garbling

$$Q = \begin{pmatrix} 1 & 0.05 & 0 \\ 0 & 0.9 & 0 \\ 0 & 0.05 & 1 \end{pmatrix}.$$

Under either information structure, the optimal contract for implementing $a = 0$ is to pay the agent $y = 1$ for all outcomes. The owner's expected profit is 8. The optimal contract for implementing ($a = 1$, $i = 1$) is $\tilde{y}_1 \approx 0.15$, $\tilde{y}_2 \approx 1.87$, and $\tilde{y}_3 \approx 22.76$, with an expected cost of 12.67. The optimal contract for implementing ($a = 1$, $i = 2$) is $y_1 \approx 3.09$, $y_2 \approx 0.02$, and $y_3 \approx 3.75$. This contract's expected cost is 3.32, and the owner's expected profit is 10.48. Therefore, the owner will induce the agent to choose the less informative information structure, $i = 2$.

Under either returns structure, the optimal contract for implementing $a = 1$ is one that punishes the manager for achieving $x = 12$ (since $x = 12$ is a relatively rare event if $a = 1$, but a relatively more common event if $a = 0$). Consequently, the manager's utility is a convex function of revenue, so she prefers the riskier—and therefore less informative—returns structure.

In this example, because the two returns structures are very 'close' to one another, there is relatively little loss of information. Would the owners implement the less informative returns structure if the two returns structures were 'far apart'? The following proposition shows the answer is no when one interprets the notion of 'far apart' as the repeated application of a mean-preserving garbling:

Proposition 7. *Consider returns structure Π^1 and mean-preserving garbling Q. Suppose that $(Q)^n$ converges to Q^∞ as n goes to ∞. In the indirect-choice problem with returns structures Π^1 and $\Pi^2 \equiv Q^\infty\Pi^1$, the owners will choose a contract that induces the agent to choose the more informative returns structure, Π^1.*

5. Conclusion

We explored agency as a possible explanation for why corporations diversify even when their shareholders could otherwise do so on their own. In evaluating alternative forms of organizing the firm and the agent's activities, owners of the firm potentially care about the returns' mean, riskiness, and informativeness.

We first examined the relationship between riskiness and informativeness. We showed that diversification that improves the informativeness of the returns structure in the Blackwell sense also reduces the firm's riskiness (Proposition 1). Thus, even if risk-neutral owners did not desire a reduction in risk *per se*, one might observe a positive correlation between diversification and risk reduction. To explore this issue further, we proposed alternative measures of informativeness appropriate for agency relationships. Using these measures, we showed (Example 1 and Proposition 3) that owners may choose returns structures (e.g. diversification strategies) that are more informative but entail increased risk.

We next turned to examination of the effects of diversification on informativeness and riskiness. In the context of an extended example, we showed that diversification that entails the spreading of managerial effort—rather than purely financial diversification—has ambiguous effects on risk and information.

Lastly, we considered situations in which the manager controls the diversification decision. We derived conditions under which the manager would choose to adopt the owners' preferred diversification strategy. Consequently, leaving the diversification decision to the manager under these conditions would be without cost to the owners. More generally, delegating the diversification decision to the manager can be costly for the owners. This is not so much because delegation makes it impossible to implement certain courses of action—the condition under which it has no impact on the set of implementable actions is relatively innocuous—but rather because of the loss of information. It is ambiguous whether the manager will, in equilibrium, choose the same diversification strategy as would the owners had they controlled the diversification decision. In Example 3, we showed that choices could be different; but, in Propositions 5 and 7, we derived conditions under which the choices would be the same.

In closing, we want to discuss the claim that diversification generates financial benefits by economizing on bankruptcy costs.[29] Without getting into a full analysis of bankruptcy here, we want to raise several issues. First, it is not obvious that diversification economizes on bankruptcy costs. In general, combining projects can raise or lower the expected costs of bankruptcy because a single failing project may be 'saved' by other (successful) projects, or it may drag all of them down.[30] Second, it is critical to understand why firms issue securities that give rise to the possibility of bankruptcy. If bankruptcy serves a useful role, then diversification to avoid bankruptcy may be costly. For example, if bankruptcy is a device to discipline managers (e.g. a manager gets in trouble only when there is a bankruptcy), then a joint venture or some other form of diversification may allow the manager to undertake projects that investors would otherwise reject.[31] Finally, one does not want to overstate the costs of bankruptcy. A firm with value as an ongoing concern may renegotiate its debts without formally going

---

[29] For an early example of a model in which this occurs, see Lewellen (1971).

[30] For more on this point, see Higgins's (1971) discussion of Lewellen (1971).

[31] Several authors have sought to model these issues formally. See e.g. Aghion and Bolton (1992), Harris and Raviv (1990), and Hart (1991).

bankrupt or may reorganize (and continue to operate) under bankruptcy. In either case, the costs are largely administrative ones, not the loss in the value of firm's productive activities.

APPENDIX

Proof of Proposition 2. Suppose, contrary to the statement of the proposition, that Π^2 is more Blackwell informative. Then there exists a stochastic transformation matrix $\mathbf{R}$ such that $\Pi^1 = \mathbf{R}\Pi^2$. Since the two returns structures yield the same expected returns conditional on the same action, $\Pi^{2\prime}(\mathbf{R} - \mathbf{I})'\mathbf{x} = \mathbf{0}$. Because Π^2 has full rank, it follows that $\mathbf{R}'\mathbf{x} = \mathbf{x}$. Thus, $\mathbf{R}$ is a mean-preserving garbling. From Blackwell's Theorem, it follows that $\pi^2(a)$ is less risky than $\pi^1(a)$—but this contradicts the assumption that $\pi^1(a)$ is strictly less risky than $\pi^2(a)$. QED

In the proofs below, we will make use of the following two facts about the individual rationality (IR) and incentive compatibility (IC) constraints stated below. One, if contract $\mathbf{v}$ satisfies these constraints, then it implements action $\hat{a}$. Two, if the optimal solution to the agency problem entails implementing action $\hat{a}$, then it must satisfy these constraints.

$$\sum_{i \in N} \pi_i(\hat{a}) v_i = K(\hat{a}) \tag{IR}$$

and

$$\sum_{i \in N} \{\pi_i(a) - \pi_i(\hat{a})\} v_i \leq K(a) - K(\hat{a}) \; \forall a \in \mathbf{A}.^{32} \tag{IC}$$

Lemma A1: If $\mathbf{v}^*$ is the solution to an agency problem in which $\pi_m(a) - \pi_m(\hat{a}) > 0 > \pi_n(a) - \pi_n(\hat{a}) \; \forall a \in \mathbf{A}\backslash\{\hat{a}\}$, then $v_m^* \leq v_n^*$.

Proof of Lemma A1: Suppose that, contrary to the hypothesis of the lemma, $\pi_m(a) - \pi_m(\hat{a}) > 0 > \pi_n(a) - \pi_n(\hat{a}) \; \forall a \in \mathbf{A}\backslash\{\hat{a}\}$ and $v_m^* > v_n^*$.

Define $\mathbf{v}^a$ by

$$v_i^a = \begin{cases} v_i^* & \text{if } i \neq m, n \\ v_0 \equiv \dfrac{\pi_m(\hat{a}) v_m^* + \pi_n(\hat{a}) v_n^*}{\pi_m(\hat{a}) + \pi_n(\hat{a})} & \text{if } i = m, n. \end{cases}$$

Because $\pi_n(\hat{a})$ cannot be zero, v_0 is well defined. It is trivial to verify that $\mathbf{v}^a$ satisfies the (IR) constraint.

Turning to the (IC) constraints, we have

---

[32] When the agent's utility is additively separable—as it is here—there is no loss in generality from assuming that the (IR) constraint is binding (see Grossman and Hart 1983).

$$\sum_{i\in N}\{\pi_i(a) - \pi_i(\hat{a})\}v_i^a = \sum_{i\in N}\{\pi_i(a) - \pi_i(\hat{a})\}v_i^* + \{v_0 - v_m^*\}\{\pi_m(a) - \pi_m(\hat{a})\}$$
$$+ \{v_0 - v_n^*\}\{\pi_n(a) - \pi_n(\hat{a})\}$$
$$< \sum_{i\in N}\{\pi_i(a) - \pi_i(\hat{a})\}v_i^* \leqslant K(a) - K(\hat{a}) \;\forall a \in A.$$

Thus, the contract v^a implements $\hat{a}$. Because the agent's expected utility is the same but the contract entails less variability, Jensen's inequality implies that the principal prefers v^a to v^*, which contradicts the optimality of v^*. QED

Proof of Proposition 3. Condition (ii) implies $\pi_n^2(\hat{a}) > 0$ for all n. Thus, if $\hat{a}$ can be implemented at first-best cost under the second returns structure, it follows from Proposition 3 of Grossman and Hart (1983) that it must be a least-cost action. But if $\hat{a}$ is a least-cost action, it can be implemented at first-best cost under either information structure. This completes the proof if $\hat{a}$ is a least-cost action. It also shows that if $\hat{a}$ is not a least-cost action, then it cannot be implemented at first-best cost (i.e. under a full-insurance contract).

Assume, henceforth, that $\hat{a}$ is not a least-cost action. Suppose that v^* is an optimal contract when the returns structure is Π^2. Pick a constant, $\beta \in (0, 1)$, such that

$$\min_{n\in N}\frac{\pi_n^2(\hat{a})}{\pi_n^1(\hat{a})} > \beta > \max_{m\in N}\frac{\pi_m^2(a) - \pi_m^2(\hat{a})}{\pi_m^1(a) - \pi_m^1(\hat{a})}.$$

Such a β exists by hypothesis. Define $\mathbf{R} \equiv \beta\mathbf{I} + [\pi^2(\hat{a})] - \beta[\pi^1(\hat{a})]$, where $[\pi]$ is the $N \times N$ matrix in which each column is π. Combining the result that $\pi_n^2(\hat{a}) > 0$ for all n with the definition of β, it follows that every element of $\mathbf{R}$ is positive. Define $\tilde{v} \equiv \mathbf{R}'v^*$, so that

$$\tilde{v}_i = \beta v_i^* + \sum_{n\in N}(\pi_n^2(\hat{a}) - \beta\pi_n^1(\hat{a}))v_n^*.$$

Define $S \equiv \{i \,|\, \pi_i^1(a) - \pi_i^1(\hat{a}) > 0\}$. Lastly, define $v_0 \equiv \max_{i\in S}v_i^*$. Note that, by Lemma A1, $v_0 \leqslant \min_{i\in N\backslash S}v_i^*$.

It is trivial to verify that $\tilde{v}$ satisfies the (IR) constraint when the information structure is Π^1. Now, consider the (IC) constraints. Using the fact that $\sum_{i\in N}\{\pi_i(a) - \pi_i(\hat{a})\} = 0$, we have

$$\sum_{i\in N}(\pi_i^1(a) - \pi_i^1(\hat{a}))\,\tilde{v}_i = \sum_{i\in N}(\pi_i^1(a) - \pi_i^1(\hat{a}))\beta v_i^*$$
$$= \sum_{i\in S}(\pi_i^1(a) - \pi_i^1(\hat{a}))\beta(v_i^* - v_0) + \sum_{i\in N\backslash S}(\pi_i^1(a) - \pi_i^1(\hat{a}))\beta(v_i^* - v_0)$$
$$\leqslant \sum_{i\in S}(\pi_i^2(a) - \pi_i^2(\hat{a}))(v_i^* - v_0) + \sum_{i\in N\backslash S}(\pi_i^2(a) - \pi_i^2(\hat{a}))(v_i^* - v_0)$$

by condition (i) of the Proposition, the construction of β, and the definition of v_0. Simplifying,

$$\sum_{i\in N}(\pi_i^1(a) - \pi_i^1(\hat{a}))\,\tilde{v}_i \leqslant \sum_{i\in N}(\pi_i^2(a) - \pi_i^2(\hat{a}))v_i^*$$
$$\leqslant K(a) - K(\hat{a}) \;\forall a \in A,$$

where the last inequality follows from the fact that $\mathbf{v}^*$ is a solution to the agency problem under returns structure Π^2. Hence, the (IC) constraints are satisfied by $\tilde{\mathbf{v}}$ under returns structure Π^1.

It remains to show that the principal prefers contract under returns structure Π^1 to contract $\mathbf{v}^*$ under returns structure Π^2. Define $\mathbf{y} \equiv (y_1, \ldots, y_N)'$, where $y_n = V^{-1}(v_n)$ (adding asterisks or tildes as appropriate). By construction $\tilde{v}_n = \mathbf{r}_{\cdot n}'\mathbf{v}^*$, where $\mathbf{r}_{\cdot n}$ is the nth column of $\mathbf{R}$. Because (i) $V^{-1}(\cdot)$ is a strictly convex function, (ii) $\mathbf{y}^*$ is not a full-insurance contract, and (iii) $\mathbf{r}_{\cdot n}$ has no zero element, Jensen's inequality implies that $\tilde{y}_n < \mathbf{r}_{\cdot n}'\mathbf{y}^*$ for all n. Hence,

$$\pi^1(\hat{a})'\tilde{\mathbf{y}} = \sum_{n \in N} \pi_n^1(\hat{a})\tilde{y}_n < \sum_{n \in N} \pi_n^1(\hat{a})(\mathbf{r}_{\cdot n}'\mathbf{y}^*) = \pi^2(\hat{a})'\mathbf{y}^*,$$

where the final equality follows from the fact that $\mathbf{R}\pi^1(a) = \pi^2(a)$. Therefore, the expected monetary compensation under the first information structure is strictly less than the expected monetary compensation under the second information structure. QED

Proof of Corollary to Proposition 3. Assumptions (i) and (ii) of the corollary imply that conditions (i) and (ii) of Proposition 3 are satisfied, because $\pi^1(\hat{a}) = \pi^2(\hat{a}) \equiv \hat{\pi}$ implies that $\min_{n \in N} \pi_n^2(\hat{a})/\pi_n^1(\hat{a}) = 1$. QED

Proof of Proposition 5. Proposition 9 of Grossman and Hart (1983) establishes that, under Assumptions A1–A4, the optimal contract, $y_{n+1} - y_n$, is non-increasing in n. Because $V(\cdot)$ is concave, it follows that $v_{n+1} - v_n$ is also non-increasing in n. This fact and Assumption A5 imply condition (4) is satisfied in the Corollary to Proposition 1. QED

Proof of Proposition 6. Suppose, contrary to the proposition, that the pair $(\hat{a}, 1)$ is not implementable (where (a, i) denotes action a and returns structure i). By Proposition 2 of Hermalin and Katz (1991), there exist sets $A_1 \subseteq A$ and $A_2 \subseteq A$ and a set of positive weights $\{\mu(a), \lambda(a)\}$ summing to one such that

$$\pi^1(\hat{a})' = \sum_{a \in A_1} \mu(a)\pi^1(a)' + \sum_{a \in A_2} \lambda(a)\pi^2(a)' \tag{5}$$

and

$$K(\hat{a}) > \sum_{a \in A_1} \mu(a)K(a) + \sum_{a \in A_2} \lambda(a)K(a). \tag{6}$$

Post-multiplying (5) by $\mathbf{x}$ and simplifying yields

$$\pi^1(\hat{a})'\mathbf{x} = \sum_{a \in A_1 \cup A_2} \hat{\mu}(a)\pi^1(a)'\mathbf{x}, \tag{7}$$

where

$$\hat{\mu}(a) = \frac{\mu(a) \cdot \mathbf{1}_{\{a \in A_1\}} + \lambda(a) \cdot \mathbf{1}_{\{a \in A_2\}}}{1 - \lambda(\hat{a}) \cdot \mathbf{1}_{\{a \in A_2\}}},$$

where $1_{(\cdot)}$ is an indicator function. By construction, $\hat{\mu}(a) > 0$ and the sum of $\hat{\mu}(a)$ over a in $(\mathbf{A}_1 \cup \mathbf{A}_2) \setminus \{\hat{a}\}$ is one. Carrying out the same simplification on (6) yields

$$K(\hat{a}) > \sum_{a \in \mathbf{A}_1 \cup \mathbf{A}_2} \hat{\mu}(a) K(a). \tag{8}$$

But (7) and (8) contradict the assumption that $\hat{a}$ satisfies the convexity of disutility property. QED

Proof of Proposition 7. Suppose the equilibrium contract, $\mathbf{v}^*$, implements $(a^*, i = 2)$. Define $\tilde{\mathbf{v}} \equiv \mathbf{Q}^{\infty\prime} \mathbf{v}^*$, and note that $\pi^1(a)' \tilde{\mathbf{v}} = \pi^2(a)' \mathbf{v}^*$.

We will now show that the contract $\tilde{\mathbf{v}}$ implements $(a^*, i = 1)$. Consider first the (IR) constraint. Because

$$\pi^1(a^*)' \tilde{\mathbf{v}} - K(a^*) = \pi^2(a^*)' \mathbf{v}^* - K(a^*) = 0,$$

the (IR) constraint is satisfied. Next consider the (IC) constraints. Because the choice of returns structure is endogenous, we have two sets of constraints

$$\{\pi^1(a)' - \pi^1(a^*)'\} \tilde{\mathbf{v}} \leqslant K(a) - K(a^*) \ \forall a \in \mathbf{A}, \tag{9}$$

and

$$\{\pi^2(a)' - \pi^1(a^*)'\} \tilde{\mathbf{v}} \leqslant K(a) - K(a^*) \ \forall a \in \mathbf{A} \tag{10}$$

Condition (9) is satisfied because

$$\pi^1(a)' \tilde{\mathbf{v}} = \pi^2(a)' \mathbf{v}^*,$$

and $\mathbf{v}^*$ implements a^* under Π^2. Consider (10). Using the fact that $\mathbf{Q}^\infty$ must be an idempotent matrix (i.e. $\mathbf{Q}^\infty \mathbf{Q}^\infty = \mathbf{Q}^\infty$), we have

$$\pi^2(a)' \tilde{\mathbf{v}} = \pi^1(a)' \mathbf{Q}^{\infty\prime} \mathbf{Q}^{\infty\prime} \mathbf{v}^* = \pi^1(a)' \mathbf{Q}^{\infty\prime} \mathbf{v}^* = \pi^2(a)' \mathbf{v}^*.$$

This equality, the fact that $\pi^1(a^*)' \tilde{\mathbf{v}} = \pi^2(a^*)' \mathbf{v}^*$, and the fact that $\mathbf{v}^*$ implements a^* under Π^2, imply (10).

Next, we show that $\tilde{\mathbf{y}}$ has lower expected cost than $\mathbf{y}^*$ (where, as before, $y_n = V^{-1}(v_n)$). $\tilde{v}_n = \mathbf{q}_{\cdot n}' \mathbf{v}^*$, where $\mathbf{q}_{\cdot n}$ is the nth column of $\mathbf{Q}^\infty$. Since $V^{-1}(\cdot)$ is a convex function, Jensen's inequality implies that $\tilde{y}_n \leqslant \mathbf{q}_{\cdot n}' \mathbf{y}^*$ for all n. This, in turn, implies that $\pi^1(a^*)' \tilde{\mathbf{y}} \leqslant \pi^2(a^*)' \mathbf{y}^*$. Thus, the expected monetary payments made by the principal to the agent are lower when a^* is implemented under returns structure 1 rather than 2. Since $\pi^1(a^*)' \mathbf{x} = \pi^2(a^*)' \mathbf{x}$, the expected gross returns are identical. It follows that the owners (weakly) prefer implementing $(a^*, i = 1)$ to implementing $(a^*, i = 2)$. QED

References

Aghion, P., and P. Bolton (1992). 'An Incomplete Contract Approach to Bankruptcy and the Financial Structure of the Firm', *Review of Economics Studies* 59: 473–94.

Alberts, W. W. (1966). 'The Profitability of Growth by Merger', in *The Corporate Merger*, W. W. Alberts and J. E. Segall (eds.). Chicago: University of Chicago Press.

Amihud, Yakov, Peter Dodd, and Mark Weinstein (1986). 'Conglomerate Mergers, Managerial Motives, and Stockholder Wealth', *Journal of Banking and Finance* 10: 401–10.

—— and Baruch Lev (1981). 'Risk Reduction as a Managerial Motive for Conglomerate Mergers', *Bell Journal of Economics* 12: 605–17.

Aron, Debra J. (1988). 'Ability, Moral Hazard, Firm Size, and Diversification', *RAND Journal of Economics* 19: 72–87.

DeMarzo, Peter M., and Darrell Duffie (1995). 'Corporate Incentives for Hedging and Hedge Accounting', *Review of Financial Studies* 8: 743–71.

Diamond, Douglas W. (1984). 'Financial Intermediation and Delegated Monitoring', *Review of Economic Studies* 51: 393–414.

—— and Robert E. Verrecchia (1982). 'Optimal Managerial Contracts and Equilibrium Security Prices', *Journal of Finance* 37: 275–88.

Gjesdal, Froystein (1981). 'Accounting for Stewardship', *Journal of Accounting* 19: 208–31.

Grossman, Sanford, and Oliver D. Hart (1983). 'An Analysis of the Principal-Agent Problem', *Econometrica* 51: 7–45.

Harris, Milton, and Artur Raviv (1990). 'Capital Structure and the Informational Role of Debt', *Journal of Finance* 45: 321–49.

Hart, Oliver (1991). 'Theories of Optimal Capital Structure: A Principal-Agent Perspective', Unpublished draft, MIT.

Hermalin, Benjamin E. (1993). 'Managerial Preferences Concerning Risky Projects', *Journal of Law, Economics, and Organization* 9: 127–35.

—— and Michael L. Katz (1991). 'Moral Hazard and Verifiability: The Effects of Renegotiation in Agency', *Econometrica* 59: 1735–53.

Higgins, Robert C. (1971). 'Discussion of "A Pure Financial Rationale for the Conglomerate Merger"', *Journal of Finance* 26: 543–5.

Holmstrom, Bengt (1979). 'Moral Hazard and Observability', *Bell Journal of Economics* 10: 74–91.

—— and Paul Milgrom (1991). 'Multitask Principal-Agent Analyses: Incentive Contracts, Asset Ownership, and Job Design', *Journal of Law, Economics, and Organization* 7: 24–52.

Kim, Son Ku (1995). 'Efficiency of an Information System in an Agency Model', *Econometrica* 63: 89–102.

Levy, Haim, and Marshall Sarnat (1970). 'Diversification, Portfolio Analysis and the Uneasy Case for Conglomerate Mergers', *Journal of Finance* 25: 795–802.

Lewellen, Wilbur G. (1971). 'A Pure Financial Rationale for the Conglomerate Merger', *Journal of Finance* 26: 521–37.

—— Claudio Loderer, and Ahron Rosenfeld (1989). 'Mergers, Executive Risk Reduction, and Stockholder Wealth', *Journal of Financial and Quantitative Analysis* 24: 459–72.

Marshall, Albert W., and Ingram Olkin (1979). *Inequalities: Theory of Majorization and Its Applications*. San Diego: Academic Press.

Marshall, William J., Jess B. Yawitz, and Edward Greenberg (1984). 'Incentives for Diversification and the Structure of the Conglomerate Firm', *Southern Economic Journal* 51: 1–23.

Mirrlees, James A. (1976). 'The Optimal Structure of Incentives and Authority within an Organization', *Bell Journal of Ecnomics* 7: 105–31.

—— (1999). 'The Theory of Moral Hazard and Unobservable Behaviour: Part I', *Review of Economic Studies* 66: 3–21.

Morck, Randall, Andrei Shleifer, and Robert W. Vishny (1990). 'Do Managerial Objectives Drive Bad Acquisitions?' *Journal of Finance* 45: 31–48.

Porter, Michael (1987). 'From Competitive Advantage to Corporate Strategy', *Harvard Business Review*, May–June, 43–59.

Samuelson, Paul A. (1963). 'Risk and Uncertainty: A Fallacy of Large Numbers', *Scientia* 98: 108–13.

Shavell, Steven (1979). 'Risk Sharing and Incentives in the Principal and Agent Relationship', *Bell Journal of Economics* 10: 55–73.

Smith, Clifford W., and Rene M. Stulz (1985). 'The Determinants of Firm's Hedging Policies', *Journal of Financial and Quantitative Analysis* 20: 391–405.

Zhang, Guochang (1998). Ownership Concentration, Risk Aversion and the Effect of Financial Structure on Investment Decisions', *European Economic Review* 42: 1751–78.

3 Adverse Selection and Insurance with *uberrima fides*

AVINASH DIXIT

- 1880 *Law Rep. Appeals Cases* 954 In policies of insurance, whether marine insurance or life insurance, there is an understanding that the contract is *uberrima fides*.
- 1959 Jowitt *Dict. Eng. Law II 1797* . . . such as to require full disclosure and the utmost good faith.

Quotation from the Oxford English Dictionary

1. Introduction

The theory of screening and mechanism design has come a long way since Mirrlees' (1971) pioneering solution of the optimum income tax problem. The general idea is that an agent who has private information that affects the principal's pay-off must be given a suitable share of the economic rent or surplus in the relationship to induce him to reveal this information by his action, that is, to achieve screening by self-selection. Other methods of obtaining the information, such as investigation or audit to obtain the information, are implicitly assumed to be too costly to use. In reality the alternative methods are used when the cost is small in relation to the benefit; for example many life insurance policies are issued only after a medical examination. But some residual asymmetry of information remains, and is too costly to remove.

In the economist's standard model of insurance with asymmetric information, Rothschild and Stiglitz (1976), the insurance company separates applicants with a low risk of loss from those with a high risk by offering a contract with only partial coverage to the low-risk types; they are made to bear just enough loss to make that contract unattractive to the high-risk types.

One should expect social institutions to evolve to cope with this problem. Common law attempts to do so by making insurance contracts subject to an understanding that the insured should make a full disclosure in utmost good faith, or *uberrima fides*, of all facts pertaining to his risk that are known to him in advance. This greatly reduces the cost of investigation. The company asks the relevant questions on its insurance application, but it need not investigate the truth of the answers unless a claim is made. At that time, if the answers are found to be false, the company can refuse to pay the claim on the grounds that the customer had not made the requisite disclosures. This prospect provides a new way to deter high-risk types from claiming to be low-risk. Separation can be achieved more easily, and in equilibrium the low-risk types can get better

I thank Alessandro Lizzeri for useful discussions, Peter Diamond, Gareth Myles, Barry Nalebuff, and Pierre Picard for perceptive comments on a previous draft, and the National Science Foundation for financial support.

coverage. Of course the Rothschild–Stiglitz model must be reworked to find out how the contracts and the equilibrium change when the requirement of *uberrima fides* is imposed. That is the aim of this paper.

Different countries apply *uberrima fides* with different degrees of strictness. In the USA, enforcement has become quite weak. Insurance companies often overlook false statements on insurance application forms unless the falsehoods are very extreme; even then, statutes of limitations apply, and in trials juries favour the insured. In Britain, the doctrine is enforced more strictly. In France the legal system is different, but a similar doctrine is enforced even more strictly. Even if the insured did not know some facts and made his assertions in good faith, he can be made to bear a portion of the loss as coinsurance if later investigation shows that these assertions were false. If bad faith can be proved, the contract is cancelled and courts can impose fines on the claimant. I find that *uberrima fides* leads to a Pareto improvement; thus the model suggests that the USA should move back towards stricter enforcement.

Economists are usually quite willing to accept that people will take full private advantage of the opportunities to conceal information (or take unobservable actions). Mirrlees (1999) regards as 'startling' the position that 'rational economic behavior cannot be morally perfidious'. The usual theory of mechanism design proposes to reward a person who refrains from such behaviour by offering him a share of the surplus. The approach of this paper uses the threat of a penalty instead of a reward. It is interesting to note that this social attempt to enforce morally superior behaviour by placing the onus of disclosure on the insured leads to an outcome that is in the rational personal interest of all.

There is a lot of literature on auditing. Townsend (1979) and Mookherjee and Png (1989) have general theoretical models, Reinganum and Wilde (1986, 1988) analyse income tax audits, Baron and Besanko (1984) deal with cost-audits of regulated firms, and Fagart and Picard (1999) analyse insurance audits of claims about the size of the loss. All these are cases of costly state verification. (In Baron and Besanko the total cost, which is a combination of type and state, is observable.) My paper deals with adverse selection (pre-contract asymmetry.) Costly verification and auditing can be thought of as response to possible fraud in *insurance claims*; pre-contract asymmetry and investigation deals with possible fraud in insurance *applications*. Some results in the adverse selection case are similar to those of the costly state verification case; in particular the importance of probabilistic auditing, and of providing a reward for truthtelling, carries over. But adverse selection is arguably a more basic and important problem of information asymmetry in insurance and therefore worth separate analysis. Also, the setting of competitive equilibrium can differ from that of a single principal designing a mechanism that typifies the auditing literature.

2. The Model

I modify the Rothschild–Stiglitz (1976) model to the minimal extent necessary for my present purpose. All individuals are expected utility maximizers, with the utility-of-wealth function $U(W)$. Each faces an idiosyncratic risk of an accident. His wealth in the no-accident state is W_N, and that in the accident state is W_A, with $W_N > W_A$. Thus the loss from the accident is $A = W_N - W_A$. There are two risk types, the low-risk or L-type with accident probability π_L, and the high-risk or H-type with accident probability π_H, where $0 < \pi_L < \pi_H < 1$. To keep the model as similar to that of Rothschild–Stiglitz and thereby highlight the new features due to *uberrima fides*, I assume that the probability of loss is private information but the size of the loss is common knowledge. But as a matter of reality, the alternative case of privately known loss size is also worth separate investigation.

Insurance companies are risk-neutral, have no administration costs, and can enter the industry freely. As in Kreps (1990: 649), I model the Rothschild–Stiglitz equilibrium as the subgame perfect Nash equilibrium in pure strategies of a game where insurance companies offer contracts, and customers choose from among these contracts.

In the Rothschild–Stiglitz model, any customer was free to choose any contract; separation was achieved by self-selection alone. Under the doctrine of *uberrima fides*, we have a new possibility. An insurance company offering a contract can label it as available only to a particular type. When applying for such a contract, a customer has to certify that he is of its type. The company can investigate this assertion at any time by paying cost c; I assume that an investigation reveals the truth accurately and unambiguously. If the assertion is found to be false, the company can void the contract *ex post facto*. Therefore an investigation will be carried out, if at all, only after a claim is made. I employ a very mild form of *uberrima fides*: when the company voids the contract, it must return the premium that was paid by the individual. This suffices to yield an equilibrium that is Pareto-superior to the separating equilibrium of the Rothschild–Stiglitz model. *Uberrima fides* in a stronger sense would let the company deny the claim and keep the premium. This stronger interpretation would yield qualitatively similar results but achieve an even greater Pareto improvement. If fines can be levied, that can yield even stronger results.

3. The Desirability of Costly Investigation

First suppose that the principle of *uberrima fides* is newly introduced in an insurance industry where a Rothschild–Stiglitz separating equilibrium prevails. Will that equilibrium survive?

Recall that in the original equilibrium, (i) the high-risk types get full and actuarially fair insurance, (ii) the low-risk types get actuarially fair but partial insurance, (iii) the low-risk types prefer their own contract to that taken up by the high-risk types, and (iv) the high-risk types are indifferent between their own contract and that intended for the low-risk types.

Write S for the shortfall of insurance for the low-risk types, that is, the difference between their final wealth in the no-accident and accident states. Using the actuarial fairness condition, it is easy to calculate that their wealth in the no-accident state will be

$$W_N - \pi_L A + \pi_L S = (1 - \pi_L)W_N + \pi_L W_A + \pi_L S = \hat{W} + \pi_L S,$$

where $\hat{W}$ is the average wealth over the two states, and that in the accident state will be

$$W_N - \pi_L A - (1 - \pi_L)S = (1 - \pi_L)W_N + \pi_L W_A - (1 - \pi_L)S$$
$$= \hat{W} - (1 - \pi_L)S.$$

Now suppose a company introduces the following contract intended for the low-risk types. To take up this contract, a customer must declare himself to be type-L and pay a premium K. If there is an accident, the company will investigate the truth of this assertion. If the customer has been truthful, the company will pay him A, so his final wealth is $W_N - K$ in both states. If the investigation reveals that the customer is in fact type-H, then the company will refund his premium but not pay anything else.

This contract will not appeal to the high-risk types: if there is no accident they simply lose their premium and end up with $W_N - K$, and if there is an accident they get their premium back but bear the loss A, and so end up with W_A. They would have been better off buying no insurance at all, and *a fortiori*, they would have been better off buying the full and fair insurance contract intended for their type in the separating equilibrium.

This contract will appeal to the low-risk types if

$$U(W_N - K) > (1 - \pi_L)U(\hat{W} + \pi_L S) + \pi_L U(\hat{W} - (1 - \pi_L)S).$$

It will be profitable for the insurance company if the premium covers the expected costs of claim and investigation, that is,

$$K > \pi_L(A + c).$$

Combining these two conditions, we see that some entrant company will offer such a contract that will then beat out the original contract for the low-risk types and destroy the original equilibrium if

$$U(\hat{W} - \pi_L c) > (1 - \pi_L)U(\hat{W} + \pi_L S) + \pi_L U(\hat{W} - (1 - \pi_L)S). \tag{1}$$

The above alternative contract based on *uberrima fides* was chosen for its simplicity rather than its optimality. In particular, as we will see below, probabilistic investigation does better than the sure investigation stipulated here. Therefore the condition (1) is sufficient, not necessary, to destroy the original Rothschild–Stiglitz equilibrium. Also, the alternative contract is not going to be a part of the new equilibrium. But the condition is useful for its simplicity. It gives a weak upper bound on the investigation cost for *uberrima fides* to make a difference.

Inspection of (1) shows that the condition is more likely to be met, other things equal, when S is larger. That is precisely when there is greater need for an alternative—when asymmetric information poses a more serious obstacle to offering full insurance to the low-risk types. If we take a second-order approximation to the right-hand side, we see the condition in a form easier to interpret. Expressing the insurance company's cost of investigation c relative to the size of the loss A, the condition becomes

$$\frac{c}{A} < \frac{1 - \pi_L}{2} R(\hat{W}) \left(\frac{S}{A}\right)^2 \frac{A}{\hat{W}} \tag{2}$$

where $R(\hat{W})$ is the coefficient of relative risk aversion evaluated at the average wealth. For example, if $\pi_L = 0.01$, $R = 2$, and $A/\hat{W} = 0.1$, $S/A = 0.5$ (that is, the loss equals 10 per cent of average wealth and low-risk types have to bear half of it in the Rothschild–Stiglitz equilibrium in order to achieve separation), then an investigation cost as high as 2.5 per cent of the loss (for example \$2,500 on a loss of \$100,000) is acceptable to a company contemplating offering a contract with *uberrima fides*. And this is only a sufficient condition.

Note the importance of the ability to investigate only when there is an accident. If the company had to investigate every application in advance, the corresponding condition would have a π_L on the right-hand side, and the upper bound on cost would be much tighter. In the above example, a cost higher than just \$25 would be too much. Thus *uberrima fides* substantially improves a company's ability to separate types.

4. Contracts and Equilibrium with Investigation

Here I assume a condition like (1) that rules out an ordinary Rothschild–Stiglitz equilibrium (RS) without investigation, and characterize competitive equilibrium when contracts based on *uberrima fides* are permitted and enforced (UF). The argument proceeds in a sequence of steps, which are laid out as Propositions for clarity.

Proposition 1. There cannot be any pooling in a UF equilibrium.

Proof. In a pooled contract the company will not conduct any investigation of type. With free entry, the contract must break even at the pool-average odds of an accident. Then the standard Rothschild–Stiglitz argument applies. The contract is a point, say P, that lies on the pool-average break-even line in (W_N, W_A) space. This point P is below the L-type's break-even line through the endowment point, so any contract in the neighbourhood of P that attracts only L-types without any investigation makes a profit. And since the indifference curve of the L-types through P is steeper than that of the H-types, such neighbouring contracts can be found. One such will be introduced by an entrant and the candidate pooling contract will be beaten. (Even under *uberrima fides*, a company can always write a contract where it *agrees* not to investigate.) ∎

Proposition 2. There cannot be a separating UF equilibrium where one company offers both types of contracts and cross-subsidizes loss on one type using profits on the other type.

Proof. An entrant could just offer the profit-making contract and get some customers. ∎

When a company can conduct an investigation, the most general contract it can offer is of the following form. Consider a customer who claims to be of type I ($I = H, L$).

If there is no accident, the customer pays the company an amount k_I. If there is an accident, the company will investigate the customer's assertion with probability p_I. If it investigates and finds that the customer has been truthful, it pays the customer x_I. If it investigates and finds that the customer has been untruthful, it pays the customer y_I. If it does not investigate, it pays the customer z_I. One can think of the k_I as the premium the customer pays in advance, and then $k_I + x_I$, etc. become the gross payments by the company to the customer in the various subcases of the accident state.

Note that the legal doctrine of *uberrima fides* allows the company to distinguish its payments in the cases of finding truth and falsehood when it carries out an investigation, that is, it allows $x_I \neq y_I$. The doctrine says nothing about what happens when the company does not carry out an investigation at all, namely whether it can write a contract with $x_I \neq z_I$. But the law does not forbid this either, and I will allow it to keep the contract as general as possible. In the concluding section I will comment on various restricted contracts.

All these amounts and investigation probabilities for both types are endogenous, to be determined as a part of the characterization of the equilibrium. Even before we start, it is obvious that the y_I are going to be set as low as the principle of *uberrima fides* allows. I interpret the principle in a weak form, where the company merely voids the contract and returns the premium to a customer caught lying, so $y_I = 0$. A stricter form would be one where the company keeps the premium, so $y_I + k_I = 0$ or $y_I = -k_I$.

Let $u_I(C)$ denote the expected utility of type I with contract C.

Proposition 3. The only pair of contracts (whether offered by one company or separate ones) that constitutes a candidate for a separating UF equilibrium is as follows. The contract C_H^* intended for the H-types gives them full and actuarially fair insurance without conducting any investigation of type. The contract $C_L(\mathrm{UF})$ for the L-types solves the following constrained optimization problem P_L:

$$u_L(C_L(\mathrm{UF})) = \max(1 - \pi_L)U(W_N - k_L) + \pi_L[p_L U(W_A + x_L) \\ + (1 - p_L)U(W_A + z_L)] \tag{3}$$

subject to the no-loss constraint:

$$(1 - \pi_L)k_L - \pi_L[p_L(c + x_L) + (1 - p_L)z_L] \geq 0 \tag{4}$$

and the incentive-compatibility condition for type H:

$$u_H(C_H^*) \geq (1 - \pi_H)U(W_N - k_L) + \pi_H[p_L U(W_A + y_L) \\ + (1 - p_L)U(W_A + z_L)]. \tag{5}$$

Proof. The contract C_H^* is the best that can be offered for H-types without cross-subsidization. It does not conduct any investigation, and does not impose any incentive-compatibility condition stopping an L-type from claiming to be an H-type; we proceed to verify that this condition is automatically satisfied by $C_L(\mathrm{UF})$.

The contract for the L-types in the Rothschild–Stiglitz model, call it $C_L(\mathrm{RS})$, solves a problem identical to P_L except that it has no possibility of investigation, which is equivalent to imposing an additional constraint $p_L = 0$ (and thereby making x_L and y_L

irrelevant). Therefore the utility of the L-types under these alternative contracts must satisfy $u_L(C_L(\text{UF})) \geqslant u_L(C_L(\text{RS}))$. The contract for the H-types is the same in our candidate UF separating equilibrium as in the RS equilibrium, namely C_H^* with full, fair insurance. And we already know that the L-type's incentive constraint is slack in the RS equilibrium: $U_L(C_L(\text{RS})) > U_L(C_H^*)$. Therefore $U_L(C_L(\text{UF})) > U_L(C_H^*)$: the L-types prefer the contract $C_L(\text{UF})$ to C_H^*.

Thus the contracts C_H^* and $C_L(\text{UF})$ are separating. And no other pair of separating contracts can survive in a competitive equilibrium. Any other contract that gives H-types equal or higher utility than $u_H(C_H^*)$ must make a loss; anything that gives them lower utility can be beaten by an entrant introducing a contract that gives them somewhat higher utility and makes a profit. And $C_L(\text{UF})$ is designed to be the best for L-types subject to the no-loss constraint and the incentive constraint of the H-types; any other separating and non-loss-making contract intended for the L-types can be beaten by an entrant profitably offering something close to $C_L(\text{UF})$. ∎

Proposition 4. A separating UF equilibrium exists for a range of population proportions of the two types larger than that for which an RS equilibrium exists.

Proof. In the candidate separating contract pair of Proposition 3, the L-types get expected utility $u_L(C_L(\text{UF}))$, which is independent of the proportions of the two types in the population. Also, $u_L(C_L(\text{UF})) < u_L(C_L^*)$, the expected utility of the L-types under the full, actuarially fair contract for their type. If the proportion of H-types in the population is small enough, a pooled contract can give the L-types expected utility close to $u_L(C_L^*)$ and the H types more than $u_H(C_H^*)$, attracting the whole population and still making a profit. Therefore the candidate pair of contracts will not be an equilibrium. This is similar to the situation in the Rothschild–Stiglitz model. But the constrained optimization problem P_L solved by $C_L(\text{UF})$ has more instruments than the similar problem solved by the contract $C_L(\text{RS})$ for the L-types in the Rothschild–Stiglitz model. So long as the solution for the UF model does not have $p_L = 0$, which is guaranteed by the condition (1), we have $u_L(C_L(\text{UF})) > u_L(C_L(\text{RS}))$. Therefore the range of population proportions where the candidate separating pair can be upset by a pooling contract is smaller under UF than in the RS case. ∎

Proposition 5. When separating equilibria under both UF and RS regimes exist, the UF equilibrium is Pareto-superior to the RS equilibrium.

Proof. We have already seen in Proposition 3 that the H-types get the same expected utility $u_H(C_H^*)$ in the two equilibria, and the L-types get higher expected utility in the UF equilibrium. ∎

Proposition 6. In a UF equilibrium, the incentive constraint of the H-types is binding. The contract for the L-types has the following properties: it stipulates probabilistic investigation, offers partial compensation for loss if no investigation is made, and if an investigation is made, then levies the highest permissible penalty if the claimant is revealed to be a type-H, and overcompensation for loss if the claimant is revealed to be truthful (type-L).

Proof. In the constrained optimization problem P_L, let ω_L be the Lagrange multiplier on the no-loss constraint, λ_H the Lagrange multiplier on the incentive compatibility constraint of type-H, and L_L the Lagrangian. Then

$$\partial L_L / \partial k_L = -(1 - \pi_L)U'(W_N - k_L) + (1 - \pi_L)\omega_L \\ + (1 - \pi_H)\lambda_H U'(W_N - k_L) \tag{6}$$

$$\partial L_L / \partial x_L = \pi_L p_L [U'(W_A + x_L) - \omega_L] \tag{7}$$

$$\partial L_L / \partial y_L = -\lambda_H \pi_H p_L U'(W_A + y_L) < 0 \tag{8}$$

$$\partial L_L / \partial z_L = (1 - p_L)[\pi_L U'(W_A + z_L) - \pi_L \omega_L - \lambda_H \pi_H U'(W_A + z_L)] \tag{9}$$

$$\partial L_L / \partial p_L = \pi_L [U(W_A + x_L) - U(W_A + z_L)] - \omega_L \pi_L (c + x_L - z_L) \\ + \lambda_H \pi_H [U(W_A + z_L) - U(W_A + y_L)]. \tag{10}$$

Since $\partial L_L / \partial y_L < 0$, it will be optimal to set y_L at the lowest permissible level, which is 0 under my weak interpretation of *uberrima fides*.

If the incentive constraint of the H-types were not binding, then $\lambda_H = 0$ and the first-order conditions for k_L, x_L, and z_L would become

$$U'(W_N - k_L) = U'(W_A + x_L) = U'(W_A + z_L) = \omega_L.$$

Therefore

$$W_N - k_L = W_A + x_L = W_A + z_L,$$

and the L-types would have full insurance, which under competition must be actuarially fair. Also, (10) would imply

$$\partial L_L / \partial p_L = -\omega_L \pi_L c < 0,$$

so $p_L = 0$. Such a contract would offer full insurance at the low-risk odds without investigation; but then the incentive constraint of the H-types would be violated.

This contradiction proves that $\lambda_H > 0$. Then (6), (7), and (9) yield the first-order conditions

$$U'(W_N - k_L) = \frac{\omega_L}{1 - \lambda_H(1 - \pi_H)/(1 - \pi_L)} \tag{11}$$

$$U'(W_A + x_L) = \omega_L \tag{12}$$

$$U'(W_A + z_L) = \frac{\omega_L}{1 - \lambda_H \pi_H / \pi_L}. \tag{13}$$

Since $\pi_H > \pi_L$, we have

$$\pi_H / \pi_L > 1 > (1 - \pi_H)/(1 - \pi_L),$$

and therefore

$$U'(W_A + x_L) < U'(W_N - k_L) < U'(W_A + z_L)$$

or

$$W_A + x_L > W_N - k_L > W_A + z_L.$$

Also (8) gives $y_L = 0$. This proves the assertions about the penalties and rewards.

Next I prove that $p_L = 1$ is impossible. If $p_L = 1$, then an H-type claiming to be an L-type, if he makes a claim, will be investigated for sure, and found to be lying. Therefore he will get $W_N - k_L$ if there is no accident, and W_A if there is an accident. He would do better buying no insurance at all, and therefore better still by taking the full, fair contract C_H^* intended for his type. Then the incentive constraint of the H-type would not be binding. That would imply $\lambda_H = 0$, which would lead to a contradiction as above.

We have ruled out $p_L = 1$, and the underlying condition on the cost of investigation (1) rules out an equilibrium with $p_L = 0$, namely the RS equilibrium. Therefore $0 < p_L < 1$. But from (10), and using $y_L = 0$, this is possible only if

$$\pi_L[U(W_A + x_L) - U(W_A + z_L)] - \omega_L \pi_L(c + x_L - z_L) + \lambda_H \pi_H[U(W_A + z_L) \\ - U(W_A)] = 0. \tag{14}$$

The three first-order conditions (11), (12), (13), the condition (14) for a probabilistic investigation, the firm's zero-profit condition, and the incentive compatibility constraint of the H-type, constitute six equations that determine the probability p_L, the premium and payments k_L, x_L, z_L, and the multipliers ω_L, λ_H, thus fixing the type-L contract in the UF equilibrium. ∎

5. Conclusion

The principle of *uberrima fides* makes available an extra set of instruments to the insurance company, namely the probability of investigation, the penalty if found lying, and the reward if found to be truthful. These can be deployed to make it harder for the high-risk types to claim low-risk status. The particular combination chosen for the type-L contract, as described in Proposition 6, achieves separation as efficiently as possible. The probability of investigation is kept below 1 so as to reduce the expected cost of investigation; the provision of partial compensation if no investigation is made reduces the attraction of this contract to the H-types; and the overcompensation if an investigation reveals truthfulness restores its attraction to the L-types. In the final outcome, the low-risk types can be offered better insurance and higher utility. The high-risk types continue to get the same fair, full insurance as in the Rothschild–Stiglitz equilibrium. Thus *uberrima fides* achieves a Pareto improvement.

However, this contract is not free from problems of its own. Moral hazard can arise in three ways, two of them familiar and one new.

First, there is moral hazard on the side of the firm, as is usually the case with probabilistic auditing. Since the firm knows that the equilibrium is separating, when a claim is made it can with safety falsely claim to have operated the random mechanism and that it came out in favour of no audit; then the firm need only give the customer the low payment z. To avoid this, the firm's randomization must be publicly verifiable.

Second, a customer may pretend to have had an accident when actually he has suffered no loss at all. This is a problem of costly state verification and needs an audit, somewhat distinct from the problem in the paper of private information about type, which needs an investigation. Of course both problems exist in reality, but the cost of an audit for the existence or size of loss will generally be smaller (easier in the case of damage to car or hospital bill, harder in case of theft because the consumer may have hidden the stuff) than the cost of investigation about type (finding out the truth about pre-existing medical conditions or family history of heart disease may be quite difficult). So although a state verification (audit) may be necessary for a large proportion or even all of the claims, it may save a lot of cost to carry out only probabilistic investigation of type.

Finally, in my model the customer may have another kind of moral hazard. In the case of an accident, he gets a low settlement with one probability and an excessively high settlement with the complementary probability. The expected utility of these may be greater than the utility in the no-accident state, that is

$$p_L U(W_A + x_L) + (1 - p_L)U(W_A + z_L) > U(W_N - k_L).$$

Then he may be actually better off with an accident than without, and therefore may create a genuine accident, not just pretend to have had a loss. I have not yet been able to rule this out (or in).

However, we can consider various restricted forms of contracts that overcome these moral hazard problems. Thus in Proposition 3 the optimization problem that yields the L-type contract can be solved subject to an additional constraint: imposing $x_L = z_L$ will ensure that the consumer is not better off with an accident, and imposing $p_L = 1$ will ensure that the company cannot pretend that its random mechanism indicated that it should not investigate in this instance. This will reduce the model to the case examined in Section 3, but it will still allow a low y_I and therefore some improvement over the conventional Rothschild–Stiglitz equilibrium.

One can also model more rigorously the issues of the credibility of the company's commitment to investigate, and various kinds of moral hazard that can combine with the adverse selection problem that was the focus here. These are topics for future research.

References

Baron, David and David Besanko (1984) 'Regulation, asymmetric information, and auditing', *Rand Journal of Economics* 15: 447–70.

Fagart, Marie-Cécile, and Pierre Picard (1999) 'Optimal insurance under random auditing', *Geneva Papers on Risk and Insurance Theory* 24: 29–54.

Kreps, David (1990) *A Course in Microeconomic Theory*. Princeton: Princeton University Press.

Mirrlees, James A. (1971) 'An exploration in the theory of optimal income taxation', *Review of Economic Studies* 38(2): 175–208.

—— (1999) 'The theory of moral hazard and unobservable behavior: Part I', *Review of Economic Studies* 66(1): 3–21.

Mookherjee, Dilip, and Ivan Png (1989) 'Optimal auditing, insurance, and redistribution', *Quarterly Journal of Economics* 104(2): 399–415.

Reinganum, Jennifer F., and Louis L. Wilde (1986) 'Equilibrium verification and reporting policies in a model of tax compliance', *International Economic Review* 27(3): 739–60.

——— ——— (1988) 'A note on enforcement uncertainty and taxpayer compliance', *Quarterly Journal of Economics* 103(4): 793–8.

Rothschild, Michael, and Joseph E. Stiglitz (1976) 'Equilibrium in competitive insurance markets: An essay on the economics of imperfect information', *Quarterly Journal of Economics* 90(4): 630–49.

Townsend, Robert (1979) 'Optimal contracts and competitive markets with costly state verification', *Journal of Economic Theory* 21(2): 265–93.

4 Strategic Experimentation: the Undiscounted Case

PATRICK BOLTON AND CHRISTOPHER HARRIS

1. Introduction

Bolton and Harris (1999) consider a game of strategic experimentation. In this game, each player divides her time in any given period between a 'safe' action and a 'risky' action. The underlying pay-off of the safe action is known. The underlying pay-off of the risky action is unknown, and can be higher or lower than that of the safe action. The actual pay-off received by any player from an action is the underlying pay-off plus noise. Once players' actions have been chosen and pay-offs realized all players observe all choices and pay-offs. Through these observations they are able to learn about the underlying pay-off of the risky action and thus revise their common beliefs and optimal choice of action. In other words, players can learn from others' current experimentation as well as their own.

Bolton and Harris provide a complete characterization of the team solution of the strategic-experimentation game, establish the existence of a unique symmetric stationary Markov-perfect equilibrium, and show how equilibrium experimentation and pay-offs vary with the number of players and the discount rate. In particular, they show that there are two major effects at work in their model, a free-rider effect and an encouragement effect. The free-rider effect arises because experimentation is a public good. The encouragement effect arises because the prospect of future experimentation by others gives a player an incentive to increase her current experimentation in order to bring forward the time at which the additional information obtained from the others' experimentation becomes available. However, Bolton and Harris only obtain a partial characterization of the unique symmetric equilibrium, and do not provide any characterization of the set of asymmetric equilibria.

In this paper, we pursue further the analysis of strategic experimentation initiated in Bolton and Harris. We begin by making an important change in the model: we add background information in the form of an exogenous noisy signal of the underlying pay-off of the risky action. This ensures that players' preferences have a well-defined limit as the discount rate converges to zero.

The undiscounted case is much easier to analyse than the discounted case. We are therefore able to give a detailed characterization of all the equilibria of the model, both symmetric and asymmetric. Using this characterization, we can show that the aggregate equilibrium pay-off of all players is maximized (subject to the incentive constraints) if and only if aggregate experimentation is maximized (subject to the incentive constraints). Furthermore, we can characterize how maximum equilibrium experimentation is achieved. Interestingly, it requires alternation between pure-strategy and mixed-strategy equilibria of the stage game: for very low values of the prior, exactly one player experiments; as common beliefs rise, two players mix; then exactly two players experiment; then three players mix; and so on. Since players' best responses can be calculated explicitly, it is straightforward to characterize the cut-offs for the prior beliefs where the equilibrium switches from nobody choosing the risky action to experimentation by one player, and then from experimentation by one player to randomization by two players, etc.

The maximal equilibria can be understood intuitively as follows. When the opportunity cost of experimentation is high, even a small amount of experimentation by the other players will deter the remaining player from experimenting. The best way of maximizing total experimentation is therefore to have the other players refrain from experimentation altogether, leaving the remaining player to undertake a full unit of experimentation. As the opportunity cost of experimentation falls, the advantage of having two players contribute to experimentation outweighs the disadvantage of the disincentive to one player that results from experimentation by the other. The best way of maximizing total experimentation is therefore to have two players mix. As the opportunity cost of experimentation falls further, it becomes feasible to persuade one player to experiment even when a second player is already experimenting for sure. The best way to maximize experimentation is therefore to have two players experiment for sure. And so on. In particular, when the opportunity cost of experimentation is high, we see a single pioneer shouldering the burden of experimentation. As the opportunity cost of experimentation falls, two players share the burden. And so on.

The main reason why the undiscounted case is easier to analyse is that, in this case, players' best responses can be calculated without first solving for their value functions. By contrast, in the discounted case, players' best responses do depend on their value functions. Hence, since closed-form solutions for the value functions cannot be obtained in the discounted case, it is not possible to provide a complete characterization of equilibrium experimentation.

Besides providing a much more detailed characterization of equilibria of the strategic experimentation game, we believe that our paper also outlines a simple methodology for characterizing equilibria of complex stochastic differential games in the special case where there is no discounting. This methodology had already been put to use in Harris (1993); it greatly facilitated our analysis of the strategic-experimentation game in Bolton and Harris (1993 and 1996); and it has subsequently been put to use in Bergemann and Valimaki (1997) and Keller and Rady (1999).

The paper is organized as follows. Section 2 describes the basic model and introduces the background signal. Section 3 defines players' objectives and shows how players' preferences converge to a well-defined limit as the discount rate converges to zero. Section 4 characterizes the dynamics of beliefs for any profile of experimentation strategies. Section 5 defines best responses and equilibrium. Section 6 characterizes best responses. Section 7 characterizes the set of equilibria. Finally, Section 8 offers some concluding remarks.

2. The Model

There are N identical players. At the outset of the game, they all believe that $\mu = l$ with probability $1 - p_0$ and $\mu = h$ with probability p_0. At time t, the players simultaneously and independently choose between two actions, action 0 (the safe action) and action 1 (the risky action). If player i chooses action a_i, then her pay-off is

$$d\pi_i(t) = \begin{cases} sdt + \sigma dZ_i(t) & \text{if } a_i = 0 \\ \mu dt + \sigma dZ_i(t) & \text{if } a_i = 1 \end{cases}.$$

All players then observe all the actions chosen and all the resulting pay-offs. They also observe a background signal

$$d\pi_0(t) = \sqrt{(x_0)}\mu dt + \sigma dZ_0(t).$$

Here: s is fixed and known; $l < s < h$; $x_0 > 0$ is the quality of the background signal; and the $dZ_i(t)$ are independently and normally distributed with mean 0 and variance dt for $0 \leqslant i \leqslant N$.

3. The Objective

The objective of player i can be stated informally as follows: maximize the expectation of the undiscounted integral of the pay-offs $d\pi_i(t)$. In order to arrive at a formal statement that embodies this objective, one can proceed in one of two ways.

The first approach is to consider the limit of the expectation of the discounted integral of the pay-offs $d\pi_i(t)$ as the discount rate goes to 0. Suppose that, at time t: the players believe that $\mu = h$ with probability $p(t)$; and player i chooses the action $x_i(t) \in \{0, 1\}$. Define the full-information pay-off $\bar{u}$ by the formula

$$\bar{u}(q) = (1 - q)s + qh,$$

and define the expected risky pay-off m by the formula

$$m(q) = (1 - q)l + qh.$$

Then:

Proposition 1. *We have*

$$\lim_{r \to 0+} \frac{1}{r}\left(\mathrm{E}\left[\int_0^\infty re^{-rt}d\pi_i(t) \right] - \bar{u}(p_0) \right)$$

$$= \mathrm{E}\left[\int_0^\infty ((1 - x_i(t))s + x_i(t)m(p(t)) - \bar{u}(p(t)))dt \right].$$

This proposition can be understood as follows. The background information provided by the signal π_0 ensures that players eventually learn the value of μ. Hence, for any reasonable strategy of player i,

$$\lim_{r \to 0+} E\left[\int_0^\infty re^{-rt}d\pi_i(t)\right] = \bar{u}(p_0).$$

For example, this is true of any Markov strategy that: (i) assigns probability 0 to the risky action when $p = 0$; (ii) assigns probability 1 to the risky action when $p = 1$; and (iii) is continuous at both $p = 0$ and $p = 1$.[1] Hence, for r near to 0, player i's preferences over her reasonable strategies are well represented by

$$\lim_{r \to 0+} \frac{1}{r}\left(E\left[\int_0^\infty re^{-rt}d\pi_i(t)\right] - \bar{u}(p_0)\right)$$

wherever this limit exists. Finally, this limit exists for all strategies of player i, reasonable or not.

Proof. Let us denote the information available at time t by $\mathcal{F}_t$. We have

$$E[x_i(t)\mu \mid \mathcal{F}_t] = E[x_i(t) \mid \mathcal{F}_t]E[\mu \mid \mathcal{F}_t]$$
$$= E[x_i(t) \mid \mathcal{F}_t]m(p(t)) = E[x_i(t)m(p(t)) \mid \mathcal{F}_t]$$

(because $x_i(t)$ is conditionally independent of μ given $\mathcal{F}_t$) and

$$E[\sigma dZ_i(t) \mid \mathcal{F}_t] = 0.$$

Hence

$$E[d\pi_i(t) \mid \mathcal{F}_t]$$
$$= E[(1 - x_i(t))(sdt + \sigma dZ_i(t)) + x_i(t)(\mu dt + \sigma dZ_i(t)) \mid \mathcal{F}_t]$$
$$= E[(1 - x_i(t))sdt + x_i(t)\mu dt + \sigma dZ_i(t) \mid \mathcal{F}_t]$$
$$= E[(1 - x_i(t))sdt + x_i(t)m(p(t))dt \mid \mathcal{F}_t].$$

Hence

$$E\left[\int_0^\infty re^{-rt}d\pi_i(t)\right] = E\left[\int_0^\infty re^{-rt}E[d\pi_i(t) \mid \mathcal{F}_t]\right]$$

$$= E\left[\int_0^\infty re^{-rt}E[(1 - x_i(t))sdt + x_i(t)m(p(t))dt \mid \mathcal{F}_t]\right]$$

$$= E\left[\int_0^\infty re^{-rt}((1 - x_i(t))sdt + x_i(t)m(p(t))dt)\right]$$

---

[1] For the formal definition of a Markov strategy, see Definition 5 below.

$$= \mathrm{E}\left[\int_0^\infty re^{-rt}((1 - x_i(t))s + x_i(t)m(p(t)))dt\right].$$

We also have

$$\bar{u}(p_0) = \mathrm{E}[\bar{u}(p(t))]$$

(because $p(t)$ follows a martingale and $\bar{u}$ is linear). Hence

$$\bar{u}(p_0) = \mathrm{E}\left[\int_0^\infty re^{-rt}\bar{u}(p_0)dt\right] = \mathrm{E}\left[\int_0^\infty re^{-rt}\bar{u}(p(t))dt\right].$$

Overall, then,

$$\frac{1}{r}\left(\mathrm{E}\left[\int_0^\infty re^{-rt}d\pi_i(t)\right] - \bar{u}(p_0)\right)$$

$$= \mathrm{E}\left[\int_0^\infty e^{-rt}((1 - x_i(t))s + x_i(t)m(p(t)) - \bar{u}(p(t)))dt\right].$$

But

$$(1 - x_i(t))s + x_i(t)m(p(t)) - \bar{u}(p(t)) \leq 0.$$

Letting $r \to 0$ and applying the monotone convergence theorem, we therefore obtain the required conclusion. ∎

The second approach is to consider the limit of the expectation of the mean of the pay-offs $d\pi_i(t)$ over the interval $[0, T]$ as T goes to $+\infty$. On this approach:

Proposition 2. *We have*

$$\lim_{T \to +\infty} T\left(\mathrm{E}\left[\frac{1}{T}\int_0^T d\pi_i(t)\right] - \bar{u}(p_0)\right)$$

$$= \mathrm{E}\left[\int_0^\infty ((1 - x_i(t))s + x_i(t)m(p(t)) - \bar{u}(p(t)))dt\right].$$

This proposition can be understood in much the same way as Proposition 1. For any reasonable strategy of player i,

$$\lim_{T \to +\infty} \mathrm{E}\left[\frac{1}{T}\int_0^T d\pi_i(t)\right] = \bar{u}(p_0).$$

Hence, for T near to $+\infty$, player i's preferences over her reasonable strategies are well represented by

$$\lim_{T \to +\infty} T \left(E \left[\frac{1}{T} \int_0^T d\pi_i(t) \right] - \bar{u}(p_0) \right),$$

wherever this limit exists. Finally, this limit exists for all strategies of player i, reasonable or not. The proof, which is analogous to that of Proposition 1, is omitted.

Propositions 1 and 2 lead us to the following definition:

Definition 3. *Player i's objective is to maximize*

$$E \left[\int_0^\infty ((1 - x_i(t))s + x_i(t)m(p(t)) - \bar{u}(p(t)))dt \right].$$

4. The Dynamics of Beliefs

Suppose that, at the outset of period t, the players believe that $\mu = h$ with probability $p(t)$. Let $x_0(t) = x_0$, and suppose that the players $i \in \{1, \ldots, N\}$ choose the actions $x_i(t) \in \{0, 1\}$. Suppose further that, at the conclusion of period t, the players believe that $\mu = h$ with probability $p(t + dt)$. Let

$$dp(t) = p(t + dt) - p(t)$$

denote the change in beliefs concerning μ; and define the information function Φ by the formula

$$\Phi(q) = \left(\frac{q(1 - q)(h - l)}{\sigma} \right)^2.$$

Then:

Proposition 4. *We have*

$$dp(t) = p(t)(1 - p(t)) \left(\frac{h - l}{\sigma} \right) \sum_{i=0}^N \sqrt{(x_i(t))} d\tilde{Z}_i(t),$$

where

$$d\tilde{Z}_i(t) = \frac{1}{\sigma} (\sqrt{(x_i(t))}(\mu - m(p(t)))dt + \sigma dZ_i(t)).$$

Moreover, conditional on the information available at time t, the $d\tilde{Z}_i(t)$ are independently and identically distributed with mean 0 and variance dt.

In particular, conditional on the information available at time t, $dp(t)$ has mean 0 and variance $(\sum_{i=0}^N x_i(t))\Phi(p(t))dt$.

Proof. See Lemma 1 of Bolton and Harris (1999). ∎

5. Definition of Equilibrium

Since the only pay-off relevant variable is the probability that $\mu = h$, and since a player's mixed action can be identified with the probability with which she chooses action 1, both the state space and the mixed-action set for our model can be taken to be the unit interval $[0, 1]$. Hence:

Definition 5. *A* **Markov strategy** *for player i is a Borel measurable function* $\xi_i : [0, 1]$ $\to [0, 1]$.

It can be shown that, for all Markov-strategy profiles and all initial beliefs, there is a unique solution to the dynamics. More precisely, put $I = \{1, 2, \ldots, N\}$, put $\xi_0(q) = x_0$ for all $q \in [0, 1]$, let $C([0, +\infty), [0, 1])$ denote the space of continuous functions from the time line $[0, +\infty)$ to the state space $[0, 1]$, let $\mathcal{P}(C([0, +\infty), [0, 1]))$ denote the space of probability measures on $C([0, +\infty), [0, 1])$, and let p denote the identity mapping on $C([0, +\infty), [0, 1])$. Then:

Proposition 6. *For all Markov-strategy profiles* $\xi = \times_{i \in I} \xi_i$ *and all initial beliefs* $p_0 \in [0, 1]$, *there is a unique* $\lambda(p_0) \in \mathcal{P}(C([0, +\infty), [0, 1]))$ *such that, with* $\lambda(p_0)$-*probability one:*

(i) $p(0) = p_0$; *and*
(ii) for all $t \in [0, +\infty)$, $dp(t)$ *has mean 0 and variance* $(\sum_{i=0}^{N} \xi_i(p(t)))\Phi(p(t))dt$.

Proof. This follows at once from the results of Engelbert and Schmidt (1985), as described in Section 5.5 of Karatzas and Shreve (1988). ∎

Proposition 6 implies that, for all Markov-strategy profiles ξ and all initial beliefs p_0, player i's expected pay-off $g_i(\xi, p_0)$ is well defined. Hence:

Definition 7. *The Markov strategy* ξ_i *is a* **perfect best response** *to the Markov-strategy profile* $\xi_{-i} = \times_{j \in I \setminus \{i\}} \xi_j$ *iff, for all* $p_0 \in [0, 1]$, ξ_i *is a best response to* ξ_{-i} *in the game in which player i has pay-off function* $g_i(\cdot, p_0)$.

Definition 8. *The Markov-strategy profile* $\xi = \times_{i \in I} \xi_i$ *is an* **equilibrium** *iff, for all* $i \in \{1, 2, \ldots, N\}$, ξ_i *is a perfect best response to* $\xi_{-i} = \times_{j \in I \setminus \{i\}} \xi_j$.

6. Characterization of Best Responses

Suppose that the players $j \in I \setminus \{i\}$ employ the Markov strategies ξ_j, and let $\Xi_{-i} = \sum_{j \in (\{0\} \cup I) \setminus \{i\}} \xi_j$. Then:

Proposition 9. *Player i's value function* $u_i : [0, 1] \to (-\infty, 0]$ *satisfies*

$$0 = \max_{\alpha_i \in [0,1]} \left\{ (1 - \alpha_i)s + \alpha_i m(p) - \bar{u}(p) + (\alpha_i + \Xi_{-i}(p)) \Phi(p) \frac{u_i''(p)}{2} \right\} \qquad (1)$$

for all $p \in (0, 1)$ *and*

$$u_i(0) = 0, \ u_i(1) = 0. \tag{2}$$

Moreover the Markov strategy ξ_i *is a perfect best response for player i iff*

$$\xi_i(p) \in \operatorname*{argmax}_{\alpha_i \in [0,1]} \left\{ (1 - \alpha_i)s + \alpha_i m(p) - \bar{u}(p) + (\alpha_i + \Xi_{-i}(p)) \Phi(p) \frac{u_i''(p)}{2} \right\} \tag{3}$$

for all $p \in (0, 1)$ *and*

$$\xi_i(0) = 0, \ \xi_i(1) = 1. \tag{4}$$

Proof. Let $H_i(p, \alpha_i, \xi_{-i}, c_i)$ denote the expectation of player i's current pay-off when the current belief is $p \in [0, 1]$, player i chooses the risky action with probability $\alpha_i \in [0, 1]$, the profile of Markov strategies employed by the other players is ξ_{-i} and player i's continuation pay-offs are given by the function $c_i : [0, 1] \to (-\infty, 0]$. Then player i's value function u_i must satisfy the Bellman equation

$$u_i(p) = \max_{\alpha_i \in [0,1]} \{ H_i(\alpha_i, p, u_i, \xi_{-i}) \} \tag{5}$$

for all $p \in [0, 1]$. Moreover the strategy ξ_i is a perfect best response for player i iff

$$\xi_i(p) \in \operatorname*{argmax}_{\alpha_i \in [0,1]} \{ H_i(\alpha_i, p, u_i, \xi_{-i}) \} \tag{6}$$

for all $p \in [0, 1]$.

Now suppose that the realized actions are $\{x_j \mid 1 \leqslant j \leqslant N\}$, and put $X_i = \sum_{j \in (\{0\} \cup I) \setminus \{i\}} x_j$. Then player i's current pay-off is

$$((1 - x_i)s + x_i m(p) - \bar{u}(p))dt$$

(by Definition 3) and her continuation pay-off is

$$c_i(p + dp) = c_i(p) + c_i'(p)dp + \frac{1}{2}c_i''(p)dp^2$$

(by Itô's Lemma), where dp has mean 0 and variance $(x_i + X_i)\Phi(p)dt$ (by Proposition 4). Hence the expectation of her current pay-off conditional on $\{x_j \mid 1 \leqslant j \leqslant N\}$ is

$$c_i(p) + \left((1 - x_i)s + x_i m(p) - \bar{u}(p) + (x_i + X_i) \Phi(p) \frac{c_i''(p)}{2} \right) dt.$$

Hence

$$H_i(\alpha_i, p, c_i, \xi_{-i}) = c_i(p)$$
$$+ \left((1 - \alpha_i)s + \alpha_i m(p) - \bar{u}(p) + (\alpha_i + \Xi_{-i}(p)) \Phi(p) \frac{c_i''(p)}{2} \right) dt \tag{7}$$

(on taking expectations over the x_j).

Next, combining (5) and (7), we obtain

$$u_i(p)$$

$$= \max_{\alpha_i \in [0,1]} \left\{ u_i(p) + \left((1 - \alpha_i)s + \alpha_i m(p) - \bar{u}(p) + (\alpha_i + \Xi_{-i}(p))\Phi(p)\frac{u_i''(p)}{2} \right) dt \right\}$$

$$= u_i(p) + \left(\max_{\alpha_i \in [0,1]} \left\{ (1 - \alpha_i)s + \alpha_i m(p) - \bar{u}(p) + (\alpha_i + \Xi_{-i}(p))\Phi(p)\frac{u_i''(p)}{2} \right\} \right) dt.$$

Hence, subtracting $u_i(p)$ from both sides and dividing both sides by dt,

$$0 = \max_{\alpha_i \in [0,1]} \left\{ (1 - \alpha_i)s + \alpha_i m(p) - \bar{u}(p) + (\alpha_i + \Xi_{-i}(p))\Phi(p)\frac{u_i''(p)}{2} \right\}$$

for all $p \in [0, 1]$. Similarly, combining (6) and (7), we obtain

$$\xi_i(p) \in \operatorname*{argmax}_{\alpha_i \in [0,1]} \left\{ (1 - \alpha_i)s + \alpha_i m(p) - \bar{u}(p) + (\alpha_i + \Xi_{-i}(p))\Phi(p)\frac{u_i''(p)}{2} \right\} \qquad (8)$$

for all $p \in [0, 1]$.

Finally, using (8) and noting that $\Phi(0) = \Phi(1) = 0$, we obtain

$$\xi_i(0) \in \operatorname*{argmax}_{\alpha_i \in [0,1]} \{(1 - \alpha_i)s + \alpha_i m(0) - \bar{u}(0)\} = \operatorname*{argmax}_{\alpha_i \in [0,1]} \{-\alpha_i(s - l)\}$$

and

$$\xi_i(1) \in \operatorname*{argmax}_{\alpha_i \in [0,1]} \{(1 - \alpha_i)s + \alpha_i m(1) - \bar{u}(1)\} = \operatorname*{argmax}_{\alpha_i \in [0,1]} \{-(1 - \alpha_i)(h - s)\}.$$

Hence $\xi_i(0) = 0$ and $\xi_i(1) = 1$. Hence the flow pay-offs in states 0 and 1 are

$$(1 - \xi_i(0))s + \xi_i(0)m(0) - \bar{u}(0) = -\xi_i(0)(s - l) = 0$$

and

$$(1 - \xi_i(1))s + \xi_i(1)m(1) - \bar{u}(1) = -(1 - \xi_i(1))(h - s) = 0.$$

Hence $u_i(0) = 0$ and $u_i(1) = 0$. ∎

The following lemma simplifies both the problem of finding player i's value function and the problem of finding player i's perfect best responses.

Lemma 10. *Equation (1) holds iff*

$$0 = \max_{\alpha_i \in [0,1]} \left\{ \frac{(1 - \alpha_i)s + \alpha_i m(p) - \bar{u}(p)}{\alpha_i + \Xi_{-i}(p)(p)} \right\} + \Phi(p)\frac{u_i''(p)}{2}. \qquad (9)$$

Moreover, if either (1) or (9) holds, then (3) holds iff

$$\xi_i(p) \in \underset{\alpha_i \in [0,1]}{\mathrm{argmax}} \left\{ \frac{(1 - \alpha_i)s + \alpha_i m(p) - \bar{u}(p)}{\alpha_i + \Xi_{-i}(p)(p)} \right\}. \tag{10}$$

Proof. This follows at once from the fact that $0 < x_0 \leqslant \alpha_i + \Xi_{-i} \leqslant x_0 + N < +\infty$. ∎

Proposition 11. *There is a unique u_i satisfying equations (1 and 2).*

Proof. In view of Lemma 10, we need only show that there is a unique u_i such that

$$0 = \underset{\alpha_i \in [0,1]}{\max} \left\{ \frac{(1 - \alpha_i)s + \alpha_i m(p) - \bar{u}(p)}{\alpha_i + \Xi_{-i}(p)} \right\} + \Phi(p) \frac{u_i''(p)}{2} \tag{11}$$

for all $p \in (0, 1)$ and

$$u_i(0) = 0, \ u_i(1) = 0. \tag{12}$$

Note first that, for any bounded $f : [0, 1] \rightarrow \mathbb{R}$,

$$0 = f(p) + \Phi(p) \frac{v''(p)}{2}$$

for all $p \in (0, 1)$ iff

$$v(p) = \int_0^1 G(p, q) f(q) dq + (1 - p)v(0) + pv(1)$$

for all $p \in [0, 1]$, where

$$G(p, q) = \begin{cases} \dfrac{2\sigma^2 p}{(h - l)^2 q^2 (1 - q)} & \text{if } p \in [0, q] \\[2ex] \dfrac{2\sigma^2 (1 - p)}{(h - l)^2 q(1 - q)^2} & \text{if } p \in [q, 1] \end{cases}$$

(by standard considerations in the theory of differential equations). Hence equations (11 and 12) hold iff

$$u_i(p) = \int_0^1 G(p, q) f(q) dq,$$

where

$$f(q) = \underset{\alpha_i \in [0,1]}{\max} \left\{ \frac{(1 - \alpha_i)s + \alpha_i m(q) - \bar{u}(q)}{\alpha_i + \Xi_{-i}(q)} \right\}.$$

Noting that neither G nor f involve u_i, we conclude that there is a unique solution of equations (11 and 12). ∎

Define the break-even probability b and the incentive to experiment β by the formulae

$$b = \frac{s - l}{h - l}$$

and

$$\beta(p) = \begin{cases} \dfrac{\bar{u}(p) - s}{s - m(p)} & \text{if } p \in [0, b) \\ +\infty & \text{if } p \in [b, 1] \end{cases}.$$

Then:

Proposition 12. *The Markov strategy ξ_i is a perfect best response for player i iff*

$$\xi_i(p) \begin{cases} = 0 & \text{if } \beta(p) < \Xi_{-i}(p) \\ \in [0, 1] & \text{if } \beta(p) = \Xi_{-i}(p) \\ = 1 & \text{if } \beta(p) > \Xi_{-i}(p) \end{cases}$$

for all $p \in [0, 1]$.

In other words, player i should experiment iff the incentive to experiment exceeds the total experimentation by the other players (including an allowance for the amount of experimentation effectively contributed by the background signal).

Proof. Elementary manipulation shows that

$$\frac{(1 - \alpha_i)s + \alpha_i m(p) - \bar{u}(p)}{\alpha_i + \Xi_{-i}(p)} = -(s - m(p)) - \frac{(\bar{u}(p) - s) - \Xi_{-i}(p)(s - m(p))}{\alpha_i + \Xi_{-i}(p)}.$$

Moreover: if $p < b$ then $s - m(p) > 0$, and so

$$(\bar{u}(p) - s) - \Xi_{-i}(p)(s - m(p)) \begin{Bmatrix} < \\ = \\ > \end{Bmatrix} 0 \text{ iff } \frac{\bar{u}(p) - s}{s - m(p)} \begin{Bmatrix} < \\ = \\ > \end{Bmatrix} \Xi_{-i}(p);$$

and if $p \geq b$ then $s - m(p) \leq 0$, and so

$$(\bar{u}(p) - s) - \Xi_{-i}(p)(s - m(p)) \geq \bar{u}(p) - s > 0. \quad ∎$$

7. Characterization of Equilibrium

Proposition 12 allows us to give a complete classification of the equilibria of our game. For all mixed-action profiles $\alpha = \times_{i=1}^{N} \alpha_i$, let k_0 be the number of players who play the safe action with probability one, let k_1 be the number of players who play the risky action with probability one, and let k_M be the number of players who play a strictly mixed action. For all $\gamma \in [0, +\infty]$, let $E(\gamma)$ be the set of mixed-action profiles α such that one of the following conditions is satisfied:

(i) $k_M = 0$, $k_1 = 0$ and $\gamma \leqslant x_0$;
(ii) $k_M = 0$, $1 \leqslant k_1 \leqslant N - 1$ and $x_0 + k_1 - 1 \leqslant \gamma \leqslant x_0 + k_1$;
(iii) $k_M = 0$, $k_1 = N$ and $\gamma \geqslant x_0 + N - 1$;
(iv) $k_M = 1$, $\gamma = x_0 + k_1$ and the player who mixes chooses the risky action with any probability in $(0, 1)$;
(v) $k_M \geqslant 2$, $x_0 + k_1 < \gamma < x_0 + k_1 + k_M - 1$ and the players who mix all choose the risky action with probability $(y - x_0 - k_1)/(k_M - 1)$.

In other words, either the incentive to experiment is so low that having no players experiment is incentive-compatible; or it is sufficiently high that at least k_1 players can be persuaded to experiment, but sufficiently low that at most k_1 players can be persuaded to experiment; or it is so high that all players can be persuaded to experiment; or it takes on a knife-edge value at which a $(k_1 + 1)^{th}$ player is indifferent between experimenting and not experimenting; or it lies in a range in which k_M players can be persuaded to mix when k_1 players experiment, provided that the probability with which the mixing-players experiment is chosen appropriately. Then:

Proposition 13. *The Markov-strategy profile* $\xi = \times_{i=1}^{N} \xi_i$ *is an equilibrium iff, for all* $p \in [0, 1]$, $\xi(p) \in E(\beta(p))$.

In other words, ξ is an equilibrium iff $\xi(p)$ is a Nash equilibrium of the stage game for all $p \in [0, 1]$.

Proof. Fix $p \in [0, 1]$, put $\alpha = \xi(p)$ and put $\gamma = \beta(p)$. Note first that, if $k_M = 0$ and $k_1 \geqslant 1$, then playing risky is incentive-compatible for those players who play risky iff $\gamma \geqslant x_0 + k_1 - 1$. Similarly, if $k_M = 0$ and $k_1 \leqslant N - 1$, then playing safe is incentive-compatible for those players who play safe iff $\gamma \leqslant x_0 + k_1$. Secondly, if $k_M = 1$ then mixing is incentive-compatible for the player who mixes iff $\gamma = x_0 + k_1$. Moreover: playing safe is less attractive for the players who play risky than it is for the player who mixes; and playing risky is less attractive for the players who play safe than it is for the player who mixes. Thirdly, if $k_M \geqslant 2$, then mixing is incentive-compatible for player i iff $\gamma = \Xi_{-i} = (\sum_{j=0}^{N} \xi_j) - \xi_i$. Hence mixing is incentive-compatible for those players who mix iff they all mix with the same probability $(y - x_0 - k_1)/(k_M - 1)$. Moreover: $(y - x_0 - k_1)/(k_M - 1) \in (0, 1)$ iff $x_0 + k_1 < \gamma < x_0 + k_1 + k_M - 1$; playing safe is less attractive for the players who play risky than it is for the players who mix; and playing risky is less attractive for the players who play safe than it is for the players who mix. ■

Proposition 13 in turn allows us to identify those equilibria that maximize aggregate pay-offs. Let $g(\xi, p_0)$ denote the aggregate pay-off when the Markov-strategy profile ξ is employed and the initial belief is p_0, let $\mathcal{E}$ denote the set of equilibria, let

$$\bar{\mathcal{E}}(p_0) = \underset{\xi \in \mathcal{E}}{\mathrm{argmax}}\, \{g(\xi, p_0)\},$$

and define $\bar{E} : [0, +\infty] \to [0, N]$ by the formula

$$\bar{E}(\gamma) = \underset{\alpha \in E(\gamma)}{\mathrm{argmax}}\, \left\{ \sum_{i \in I} \alpha_i \right\}.$$

Then:

Proposition 14. *For all $p_0 \in [0, 1]$, $\xi \in \bar{\mathcal{E}}(p_0)$ iff $\xi(p) \in \bar{E}(\beta(p))$ for all $p \in [0, 1]$.*

In other words, for any given initial belief, an equilibrium maximizes the aggregate pay-off iff it maximizes total experimentation in every state. In particular, if an equilibrium maximizes the aggregate pay-off for some initial belief, then it maximizes the aggregate pay-off for all initial beliefs.

Proof. Suppose that ξ is an equilibrium. Then Proposition 9 and Lemma 10 imply that

$$0 = \frac{(1 - \xi_i(p))s + \xi_i(p)m(p) - \bar{u}(p)}{\xi_i(p) + \Xi_{-i}(p)} + \Phi(p)\frac{u_i''(p)}{2} \tag{13}$$

for $p \in (0, 1)$ and

$$u_i(0) = u_i(1) = 0. \tag{14}$$

Put $v = \sum_{i \in I} u_i$. Then, summing (13) and (14) over i, we obtain

$$0 = \frac{-N(\bar{u}(p) - s) - (s - m(p))\sum_{i \in I}\xi_i(p)}{x_0 + \sum_{i \in I}\xi_i(p)} + \Phi(p)\frac{v''(p)}{2} \tag{15}$$

for $p \in (0, 1)$ and

$$v(0) = v(1) = 0. \tag{16}$$

Moreover, rearranging (15), we obtain

$$0 = -(s - m(p)) - \frac{N(\bar{u}(p) - s) - x_0(s - m(p))}{x_0 + \sum_{i \in I}\xi_i(p)} + \Phi(p)\frac{v''(p)}{2}.$$

As in the proof of Proposition 11, it follows that (15 and 16) hold iff

$$v(p) = \int_0^1 G(p, q)f(q, \xi(q))dq + (1 - p)v(0) + pv(1)$$

for $p \in [0, 1]$, where

$$G(p, q) = \begin{cases} \dfrac{2\sigma^2 p}{(h - l)^2 q^2 (1 - q)} & \text{if } p \in [0, q] \\[4mm] \dfrac{2\sigma^2 (1 - p)}{(h - l)^2 q(1 - q)^2} & \text{if } p \in [q, 1] \end{cases}$$

and

$$f(q, \alpha) = -(s - m(q)) - \frac{N(\bar{u}(q) - s) - x_0(s - m(q))}{x_0 + \sum_{i \in I} \alpha_i}.$$

It follows at once that $\xi \in \bar{E}(p_0)$ iff

$$\xi(q) \in \operatorname*{argmax}_{\alpha \in E(q)} \{f(q, \alpha)\}$$

for $q \in [0, 1]$. Finally, $\xi_i(q) = 0$ whenever $\beta(q) < x_0$,

$$N(\bar{u}(q) - s) - x_0(s - m(q)) > 0$$

whenever $\beta(q) \in [x_0, x_0 + N - 1]$, and $\xi_i(q) = 1$ whenever $\beta(q) > x_0 + N - 1$. Hence

$$\operatorname*{argmax}_{\alpha \in E(q)} \{f(q, \alpha)\} = \bar{E}(\beta(q)).$$

This completes the proof. ∎

Figure 4.1 depicts the total-experimentation correspondence $\hat{E}$ given by the formula $\hat{E}(\gamma) = \{\sum_{i \in I} \alpha_i \mid \alpha \in E(\gamma)\}$ in the case $N = 3$ and $x_0 = 2$. It suggests that, in order to maximize total experimentation: there should initially be a single pioneer who

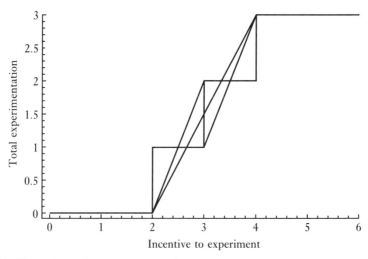

FIG. 4.1. *The total-experimentation correspondence*

experiments alone; then two pioneers should share the burden of experimentation; then three pioneers should share the burden of experimentation; and so on.

The following proposition gives an explicit characterization of $\bar{E}(\gamma)$.

Proposition 15. *For all $l \in \{1, 2, \ldots, N - 1\}$:*

(i) *for all $\gamma \in [x_0 + l - 1, x_0 + l - 1 + \frac{1}{l+1})$, $\alpha \in \bar{E}(\gamma)$ iff $k_M = 0$ and $k_1 = l$;*

(ii) *for all $\gamma \in (x_0 + l - 1 + \frac{1}{l+1}, x_0 + l)$, $\alpha \in \bar{E}(\gamma)$ iff $k_M = l + 1$ and $k_1 = 0$;*

and, in the knife-edge case in which $\gamma = x_0 + l - 1 + \frac{1}{l+1}, \alpha \in \bar{E}(\gamma)$ iff either $k_M = 0$ and $k_1 = l$, or $k_M = l + 1$ and $k_1 = 0$.

In particular: for $\gamma \in [x_0, x_0 + \frac{1}{2})$, exactly one player plays risky; for $\gamma \in (x_0 + \frac{1}{2}, x_0 + 1)$, exactly two players randomize; for $\gamma \in [x_0 + 1, x_0 + 1 + \frac{1}{3})$, exactly two players play risky; for $\gamma \in (x_0 + 1 + \frac{1}{3}, x_0 + 2)$, exactly three players randomize; and so on up to $l = N - 1$.

Proof. Note first that any $\alpha \in E(\gamma)$ in which both $k_1 > 0$ and $k_M > 0$ is dominated by the corresponding equilibrium $\hat{\alpha} \in E(\gamma)$ in which $\hat{k}_1 = 0$ and $\hat{k}_M = k_1 + k_M$. Hence we can confine attention to equilibria in which either $k_1 = 0$ or $k_M = 0$. Secondly, any $\alpha \in E(\gamma)$ in which $k_1 = 0$ and $k_M \geq 3$ is dominated by the corresponding equilibrium $\hat{\alpha} \in E(\gamma)$ in which $\hat{k}_1 = 0$ and $\hat{k}_M = k_M - 1$ if $\gamma \in (x_0, x_0 + k_M - 2)$. Hence equilibria in which $k_1 = 0$ and $k_M \geq 2$ are only relevant when $\gamma \in (x_0 + k_M - 2, x_0 + k_M - 1)$. Thirdly, any $\alpha \in E(\gamma)$ in which $k_1 \leq N - 1$ and $k_M = 0$ is dominated by the corresponding equilibrium $\hat{\alpha} \in E(\gamma)$ in which $\hat{k}_1 = k_1 + 1$ and $\hat{k}_M = 0$ if $\gamma = x_0 + k_1$. Hence equilibria in which $k_1 \leq N - 1$ and $k_M = 0$ are only relevant when $\gamma \in [x_0 + k_1 - 1, x_0 + k_1)$. Finally, for all $l \in \{1, 2, \ldots, N - 1\}$ and all $\gamma \in [x_0 + l - 1, x_0 + l)$, the equilibrium in which $k_1 = l$ and $k_M = 0$ dominates the equilibrium in which $k_1 = 0$ and $k_M = l + 1$ if $\gamma \in [x_0 + l - 1, x_0 + l - 1 + \frac{1}{l+1}]$, and vice versa if $\gamma \in (x_0 + l - 1 + \frac{1}{l+1}, x_0 + l)$. ∎

8. Conclusion

As we have seen, the characterization of perfect best responses becomes very simple in the limit case where there is no discounting. As a result, it is possible to provide a complete classification of equilibria for this limiting case. The analysis of this paper therefore provides an illustration of the important simplifications that may be obtainable in the case of no discounting for the analysis of stochastic differential games. We believe that this methodology can be applied to problems other than experimentation and learning, and may provide a useful key to solve problems that have previously been thought to be intractable.

References

Bergemann, D., and Valimaki, J. (1997) 'Market Diffusion with Two-sided Learning', *RAND Journal of Economics* 28: 773–95.

——and Valimaki, J. (2000) 'Experimentation in Markets', *Review of Economic Studies* (forthcoming).

Berry, D. A., and Fristedt, B. (1985) *Bandit Problems.* Chapman & Hall: New York.

Bolton, P., and Harris, C. (1993) 'Strategic Experimentation', STICERD Theoretical Economics Discussion Paper TE/93/261, London School of Economics, January.

——— (1996) 'Strategic Experimentation: A Revision', Discussion Paper 9627, CentER Tilburg University.

——— (1999) 'Strategic Experimentation', *Econometrica* 67: 349–74.

Engelbert, H. J., and Schmidt, W. (1985) 'On Solutions of Stochastic Differential Equations without Drift', *Zeitschrift für Wahrscheinlichkeitstheorie und verwandte Gebiete* 68: 287–317.

Harris, C. (1993), 'Generalized Solutions of Stochastic Differential Games in One Dimension', Industry Studies Program Discussion Paper 44, Boston University, December.

Karatzas, I. (1984) 'Gittins Indices in the Dynamic Allocation Problem for Diffusion Processes', *Annals of Probability* 12: 173–92.

——and Shreve, S. E. (1988) *Brownian Motion and Stochastic Calculus.* Springer-Verlag, New York.

Keller, G., and Rady, S. (1999) 'Optimal Experimentation in a Changing Environment', *Review of Economic Studies* 66: 475–509.

Krylov, N. V. (1980) *Controlled Diffusion Processes.* Springer-Verlag, New York.

Mandelbaum, A. (1987) 'Continuous Multi-Armed Bandits and Multi-Parameter Processes', *Annals of Probability* 15: 1527–56.

Smith, L. (1991) 'Error Persistence and Experimental versus Observational Learning', Foerder Discussion Paper, Tel-Aviv University and MIT.

5 Approximate Common Knowledge in a Search Model

HYUN SONG SHIN

1. Introduction

In a single-person decision problem, pay-offs are determined by one's action and the state of the world. When a decision-maker receives a message which rules out some states of the world, this information can be utilized directly by disregarding these states in one's deliberations. However, the same is not true in an environment where pay-offs depend on the actions of other individuals, as well as the state of the world. Since my pay-off depends on your actions and your actions are motivated by your beliefs, I care about the range of possible beliefs you may hold. So, when I receive a message which rules out some states of the world, it may not be possible to disregard these states in my deliberations, since some of these states may carry information concerning your beliefs. Furthermore, your beliefs at these neighbouring states may depend on your beliefs concerning my beliefs at a further set of states. The reasoning does not stop here. Unless there is some feature of the framework which curtails this sequence of iterated beliefs, higher-order beliefs of all orders will be relevant for my decision now. In this way, states which are *known* not to have occurred may nevertheless exercise an influence on the equilibrium outcome due to such 'infection' of actions across the state space.

The role of common knowledge in determining equilibrium in incomplete information games is implicit in Harsanyi's (1967) discussion of Bayesian equilibrium, but the explication of the precise role of departures from common knowledge has received concerted attention only recently. Rubinstein (1989) and Monderer and Samet (1989) set the stage for the recent discussion, and Carlsson and Van Damme (1993), Sorin (1993), Morris, Rob, and Shin (1995), Chwe (1995a, b), Kajii and Morris (1997), and Morris (2000) and have developed these arguments further.[1]

These developments have been in games with finite action sets. One consistent theme which has emerged has been the importance of the notion of common *p*-belief, as introduced by Monderer and Samet (1989) in characterizing equilibrium. However, relatively little is known about the effect of departures from common knowledge when action sets are continuous. This is an unsatisfactory state of affairs for a number of reasons.

I am grateful to Raquel Fernandez, In Ho Lee, George Mailath, Stephen Morris, Kevin Roberts, and seminar participants at LSE, QMW, and Bonn for their comments. An earlier version of this paper was entitled 'Defining a Notion of Confidence in an Economy with Differential Information'.

[1] For a survey, see Morris and Shin (1997). A parallel literature on the relationship between common knowledge and trade in financial markets has also emerged, such as Sonsino (1995) and Neeman (1996).

Many games derived from economic models are most naturally dealt with by assuming that action sets are continuous, and the lack of a proper framework for analysing such games is a serious gap. Furthermore, it is already known that for a small class of such games (coordination games with continuous action sets), no amount of common p-belief is enough to approximate equilibria under common knowledge.[2] This is in great contrast to the approximation theorems for finite games, and suggests that rather different types of arguments are needed to deal with games with continuous action sets.

The main contribution of this paper is the introduction of a technique which formalizes and quantifies the consequences of departures from common knowledge for continuous action games. The main innovation is a technique involving the construction of a Markov chain over the types in a Bayesian game, in which I show that the absence of common knowledge of fundamentals corresponds in a natural way to features of this Markov chain, in particular to the existence of an absorbing state. In this context, the equilibrium action of type k can be characterized as follows. Imagine that the Markov chain starts from state k. Every time it visits a state j, a non-negative 'prize' associated with this state is collected. The equilibrium action of type k is then the expected value of the accumulated prize before the system eventually reaches the absorbing state.

It is then shown how such a framework provides the basis for a formal analysis of an 'infection' argument analogous to the finite action case, but one which differs significantly in terms of its mode of operation. The additional richness of structure introduced by continuous actions means that no simple characterization of equilibrium can be given in terms of common p-belief.

For concreteness, the development of the theory is conducted in terms of a simple search model in the spirit of Diamond (1982), in which a small idiosyncratic component to signals entails a failure of common knowledge of the fundamentals. In an economy with a large number of disparate agents, failures of common knowledge will be the rule rather than the exception. Although an individual may have a window on to the world in the form of a signal concerning the fundamentals, if signals have an idiosyncratic component, failures of common knowledge are to be expected even when the idiosyncratic component is small. I address the issue of whether such departures from common knowledge will matter in terms of equilibrium activity, and if so, by how much.

The insight generated by this analysis is useful in adjudicating between two types of explanations of low economic activity. On the one hand, there are those explanations, typified by the real business cycle theory of Kydland and Prescott (1982), which appeal to the unfavourable fundamentals of the economy. On the other hand, there are explanations which emphasize coordination failures in the presence of multiple equilibria (for instance, Cooper and John 1988). Empirical investigations, such as Dagsvik and Jovanovic (1994) appeal to this dichotomy in asking whether the Great Depression was due to bad fundamentals or to a coordination failure. However, if departures from common knowledge rule out outcomes with high activity, then the fundamentals–coordination-failure dichotomy is too restrictive. Merely showing that the

---

[2] Shin and Williamson (1996).

fundamentals are consistent with high activity does not demonstrate that low activity was simply the result of failing to coordinate on the correct equilibrium. For high activity to be sustained as an equilibrium outcome, something more is required. The fundamentals must be sufficiently transparent to all individuals that they are close to being common knowledge.

The culmination of the analysis is the proposal of a formal definition of 'confidence' in this search economy. The measure of confidence has a counterpart in the induced Markov chain in terms of the expected time to absorption, and has the following features.

- The higher is confidence, the higher is the search intensity and welfare.
- The discrepancy between the equilibrium outcome and the outcome justified by the fundamentals (i.e. the discrepancy between the actual outcome and the best feasible outcome) can be explained by the shortfall in confidence.

Most importantly, the framework of this paper allows us to quantify such effects. The main results and arguments are presented after we have outlined the basic economy (in the next section) and examined its welfare properties (Section 3). We begin with the model.

2. The Model

Our model is concerned with the activities of a continuum of individuals, indexed by the interval [0, 1]. Each individual is endowed with $\bar{\ell}$ units of labour, which may either be taken as leisure, or which may be employed towards the consumption of an indivisible traded good, as described below. Everyone has the identical utility function

$$\alpha c + \ell, \tag{1}$$

where ℓ is the consumption of leisure, $\alpha > 1$ is a constant representing the consumption value of the traded good, and c is the number of units of the indivisible traded good consumed. An individual consumes either one or zero units of the traded good.

Labour input is necessary for the consumption of the traded good for two reasons. Firstly, there is a cost of production associated with the indivisible consumption good. For individual i, the cost of producing the consumption good (in units of labour) is $g_i \geq 0$. Secondly, as in Diamond (1982), the consumption good must be traded with that of another individual in the economy before it can be consumed. A trading partner must be found during a process of search, to be outlined below. Due to the indivisibility of the traded good, the terms of trade are assumed to be one to one whenever trade takes place.

The search intensity of individual i is a number in the interval [0, 1], and is denoted by s_i. Search activity incurs a disutility of effort, represented by a quadratic cost of effort

$$s_i^2/2, \tag{2}$$

measured in units of labour. The matching process is governed by the profile of search intensities $\{s_i\}$ of all the individuals in the economy. Given a profile of search intensities, the *average search intensity* is denoted by s^*. If the search intensity of individual i is s_i and the average search intensity is s^*, the probability of trader i meeting a trading partner in the search process is given by the product

$$s^* s_i. \tag{3}$$

The final part of the description of our search economy concerns the structure of uncertainty concerning g_i. Each g_i is given by the sum:

$$g_i = f + \eta_i, \tag{4}$$

where f is a random variable taking values in the set $\{0, \Delta, 2\Delta, 3\Delta, \ldots\}$, where Δ is a small positive number representing the smallest unit of account in the economy. The random variable f represents the component of each trader's cost of production which is common across individuals. It should be seen as the aggregate shock to production costs in the economy. We denote by

$$p(k) \tag{5}$$

the probability that f takes the value $k\Delta$, and assume that $p(k) > 0$ for all k. The random variable η_i represents the idiosyncratic shock to the production cost of individual i, and takes two values only. In particular

$$\eta_i = \begin{cases} \Delta & \text{with prob } \tfrac{1}{2} \\ 0 & \text{with prob } \tfrac{1}{2}. \end{cases} \tag{6}$$

The idiosyncratic shock η_i is independent of f, and is independent across individuals. Each individual i observes his own cost (the realization of g_i), but does not observe the realizations of f or η_i separately.

After individual i observes g_i, he decides whether or not to produce the traded good. If the individual decides to produce, he decides how hard to search for a trading partner, by choosing the search intensity s_i. The pay-off of individual i falls under three cases. If i is successfully matched with a trading partner after having searched with intensity s_i, his pay-off consists of the consumption of the traded good (given by α) plus the consumption of the available leisure (given by $\bar{\ell} - g_i - s_i^2/2$). Thus, the pay-off is:

$$\alpha + \bar{\ell} - g_i - \frac{s_i^2}{2}. \tag{7}$$

If i has produced the traded good but has been unsuccessful in meeting a trading partner after having searched with intensity s_i, his pay-off is:

$$\bar{\ell} - \frac{s_i^2}{2} - g_i. \tag{8}$$

Finally, if i has decided not to produce, his pay-off is simply the consumption of the endowment $\bar{\ell}$. A *strategy* for individual i can then be represented as a function:

$$s_i : \{0, 1, 2, 3, \ldots \} \rightarrow [0, 1], \tag{9}$$

where $s_i(k)$ denotes the level of search intensity chosen by individual i given $g_i = k\Delta$. It will be understood that i has undertaken production if and only if the search intensity is non-zero. A profile of strategies $\{s_i\}$ is an *equilibrium* of our economy if, for any individual i and for any $k \in \{0, 1, 2, \ldots \}$, the action $s_j(k)$ maximizes j's expected pay-off conditional on the observation of $g_j = k\Delta$, given the strategies of all other individuals in the profile $\{s_i\}$.

3. A Welfare Benchmark

Before we embark on the analysis of the economy described above, it will be useful to outline the welfare properties of a variant of our search economy in which all individuals have *identical* costs of production. This will serve as a benchmark for the welfare analysis of the equilibria to be characterized in the economy with idiosyncratic components in costs.

Thus, for this section only, we will suppose that there is no idiosyncratic shock to the cost of production, and that each trader i has the identical cost of production:

$$g_i = f. \tag{10}$$

In this case, the realization of f will be common knowledge among the individuals in the economy. An equilibrium strategy is then trivially defined by the solution of each one-shot, complete information game, indexed by the realization of f.

The analysis of the one-shot game falls under two cases, depending on whether an individual's cost of production is above or below $\bar{g}$, where

$$\bar{g} \equiv \alpha - \tfrac{1}{2}. \tag{11}$$

If the cost of production exceeds $\bar{g}$, then it is a dominant action for a trader not to produce the traded good. This is so, since a trader's pay-off cannot exceed $\alpha s_i + \bar{\ell} - s_i^2/2 - g_i$, which in turn is less than $\bar{\ell}$ if $g_i > \bar{g}$. But since an individual can guarantee a pay-off of $\bar{\ell}$ by not producing the traded good, no production will take place, and no search is undertaken. Thus, if the cost of production for everyone exceeds $\bar{g}$, the unique equilibrium is that in which $s_i = 0$ for all i.

Even when the realization of f is below $\bar{g}$, there is an equilibrium in which $s_i = 0$ for all i. This is so, since if no one else searches, it is optimal not to search oneself. However, there is another, Pareto-superior equilibrium, in which traders exploit the scope for mutually beneficial trade. Indeed, this equilibrium results in an efficient allocation. The marginal cost of search activity by trader i is s_i, while the marginal benefit is αs^*, where s^* is the average search intensity. Thus, if $s^* = 1$, the optimal search intensity is $s_i = 1$, so that the resulting average search intensity will, indeed, be equal to 1. Furthermore, since $g_i \leq \bar{g}$, individual i cannot do better by not producing. The efficiency of the resulting allocation is also apparent, since trader i's pay-off is bounded above by $\alpha s_i + \bar{\ell} - s_i^2/2 - g_i$ (the probability of meeting a trading partner cannot exceed one's own search intensity).

For the sake of completeness, we should observe that there are no other equilibria in the one-shot game. If there were, it must involve a level of search for some trader which is an interior solution. A necessary condition for s_i to be an interior best reply to s^* is that $s_i = \alpha s^*$. But this is ruled out by the fact that $\alpha > 1$ and that all individuals have the identical best reply to s^*. Thus, when $k\Delta \leq \bar{g}$, the equilibrium value of $s_i(k)$ is either 1 or 0. No other value of $s_i(k)$ can be supported in equilibrium.

In summary, our benchmark case gives rise to a particularly simple set of equilibrium outcomes, which we shall summarize as follows.

Proposition 1. Equilibrium search is zero if $f > \bar{g}$, and is either 1 or 0 if $f \leq \bar{g}$.

Since maximum search gives rise to the efficient outcome, the *ex ante* efficient equilibrium is one in which all individuals engage in maximum search whenever the cost of production is below $\bar{g}$. That is, $s(k) = 1$ for $k \leq \bar{g}\Delta$, and $s(k) = 0$ for $k > \bar{g}/\Delta$.

4. Equilibrium with Noise

The idiosyncratic component in the cost of production induces a failure of common knowledge of the fundamentals. In particular, there is a failure of common knowledge of the event that everyone's cost of production is lower than the benchmark $\bar{g}$, and hence that full search yields the efficient outcome. To see this, note that everyone's cost level is below $\bar{g}$ if and only if the realization of f is $\bar{g} - \Delta$ or lower. Denote this event by A. However, it is clear that A is never common knowledge; everyone knows A if $g_i < \bar{g} - 2\Delta$, which in turn implies that $f < \bar{g} - 3\Delta$, everyone knows that everyone knows A if $f < \bar{g} - 5\Delta$, and so on, so even if costs are zero, only a finite number of iterations of knowledge are possible.

An event is said to be common *p*-belief if, whenever this event is true, everyone puts probability at least p to this event (Monderer and Samet 1989). In our model, the event A is common *q*-belief, where

$$q = \frac{p(\bar{g} - \Delta)}{p(\bar{g} - \Delta) + p(\bar{g})}. \tag{12}$$

This is so, since whenever the event A occurs (so that everyone's cost is at most $\bar{g} - \Delta$), everyone puts posterior weight at least q to the event A.

For finite action games, and in particular for binary games, the degree to which the pay-offs are common *p*-belief largely determines the equilibrium of the incomplete information game. The layers of iterated knowledge plays little role, and Rubinstein's (1989) e-mail game is a striking example of this irrelevance. However, as shown below, when action sets are continuous, the layers of iterated knowledge come into play, as well as other features of the information structure. The task will be to formulate a framework which will be able to keep track of all these effects.

I summarize the salient properties of equilibrium with idiosyncratic shocks by means of three propositions. The arguments and proofs are presented separately in the following section. The results are stated in terms of strategies in which search is positive if and only if production cost is lower than some switching point m. We reserve the term *switching strategy* for such a strategy. In other words, $s(\cdot)$ is a switching strategy if there is $m > 0$ such that $s(k) > 0$ if and only if $k < m$. Since optimal search will be zero for very large values of g, in any equilibrium, our focus on switching strategies will allow us to concentrate on equilibria which favour search. In spite of this, it will be shown that equilibrium search can be very low.

Proposition 2. Equilibrium search is decreasing with the cost of production. That is, $s(0) \geq s(1) \geq s(2) \ldots \geq s(k) \geq \ldots$ for any symmetric switching equilibrium s. Moreover, if $0 < s(k) < 1$, then $s(k) > s(k + 1)$.

Proposition 3. For any $\epsilon > 0$, there is $\alpha > 1$ such that, for any symmetric equilibrium switching strategy s, $s(k) < \epsilon$ for all k.

Proposition 4. If s is a symmetric equilibrium switching strategy and g is the highest cost level for which there is positive search, then

$$ g \leq \frac{1}{2}\left(\frac{\alpha}{2 - \alpha} \frac{p(k - 1)}{p(k - 1) + p(k)} \right)^2. \tag{13} $$

The first proposition is a monotonicity result concerning equilibrium search. It guarantees that the level of search in a switching equilibrium is increasing as the cost of production falls. This is in contrast to the perfect information case, where equilibrium search is not monotonic in cost.

Proposition 2 points to the importance of the number of layers of *iterated knowledge* of the fundamentals. A lower value of f implies a larger number of layers of knowledge of the event that full search is the efficient outcome. Proposition 2 then states that an extra layer of knowledge that full search is efficient will increase the level of search activity. In particular, the highest possible search in equilibrium will occur when $f = 0$. This is in contrast to finite action games, where additional layers of iterated knowledge play little role.

By itself, proposition 2 does not convey the full picture of the severe disruption to search activity resulting from the failure of common knowledge. However, we see from proposition 3 something of the impact of the idiosyncratic component in cost. Proposition 3 is the continuous action analogue of the 'infection' argument in finite action games, and states that equilibrium search is close to zero for *any* level of cost when α is chosen appropriately from the admissible range. This is in great contrast to the outcome in the benchmark case as summarized in proposition 1. When there is common knowledge of the cost of production, maximum search can always be supported as an equilibrium provided the cost of production is below $\bar{g}$. In contrast, proposition 3 demonstrates the possibility of search activity being driven down to zero, even though the realization of f (the underlying common component in cost) is sufficiently low that everyone knows that maximum search is efficient and feasible.

Proposition 3 also reinforces the monotonicity result, as given by proposition 2, since low values of α are guaranteed to generate equilibria in which equilibrium search is strictly below 1.

Proposition 4 gives us another window on the disruption to search activity entailed by the idiosyncratic component in cost. It gives a necessary condition for positive search in equilibrium. If the inequality (13) is violated, we can be sure that search is zero in equilibrium. A quick glance at (13) shows that violation of this inequality may occur even when cost is comparatively low, and certainly lower than the benchmark level $\bar{g}$ identified in the last section. For instance, suppose that $\alpha = 1.2$, so that $\bar{g} = 0.7$. We know from the analysis of the benchmark case that, if it were common knowledge that everyone's cost is below $\bar{g}$, efficient search can be supported as an equilibrium. However, according to (13), equilibrium search is positive only if the cost level falls below $\frac{1}{2}(\frac{\alpha}{2-\alpha} \frac{p(k-1)}{p(k-1)+p(k)})^2$. If we suppose that the density $p(\cdot)$ is approximately uniform over the relevant range, this is approximately $\frac{1}{4}$. In other words, unless the cost of production is as low as $\frac{1}{4}$, equilibrium search is zero in spite of the fact that maximum search is the efficient outcome provided everyone's cost is below 0.7. Finally, it is worth noting that in all three results the size of Δ plays no essential role in our analysis. Even for small Δ, the effects outlined above survive.

Before we embark on the formal constructions employed in proving our results, it is instructive to go through an informal argument, so as to fix our intuitions. Let us place ourselves in the shoes of a typical individual i in this economy, and let us suppose that the realization of g_i is well below $\bar{g}$ so that i knows that the efficient outcome is for everyone to engage in maximum search. Although i knows that maximum search is the efficient outcome, i's individual incentives are such that search is only justified if others are engaged in search. Thus, in order to decide how much search should be undertaken, i must consider the actions of others, and in turn their *beliefs*, since others' actions are motivated by their beliefs. Suppose that $g_i = k\Delta$. Then, there are two possible values of f, namely $k\Delta$ and $(k-1)\Delta$. If it is the former, then half of the population will have the cost $k\Delta$, while the other half will have cost $(k+1)\Delta$. It is then necessary to consider (among other things) what would be optimal for a typical individual if the cost level were $(k+1)\Delta$. But then, an exactly analogous line of reasoning suggests that, in order to work out one's optimal search effort given cost $(k+1)\Delta$, it is necessary to consider what would be optimal for a typical individual if the cost level were $(k+2)\Delta$. With each round in this iterative reasoning, successively higher levels of cost become relevant. Moreover, i's incentive to search is increasing in the search activity of others, so that i's incentive to search would be raised if the search activity of others were high given cost $(k+1)\Delta$, $(k+2)\Delta$, and higher levels. Eventually in this line of reasoning, we must consider what would be optimal for a typical individual for cost levels above $\bar{g}$. When cost exceeds $\bar{g}$, it is a dominant action not to produce. Depending on the degree to which i's incentive to search is affected by the search intensity of others, the knowledge that others will not produce when cost exceeds $\bar{g}$ has a potential effect on i's search at lower cost levels.

When the consumption value of the traded good is high, this sort of effect can be expected to be small or non-existent, since the potential rewards to search activity is sufficiently high for traders to overcome the strategic effects described above. However, when α is relatively small (when it is close to 1), the potential reward to search is more marginal, and depends to a greater extent on how hard others are searching. In this setting, the strategic effects could be expected to be much more prominent. Thus, it is no surprise that in propositions 3 and 4, the overall level of search depends on the consumption value of the traded good. When it is close to 1, equilibrium search is driven down to zero as the strategic effects begin to dominate.

5. Markov Chain over Types

For the formal argument, I define a Markov chain with a countable number of states, indexed by the set of natural numbers $N = \{0, 1, 2, \ldots\}$. The one-step transition probability from state k to state j is denoted by $\phi(k, j)$ and is defined as follows. For the state $0 \in N$,

$$\phi(0, j) = \begin{cases} \frac{1}{2} & \text{if } j = 0 \text{ or } j = 1 \\ 0 & \text{otherwise} \end{cases}. \tag{14}$$

For state $k > 0$,

$$\phi(k, j) = \begin{cases} p(k-1)/(p(k-1) + p(k)) & \text{if } j = k - 1 \\ p(k)/(p(k-1) + p(k)) & \text{if } j = k + 1 \\ 0 & \text{otherwise.} \end{cases} \tag{15}$$

This is a Markov chain on the line in which a one-unit transition is possible either to the left or to the right, with probabilities $p(k-1)/(p(k-1) + p(k))$ and $p(k)/(p(k-1) + p(k))$ respectively. From state 0, a transition is possible to state 1 or back to state 0, with equal probability. We then have the following preliminary result.

Lemma 1. For any symmetric equilibrium s,

   (i) If $s(k) > 0$, then $s(k) \geqslant \sum_j \phi(k, j)s(j)$,
   (ii) $s(k) \leqslant \sum_j \phi(k, j)s(j) + F(\alpha)$, where $F(\alpha) = 2(\alpha - 1)/(2 - \alpha)$.

   Clause (i) states that positive search in equilibrium can be described as a *supermartingale* with respect to the Markov chain defined by the transition probabilities $\phi(\,.\,,\,.\,)$. This is so, since if we denote the Markov chain by $\{X_n\}$, then $E(s(X_{n+1}) \mid X_n = k) = \sum_j \phi(k, j)s(j) \leqslant s(k)$, so that $s(X_n) \geqslant E(s(X_{n+1}) \mid X_n)$. Hence, $\{s(X_n)\}$ is a supermartingale with respect to $\{X_n\}$. Functions such as $s(\cdot)$ which satisfy clause (i) are known as *superregular* functions with respect to ϕ (Karlin and Taylor 1981: 45). Clause (ii) tells us that the difference between $s(X_n)$ and $E(s(X_{n+1}) \mid X_n)$ can be bounded by a constant which depends only on the consumption value of the traded good.

Proof of Lemma 1. Suppose s is a symmetric equilibrium, and consider the optimal action of trader i who has observed the realization $g_i = k\Delta$, where $k > 0$. Conditional on this observation, trader i allows two possible realizations of f, namely $k\Delta$ and $(k - 1)\Delta$, with the following probabilities

$$pr(f = k\Delta \mid g_i = k\Delta) \qquad = \frac{\frac{1}{2}p(k)}{\frac{1}{2}p(k - 1) + \frac{1}{2}p(k)} = \phi(k, k + 1)$$

$$pr(f = (k - 1)\Delta \mid g_i = k\Delta) = \frac{\frac{1}{2}p(k - 1)}{\frac{1}{2}p(k - 1) + \frac{1}{2}p(k)} = \phi(k, k - 1). \tag{16}$$

When $f = k\Delta$, half of the traders have cost level $k\Delta$, while the other half have cost $(k + 1)\Delta$. Those with cost level $k\Delta$ take action $s(k)$, while those with cost $(k + 1)\Delta$ take action $s(k + 1)$. Hence, when $f = k\Delta$, the average search intensity is given by

$$s^*(k) = \frac{s(k) + s(k + 1)}{2}. \tag{17}$$

Similarly, when $f = (k - 1)\Delta$, average search intensity is given by

$$s^*(k - 1) = \frac{s(k - 1) + s(k)}{2}. \tag{18}$$

Then, for individual i, the expected search intensity conditional on $g_i = k\Delta$, which we shall denote by $E(s^* \mid k)$, is given by the weighted sum:

$$E(s^* \mid k) = s^*(k - 1) \cdot pr(f = (k - 1)\Delta \mid g_i = k\Delta)$$
$$+ s^*(k) \cdot pr(f = k\Delta \mid g_i = k\Delta),$$

which simplifies to:

$$\frac{\phi(k, k - 1)s(k - 1) + s(k) + \phi(k, k + 1)s(k + 1)}{2}. \tag{19}$$

The expected pay-off of individual i conditional on $g_i = k\Delta$ is thus given by

$$\alpha E(s^* \mid k)s(k) + \bar{\ell} - \frac{s(k)^2}{2} - k\Delta. \tag{20}$$

Let us first consider the case where the optimal $s(k)$ is an interior solution. Then optimal $s(k)$ satisfies the first-order condition:

$$s(k) = \alpha E(s^* \mid k), \tag{21}$$

so that

$$s(k) = \frac{\alpha}{2}\{\phi(k, k - 1)s(k - 1) + s(k) + \phi(k, k + 1)s(k + 1)\}$$

$$= \frac{\alpha/2}{1 - (\alpha/2)}\{\phi(k, k - 1)s(k - 1) + \phi(k, k + 1)s(k + 1)\} \tag{22}$$

$$= \frac{\alpha}{2 - \alpha}\sum_j \phi(k, j)s(j).$$

Thus, at an interior solution[3] $s(k) > \sum_j \phi(k,j)s(j)$. When the constraint $s(k) \leq 1$ binds, we have $s(k) = 1 \geq \sum_j \phi(k,j)s(j)$. Thus, clause (i) of the lemma holds. To see that clause (ii) holds, note that it holds trivially if $s(k) = 0$. Thus, suppose $s(k)$ is positive. Then, from (22),

$$s(k) = \min\left\{1, \frac{\alpha}{2-\alpha}\sum_j \phi(k,j)s(j)\right\}. \tag{23}$$

Thus,

$$s(k) - \sum_j \phi(k,j)s(j) \leq \left[\frac{\alpha}{2-\alpha} - 1\right]\sum_j \phi(k,j)s(j) \leq F(\alpha), \tag{24}$$

which is clause (ii) of lemma 1.

In order to complete the proof of lemma 1, we need to consider $s(0)$, the optimal action of trader i given $g_i = 0$. Given the observation $g_i = 0$, individual i knows for sure that $f = 0$. When $f = 0$, half of the traders have cost level 0 and search with intensity $s(0)$, while the other half have the cost level Δ and search with intensity $s(1)$. Hence, the average search intensity conditional on $g_i = 0$ is given by

$$E(s^* \mid 0) = s^*(0) = \frac{s(0) + s(1)}{2} = \sum_j \phi(0,j)s(j). \tag{25}$$

The expected pay-off of individual i conditional on $g_i = 0$ is $\alpha E(s^* \mid k)s(k) + \bar{\ell} - s(k)^2/2$. Thus, the optimal $s(0)$ is given by

$$s(0) = \min\left\{1, \frac{\alpha}{2-\alpha}\sum_j \phi(0,j)s(j)\right\}. \tag{26}$$

Hence, both clauses of lemma 1 hold for $k = 0$. This completes the proof of lemma 1.

Apart from the Markov chain defined on N, we introduce a related class of *finite* Markov chains. Define the *m-truncated Markov chain* to be the finite Markov chain on the state space $\{0, 1, 2, \ldots, m\}$, in which state m is an absorbing state, while the transition probabilities from all other states $k < m$ are given by $\phi(k,j)$. In other words, the transition probabilities are given by $q(i,j)$, where

$$q(i,j) = \begin{cases} \phi(i,j) & \text{if } i < m \\ 1 & \text{if } i = j = m. \end{cases} \tag{27}$$

Then, consider the *first-passage probabilities* for this chain. Denote by

$$\psi^{(n)}(i,j) \tag{28}$$

---

[3] Notice that an interior solution implies that $\alpha < 2$. When α is larger than 2, maximum search takes place, irrespective of the search level at other states.

the probability that, when the system starts from state i, it makes a transition to state j *for the first time* after n transitions. In other words,

$$\psi^{(n)}(i, j) = prob(X_n = j \text{ and } X_r \neq j, \text{ for } r = 1, 2, \ldots, n - 1 \mid X_0 = i). \tag{29}$$

From lemma 1(i), for any $i < m$, we have the inequality:

$$s(i) \geqslant \sum_j q(i, j)s(j) = \sum_{j \neq k} q(i, j)s(j) + q(i, k)s(k). \tag{30}$$

Iterating this inequality gives:

$$
\begin{aligned}
s(i) &\geqslant \sum_{j \neq k} q(i, j)s(j) + q(i, k)s(k), \\
&\geqslant \sum_{j \neq k} q(i, j)\left(\sum_{r \neq k} q(j, r)s(r) + q(j, k)s(k)\right) + q(i, k)s(k) \\
&= \sum_{j, r \neq k} q(i, j)q(j, r)s(r) + \sum_{j \neq k} q(i, j)q(j, k)s(k) + q(i, k)s(k) \\
&= \sum_{j, r \neq k} q(i, j)q(j, r)s(r) + \psi^{(2)}(i, k)s(k) + \psi^{(1)}(i, k)s(k),
\end{aligned}
$$

where we have used the fact that $\psi^{(1)}(i, k) = q(i, k)$ and $\psi^{(2)}(i, k) = \sum_{j \neq k} q(i, j)q(j, k)$. By iterating the substitution of inequality (30), we have:

$$s(i) \geqslant \sum_{n=1}^{m} \psi^{(n)}(i, k)s(k), \text{ for all } m. \tag{31}$$

Thus, if we define $\psi^*(i, k) \equiv \sum_{n=1}^{\infty} \psi^{(n)}(i, k)$, the number $\psi^*(i, k)$ gives the probability that the system *ever* visits state k from state i. Then, from (31),

$$s(i) \geqslant \psi^*(i, k)s(k). \tag{32}$$

Proposition 1 follows from this inequality. Since m is the only absorbing state, the probability that the system visits state m from any state is 1. Thus, $\psi^*(i, m) = 1$ for all i. Moreover, in making a transition from state i to state m, the system must eventually visit every state between i and m, since only one-unit transitions are possible. Thus, for any two states i and k such that $i < k$, we have $\psi^*(i, k) = 1$, so that

$$s(i) \geqslant s(k), \text{ for all } k > i. \tag{33}$$

To complete the proof of proposition 1, we note from (23) that when equilibrium $s(i)$ is less than 1, the inequality (31) holds strictly, so that $s(i) > s(k)$ if $s(i) < 1$. ∎
We can then characterize equilibrium search as follows.

Lemma 2. Suppose $v(k, j)$ is the expected number of visits to state j when the system starts from state k in the m-truncated Markov chain. Then, $v(k, j) < \infty$ for any $j, k < m$. Moreover, if s is a symmetric equilibrium for which m is the smallest integer such that $s(m) = 0$, then for any $k < m$,

$$s(k) = \sum_{j < m} v(k, j)\left(s(j) - \sum_i \phi(j, i)s(i)\right). \tag{34}$$

Lemma 2 provides an intriguing interpretation of equilibrium search. Imagine that the Markov chain starts off at state $k < m$. Also, imagine that every time the system visits state $j < m$, a 'prize' equal to $s(j) - \Sigma_i \phi(j, i)s(i)$ is won. This prize is non-negative, by lemma 1(i). Then, equation (34) tells us that the equilibrium search intensity $s(k)$ is given by the expected value of the accumulated prize when the system starts out from state k.

Proof of Lemma 2. From any state $k < m$, a transition is possible to both of its neighbours with positive probability. However, since m is an absorbing state, all states other than m are transient in this chain. Denote by Q the $m \times m$ matrix which describes the transitions among the transient states. The $(k, j)^{th}$ entry of Q is thus given by $\phi(k - 1, j - 1)$. Note that all rows of Q sum to 1, except for the last row. The last row is given by:

$$(0, 0, 0, \ldots, 0, 0, \phi(m - 1, m - 2), 0), \tag{35}$$

so that the sum of entries is $\phi(m - 1, m - 2)$, which is strictly less than 1.

Now, consider the switching strategy $s(\cdot)$. If we denote by s the column vector:

$$s = \begin{bmatrix} s(0) \\ s(1) \\ \vdots \\ s(m - 1) \end{bmatrix}, \tag{36}$$

then lemma 1(i), together with the fact that $s(m) = 0$ implies that

$$s \geqslant Qs. \tag{37}$$

Also, for any positive integer k, we have the identity:

$$s = Q^{k+1}s + (I + Q + \ldots + Q^k)(s - Qs). \tag{38}$$

Since the matrix Q describes the transitions among the transient states, the series $I + Q + \ldots + Q^k$ converges to some finite $m \times m$ matrix $V \equiv \Sigma_{k=0}^{\infty} Q^k$, whose $(i, j)^{th}$ entry is the expected number of visits to state j when the process starts at state i. Indeed, $I - Q$ is non-singular, and $V = (I - Q)^{-1}$. Clearly, Q^k tends to the zero matrix as k becomes large. Since $s \geqslant Qs$, the second term on the right-hand side of (38) is increasing in k. We may thus appeal to monotone convergence in passing to the limit in (38) to yield

$$s = V(s - Qs), \tag{39}$$

which is lemma 2.

The argument for proposition 3 can then proceed as follows.

Proof of Proposition 3. Suppose $\{\alpha^0, \alpha^1, \alpha^2, \ldots, \alpha^t, \ldots\}$ is a decreasing sequence of values of α which converges to 1. Let m^t be the smallest integer such that

$$m^t > (\alpha^t - \frac{1}{2})/\Delta. \tag{40}$$

Then, for the economy in which the consumption value of the traded good is α^t, we have $\Delta m^t > \alpha^t - \frac{1}{2}$, so that $s(m^t) = 0$ is a dominant action for any individual in this economy.

Since $\{\alpha^0, \alpha^1, \alpha^2, \ldots, \alpha^t, \ldots\}$ is a decreasing sequence, $m^t \leqslant m^0$, for all t. Thus, if we denote by $v^t(k, j)$ the expected number of visits to state j when the m^t-truncated Markov chain starts at state k, then for any states $k, j < m^t$,

$$v^t(k, j) \leqslant v^0(k, j). \tag{41}$$

Meanwhile, from lemma 1(ii), we know that for any symmetric equilibrium switching strategy $s^t(\cdot)$ for the economy parametrized by α^t,

$$s^t(k) - \sum_j \phi(k, j)s^t(j) \leqslant F(\alpha^t). \tag{42}$$

Thus, we have the following sequence of inequalities.

$$s^t(k) = \sum_{n<m^t} v^t(k, n)\left(s^t(n) - \sum_i \phi(n, i)s^t(i) \right) \qquad \text{(from lemma 2)}$$

$$\leqslant \sum_{n<m^t} v^0(k, n)\left(s^t(n) - \sum_i \phi(n, i)s^t(i) \right) \qquad \text{(from (41))}$$

$$\leqslant \sum_{n<m^0} v^0(k, n)\left(s^t(n) - \sum_i \phi(n, i)s^t(i) \right) \qquad \text{(since } m^t \leqslant m^0\text{)}$$

$$\leqslant F(\alpha^t) \sum_{n<m^0} v^0(k, n) \qquad \text{(from (42))}$$

Moreover, $F(\alpha^t) \to 0$ as $t \to \infty$. Thus, for any $\epsilon > 0$, there is an element α^t in the sequence $\{\alpha^0, \alpha^1, \alpha^2, \ldots\}$ such that, for any equilibrium $s^t(\cdot)$ for this economy,

$$\epsilon > F(\alpha^t) \sum_{n<m^0} v^0(k, n) \geqslant s^t(k). \tag{43}$$

This is the statement of proposition 3.

It now remains for us to prove proposition 4. We can be quite economical with the argument here, since many of the steps have been outlined already. Thus, suppose that k is the largest integer such that $0 < s(k) < 1$ in a symmetric equilibrium s. Then, from (23) and the fact that $s(k + 1) = 0$, we have

$$s(k) \leqslant \phi(k, k-1)s(k-1) \leqslant \phi(k, k-1) = \frac{p(k-1)}{p(k-1) + p(k)}. \tag{44}$$

Meanwhile, since $s(k) < 1$, it satisfies the first-order condition given by (21), so that the expected pay-off (as given by (20)) is

$$\frac{s(k)^2}{2} + \bar{\ell} - k\Delta. \tag{45}$$

Since a trader can guarantee a pay-off of $\bar{\ell}$ by not producing at all, positive $s(k)$ is optimal only if this expected pay-off is no smaller than $\bar{\ell}$. That is, $s(k) \geq \sqrt{(2k\Delta)}$. When taken together with (44), we have the statement of proposition 4.

6. A Proposal

In the light of our discussion of the properties of equilibrium search, we are now in a position to propose a definition of the degree of confidence in our economy. The proposal arises from the characterization of equilibrium search given by lemma 2. Lemma 2 states that equilibrium search given some cost level can be interpreted as the expected aggregate prize generated in a Markov chain, when the system starts at the corresponding state.

Let m be the smallest integer such that $m\Delta > \bar{g}$, so that $m\Delta$ is the smallest cost level for which not producing is the dominant action. Consider, then, the m-truncated Markov chain, and denote by $v(i, j)$ the expected number of visits to state j when the system starts in state i. For $i, j < m$, $v(i, j)$ is finite. Furthermore, if we now sum across j these expected number of visits, the resulting number is the expected number of visits to the set of transient states of the m-truncated Markov chain. In other words, it is the *expected time to absorption*. We shall propose the expected time to absorption from state i as our proposed measure of confidence given cost level i. That is, the level of confidence of an agent who has cost level $i\Delta$ is given by:

$$\sum_{j} v(i, j). \tag{46}$$

The level of confidence of the whole economy could then be defined as the average of the individual levels of confidence. Since the Markov chain is defined on the line where 0 is a reflecting barrier and m is an absorbing barrier, for two states i, k where $i < k$, the expected time to absorption from state i is higher than that from state k. However, we know from proposition 2 that equilibrium search is higher at state i than at k. Hence, equilibrium search (and hence welfare) is increasing in our measure of confidence.

The main virtue of our proposed measure of confidence is that it ties in directly with the mechanism at work whereby the absence of common knowledge impinges on equilibrium outcomes. The fact that a transition is possible to the absorbing state from any state of the Markov chain has a direct counterpart in the absence of common knowledge, and the degree to which common knowledge fails is mirrored by the expected time to absorption. In this sense, our proposed measure of confidence gives an indication of the *impact* of the absorbing state m.

Above all, our proposed definition of confidence allows us to distinguish between states which have identical first-best levels of search, but which give rise to distinct outcomes in equilibrium. As we noted in Section 3 on the welfare properties of our economy, whenever everyone's cost of production is below $\bar{g}$, the efficient outcome is for everyone to search with maximum intensity. Indeed, if it were *common knowledge* that everyone's cost is below $\bar{g}$, this allocation can be supported as an equilibrium. However, in the absence of common knowledge, the outcome is determined by the induced Markov chain, and our definition of confidence summarizes this effect.

An examination of the main steps in our construction provides clues as to what the ingredients of a more general argument might be. We have already alluded to the role played by the failure of common knowledge and how this constrains the actions of the types. Equally important is the *nature* of this constraint. It is important for our argument that the actions of the types are *strategic complements* in the sense that the best reply of a type is increasing in the actions of other types (Bulow, Geanakoplos, and Klemperer 1985; Milgrom and Roberts 1990). Thus, an individual will search harder if others are searching harder. This is why, if some of the types are not searching at all, this has repercussions across all the types, as traders react by lowering their search intensities, even though they all know that better outcomes are feasible.

References

Bulow, J., J. Geanakoplos and P. Klemperer (1985) 'Multi-Market Oligopoly: Strategic Substitutes and Complements', *Journal of Political Economy* 93: 488–511.

Carlsson, H., and E. van Damme (1993) 'Global Games and Equilibrium Selection', *Econometrica* 61: 989–1018.

Chwe, M. S.-Y. (1995*a*) 'Strategic Reliability of Communication Networks', *GSB Discussion Paper* 21, University of Chicago.

—— (1995*b*) 'The Reeded Edge and the Phillips Curve: Money Neutrality, Common Knowledge, and Subjective Beliefs', *GSB Discussion Paper* 22, University of Chicago.

Cooper, R., and A. John (1988) 'Coordinating Coordination Failures in Keynesian Models', *Quarterly Journal of Economics* 103: 441–63.

Dagsvik, J., and B. Jovanovic (1994) 'Was the Great Depression a Low Level Equilibrium?', *European Economic Review* 38: 1711–29.

Diamond, P. (1982) 'Aggregate Demand Management in Search Equilibrium', *Journal of Political Economy* 91: 410–19.

Harsanyi, J. (1967) 'Games with Incomplete Information Played by Bayesian Players, parts I, II, III', *Management Science* 14: 159–82, 320–34, 486–502.

Kajii, A., and S. Morris (1997) 'Robustness of Equilibria to Incomplete Information', *Econometrica* 65: 1283–1309.

Karlin, S., and H. Taylor (1981) *A Second Course in Stochastic Process.* Academic Press: New York.

Kydland, F. E., and E. C. Prescott (1982) 'Time to Build and Aggregate Fluctuations', *Econometrica* 50: 1345–70.

Milgrom, P., and J. Roberts (1990) 'Rationalizability, Learning and Equilibrium in Games with Strategic Complementarities', *Econometrica* 58: 1255–78.

Monderer, D., and D. Samet (1989) 'Approximating Common Knowledge with Common Beliefs', *Games and Economic Behavior* 1: 170–90.

Morris, S. (2000) 'Contagion', *Review of Economic Studies* 67: 57–78.

—— R. Rob and H. S. Shin (1995) '*p*-Dominance and Belief Potential', *Econometrica* 63: 145–58.

—— and H. S. Shin (1997) 'Approximate Common Knowledge and Coordination: Recent Lessons from Game Theory', *Journal of Logic, Language and Information* 6: 171–90.

Neeman, Z. (1996) 'Common Beliefs and the Existence of Speculative Trade', *Games and Economic Behavior* 16: 77–96.

Rubenstein, A. (1989) 'The Electronic Mail Game: Strategic Behavior under Almost Common Knowledge', *American Economic Review* 79: 385–91.

Shin, H. S., and T. Williamson (1996) 'How Much Common Belief is Necessary for a Convention?', *Games and Economic Behavior* 13: 252–68.

Sonsino, D. (1995) ' "Impossibility of Speculation" Theorems with Noisy Information', *Games and Economic Behavior* 8: 406–23.

Sorin, S. (1993) 'On the Impact of an Event', Ecole Normale Superieure, mimeo.

Part III

WELFARE ECONOMICS

6 Wealth and Welfare

PARTHA DASGUPTA

1. Two Indices of Welfare

In a little-cited 1969 article, Jim Mirrlees explored the welfare significance of real national income in a timeless, optimizing economy. Real national income had previously been interpreted as a welfare measure, but only in the context of a full optimum (e.g. Lindahl 1934; Hicks 1940). Mirrlees (1969) studied a second-best economy, of the kind subsequently made famous by Diamond and Mirrlees (1971), one which is fully competitive, but where optimum lump-sum transfers are not feasible.

As it happens, the argument Mirrlees deployed is easily extendable. Dasgupta (1993: ch. 7) studied a timeless, optimizing economy, which is given to a pluralist conception of social welfare and which faces any number of constraints (technological, transaction, institutional, information, or whatever). The general theorem on the welfare significance of real national income reads as follows: provided the economy's optimization problem satisfies the Kuhn–Tucker conditions, associated with any social welfare function (be it welfarist or non-welfarist) and any set of technological, institutional, transaction, and information constraints, there exists a set of person-specific accounting prices for goods and services that can be used for the construction of an index of real national income. The index has the property that, at those accounting prices, changes in real national income (changes in comparative static terms, that is) reflect changes in social welfare (again, in comparative static terms). Moreover, changes in the income of a group (e.g. expectant mothers, the elderly, and so forth) reflect changes in the welfare of that group. Furthermore, changes in the income generated in each sector reflect changes in its contribution to social welfare. And so on.

Thus, suppose we were confident that accounting prices have been estimated with reasonable accuracy. Then, for the purposes of welfare comparisons there would be no need to augment real national income with 'socio-economic indicators', such as those in use by the World Bank in its annual *World Development Report* and the United Nations Development Programme in its annual *Human Development Report*, for example, literacy, infant survival, maternal mortality, and so forth. Of course, we would still want to have such indicators, should we be interested in knowing what they are. But we would not need them in order to compare social welfare across groups. Real national income would be an adequate summary index of the 'quality of life' in a timeless, optimizing economy, no matter how pluralistically social welfare were to be construed

I am most grateful to Karl-Göran Mäler of the Stockholm School of Economics, collaboration with whom led to the formal results reported here (see Dasgupta and Mäler 2000).

and no matter how constrained the government were to find itself. The reach of the theorem goes far beyond that of the Second Fundamental Theorem of Welfare Economics.

In a widely cited work, Little and Mirrlees (1968) showed us the welfare significance of the present discounted value of the flow of social profits of an act of investment. The Little–Mirrlees theorem can be extended to dynamic optimizing economies, given to pluralist conceptions of life and facing any number of constraints (technological, transaction, institutional, information, or whatever). The theorem reads as follows: imagine that the economy has in place a decentralization scheme that contains a separate production sector. Provided the economy's optimization problem satisfies the Kuhn–Tucker conditions, associated with any intertemporally additive social welfare function (be it welfarist or non-welfarist) and any set of technological, institutional, transaction, and information constraints, there exists a set of person-specific accounting prices for goods and services which can be used to compute the present discounted value (PDV) of the flow of social profits of small investment projects. If the PDV of the flow of social profits of a small project is positive (negative), the project's acceptance would increase (decrease) intertemporal social welfare.[1]

Thus, suppose we were confident that accounting prices have been estimated with reasonable accuracy. Then the PDV of the flow of social profits could serve as an index of social welfare, in the sense that it could be used for project selection.

Mirrlees (1969) was explicit that the economy he was studying was timeless. It was therefore natural that he would interpret the linear index he obtained to represent social welfare as real national income, which is a flow. In contrast, Little and Mirrlees (1968) were interested in an economy moving through time. The PDV of the flow of social profits is a stock concept.

The question arises if there is a connection between the two.

The question is of interest because it has become all too customary to regard real national income's counterpart, net national product (NNP), as a welfare index for dynamic economies. In recent years there has been renewed interest among economic theorists in the concept of NNP because it has become clear that environmental pollution and resource depletion ought to find expression in NNP if NNP is to reflect what it is believed to reflect. The term 'green NNP' is an expression of this belief. In the space of only a few years the term has gained such currency that it is today a commonplace to say that in estimating NNP deduction ought to be made from gross national product (GNP) of not only the depreciation of physical and human capital, but also the depreciation of natural capital and the social losses that are incurred owing to increases in the stock of environmental pollution. Dasgupta and Mäler (1991, 2000) have shown that NNP can be used to evaluate policy reforms, but only those that are of brief duration. But it has become customary to use NNP, at constant prices, for many more purposes. Economists writing on the subject have gone farther and argued that

---

[1] Little and Mirrlees (1974) developed their earlier ideas more formally. However, they didn't prove the theorem in the full generality in which I have just stated it. But it is easy enough to extend their arguments. Arrow and Kurz (1970) developed the same arguments in the context of a somewhat different set of second-best constraints.

NNP can be used to measure sustainable consumption.[2] I show below the sense in which the claim is justified.

Both Mirrlees (1969) and Little and Mirrlees (1968) assumed that governments choose policies so as to maximize social welfare. As an assumption it is so strong that the recommendations flowing from it are not applicable to the world we have come to know. The question arises if Mirrleesian prescriptions, in their general form, can be extended to economies pursuing non-optimal economic policies. My second purpose here is to show that they can be so extended.

2. Why Measure Welfare?

Before offering a formal model it is as well to ask why we need measures of social welfare. There are at least three reasons.

First, we may wish to compare the states of affairs in different places (e.g. countries), or between different groups of people (e.g. the poor in comparison with the rich, or men in comparison with women), at a given point in time. Secondly, we need welfare indices because we frequently wish to make welfare comparisons over time of people in the same place (e.g. the same country) or members of a particular group (e.g. the poor or rich, suitably defined, or women). For example, we may ask if a country is doing better today than it did a decade ago, and so forth. And thirdly, we seek welfare indices because we need ways to evaluate alternative economic policies.

Since policy evaluation and welfare comparisons of groups across time and of groups at a given point of time involve different considerations, there is no obvious reason why the indices most useful for the three sets of exercises would be the same. In this paper we will confirm that they do indeed differ. I show that for the latter two purposes the correct linear index of social welfare in dynamic economies is their *wealth*, *not* their NNP. Wealth in a dynamic economy is the appropriate counterpart of real national income in a timeless economy. I show that NNP comparisons at constant accounting prices are neither here nor there, in that NNP should not be used for making welfare comparisons, be they comparisons across groups or over time. I show too that NNP at constant accounting prices should not be used for project evaluation if projects have longevity. The PDV of the flow of social profits is the correct welfare index for the evaluation of small investment projects. This set of results allows us to relate Mirrlees (1969) and Little and Mirrlees (1968).

As mentioned earlier, in unifying Mirrlees' insights, I generalize the context in which the analysis is undertaken by including economies that are not pursuing optimum programmes. So, for example, investment projects will be regarded as perturbations to 'arbitrary' economic forecasts, a viewpoint adopted in Dasgupta, Marglin, and Sen (1972). It transpires that the generalization is non-trivial, because we do not have to assume that economies have convex structures. I show that, despite non-convexities, accounting

---

[2] See e.g. Solow (1986, 1992), Hartwick (1990, 1994), Asheim (1994, 1997, 2000), Aronsson, Johansson, and Löfgren (1997), Aronsson and Löfgren (1998), and Weitzman (1998, 2000).

prices can be defined and used for the construction of an index of wealth. I show also that despite non-convexities social cost–benefit analysis of (small) investment projects can be conducted with the help of accounting prices. In short, the theory I report here extends Little and Mirrlees (1968) to dynamic economies with non-convexities.[3]

3. The Model

Consider an economy where the production of goods and services requires labour, manufactured capital, and natural resources. The economy is deterministic. Time is continuous and is denoted by t ($\geqslant 0$). Assume that there is an all-purpose, non-deteriorating durable good, whose stock at t is K_t ($\geqslant 0$). The good can be either consumed or reinvested for its own accumulation. I assume that both population size and the stock of human capital are constant, which means that we may ignore them. The all-purpose good can be produced with its own stock (K), labour (L), and the flow of natural resources (R) as inputs. I write the production function as $F(K, L, R)$. Production of the all-purpose durable good at date t is then $F(K_t, L_t, R_t)$. I take it that F is an increasing and continuously differentiable function of each of its variables. But I do *not* assume F to be concave. It transpires that I do not need to, given that I am developing welfare economics in a reformist economy, not an optimizing one.

Let C_t ($\geqslant 0$) denote aggregate consumption at t. Net accumulation of physical capital satisfies the condition:

$$\mathrm{d}K_t/\mathrm{d}t = F(K_t, L_t, R_t) - C_t. \tag{1}$$

It helps to interpret natural resources in broad terms. It enables us to consider a number of issues. We should certainly include in the natural-resource base the multitude of capital assets that provide the many and varied ecosystem services upon which life is based. But we should add to this minerals and fossil fuels. Note too that environmental pollution can be viewed as the reverse side of environmental resources. In some cases the emission of pollutants amounts directly to a degradation of ecosystems (e.g. loss of biomass); in others it amounts to a reduction in environmental quality (e.g. deterioration of air and water quality), which also amounts to degradation of ecosystems. This means that for analytical purposes there is no reason to distinguish resource economics from environmental economics, nor resource management problems from pollution management problems (Dasgupta 1982). To put it crudely, 'resources' are a 'good', while 'pollution' (the degrader of resources) is a 'bad'. So I work with an aggregate stock of natural resources, whose size at t is denoted by S_t ($\geqslant 0$). For simplicity of exposition I assume that resource extraction is costless.

Let the natural rate of regeneration of the resource base be $M(S_t)$, where $M(S)$ is a continuously differentiable function.[4] The dynamics of the resource base can be expressed as:

---

[3] The model I present below to demonstrate this is a stripped-down version of the model developed for the same purpose in Dasgupta and Mäler (2000).

[4] If the resource in question were minerals or fossil fuels, S_t would denote known reserves at t and we would have $M(S) = 0$ for all S.

$$dS_t/dt = M(S_t) - R_t. \tag{2}$$

I formulate the idea of social welfare in a conventional manner and ignore those many matters which arise when households are heterogeneous. I do this so as to keep the notation tidy. Following the classic articles of Koopmans (1960, 1972), I assume that social welfare at t ($\geqslant 0$) is of the 'utilitarian' form, $\int_t^\infty U(C_\tau, L_\tau)e^{-\delta(\tau - t)}d\tau$, where U is strictly concave, increasing in C, decreasing in L (at least at large enough values of L), and continuously differentiable in both C and L. δ (> 0), a constant, is the 'utility' discount rate. The analysis that follows does not require that U be concave. I assume it nonetheless to be concave for ethical and empirical reasons.

4. Resource Allocation Mechanisms

Let $(C_t, L_t, R_t, K_t, S_t)_0^\infty$ denote an *economic programme*, from the present ($t = 0$) to the indefinite future. Welfare economics capable of speaking only to optimizing governments would be of very limited interest. For it to be of practical use, welfare economics should be able to cover economies where governments not only do not optimize, but perhaps cannot even ensure that economic programmes resulting from its policies are intertemporally efficient.

For concreteness, consider an economy facing the technological constraints in equations (1) and (2). In addition, it faces institutional constraints (sometime called transaction and information constraints) which I will formalize presently. The initial capital stocks (K_0, S_0) are given and known. By the institutional structure of the economy I mean market structures, the structure of property-rights, tax rates, and so forth. We take it that the institutional structure is given and known. If in addition we knew the behavioural characteristics of the various agencies in the economy (i.e. those of households, firms, the government, and so on), it would be possible to make a forecast of the economy, by which I mean a forecast of the economic programme $(C_t, L_t, R_t, K_t, S_t)_0^\infty$ that would be expected to unfold. Let us call this relationship a *resource allocation mechanism*. So, a resource allocation mechanism is a mapping from initial capital stocks (K_0, S_0) *into* the set of economic programmes $(C_t, L_t, R_t, K_t, S_t)_0^\infty$ satisfying equations (1) and (2).

I formalize this. Write

$$\Omega_t \equiv (K_t, S_t), \text{ and} \tag{3}$$

$$(\xi_\tau)_t^\infty \equiv (C_\tau, L_\tau, R_\tau, K_\tau, S_\tau)_t^\infty, \text{ for } t \geqslant 0. \tag{4}$$

Next let $\{t, \Omega_t\}$ denote the set of possible t and Ω_t pairs, and $\{(\xi_\tau)_t^\infty\}$ the set of economic programmes from t to the indefinite future. A resource allocation mechanism, α, can then be expressed as a mapping

$$\alpha: \{t, \Omega_t\} \to \{(\xi_\tau)_t^\infty\}. \tag{5}$$

α would depend on calender time if knowledge, or population, or terms of trade were to change autonomously over time.[5] If they were not to display any exogenous shift, α would be independent of t. For reasons to be discussed in Section 12, we will pay particular attention to the case where α is autonomous. So I assume that α does not depend on calendar time (i.e. it is time-consistent).

It bears re-emphasis that I do *not* assume α to sustain an optimum economic programme, nor even do I assume that it sustains an efficient programme. The following analysis is valid even if α is riddled with economic distortions and inequities.

To make the dependence of the economic forecast on α explicit, let $(C_t(\alpha), L_t(\alpha), R_t(\alpha), K_t(\alpha), S_t(\alpha))_0^\infty$ denote the forecast at $t = 0$. Consider date t (≥ 0). Use (3)–(5) to define

$$V_t(\alpha, \Omega_t) \equiv \int_t^\infty e^{-\delta(\tau - t)} U(C_\tau(\alpha), L_\tau(\alpha)) d\tau. \tag{6}$$

The right-hand-side (RHS) of equation (6) is social welfare at t. In the theory of optimum programming V_t is called the 'value function' at t (Bellman 1957).[6]

Before putting the concept of resource allocation mechanism to work, it is as well that we discuss examples by way of illustration. Imagine first that all capital assets are private property and that there is a complete set of competitive forward markets capable of sustaining a unique equilibrium. In this case α would be defined in terms of this equilibrium. (If equilibrium were not unique, a selection rule among the multiple equilibria would need to be specified.) Most studies on green accounting (e.g. Heal 1998) are implicitly based on this mechanism.

Of particular interest are situations where some of the assets are not private property. Consider, for example, the class of cases where K is private property, but S is not. It may be that S is a local common-property resource, not open to outsiders. If S is managed efficiently, we are back to the case of a competitive equilibrium allocation, albeit one not entirely supported by market prices, but in part by, say, social norms.

On the other hand, it may be that local institutions are not functioning well (e.g. because social norms are breaking down), in that the marginal private benefits from the use of S exceed the corresponding marginal social benefits. Suppose in addition that decisions bearing on the net accumulation of K is guided by the profit motive. Then these behavioural rules together help determine α. In a similar manner, we could characterize α for the case where S is open-access.

These observations imply that institutional assumptions underlie the notion of resource allocation mechanism. Aspects of the concept of 'social capital' (Putnam 1993) would appear as part of the defining characteristics of α, as would ideas relating to 'social capability' (Abramovitz 1986), and 'social infrastructure' (Hall and Jones 1999); other aspects would be reflected as factors in the production function F.[7]

---

[5] There are exceptions to this statement in extreme cases, namely closed economies where production is subject to constant-returns-to-scale, population changes exponentially, technical change is Harrod-neutral, there are no environmental resources, and social well-being is based on classical utilitarianism (Mirrlees 1967). In such an economy α would be a mapping from the set of capital assets per efficiency unit of labour into the set of economic programmes, where the programmes are expressed in efficiency units of labour.

[6] In all this, we take it that V_t is well defined. The assumption that $\delta > 0$ is crucial for this.

[7] The analytics underlying the idea of social capital are explored in Dasgupta (1999).

The crucial assumption I now make is that V_t is differentiable in each of the two components of Ω. I apologize for imposing a technical condition on something which is endogenous, but space forbids that we explore here the various conditions of an economy's fundamentals (behavioural characteristics of the various agencies and properties of the various production functions and ecological processes; initial set of property rights; and so forth) which would guarantee a differentiable value function.

In any event, it is not easy to judge if V_t is differentiable everywhere. The mathematical properties of V_t depend upon the mathematical properties of α. But it is not easy to judge if α is 'smooth'. An economy's underlying institutional structure is incorporated in α, and there are no obvious limits to the kinds of institution one can envision. So one looks at what might be termed 'canonical' institutions. Analytically, the most well understood are those which support optimum economic programmes. What do we know about them?

We know that if production functions are concave and differentiable everywhere, then for optimum economic programmes V_t is differentiable in each of the components of Ω. Let us therefore consider cases where the production functions are *not* concave. Now, we know that even if production functions are differentiable, optimum resource allocation mechanisms can have discontinuities. However, Skiba (1978) showed that even at those values of Ω where V_t is non-differentiable (such points are, in any event, non-generic), it is continuous. If, nevertheless, V_t possesses right- and left-partial derivatives (and it does in the examples we have studied), social cost–benefit analysis of policy reforms can be conducted at the optimum with the aid of accounting prices, using the PDV of the flow of social profits as the criterion of choice. The same could be expected to be true for the case of market economies subject to fixed distortions, such as those considered by Dasgupta, Marglin, and Sen (1972) and Little and Mirrlees (1974) in their development of the theory of social cost–benefit analysis of investment projects.

Experience with non-linear dynamical systems suggests that, if α is *non*-optimal, V_t is discontinuous at certain values of Ω. Accounting prices would not be definable at such points.[8] Note though that for αs that would be thought of as being empirically interesting, points of discontinuity are non-generic. So, unless the economy were by fluke at such a point, V_t would be differentiable within a small neighbourhood of the initial capital stocks. It would seem, therefore, that the demand that V_t be differentiable does not rule out much of practical significance. The theory I offer here is valid for a considerably more general set of environments than is usual in writings on welfare economics.

5. Local Accounting Prices and their Dynamics

Define,

$$p_t(\alpha) \equiv \partial V_t(\alpha, \Omega_t)/\partial K_t; \text{ and } r_t(\alpha) \equiv \partial V_t(\alpha, \Omega_t)/\partial S_t. \tag{7}$$

---

[8] However, if the location of these points on the stock space were uncertain and the uncertainty a smooth probability distribution, the expected value of V_t would be continuous. I conjecture that in this case accounting prices exist.

These are *local accounting prices*, or *accounting prices* for short. They measure social scarcities of the economy's capital assets along the economic forecast.

How might local accounting prices be estimated? If households are not rationed in any market and externalities are negligible, market prices would be the reasonable estimates. However, when households are rationed or externalities are rampant, estimating local accounting prices involves more complicated work. For example, in the presence of environmental externalities market prices need to be augmented by the external effects (see, for example, Freeman (1992) for an excellent account of current evaluation techniques). If households are rationed, one has to estimate 'willingness-to-pay'. And so on.

What are the dynamics of accounting prices? To study this, note that the current-value Hamiltonian associated with α can be expressed as

$$H_t = U(C_t, L_t) + p_t(F(K_t, L_t, R_t) - C_t) + r_t(M(S_t) - R_t). \tag{8}$$

Recall equation (6), which we rewrite here as:

$$V_t(\alpha, \Omega_t) \equiv \int_t^\infty e^{-\delta(\tau - t)} U(C_\tau, L_\tau) d\tau. \tag{9}$$

V_t is social well-being at t. Differentiating V_t with respect to t we obtain

$$dV_t/dt = \delta V_t - U(C_t, L_t). \tag{10}$$

But $V_t = V_t(\alpha, \Omega_t)$. Using (7), we conclude also that

$$dV_t/dt = p_t dK_t/dt + r_t dS_t/dt + \partial V_t/\partial t. \tag{11}$$

Now combine equations (8), (10)–(11) to obtain

$$H_t = \delta V_t - \partial V_t/\partial t. \tag{12}$$

We can use equations (8) and (12) to conclude that

$$dp_t/dt = -\partial H_t/\partial K_t + \delta p_t; \text{ and } dr_t/dt = -\partial H_t/\partial S_t + \delta r_t. \tag{13}$$

The equations embodied in (13) define the dynamics of local accounting prices. It will be noticed that they are formally the same as the Pontryagin conditions for the evolution of accounting prices in an optimizing economy. Note also that all future effects on the economy of changes in the structure of assets are reflected in local accounting prices. That is why they are useful objects.

As α has been assumed not to depend on calendar time, V_t does not depend on it either. So equation (12) reduces to

$$H_t = \delta V_t. \tag{14}$$

Equation (14) is fundamental in intertemporal welfare economics. It says that the Hamiltonian equals the return on social well-being even in a non-optimizing economy.

6. The Hamiltonian as Constant-Equivalent Utility

It has been argued repeatedly in the theoretical literature on green NNP (see especially Weitzman, 1998) that NNP measures 'constant-equivalent consumption'. I now look into this interpretation.

Continue to assume that $\partial V_t / \partial t = 0$. Since $\delta[\int_t^\infty e^{-\delta(\tau-t)}d\tau] = 1$, equation (14) can be written as

$$H_t = H_t \left\{ \delta \left[\int_t^\infty e^{-\delta(\tau-t)}d\tau \right] \right\} = \delta \left[\int_t^\infty e^{-\delta(\tau-t)}H_t d\tau \right] = \delta V_t,$$

from which we have

$$H_t \left[\int_t^\infty e^{-\delta(\tau-t)}d\tau \right] = \int_t^\infty e^{-\delta(\tau-t)}H_t d\tau = V_t \equiv \int_t^\infty e^{-\delta(\tau-t)}U(C_\tau, L_\tau)d\tau. \tag{15}$$

Equation (15) can be summarized as:

Proposition 1. *Along an economic programme the Hamiltonian at each date equals the constant-equivalent flow of utility starting from that date.*

This result was proved for optimum economic programmes by Weitzman (1976), who restricted his analysis to linear utility functions (specifically that $U(C, L) = C$). Since in this case the Hamiltonian *is* NNP, Weitzman interpreted NNP as the constant-equivalent consumption. The interpretation is today in wide usage. The attraction of NNP is that it is *linear* in quantities (the weights being accounting prices). If U is non-linear, the Hamiltonian is non-linear and is of little direct practical use. In what follows I develop linear indices of social welfare. In the following three sections I do this in the context of welfare comparisons across time and space when the criterion of comparison is *sustainable development*. In Sections 10–11 I develop linear indices for evaluating policy reform. We will confirm that NNP figures nowhere in all this.

7. Sustainable Development

World Commission (1987) defined 'sustainable development' as an economic programme in which, loosely speaking, the well-being of future generations is not jeopardized. There are a number of possible interpretations of this.[9] Consider the following:

---

[9] See Pezzey (1992) for a thorough treatment. It should be noted that to ask if economic development is sustainable is different from asking if a given level of consumption is sustainable. See below in the text.

(a) An economic development is sustainable if $dU_t/dt \geq 0$, where $U_0 \geq \lim U_t$ as $t \to -0$.
(b) An economic development is sustainable if $dU_t/dt \geq 0$.
(c) An economic development is sustainable if $dV_t/dt \geq 0$,

where $V_t(\alpha, \Omega_t) \equiv \int_t^{\infty} e^{-\delta(\tau-t)} U(C_\tau, L_\tau) d\tau$.

It is clear that (a) lacks ethical foundation. For example, it may be desirable to reduce U in the short run in order to accumulate assets in order that the flow of U is still higher in the future. In this sense (b) offers greater flexibility in ethical reasoning: it permits initial sacrifices in the current standard of living, U (a burden assumed by the generation engaged in the reasoning), but requires that no future generation should have to experience a decline in their standard of living.

Consider the resource allocation mechanism α. The mechanism allows one to make an economic forecast. Suppose (b) were to be adopted as the definition of sustainable development. Now

$$dU_t/dt = U_C dC_t/dt + U_L dL_t/dt. \tag{16}$$

From equation (16) we may conclude with:

Proposition 2. *If sustainable development is taken to mean that, starting from now, utility must never decline, then an economic programme corresponds to sustainable development if, and only if, the value of changes in the flow of consumption services is always non-negative.*

8. Welfare Comparisons across Time

In contrast to (b) above, the focus of (c) as a notion of sustainable development is social welfare, V. The criterion permits the first generation to make initial sacrifices in V (relative to the past), but requires that social welfare should never decline in the future. Note that, while (b) implies (c), (c) does not imply (b).[10] In short, (c) is more general. In what follows, we adopt (c) as our notion of sustainable development and develop criteria for judging if a given economic programme represents sustainable development.

Continue to assume that $\partial V_t/\partial t = 0$. Differentiating both sides of equation (15) with respect to time, we have

$$dH_t/dt = \delta dV_t/dt. \tag{17}$$

Use (7) to define

$$I_t^K \equiv p_t dK_t/dt; \text{ and } I_t^S \equiv r_t dS_t/dt, \tag{18}$$

which are net investments in the two types of capital assets, respectively, expressed in utility numeraire. We may then define aggregate net investment as,

---

[10] For an arbitrary α this is a trivial matter to confirm. Interestingly, Asheim (1994) has identified cases where even an optimum economic programme may satisfy (c), while violating (b).

$$I_t = I_t^K + I_t^{S}.^{11} \tag{19}$$

It follows from equations (10), (13), and (15)–(19) that

$$U_C \mathrm{d}C/\mathrm{d}t + U_L \mathrm{d}L/\mathrm{d}t + \mathrm{d}I_t/\mathrm{d}t = \delta I_t. \tag{20}$$

Equation (20) enables us to obtain two alternative indicators of sustainable development. The first can be obtained from the RHS of equation (20). For it implies

Proposition 3. *Social welfare increases over time if, and only if, net investment in the economy's capital assets is positive.*

The result has intuitive appeal. It says that social welfare is higher today than it was yesterday if the economy is wealthier today. Here, an economy's 'wealth' is interpreted as the accounting value of all its capital assets, and wealth comparisons are made at constant prices. In a famous article Samuelson (1961) argued in connection with national income accounting that welfare comparisons should deal with 'wealth-like' entities. Proposition 3 formalizes that insight. Since, by definition, net investment is positive if and only if, consumption is less than net national product (NNP), Proposition 3 offers an interpretation of NNP as an index of sustainable development.

Note, however, that what we have obtained is an equivalence result: Proposition 3 cannot on its own tell us if sustainable development is feasible. Whether the economy is capable of growing wealthier indefinitely depends, among other things, on the extent to which different assets are substitutable in production.[12]

An equivalent way of characterizing sustainable development is to use the LHS of equation (20). I state the result as:

Proposition 4. *Social welfare increases (decreases) over time if the value of net changes in the flow of consumption services plus the change in the value of net aggregate investment is positive (negative).*

For making intertemporal welfare comparisons it is customary to compare NNP over time at constant prices. Proposition 4 says that this is not a correct procedure unless the economy is stationary (i.e. $\mathrm{d}p_t/\mathrm{d}t = \mathrm{d}r_t/\mathrm{d}t = 0$). I conclude that intertemporal NNP comparisons are far less informative about changes in social welfare over time than is commonly believed. Indeed, they would be highly misleading indicators if relative prices were changing significantly.

Proposition 3 says that there has to be *genuine* saving if social welfare is to be sustainable. Since it is possible for a country's GNP to increase over an extended period even while her wealth is declining, time series of GNP per head could mislead.

Hamilton and Clemens (1999) have provided estimates of genuine saving in a number of countries. Among the resources that make up natural capital, only forests, oil and minerals, and pollution were included (not included were such vital resources as

---

[11] Note that the summation in equation (18) does *not* imply any assumptions regarding substitution possibilities among the three kinds of capital assets. Whatever substitution possibilities there may be would be reflected in the local accounting prices.

[12] For an account of this, see Dasgupta and Heal (1979: ch. 7).

water). So there is an undercount. Moreover, the accounting prices used to value natural capital were crudely estimated. Nevertheless, one has to start somewhere. The figures imply that sub-Saharan Africa, the Middle East, Pakistan, and Bangladesh have been depleting their capital assets over several decades: they are becoming poorer even if their GNP per capita are increasing. For example, Pakistan's genuine saving rate (genuine saving divided by GNP) is estimated by Hamilton and Clemens (1999) to have on average been about 0.04 since the 1970s. If we were to assume that the output-capital ratio is a generously high 0.25 per year, population would have had to grow at a rate less than 0.04×0.25 per year (= 1 percent per year) in order for Pakistan to have accumulated wealth on a per capita basis. Pakistan's population has been growing at about 3 percent per year for a long while. And these estimates don't account for inequalities in the ownership of assets among the people of Pakistan. If, as ideally one would, use were made of distributional weights in the estimation of accounting prices to value capital assets, the figures would reveal an even greater decumulation of wealth. The data presented in Hamilton and Clemens (1999) are far too incomplete, but the possibility that large parts of India too have been dissaving cannot be ruled out.

9. Welfare Comparisons across Space

In both popular and academic writings cross-country comparisons of GNP per head are today a commonplace method for comparing social welfare across countries. The analysis in the previous section suggests not only that this practice is wrong, but also that replacing GNP by NNP would not rescue matters. So the question is what index should be used instead? I look into this.

It is simplest to consider a continuum of closed economies, parametrized by x (a scalar).[13] We may interpret differences among economies in terms of differences in initial endowments, or behavioural characteristics, or the resource allocation mechanisms guiding them. But in order to make meaningful comparisons of social welfare, we must be able to ascribe the same value-function to all countries, that is, the same utility function $U(\cdot)$ and the same δ.

Consider a date when the cross-country comparisons are to be made. To keep the notation simple, I drop the time subscript. Let H_x be the Hamiltonian in country x and V_x the value function there. Recall equation (14). In the present case it reads as $H_x = \delta V_x$. An argument identical to the one establishing equation (20) then yields

$$
\delta[p_x dK_x/dx + r_x dS_x/dx + \partial V_x/\partial x] = U_C dC_x/dx + U_L dL_x/dx \\
+ dI_x/dx + \partial H_x/\partial x,
$$

(21)

where I_x is net aggregate investment in country x.

---

[13] I assume a continuum of economies in order to make use of the calculus. It simplifies the computations. The analysis that follows can be easily adapted for the case where there is a discrete number of economies.

For tractability, the interesting special case to consider is $\partial V_x/\partial x = \partial H_x/\partial x = 0$.[14] From the LHS of equation (21) we conclude:

Proposition 5. *Social welfare in a country is higher (lower) than in any of its immediate neighbours if in the aggregate it is wealthier (less wealthy).*

Proposition 5 formalizes the insight in Samuelson (1961) that in making welfare comparisons across countries, one should compare their wealths. It corresponds to proposition 3.

An equivalent indicator for making welfare comparisons can be obtained from the RHS of equation (21):

Proposition 6. *Social welfare in a country is higher (lower) than in any of its immediate neighbours if the value of the difference in the flow of consumption services between them plus the difference in the value of aggregate net investment between them is positive (negative).*

Notice that the recommendation in proposition 6 (which corresponds to Proposition 4) would not amount to NNP comparisons across countries unless local accounting prices were the same (i.e. $dp_x/dx = dr_x/dx = 0$). I conclude that cross-country comparisons of NNP tell us nothing about differences in social welfare excepting under empirically uninteresting circumstances.

Equation (21) is exact, but the pair of (linear) indicators we have obtained in Propositions 5 and 6 serve their purpose accurately only when $\partial V_x/\partial x = 0$. I believe this to be a strong condition. If, as I suspect is the case, $\partial V_x/\partial x$ is not even approximately zero, there are no simple linear indices to be had for making cross-country welfare comparisons.

10. Evaluation of Permanent Policy Change

The technique developed for cross-country comparisons of social welfare can also be used for evaluating a permanent change in some parameter of the economy (e.g. tax rates). Retracing the arguments in Section 5, we may perturb equation (14) to obtain

$$\Delta H_t = \delta[\Delta V_t]. \tag{22}$$

Using equations (18)–(20) in equation (22), we obtain

$$\delta[\Delta V_t] = \Delta H_t = U_C \Delta C_t + U_L \Delta L_t + \Delta I_t. \tag{23}$$

From equation (23) we have:

Proposition 7. *If the value of the changes in consumption services plus the change in the value of net investment occasioned by a permanent change in a parameter characterizing an economy is positive (negative), social well-being increases (decreases).*

---

[14] The condition requires that the same resource allocation mechanism prevails in all countries. The condition is strong.

11. Project Evaluation

Investment projects, if accepted, would be perturbations to the resource allocation mechanism α. Let us consider projects that are small and have longevity. How should they be evaluated?

Consider a new project that would involve small quantities of manufactured capital, labour, and natural resources to produce the all-purpose commodity Y. I denote the project's output and inputs at t as the vector $(\Delta Y_t, \Delta K_t, \Delta L_t, \Delta R_t)$.[15]

The project's acceptance would perturb aggregate consumption and labour supply in a manner dictated by α. Denote the perturbation at t by the vector $(\Delta \tilde{C}_t, \Delta \tilde{L}_t)$. It would affect U_t by the amount $(U_C \Delta \tilde{C}_t + U_L \Delta \tilde{L}_t)$. In practice $(\Delta \tilde{C}_t, \Delta \tilde{L}_t)$ is very hard to estimate. Accounting prices are useful because they enable one to estimate $(\Delta \tilde{C}_t, \Delta \tilde{L}_t)$ indirectly by estimating the project's social profit. The usefulness of the move is best appreciated when it is recalled that in each year in the life of any economy large numbers of projects have to be evaluated. Clearly, it would be simpler if, instead of estimating $(\Delta \tilde{C}_t, \Delta \tilde{L}_t)$ for each project, use were made of a macroeconomic model to estimate accounting prices for use in all projects that come up for scrutiny. Of course, since the economy's asset structure changes over time, accounting prices need to be revised continually (equation (7)). The arguments that follow formalize the theory of social cost–benefit analysis developed in Dasgupta, Marglin, and Sen (1972).

Utility is chosen as numeraire. Recall that the accounting price of manufactured capital is p_t (equation (7)). So the corresponding accounting rental rate is δp_t. It is most unlikely that consumption and investment have the same accounting price in an imperfect economy. Therefore, we need to decompose ΔY_t into its two components: consumption and accumulation of manufactured capital. Knowledge of α enables one to estimate them.[16] I write them as ΔC_t and $\Delta(dK_t/dt)$, respectively.

Finally, let w_t denote the accounting wage rate. How would we estimate it? Dasgupta, Marglin, and Sen (1972) suggested that if we know α, we should be able to estimate $\Delta \tilde{L}_t/\Delta L_t$. This means that $w_t = -(\Delta \tilde{L}_t/\Delta L_t)U_L$. So, for example, $w_t = -U_L$ if $\Delta \tilde{L}_t = \Delta L_t$, and $w_t = 0$ if $\Delta \tilde{L}_t = 0$. In 'labour-surplus economies' one would typically find $0 < -(w_t/U_L) < 1$.

It follows that:

$$U_C \Delta \dot{C}_t + U_L \Delta \tilde{L}_t = U_C \Delta C_t + p_t \Delta(dK_t/dt) - \delta p_t \Delta K_t - w_t \Delta L_t - r_t \Delta R_t. \quad (24)$$

But the RHS of equation (24) is the project's social profit at t. Let ΔV_0 be the change in social welfare if the project, starting at $t = 0$, were accepted. If follows that

$$\Delta V_0 = \int_0^\infty [U_C \Delta C_t + p_t \Delta(dK_t/dt) - \delta p_t \Delta K_t - w_t \Delta L_t - r_t \Delta R_t]e^{-\delta t}dt.$$

So we have a criterion for project evaluation:

Proposition 8. *Small investment projects should be accepted if and only if the present discounted value of social profits is positive.*

---

[15] If the project has been efficiently designed, then we would have $\Delta Y_t = F_K \Delta K_t + F_L \Delta L_t + F_R \Delta R_t$.
[16] See Dasgupta, Marglin, and Sen (1972) for practical methods of estimation.

12. Technological Change and Growth Accounting

It has been customary in the economics literature to regard technical progress as shifts in production functions. In what follows I explore this route by introducing technical progress in the production of the final good. I want here to justify the assumption I have made throughout that the resource allocation mechanism, α, is independent of time.

We need to extend our notation. Denote by E_t the expenditure on research and development (R&D). Now define Z_t by the equation

$$dZ_t/dt = E_t, \tag{25}$$

Z can be thought of as knowledge. Imagine that output of the produced consumption good at t can be expressed as

$$Y_t = e^{\lambda t}Q(Z_t)F(K_t, L_t, R_t), \tag{26}$$

where $\lambda \geqslant 0$ and $Q'(Z) \geqslant 0$. Technical progress in the production of the final good appears here as the term $e^{\lambda t}Q(Z_t)$. It combines exogenous factors (λ) with endogenous ones (Z).

The question arises what factors contribute to changes in GNP over time. To see what the answer could be, consider that GNP in our model economy is given by (26). Differentiating both sides of equation (26) with respect to t, rearranging terms, and dropping the time subscript from variables for the sake of notational simplicity, we obtain the growth accounting identity as

$$(dY/dt)/Y \equiv \lambda + (Q'(Z)dZ/dt)/Q(Z) + (F_K dK/dt)/F$$
$$+ (F_L dL/dt)/F + (F_R dR/dt)]/F. \tag{27}$$

The sum of the first two terms on the RHS of equation (27) measures the percentage rate of change in 'total factor productivity', while the remaining terms together represent the contributions of changes in the 'factors of production' to the percentage rate of change in GNP. Since λ is an exogenous factor, it is unexplained within the model. This is the famous 'residual'. When it is not zero, λ could well be the most important determinant of $\partial V_t/\partial t$.

Solow (1957) used a reduced-form of the production function in (26) to estimate the contribution of changes in the factors of production to growth of non-farm GNP per 'man-hour' in the US economy over the period 1909–49, and discovered that it was a mere 12 per cent of the average annual rate of growth.[17] In other words, 88 per cent of the growth was attributable to the residual. (Solow's estimate of λ was 1.5 per cent per year.) A significant empirical literature since then has shown that when K is better measured (e.g. by accounting for changes in the utilization of capacity and changes in what is embodied in capital) and when account is taken of human-capital formation, the residual is small for the non-farm sector in the US economy.[18]

---

[17] Solow assumed in particular that $Q'(Z) = 0$.
[18] Jorgenson (1995) contains a masterly account of this complex literature.

This is congenial to intuition. We should doubt if it is prudent to postulate ever-lasting increases in total factor productivity, let alone in *per capita* output. To do so would be to place an enormous burden of proof on an experience which is not much more than a few hundred years old. Extrapolation into the past is a sobering exercise: over the long haul of time (say, a few thousand years), the residual has been not much more than zero.

It is in any case hard to believe that serendipity, unbacked by R&D effort and investment in physical capital (learning by doing), can be a continual source of productivity growth. A positive value of λ would imply that the economy is guaranteed a 'free lunch' forever. To be sure, such an assumption would ensure that growth in aggregate consumption is sustainable. In fact, that would be its attraction: it would enables us to assume away problems of environmental and resource scarcities. But there are no theoretical or empirical grounds for presuming that it is a reasonable assumption. At this point in our understanding of the process by which discoveries are made, it makes greater sense to set $\lambda = 0$ in (27) (which would imply that $\partial V_t / \partial t = 0$).[19] This thought is reinforced by the observation that most environmental resources go unrecorded in growth accounting. The implication is obvious: *when we regress growth in GNP on growth in inputs which exclude the use of environmental resources, we obtain too high an estimate of λ if in fact the use of such resources has been growing.* In adopting this position, I am not suggesting that there is no such thing as technical change, but rather, that of the first two terms on the right-hand-side of equation (27), it is the second term which is significant. It denotes the contribution of technical change to productivity growth.

13. Summary

Green NNP has widely been interpreted to be constant-equivalent consumption. In this paper I have shown that, excepting for the uninteresting case where instantaneous utility is linear in consumption (or else homogeneous of degree less than one), this interpretation is false. What is true is that the Hamiltonian equals constant-equivalent utility (Proposition 1). However, since the Hamiltonian is typically a non-linear function of consumption and leisure, it is of little practical use.

This implies that in a dynamic economy NNP at constant accounting prices is not the counterpart of real national income. The appropriate counterpart is *wealth*. In mak-

---

[19] Lau (1996) reports on a series of studies that have specified the aggregate production function to be of the form $Y_t = F(A_t K_t^a H_t^{(1-a)}, L_t)$, where K is physical capital, H is human capital, A is the augmentation factor of the composite capital, L is the number of labour-hours, and $0 < a < 1$. The studies have uncovered that, since the end of the Second World War, the contribution of technical progress (i.e. the percentage rate of change in A_t) to growth in Y_t in today's newly industrialized countries has been negligible. He also reports that, if new knowledge is taken to be embodied in new capital-equipment, the contribution of growth in the value of A_t to growth in Y_t among western industrialized economies has been a mere 10%, that of growth in physical capital some 75%, while the contributions of growth in human capital and labour-hours have each been some 7%. Lau also notes that the studies are silent on whether technical progress in Western industrialized economies has been exogenous or the fruit of expenditures on research and development.

ing welfare comparisons of a given group across time or of different groups at the same point in time, wealth is the index one should use. Thus, for example, when we compare the welfare of nations we should compare their wealths (*per capita*), not their incomes (Propositions 3 and 5). On the other hand, the PDV of the flow of social profits is the correct index for evaluating (small) investment projects (Proposition 8). Investment projects yielding positive PDV increase social welfare, those yielding negative PDV decrease social welfare. The temptation to use one index for all purposes should be resisted.

References

Abramovitz, M. (1986), 'Catching Up, Forging Ahead, and Falling Behind', *Journal of Economic History* 56: 385–406.

Aronsson, T., P.-O. Johansson, and K.-G. Löfgren (1997), *Welfare Measurement, Sustainability and Green National Accounting* (Cheltenham: Edward Elgar).

—— and K.-G. Löfgren (1998), 'Green Accounting: What Do We Know and What Do We Need to Know?', in T. Tietenberg and H. Folmer (eds.), *The International Yearbook of Environmental and Resource Economics 1998/1999* (Cheltenham: Edward Elgar).

Arrow, K. J., and M. Kurz (1970), *Public Investment, the Rate of Return and Optimal Fiscal Policy* (Baltimore: Johns Hopkins University Press).

Asheim, G. (1994), 'Net National Product as an Indicator of Sustainability', *Scandinavian Journal of Economics* 96: 257–65.

—— (1997), 'Adjusting Green NNP to Measure Sustainability', *Scandinavian Journal of Economics* 99: 355–70.

—— (2000), 'Green National Accounting: Why and How?', *Environment and Development Economics* 5(1&2): 25–48.

Bellman, R. (1957), *Dynamic Programming* (Oxford: Oxford University Press).

Dasgupta, P. (1982), *The Control of Resources* (Cambridge, Mass.: Harvard University Press).

—— (1993), *An Inquiry into Well-Being and Destitution* (Oxford: Clarendon Press).

—— (1999), 'Economic Progress and the Idea of Social Capital', in P. Dasgupta and I. Serageldin (eds.), *Social Capital: A Multifaceted Perspective* (Washington, DC: World Bank).

—— and G. M. Heal (1979), *Economic Theory and Exhaustible Resources* (Cambridge: Cambridge University Press).

—— and K.-G. Mäler (1991), 'The Environment and Emerging Development Issues', *Proceedings of the Annual World Bank Conference on Development Economics, 1990* (Suppl. to the *World Bank Economic Review* and the *World Bank Research Observer*): 101–32.

—— —— (2000), 'Net National Product, Wealth and Social Well-Being', *Environment and Development Economics* 5: 69–93.

—— S. Marglin, and A. Sen (1972), *Guidelines for Project Evaluation* (New York: United Nations).

Diamond, P. A., and J. A. Mirrlees (1971), 'Optimal Taxation and Public Production: Parts 1 and 2', *American Economic Review* 62.

Freeman III, A. M. (1992), *The Measurement of Environmental and Resource Values* (Washington, DC: Resources for the Future).

Hall, R. E., and C. I. Jones (1999), 'Why Do Some Countries Produce So Much More Output per Worker than Others?', *Quarterly Journal of Economics* 114: 83–116.

Hamilton, K., and M. Clemens (1999) 'Genuine Savings Rates in Developing Countries', *World Bank Economic Review* 13: 333–56.

Hartwick, J. (1990), 'Natural Resources, National Accounting, and Economic Depreciation', *Journal of Public Economics* 43: 291–304.

—— (1994), 'National Wealth and Net National Product', *Scandinavian Journal of Economics* 96: 253–6.

Heal, G. M. (1998), *Valuing the Future: Economic Theory and Sustainability* (New York: Columbia University Press).

Hicks, J. R. (1940), 'The Valuation of Social Income', *Economica* 7: 105–24.

Jorgenson, D. (1995), *Productivity: Postwar U.S. Economic Growth* (Cambridge, Mass.: MIT Press).

Koopmans, T. C. (1960), 'Stationary Ordinal Utility and Impatience', *Econometrica* 28: 287–309.

—— (1972), 'Representation of Preference Orderings over Time', in C. B. McGuire and R. Radner (eds.), *Decision and Organization* (Amsterdam: North-Holland).

Lau, L. (1996), 'The Sources of Long-Term Economic Growth: Observations from the Experiences of Developed and Developing Countries', in R. Landau, T. Taylor, and G. Wright (eds.), *The Mosaic of Economic Growth* (Stanford, Calif.: Stanford University Press).

Lindahl, E. (1934), 'The Concept of Income', in G. Bagge (ed.), *Economic Essays in Honor of Gustaf Cassel* (London: George Allen & Unwin).

Little, I. M. D., and J. A. Mirrlees (1968), *Manual of Industrial Project Analysis in Developing Countries: Social Cost Benefit Analysis* (Paris: OECD).

Little, I. M. D., and J. A. Mirrlees (1974), *Project Appraisal and Planning for Developing Countries* (London: Heinemann).

Mirrlees, J. A. (1967), 'Optimum Growth When the Technology is Changing', *Review of Economic Studies* 34 (Symposium Issue): 95–124.

—— (1969), 'The Evaluation of National Income in an Imperfect Economy', *Pakistan Development Review* 9(1): 1–13.

Pezzey, J. (1992), 'Sustainable Development Concepts: An Economic Analysis', World Bank Environment Paper 2 (Washington, DC: World Bank).

Putnam, R. D., with R. Leonardi and R. Y. Nanetti (1993), *Making Democracy Work: Civic Traditions in Modern Italy* (Princeton, NJ: Princeton University Press).

Samuelson, P. A. (1961), 'The Evaluation of "Social Income": Capital Formation and Wealth', in F. A. Lutz and D. C. Hague (eds.), *The Theory of Capital* (London: Macmillan).

Skiba, A. K. (1978), 'Optimal Growth with a Convex-Concave Production Function', *Econometrica* 46(3): 527–40.

Solow, R. M. (1957), 'Technical Change and the Aggregate Production Function', *Review of Economics and Statistics* 39(3): 312–20.

—— (1986), 'On the Intergenerational Allocation of Exhaustible Resources', *Scandinavian Journal of Economics* 88: 141–9.

—— (1992), 'An Almost Practical Step Toward Sustainability', 40th Anniversary Lecture, Resources for the Future, Washington, DC.

Weitzman, M. L. (1976), 'On the Welfare Significance of National Product in a Dynamic Economy', *Quarterly Journal of Economics* 90(1): 156–62.

—— (1998), 'On the Welfare Significance of National Product Under Interest Rate Uncertainty', *European Economic Review* 42: 1581–94.

—— (2000), 'The Linearized Hamiltonian as Comprehensive GDP', *Environment and Development* 5(1&2): 55–68.

World Commission (1987), *Our Common Future* (New York: Oxford University Press).

7   Adjusting One's Standard of Living: Two-Period Models

P. DIAMOND AND J. MIRRLEES

Foreword by PD

In the summer of 1967, Jim and I began collaborating on optimal taxation. Our paper was essentially finished that summer, although it was a number of years before it appeared in print. Since then, we have collaborated continuously and have published eight more papers plus one forthcoming. At one point, we contemplated writing a graduate text. We got as far as a table of contents and an allocation of who would write the first version of each chapter—for our working style, after initial results, was to alternate writing complete drafts. But, neither of us was really interested in taking on a task of the magnitude needed to write a book we would be satisfied with, and the project had a mercifully quick ending.

Collaboration with Jim has been a source of great pleasure for me, as well as a way to write papers that, I believe, are different from what either of us would have done alone. I can also attest to the positive impact on papers that I wrote by myself. Whether in Cambridge, Oxford, or other locales, such as the Mull of Kintyre, I always relished being with Jim, with work on the papers being both an end and a justification for getting together. As much as possible, these meetings were family affairs, made far better by the presence of Gill and Kate, not to mention Catriona, Fiona, Matt, and Andy.

Almost all of the papers we started we have finished. However, there are a few incomplete papers in our file drawers. I have resurrected one that was last revised in March 1982 and completed it as my contribution for this occasion—I hope Jim doesn't object to the revisions and additions. While there has been relevant literature in the interim, the issue addressed still seems to me important, indeed pressing, as both research and legislation address social security reform. I have not attempted to bring the references in the paper fully up to date.

1. Introduction

Because of the tractability it provides, use of an intertemporally additive utility function is widespread. It is used for abstract theoretical work, and it is used for simulations. Yet, we know that preferences are not intertemporally additive; tastes are affected

We are grateful to Mike Whinston, Saku Aura, and Tom Davidoff for research assistance and to the Social Security Administration and the National Science Foundation (under grant SBR-9618698) for research support.

by experience. We know this for individual products, where experience with a good can add to or subtract from later enjoyment of the same good. And we know this for consumption in the aggregate. The way in which savings provide for consumption late in life should accordingly allow for the influence of earlier consumption levels on later 'needs'. Thus, we explore simple forms of intertemporal connection that would capture some of the intertemporal interaction and yet remain tractable. We draw a distinction between two simple forms of interaction, and then ask straightforwardly with what further assumptions some results that assumed additivity of preferences carry over to these simple forms. The results examined are both about individual savings and the design of an optimal social security system for a representative agent in the presence of asymmetric information about the ability to continue work in the range of ages we consider early retirement.

In addition to assuming that preferences are intertemporally additive, the common formulation also assumes that preferences are the same in every period. Like additivity, this assumption is clearly wrong. However, we chose to continue to use this assumption, not examining how to formulate plausible age-varying preferences.

Although we do not explore it in detail, the models suggest a route into modelling individual savings where people are not successfully optimizing. Since widespread inadequate savings for retirement is seen by some as a justification for the existence of mandatory social security systems, modelling savings is an important question. Simulations of the effects of social security that omit justifications for the existence of the programme are bound to find it costly and without benefit. But this is an inadequate basis for simulations. The approach we took to non-optimizing behaviour was simply to assume that people ignored the intertemporal link between current consumption and the future marginal utility of consumption, even though they correctly forecast future marginal utility. We have not explored any justification for this assumption, but merely followed convenient mathematics. This is a less satisfactory approach than building on psychological insights about intertemporal decisions, such as the work on hyperbolic and quasi-hyperbolic discounting (Ainslie 1992; Laibson 1997), an approach which I am applying to retirement issues together with Botond Koszegi (1999).

We introduce a simple model of savings, in which consumption affects a variable we call the 'standard of living', which in turn affects the utility of future consumption. This approach fits with the common vocabulary of thinking about pensions in terms of replacement rates. Using a two-period certainty model, we examine two different simple ways that the standard of living could enter the instantaneous utility function, and then compare savings behaviour of naïve and sophisticated savers, differing in their perception of the link between present consumption and future instantaneous utility (Section 2). In Section 3, we examine savings under certainty. In Section 4 we examine savings under uncertainty to relate this model to the analysis of H. Leland (1968). In Section 5, the analysis is applied to earnings uncertainty. In Section 6, we summarize our earlier work on social insurance with uncertainty only in the second period (1978, forthcoming) and relate the standard-of-living models to the assumptions used there. In Section 7, we consider an alternative model where individuals face uncertainty in both periods, examining the optimal wage path assuming that both moral hazard constraints are binding. In Section 8, we consider the question of when both moral hazard constraints do bind. In Section 9, concluding remarks consider further research opportunities.

Although it has been common to assume an additive intertemporal utility function, there are previous analyses that have also sought simple generalizations, as we do. G. Heal and H. Ryder (1973) have examined an optimal growth model using the assumptions we describe as the addiction model. P. Samuelson (1971) has extended the turnpike theorem to a similar case. H. Houthakker and L. Taylor (1970) have done similar analysis for the demand for durables. In alternative formulations, M. Kurz (1968) included wealth in the instantaneous utility function while S. Chakravarty and A. Manne (1968) included the rate of growth of consumption. Our treatment of naïve savers is related to the analysis of changing preferences of C. Weizsacker (1971) and R. Pollak (1970). There is now a sizeable literature directly addressing addiction, both with and without quasi-hyperbolic discounting (Becker and Murphy 1988; Gruber and Koszegi 1999).

2. Modelling the Standard-of-Living Effect

We start by considering individual savers with lifetime utility functions, U, defined over first- and second-period consumptions (c_1 and c_2). (For the present we ignore the question of labour supply.)

$$U(c_1, c_2) = u(c_1, s_0) + \delta u(c_2, s_1),$$ (1)

where δ is the utility discount factor and s_i the standard of living to which the individual has become accustomed by the end of period i. We assume that s_0 is given and think of it as the standard of living at age 40, with each period covering 15 to 20 years.[1] We assume that the accustomed standard of living adjusts according to the equation ($\alpha > 0$).

$$s_1 = \frac{s_0 + \alpha c_1}{1 + \alpha}.$$ (2)

For a well-behaved choice problem once we extend the model to take expected values, we assume that U is concave in both variables. A sufficient condition for this would be the concavity of u in both variables, which we also assume. We naturally assume a positive instantaneous marginal utility of consumption, $u_c > 0$.

To reflect on additional assumptions, we distinguish two separate cases. One incorporates the view that it is 'relative consumption' that matters. In this case the greater the standard of living to which the individual has become accustomed, the lower the level of instantaneous utility and the greater the marginal utility of consumption:

---

[1] We do not incorporate any pure age effects in the analysis.

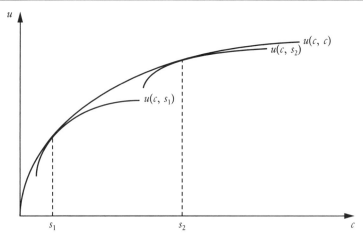

FIG. 7.1. *Short-run and long-run utility functions*

$$u_s < 0, \ u_{cs} \geqslant 0. \tag{3}$$

Pure examples of a relative consumption view (with v concave and increasing) are:

$$u = v(c - s)$$
$$u = v(c/s).$$

We refer to the assumptions in (3) as the 'addiction' model.

As an alternative approach, we can consider individuals who adapt their habits (spending patterns) to the expenditure level they have become accustomed to. Such individuals have greater instantaneous utility from long-run adjustments to a changed expenditure level than from short-run changes. This idea is shown in pure form in Figure 7.1, depicting the short-run and long-run utility functions. In this case, the plausible assumptions are

$$(s - c)u_s \leqslant 0, \ u_{cs} \geqslant 0, \ u_s(c, c) = 0. \tag{4}$$

Pure examples satisfying these assumptions are:

$$u = v(c - s) + sv'(0)$$
$$u = v(c/s) + v'(1)\log s,$$

where v' is the derivative. We refer to this model as the 'habit' model.

With both models it seems reasonable to add the condition that consumption is more important than standard of living in determining marginal utility.

$$u_{cc} + u_{cs} \leqslant 0. \tag{5}$$

3. Savings under Certainty

Consumer choice for a two-period model can be stated as

$$\text{Max } u(c_1, s_0) + \delta u\left(c_2, \frac{s_0 + \alpha c_1}{1 + \alpha}\right) \tag{6}$$

$$\text{s.t. } c_1 + c_2/r = A,$$

where r is one plus the interest rate.

The first-order condition for individual choice is

$$u_c(1) + \frac{\delta \alpha}{1 + \alpha} u_s(2) = \delta r u_c(2), \tag{7}$$

where $u_c(1)$ means the instantaneous marginal utility of consumption evaluated at period 1 values (c_1, s_0).

Differentiating the first-order condition, we can express the income derivative of consumption as

$$\frac{dc_1}{dA} = -\frac{\left(\dfrac{r\delta\alpha}{1 + \alpha}\right) u_{cs}(2) - \delta r^2 u_{cc}(2)}{u_{cc}(1) + \delta r^2 u_{cc}(2) - \dfrac{2\delta \alpha r}{(1 + \alpha)} u_{cs}(2) + \dfrac{\delta \alpha^2}{(1 + \alpha)^2} u_{ss}(2)}. \tag{8}$$

With u concave and $u_{cs} \geq 0$, as is assumed in both formulations, present and future consumption are both normal goods. It is interesting to compare sophisticated choice as given in (7) with the particular version of naïve choice given by a correct perception of the marginal utility of consumption, but a failure to recognize the connection between c_1 and $u_c(2)$. That is, consider a naïve equilibrium given by

$$u_c(1) = \delta r u_c(2). \tag{9}$$

This would be the case if an individual looked at the marginal utility of consumption of a similarly situated (in terms of consumption) older individual to form an estimate of $u_c(2)$, but did not look at how a change in consumption in period 1 affected marginal utility in the later period. With the addiction model, $u_s < 0$ and sophisticated choice has more savings than naïve choice. With the habit model, the analysis depends on the level of s_0. When s_0 equals the sophisticated choice level of c, then sophisticated choice is closer to the constant consumption path than is the naïve choice equilibrium.

4. Savings under Uncertainty

We now assume that individuals want to maximize the expected value of lifetime utility. We assume that lifetime resources, A, are a random variable, whose value becomes

TABLE 7.1. *Sufficient conditions for savings to increase with risk*

Utility function	Mean preserving spread	Mean utility preserving spread
General function $U(c_1, c_2)$	$rU_{122} - U_{222} < 0$	$U_2(rU_{122} - U_{222}) - U_{22}(rU_{12} - U_{22}) < 0$
Additive function $u(c_1) + \delta u(c_2)$	$u''' > 0$	$u'u''' - u''u'' > 0$
Standard of living $u(c_1, s_0) + \delta u(c_2, s_1)$	$ru_{ccc} - \dfrac{\alpha}{1+\alpha} u_{ccs} > 0$	$u_c \left(ru_{ccc} - \dfrac{\alpha}{1+\alpha} u_{ccs} \right) - u_{cc}\left(ru_{cc} - \dfrac{\alpha}{1+\alpha} u_{cs} \right) > 0$

known after the choice of c_1. With this modification of the choice problem given in (6), the first-order condition becomes

$$u_c(1) = E\left[\delta r u_c(2) - \frac{\delta \alpha}{1+\alpha} u_s(2) \right]. \tag{10}$$

We want to examine the response of first-period consumption to an increase in risk in lifetime income, a question posed by H. Leland (1968). In Table 7.1 we state sufficient conditions for savings to increase with riskiness using the definitions of mean preserving increase in risk of Rothschild and Stiglitz (1970) and mean utility preserving increase in risk of Diamond and Stiglitz (1974). The table states the conditions for a general two-period utility function and then specializes them for the additive and standard-of-living special cases.

5. Earnings Uncertainty

We now consider the situation where the source of uncertainty about lifetime utility is uncertainty about second-period earnings. We write utility, U, as a function of first-period consumption, second-period consumption, and the number of periods worked. The uncertainty for the individual is about the ability to work in the second period, with the probability of being able to work being given by θ. Thus, for an individual planning on two periods of work if able, expected utility can be written as[2]

$$\text{Max}_c [\theta U(c, W + w - rc, 2) + (1 - \theta)U(c, W - rc, 1)], \tag{11}$$

where w is the second-period wage and W is non-random income measured in second-period units. The first-order condition for this consumption choice problem is

$$\theta(U_1(2) - rU_2(2)) + (1 - \theta)(U_1(1) - rU_2(1)) = 0, \tag{12}$$

---

[2] Adding an additive disutility of being unable to work would make no change in the analysis.

where $U_i(j)$ is the ith partial derivative of U evaluated where j periods of work are done.

Now let us consider similar questions to that asked in the previous section—what happens to c in response to changes in w or W that keep expected income or expected utility constant? The first step in the analysis is the calculation of the response of c to changes in w and W separately. To calculate these derivatives, let us write the second-order condition as

$$D = \theta(U_{11}(2) - 2rU_{12}(2) + r^2U_{22}(2)) + (1 - \theta)(U_{11}(1) - 2rU_{12}(1) + r^2U_{22}(1)) < 0. \tag{13}$$

Then, by differentiating the first-order condition, we have the following comparative statics:

$$\frac{\partial c}{\partial w} = -D^{-1}[\theta(U_{12}(2) - rU_{22}(2))] \tag{14}$$

$$\frac{\partial c}{\partial W} = -D^{-1}[\theta(U_{12}(2) - rU_{22}(2)) + (1 - \theta)(U_{12}(1) - rU_{22}(1))].$$

To calculate the change in consumption for an increase in risk, expected income held constant, we need to increase w while decreasing W, recognizing that w is only received with probability θ. Thus, we have:

$$\frac{\partial c}{\partial w} - \theta\frac{\partial c}{\partial W} = -D^{-1}\{[\theta(U_{12}(2) - rU_{22}(2))] - \theta[\theta(U_{12}(2) - rU_{22}(2)) + (1 - \theta)(U_{12}(1) - rU_{22}(1))]\}$$
$$= -D^{-1}\theta(1 - \theta)[(U_{12}(2) - rU_{22}(2)) - (U_{12}(1) - rU_{22}(1))] \tag{15}$$

if the disutility of labour is additive, this expression is signed by the conditions in Table 7.1. This follows abstractly from this being a special case of the analysis behind the table. It can also be seen directly by noting that the difference between terms in (15) is signed by the condition in the table. Without additive disutility of labour, there is an additional term, the sign of which depends on whether $U_{12} - rU_{22}$ is raised or lowered by work.

Similarly, to consider the mean utility preserving spread, we need to weight the changes in w and W by their impacts on expected utility. Thus the relevant derivative is:

$$\frac{\partial c}{\partial w} - \theta U_2(2)\frac{\partial c}{\partial W}/(\theta U_2(2) + (1 - \theta)U_2(1))$$

$$= \frac{\partial c}{\partial w} - \theta\frac{\partial c}{\partial W} + \frac{\partial c}{\partial W}\theta(1 - \theta)(U_2(2) - U_2(1))/(\theta U_2(2) + (1 - \theta)U_2(1)). \tag{16}$$

We have not examined a direct argument from the condition in Table 7.1.

In the additive model, U_{12} is zero and the effect of labour in the second period on $U_{12} - rU_{22}$, needed in (15) above, depends on the direct impact of labour on U_{22} and the sign of U_{222}, which depends on u'''.

In the standard-of-living model, however, we need to consider more carefully the instantaneous utility function, $u(c, s, h)$ (where h is hours of work). We shall consider the special cases considered above. With the addiction model we considered the two special cases

$$
\begin{aligned}
U(c_1, c_2, h_1, h_2) &= u(c_1 - s_0, h_1) + \delta u(c_2 - s_1, h_2) \\
U(c_1, c_2, h_1, h_2) &= u(c_1/s_0, h_1) + \delta u(c_2/s_1, h_2)
\end{aligned}
\tag{17}
$$

Differentiating we have

$$
\begin{aligned}
U_2 &= \delta u_1(2), \ U_{12} - rU_{22} = -\delta u_{11}\frac{\alpha}{1 + \alpha} - r\delta u_{11} = -\delta u_{11}\left(\frac{\alpha}{1 + \alpha} + r\right) \\
U_2 &= \delta u_1(2)s_1^{-1}, \ U_{12} - rU_{22} = -\delta u_1 s_1^{-2}\frac{\alpha}{1 + \alpha} - \delta u_{11}c_2 s_1^{-3}\frac{\alpha}{1 + \alpha} - r\delta u_{11}s_1^{-2}.
\end{aligned}
\tag{18}
$$

Thus, with the difference addiction model we need to inquire how u_{11} varies with labour supply. With the ratio addiction model, we also need to ask how u_1 varies with labour supply.

With the habit models, we have the same structure since the additive terms in standard of living do not show up in $U_{12} - rU_{22}$.

6. Social Insurance

In our forthcoming paper we consider a social insurance plan to ease the wage uncertainty problem depicted in Section 4. That is, we consider a social security system that is providing insurance relative to the length of working life. The government selects w and W to maximize expected utility as given in (11) subject to two constraints. One constraint is the resource constraint. The second constraint is a moral hazard constraint, that expected utility for a worker planning on two periods of work, if able, be at least as large as expected utility with a plan of no work in the second period.

We showed that the moral hazard constraint was binding provided the following plausible condition was satisfied

$$
\begin{aligned}
&\text{Max}_c \ U(c_2, W + w - rc_2, 2) = \text{Max}_c \ U(c_1, W \quad rc_1, 1) \\
&\text{implies } U_2(2) < U_2(1).
\end{aligned}
\tag{19}
$$

In addition, we considered the further tool of wealth taxation. We showed that wealth should be taxed or subsidized as a worker planning on two periods of work saved less or more than a worker planning on one period of work who had the same expected utility. In this section, we examine conditions on the additive and standard-of-living models that are sufficient to satisfy the moral hazard assumption (19) and the wealth taxation condition.

If utility is additive, then we can write instantaneous utilities as $u(c, 1)$ or $u(c, 0)$ as individuals are working or not. A sufficient condition to imply that the moral hazard constraint is binding is then

$$u(c, 1) = u(c', 0)$$
$$\text{implies } u_c(c, 1) < u_c(c', 0). \tag{20}$$

That is, compensating people sufficiently to just induce work results in a lower marginal utility of consumption for workers. Thus there would be a gain from redistributing to non-workers, which must violate the moral hazard constraint if we are to have an optimum. Conditions (19) and (20) can also be reversed in the sense that reversal of the inequalities in both cases implies that the first-best solution is feasible.

Turning to the standard-of-living model we can consider the analogous one-period condition

$$u(c, s, 1) = u(c', s, 0)$$
$$\text{implies } u_c(c, s, 1) < u_c(c', s, 0). \tag{21}$$

As with (20), (21) is sufficient to imply that the moral hazard condition is binding.

It seems to us that the plausible case of the savings condition is that someone planning on two periods of work if able would consume more than if planning on only one period of work, $c_2^* > c_1^*$. In turn, this implies the desirability of taxing wealth. We explore this condition first in the general model by exhibiting a sufficient condition to imply $c_2^* > c_1^*$.

$$\text{Max}_c \ U(c_1, W - rc_1, 1) = \text{Max}_{c'} \ U(c_2', W + w - rc_2', 2)$$
$$\text{implies } c_1^* < c_2'^*. \tag{22}$$

That is, we consider two certainty problems with one and two periods of work and equal levels of utility. The one-period certainty problem is the same as the uncertainty problem for a worker planning on only one period of work. However, the two-period certainty problem is different from the uncertainty problem with a plan of two periods of work if able. Thus the distinction in the notation. The assumption in (22) is that comparing the two certainty problems, the individual with greater lifetime income then consumes more in the first period. We depict (22) in Figure 7.2, where we have drawn utility as a function of consumption, with w chosen to equate optimized utility, as in (22), showing the condition that $c_1^* < c_2'^*$. If we also consider the level of consumption that maximizes expected utility for this wage conditional on planning on two periods of work if able, c_2^*, we would have $c_1^* < c_2^* < c_2'^*$. However, at this wage, expected utility for someone planning on two periods of work if able (but subject to disability risk) would be less than utility of a one period worker. To equate expected utilities we need to raise w, but not to a point where $U(c_1^*, W + w' - rc_1^*, 2)$ exceeds $\bar{U}$. Thus the expected utility equating wage w' must give a picture like the dashed curve in Figure 7.2. It is clear from the figure (using normality) that c_2^* is greater than c_1^*.

We turn now to examining analogs to (22) in the context of additive and standard-of-living models. In the additive model, (23) (which is the familiar moral hazard condition) is sufficient to imply (22):

$$u(c, 1) = u(c', 0)$$
$$\text{implies } u_c(c, 1) < u_c(c', 0). \tag{23}$$

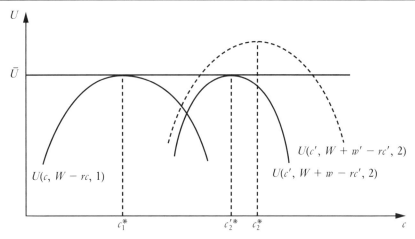

FIG. 7.2. *One and two periods of work and equal levels of utility*

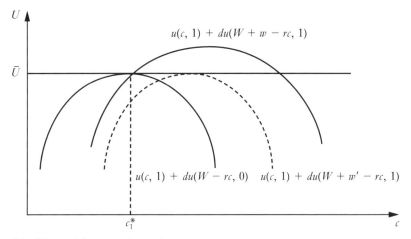

FIG. 7.3. *First-period consumption and wage*

The argument proceeds in a similar fashion. Consider the wage, w, which just equates second-period utilities, first-period consumption held constant at the optimal level given no work in the second period, c_1^*. That is, the wage w is chosen so that utility with this wage and an extra period of work would be the same if first-period consumption did not change. Allowing first-period consumption to vary implies that optimized utility must be higher; while (23) implies that the slope of the utility function is positive at c_1^*, as shown in Figure 7.3. Lowering the wage lowers the utility curve at all levels of first-period consumption, resulting in a utility equating wage, w', as shown by the dashed curve. With the standard-of-living model the argument is identical to that with the additive model and the sufficient condition for (22) is

$$u(c, s, 1) = u(c', s, 0)$$
$$\text{implies } u_c(c, s, 1) < u_c(c', s, 0) \tag{24}$$

7. Wage Profile

In the model described above, there is uncertainty in only one period. Thus one cannot draw conclusions on the optimal time shape of the net financial return to working. In our previous paper, we considered an alternative model where there was uncertainty in both periods. There are then two moral hazard constraints—that a two-period work plan be at least as good as one- and zero-period work plans. That is, since there will now be some people unable to work at all, there is a need to provide income for someone who does no work at all. But this should not be so large as to induce everyone to stop working. Considering the additive model with the one-period moral hazard assumption, we reached two conclusions. Both moral hazard constraints were binding and the second-period wage exceeded the first period wage.

In this section we will assume that both moral hazard constraints are binding and examine sufficient conditions for a rising wage. In the next section we will examine sufficient conditions for both constraints to bind.

We continue to assume that the impact of disability on utility is additive and that individuals know their disability before choosing current consumption. We assume that someone doing no work is given a lifetime wealth level of W. Someone working in the first period receives an additional amount w_1. Someone who also works in the second period receives a further increment w_2. Then, we have three possible individual plans for an individual who is able to work in the first period, based on plans to work none, one, or two periods if able.

$$
\begin{aligned}
V_0(W) &\equiv Max_{c_c}\, U(c_0, W - rc_0, 0) \\
V_1(W, w_1) &\equiv Max_{c_1}\, U(c_1, W + w_1 - rc_1, 1) \\
V_2(W, w_1, w_2) &\equiv Max_{c_2}\, (\theta U(c_2, W + w_1 + w_2 - rc_2, 2) \\
&\quad + (1 - \theta)U(c_2, W + w_1 - rc_2, 1)).
\end{aligned} \tag{25}
$$

We now examine the implications of equal expected utility with all three plans,

$$V_0(W) = V_1(W, w_1) = V_2(W, w_1, w_2). \tag{26}$$

First, we note that concavity would imply a rising wage if individuals were facing a certainty problem. Denoting the wages that solve equal utility in the certainty problems by w'_i, we have:

$$
\begin{aligned}
Max_{c_0}\, U(c_0, W - rc_0, 0) &= Max_{c_1}\, U(c_1, W + w'_1 - rc_1, 1) \\
&= Max_{c_2}\, U(c_2, W + w'_1 + w'_2 - rc_2, 2) \\
\text{implies } w'_1 &< w'_2.
\end{aligned} \tag{27}
$$

Since a worker planning on a single period is not subject to uncertainty, the equal utility conditions with and without uncertainty are the same. Therefore, (26) and (27) give us $w_1 = w_1'$. To complete the proof we argue that $w_2 \geqslant w_2'$. From the definition of V we have:

$$
\begin{aligned}
V_2(W, w_1, w_2') &= Max_{c_2}\ (\theta U(c_2, W + w_1 + w_2' - rc_2, 2) \\
&\quad + (1 - \theta)U(c_2, W + w_1 - rc_2, 1)) \\
&\leqslant \theta Max_c\ U(c, W + w_1 + w_2' - rc, 2) \\
&\quad + (1 - \theta)Max_c\ U(c, W + w_1 - rc, 1) = V_1(W, w_1).
\end{aligned}
\tag{28}
$$

We note that we would have a strict inequality in (28) if first-period consumptions are different in the two certainty problems.

We also note that $w_1 > 0$ if labour is disliked and w_2 is not greater than the marginal product of labour. The latter conclusion follows from considering a small decrease in w_2. This leads workers to plan on only one period of work, while having no effect on expected utility, by the equal expected utility condition. For w_2 to be optimal, therefore, work in the second period must not lose revenue for the government.

This result is stated in terms of wages measured in second-period units of account. With a positive discount rate we have the further result that wages rise in current units of account.

8. Moral Hazard Constraints

We now examine sufficient conditions for both moral hazard constraints to be binding. Recognizing that the fraction $(1 - \theta_1)$ of the population is disabled at the start of period one, while the remainder of the population is induced to plan on two periods of work if able, the social choice problem can be stated as

$$
\begin{aligned}
&Max_{W, w_1, w_2}\ (1 - \theta_1)V_0(W) + \theta_1 V_2(W, w_1, w_2) \\
&\text{subject to } W + \theta_1(w_1 - mr) + \theta_2(w_2 - m) = A \\
&V_2 \geqslant V_1,\ V_2 \geqslant V_0,
\end{aligned}
\tag{29}
$$

where m is the marginal product. We solve this problem in two steps. For a given W, we do the suboptimization in w_1 and w_2, ignoring the constraint $V_2 \geqslant V_0$. Then, we consider the choice of the optimal W. This sequence is permissible since V_0 does not depend on w_1 and w_2, and w_1 and W are perfect substitutes as control variables in the suboptimization if the income of those disabled at the start is held constant. The suboptimization is

$$
\begin{aligned}
&Max_{w_1, w_2}\ \theta_1 V_2(W, w_1, w_2) \\
&\text{subject to } \theta_1(w_1 - mr) + \theta_2(w_2 - m) = A - W \\
&\quad\quad V_2 \geqslant V_1.
\end{aligned}
\tag{30}
$$

The suboptimization problem is the same one considered in Section 5 above. Thus, with the moral hazard condition, we know that at the optimum $V_2 = V_1$. Thus there are two types of solutions to (29) depending on whether the remaining moral hazard

TABLE 7.2. *Summary of results*

General model	Additive	Standard of living
Model with uncertainty in second period only		
(19) → Moral hazard constraint binds	(20) → (19)	(21) → (19)
(22) → Optimal to tax wealth	(20) → (22)	(21) → (22)
Model with uncertainty in both periods		
(19), (32), (33) → Rising wage	(20) → (19), (32), (33)	(21) → (19), (32), (33)
(19), (34), (35) → Both constraints bind, (33)	(20) → (33)	(21) → (19), (34), (35)

constraint is binding. If it is, $V_0 = V_2$. Otherwise, $V'_0(W) = \lambda$ where λ is the Lagrangian on the resource constraint in (30). We look for conditions to rule out the latter type of solution.

Setting up (30) as a Lagrangian problem, and differentiating with respect to w_1, we have

$$\theta_1 \frac{\partial V_2}{\partial w_1} - \lambda\theta_1 - \mu\left(\frac{\partial V_2}{\partial w_1} - \frac{\partial V_1}{\partial w_1}\right) = 0. \tag{31}$$

Thus a sufficient condition to rule out the solution with $V_2 > V_0$ is to have the following two conditions:

$$V_1 = V_2 \text{ implies} \frac{\partial V_1}{\partial w_1} - \frac{\partial V_2}{\partial w_1} > 0. \tag{32}$$

$$V_0 = V_1 \text{ implies} \frac{\partial V_0}{\partial W} > \frac{\partial V_1}{\partial w_1}. \tag{33}$$

Condition (33) is the familiar moral hazard condition applied to first-period work and is a reasonable additional assumption (along with (19)) in the general case. It is satisfied by the one-period assumptions (20) and (21) in the additive and standard-of-living models.

In our earlier paper, we showed that (32) was satisfied in the additive model by the condition $c_1^* < c_2^*$, which, in turn, was implied by the moral hazard condition. That is, as summarized in Table 7.2, the assumption in (20) was sufficient for the two results that the wage would rise if both moral hazard constraints were binding and that both constraints would bind. We now complete the argument that the standard-of-living model (21) is sufficient for both results by considering sufficient conditions for the general case and showing that they are implied by (21).

While (32) is similar to the moral hazard assumptions we have made above, it differs in that it involves choice under uncertainty rather than comparing two choices under certainty. In the additive model, this problem is avoided since marginal utility in the first period is not random. In the standard-of-living and general models, marginal utility of first-period consumption depends on the level of second-period consumption, and so is a random variable.

For the general case, a set of sufficient conditions[3] for (32) is (34), (35), and (19)

$$U_{11} \leqslant rU_{12}. \tag{34}$$

$$U_{12} \geqslant rU_{22}. \tag{35}$$

We note that (34) and (35) are normality conditions for present and future consumption and are satisfied in the standard-of-living model.

Bringing together the definitions and conditions, and notationally combining $W + w$, into W, we have

$$
\begin{aligned}
&c_1^* \text{ maximizes } U(c_1, W - rc_1, 1)\\
&c_2^* \text{ maximizes } [\theta U(c_2, W + w_2 - rc_2, 2) + (1 - \theta)U(c_2, W - rc_2, 1)]\\
&V_1(W) \equiv U(c_1^*, W - rc_1^*, 1) = \theta U(c_2^*, W + w_2 - rc_2^*, 2)\\
&\qquad\qquad\qquad\qquad\qquad + (1 - \theta)U(c_2^*, W - rc_2^*, 1) \equiv V_2(W, w_2).
\end{aligned}
\tag{36}
$$

We are proving the equivalent statement of (32):

$$
\begin{aligned}
U_2(c_1^*, W - rc_1^*, 1) &> \theta U_2(c_2^*, W + w_2 - rc_2^*, 2)\\
&+ (1 - \theta)U_2(c_2^*, W - rc_2^*, 1).
\end{aligned}
\tag{37}
$$

Define w_2' by

$$\mathrm{Max}_{c_2} \, U(c_2, W + w_2' - rc_2, 2) = V_1(W). \tag{38}$$

Denote the optimizing level of c_2 as c_2'. From the definition, we see that $w_2' \leqslant w_2$ with a strict inequality if $c_1^* \neq c_2^*$. From the moral hazard condition, (19), and the fact that c_2' and c_1^* are optimizing values, we have

$$
\begin{aligned}
r^{-1}U_1(c_2', W + w_2' - rc_2', 2) &= U_2(c_2', W + w_2' - rc_2', 2)\\
&< U_2(c_1^*, W - rc_1^*, 1) = r^{-1}U_1(c_1^*, W - rc_1^*, 1).
\end{aligned}
\tag{39}
$$

Since c_2' and c_2^* are both optimizing values and U is concave we have

$$
\begin{aligned}
r^{-1}U_1(c_2^*, W + w_2 - rc_2^*, 2) &= U_2(c_2^*, W + w_2 - rc_2^*, 2)\\
&\leqslant U_2(c_2', W + w_2' - rc_2', 2)\\
&= r^{-1}U_1(c_2', W + w_2' - rc_2', 2)
\end{aligned}
\tag{40}
$$

with a strict inequality if $w_2' < w_2$. Combining (39) and (40) we have

$$U_2(c_2^*, W + w_2 - rc_2^*, 2) < U_2(c_1^*, W - rc_1^*, 1) \tag{41}$$

and

$$U_1(c_2^*, W + w_2 - rc_2^*, 2) < U_1(c_1^*, W - rc_1^*, 1). \tag{42}$$

---

[3] This result is due to M. Whinston.

We proceed by considering separately the different relative sizes of c_1^* and c_2^*. If $c_1^* = c_2^*$, (41) implies (37). If $c_1^* > c_2^*$, then, by (35) we have

$$U_2(c_1^*, W - rc_1^*, 1) > U_2(c_2^*, W - rc_2^*, 1). \tag{43}$$

(41) and (43) imply (37). If $c_1^* < c_2^*$, then, by (34) we have

$$U_1(c_1^*, W - rc_1^*, 1) > U_1(c_2^*, W - rc_2^*, 1). \tag{44}$$

(42) and (44) imply (37) since c_1^* and c_2^* are both optimizing values. This completes the proof.

Summarizing the extensions of our earlier work, we have the results in Table 7.2.

9. Concluding Remarks

Exploring non-additive preferences is both tractable and important. Habit formation implies a different degree of risk-aversion to resource changes that are learned about early in life relative to those learned about late in life (beyond what would be present anyway with additive preferences). It gives added importance to errors in planning that result in large drops in consumption at and after retirement. It gives a starting place for an analytical underpinning for thinking about pensions in terms of replacement rates. It can be used as a way to think about the averaging period used for defining benefits in defined-benefit plans. Moreover, it will change evaluations of the risks associated with different types of pension plans—such as a comparison of defined benefit and defined contribution plans. With social security reform on the agenda of so many countries and with more economists thinking about these programmes, it is important to avoid taking over-simple models too seriously, even if an over-simple description of preferences is embedded in a very complex dynamic simulation. One way to combat this natural tendency is by having more general models. While this paper does not get very far in examining a generalization, it is a start that may be a useful jumping-off place.

References

Ainslie, George (1992), *Picoeconomics: The Strategic Interaction of Successive Motivational States within the Person*. Cambridge: Cambridge University Press.

Becker, G., and K. Murphy (1988), 'A Theory of Rational Addiction', *Journal of Political Economy* 96: 675–700.

Chakravarty, S., and A. Manne (1968), 'Optimum Growth when the Instantaneous Utility Function Depends upon the Rate of Change in Consumption', *American Economic Review* 58: 1351–4.

Diamond, P., and B. Koszegi (1999), 'Quasi-hyperbolic Discounting and Retirement', unpublished.

—— and J. Mirrlees (1978), 'A Model of Social Insurance with Variable Retirement', *Journal of Public Economics* 10: 295–336.

——— ——— (forthcoming), 'Social Insurance with Variable Retirement and Private Savings', *Journal of Public Economics*.

Diamond, P., and J. Stiglitz (1974), 'Increases in Risk and in Risk Aversion', *Journal of Economic Theory* 8: 337–60.

Gruber, J., and B. Koszegi (1999), 'Time-inconsistent Theories of Addiction', unpublished, MIT.

Heal, G., and H. Ryder (1973), 'Optimum Growth with Intertemporally Dependent Preferences', *Review of Economic Studies* 60: 1–32.

Houthakker, H., and L. Taylor (1970), *Consumer Demand in the United States: Analyses and Projections*. Cambridge, Mass.: Harvard University Press.

Kurz, M. (1968), 'Optimal Economic Growth with Wealth Effects', *International Economic Review* 9: 348–57.

Laibson, David (1997), 'Golden Eggs and Hyperbolic Discounting', *Quarterly Journal of Economics*.

Leland, H. (1968), 'Savings and Uncertainty: The Precautionary Demand for Saving', *Quarterly Journal of Economics* 82: 465–73.

Pollak, R. (1970), 'Habit Formation and Dynamic Demand Functions', *Journal of Political Economy* 78: 745–63.

Rothschild, M., and J. Stiglitz (1970), 'Increasing Risk: I A definiton, *Journal of Economic Theory* 2: 225–43.

Samuelson, P. A. (1971), 'Turnpike Theorems Even Though Tastes are Intertemporally Dependent', *Western Economic Journal* 9: 21–5.

Weiszacker, C. C. von (1971), 'Notes on Endogenous Changes of Tastes', *Journal of Economic Theory* 3: 345–72.

8 Who Should Provide Public Goods?

JUN-ICHI ITAYA, DAVID de MEZA, AND GARETH D. MYLES

1. Introduction

This paper asks a simple question: who should provide public goods? It may seem surprising that we do not yet have a satisfactory answer to what is one of the core issues of public policy. We know the quantity of public goods that should be provided (Samuelson 1954), how successful private provision would be under a variety of motives for giving (Andreoni 1990; Cornes and Sandler 1996), and how taxes interact with provision when either the government (Atkinson and Stern 1974) or private individuals (Itaya, de Meza, and Myles 1996) provide the public goods. But there has been no analysis of how private and public provision should be best combined. This is a significant gap in our understanding of a major policy question.

In contrast to the paucity of theoretical work, the issue of who should provide public goods is one which has received considerable airing in political circles. There has been increasing discussion of the extent to which it is possible to rely on private individuals to provide public goods for themselves and a retrenchment of the government from the provision of numerous goods and services. This has left a situation in which some public goods are provided entirely by the government, some by private contributions alone and others through a mix of the two. For example, medical research is supported by a combination of private and public finance.[1] Defence provision is almost entirely government finance. Public-sector broadcasting in the USA is supported by voluntary contributions but is publicly financed in the UK. As well as investigating the theoretical problem, an analysis of who should provide may also shed light on the reasons underlying these differences in financing methods.

For a pure public good, the Samuelson rule provides a characterization of Pareto-optimal allocations. Such allocations represent the first best and are a guide to the quantity that should be provided but say little about the best mechanism for provision. Except in special cases,[2] when the government is the only provider of public goods, Samuelson-rule allocations will only be attainable if the government is able to levy optimal lump-sum taxes. As is well known from the work of Mirrlees (1986), implementation of such taxes faces insurmountable problems. At the opposite extreme, it is also known that total reliance on private provision will lead to an allocation that is

Thanks are due to Richard Cornes, Todd Sandler, and seminar audiences at Exeter, Iowa State, UBC, Toronto, Western Ontario, QMW, the APET meeting in Tuscaloosa, and the Public Finance Weekend at Essex.

[1] Research into the treatment of illnesses such as cancer is financed by government grants, profit-making companies, and charities. A successful treatment may be excludable but is a public good in that a breakthrough is non-rival and all members of the population may potentially benefit.

[2] Such as when incomes are fixed so that linear taxes can be non-distortionary.

not Pareto optimal. This result was initially derived in models (such as Chamberlin 1974 and McGuire 1974) that assumed individuals cared only about private consumption and the quantity of the public good. With such preferences, a number of very clear-cut conclusions emerge such as the irrelevance of income redistribution and the fact that in a large economy there is one-to-one crowding out of private by public contributions. However, empirical and experimental evidence conflicts with these findings. This has led to the development of the warm-glow formulation of preferences in which individuals derive utility from the act of giving itself. This model still retains the inefficiency but eliminates most of the contentious results. It does this, though, at the expense of not providing any clear-cut findings.

In the existing literature Atkinson and Stern (1974) provide a characterization of optimal commodity taxes when it is assumed that the government is the sole provider of a public good. In the same situation, Boadway and Keen (1993) analyse the optimal structure of income taxation. At the other extreme, Itaya, de Meza, and Myles (1996) consider both sets of tax instruments when public goods are provided by private contributions alone. The important feature of the latter analysis is the corner solutions for individual choices and the consequent motive that emerges for inequality-worsening income redistribution. The role of corner solutions will become apparent in Section 3.

As we have already noted, what is missing is any integration of these alternative strands. This is what we attempt in the present paper. In general terms the underlying issue can be introduced as follows. We know that private contributions generally lead to an inefficient outcome even with warm-glow preferences. We also know that the government can only finance public provision through distortionary taxes. Simple intuition would then suggest that the optimal policy will balance these effects and lead to a mixture of public and private provision. It may further be expected that in some cases one of these effects may more than offset the other so that a corner solution with only private or only public provision.

Unfortunately, the analysis does not prove to be this simple. It is necessary to distinguish between a number of different forms of preferences and assumptions on consumers' knowledge about the government's reaction to changes in their behaviour. These yield widely differing conclusions. In particular, we need to address the validity of the 'see-through'[3] assumption and whether giving obtains a warm glow. And, if a warm glow is obtained, is this quantity-driven or value-driven? It is looking at these alternative cases and assessing their relevance that forms the paper's contents. Having determined the nature of the correct policy for each situation, we then discuss the relevance of each and methods for inferring from data which are most appropriate.

For the greatest part of the paper we adopt the standard model of a benevolent government that acts as correctly as possible given its limited information. This idealistic view of government may be far too generous. Indeed, a primary reason for supporting the private provision of public goods may be that the government cannot be trusted to 'get it right'. It may be grossly inefficient or supply the wrong public

---

[3] This assumption is defined in Section 2.

goods. Alternatively, the government may be unable to set anything like the correct taxes or may fail to collect them effectively. We do offer comments on some of these observations below, but all of them should be borne in mind when assessing our results.[4]

The major finding that emerges from the analysis is the extent to which it is desirable to rely on private financing of public goods. In some cases all finance should be private and in most others there should be a mix of public and private. Viewed differently, it appears to be preferable for the government to provide incentives, via the price mechanism, for individuals to voluntarily supply public goods rather than to supply the public goods itself. The common textbook perception is that the market failure resulting from the existence of public goods naturally implies government provision. This is not the case.

Section 2 discusses the ingredients of the model. Section 3 analyses provision of public goods under the see-through assumption. Non-see-through is analysed in Section 4. Extensions of the basic model are described in Section 5. Section 6 discusses the results. Conclusions are given in Section 7.

2. Key Ingredients

Here we define and discuss alternative specifications of preferences and assumptions on consumers' information about government behaviour employed in the following sections. Some suggestions about interpretations and appropriate applications are also made.

To fix ideas, consider an economy with a single private good, a single public good, and H consumers each with a fixed income M^h. The consumption of the private good by consumer h is denoted by x^h and the contribution to the public good by g^h. Government provision of the public good is denoted Γ and total provision, $\Gamma + \sum_{h=1}^{H} g^h$, by G. The production technology is linear and both the public and private good have a per-unit production cost of one. The consumer prices of the private and public good are $q_x = 1 + t_x$ and $q_G = 1 + t_G$ respectively, where t_x and t_G are the commodity taxes. At these prices, the value of the public good provision by h is $v^h = q_G g^h$.[5]

2.1. Preferences

The first distinction that needs to be drawn is between different forms of preferences. As will become clear, the nature of preferences is of major importance in determining the properties of equilibrium and optimal policy.

2.1.1. Instrumental preferences
The early literature on the private provision of public goods focused on the case in which consumers cared about consumption of the private good and the total provision of the public good. In this case, the utility function can be written

---

[4] The consequences of an inefficient government are developed further in Myles (2000).
[5] A general equilibrium interpretation of the model would have M as a labour endowment which is supplied inelastically.

$$U^h = U^h(x^h, G). \tag{1}$$

The form of preferences in (1) will be termed *instrumental preferences* in what follows. This terminology is adopted because the consumer's utility is derived solely from the total quantity of the public good and there is no benefit *per se* from the level of individual contribution.

The implications of this form of preference have been extensively studied and surveys of the literature can be found in Cornes and Sandler (1996), Itaya, de Meza, and Myles (1999), and Myles (1995). The essential consequence of this formulation is that the Nash equilibrium reached in the absence of any government intervention is not Pareto optimal. Furthermore, the equilibrium is invariant to reallocations of income that do not alter the set of contributors, in large populations any government provision crowds out private provision on a one-for-one basis and, if there are income differences, only the richest consumer contributes. Empirical and experimental evidence has provided conflicting evidence on whether these results hold in practice. These have lead to questions about the appropriateness of this model.

These observations point to the conclusion that instrumental preferences lead to private provision only in small populations, say within the family. This statement is based upon the observation that a positive level of provision is only likely to arise if a contributor captures a substantial fraction of the benefits. This condition is easily met when the population is small but only the richest can be non-negligible when the population is large. It is this property that leads to the conflicts between this model and the data, since it is an empirical fact that charitable donations are significant for many consumers even in large populations. Instrumental preferences therefore have a role to play in some applications of the private contribution model. As a representation of the motivation for the bulk of personal charitable donations, they are of questionable validity.

2.1.2. Warm-glow preferences

One response to these difficulties has been the introduction of *warm-glow preferences*.[6] With such preferences, a contribution to the public good generates a utility benefit from both the addition to the quantity of the public good and from the act of charity itself. Essentially, contributing makes consumers feel good about themselves and generates a 'warm glow' of self-approval. Such preferences ensure that contributions remain positive in large populations since the warm glow is essentially a private good and remains significant even if the addition to the stock of public good is negligible. Furthermore, neither the crowding-out or invariance results apply in an economy with warm-glow preferences. Despite this, the equilibrium will not in general be Pareto optimal since the externality effect of contributions is not taken into account by consumers.

The form of warm glow introduced by Andreoni (1990) can be written as

$$U^h = U^h(x^h, g^h, G), \tag{2}$$

---

[6] Another has been to consider alternative forms of conjecture in the game played between the consumers. This line of reasoning does not appear to have been successful, see Myles (1995) for further discussion.

where the extent of the glow depends on the quantity of the public good contributed. We choose to term this the *quantity warm-glow*. An obvious alternative to (2) is the *value warm-glow* given by

$$U^h = U^h(x^h, v^h, G).\tag{3}$$

In the preferences described by (3), it is the market value of the contribution that is relevant for the warm glow whereas in (2) it is what is purchased with the contribution that counts.

The two formulations of the utility function suggest rather different motivations for donations. According to (2), what matters to the individual is the benefit to others reflecting something of a utilitarian outlook.[7] In contrast, the preferences represented by (3) are more self-centred in embodying the view that making a sacrifice for others is appropriate irrespective of the practical good it does. There is further discussion of these issues in Section 6.

2.2. See-through

A further issue is the extent to which consumers take into account the implications of their choices on government revenue and, hence spending, decisions. In a large economy it is reasonable that if a consumer buys more of a highly taxed good they ignore the feedback arising from the fact that more of the public good will be provided by the government or else some tax will be cut or subsidy raised. In a small economy rational consumers will anticipate significant feedbacks.

When consumers anticipate significant reaction by the government, we say that the *see-through* assumption applies (see Boadway, Pestieau, and Wildasin 1989). In a small economy with a government that is committed to providing the public good, the application of economic rationality makes it hard to avoid concluding that this assumption must be satisfied. Despite this, it is not impossible to conceive of a situation in which consumers act in ignorance or else feedback effects are small. In such cases we say *non-see-through* holds. When a large economy is considered, as in the Mirrlees (1971) model of income taxation, the see-through assumption is not an issue since the effect of a change in action by a single consumer has a negligible effect upon the government's behaviour. In a large but finite economy, non-see-through is approximately valid in the same way the competitive assumption can only be approximately true in a finite economy.[8]

As will be seen below, the policy choice that arises when the see-through assumption is imposed is quite distinct from that when it is not. This shows that the choice of which to adopt is not an inconsequential modelling issue. In assessing the results we derive, it is worth holding in mind the suggested settings for each.

---

[7] Of course, this is not full utilitarianism even in reduced form due to the asymmetric treatment of the donor's contribution.

[8] The issue of see-through is circumvented in Diamond and Mirrlees (1971) by the assumption that government revenue is spent on a good which does not directly affect utility.

3. Provision with See-through

Throughout we adopt the standard assumption that consumers are engaged in a Nash contribution game with each maximizing utility taking the contributions of the others as fixed. Although we have noted inconsistencies between some of the models using this assumption and the data, it appears to be the structure of preferences that is at fault, not the underlying nature of the game. Where we differ from existing treatments is that we permit the government to levy taxes and to supply the public good—if it chooses to do so. The intention is to determine the optimal mix of government and private contribution to the public good and to characterize optimal pricing policy. In contrast to much of the tax literature, the latter is given lower prominence than the division of funding.

3.1. Instrumental preferences

With the see-through assumption and instrumental preferences, it is clear that Bernheim's (1986) equivalence result applies. That is, if all consumers contribute towards provision of the public good, the equilibrium of the provision game is independent of any tax system which does not change the set of contributors. To show this, denote the tax on income by $T(M^h)$ so the budget constraint of h is

$$M^h - T(M^h) = q_x x^h + q_G g^h. \tag{4}$$

Government provision of the public good is

$$\Gamma = \sum_{h=1}^{H} [T(M^h) + [q_x - 1]x^h + [q_G - 1]g^h]. \tag{5}$$

Using (4) and (5), total provision of the public good is

$$G = \Gamma + \sum_{h=1}^{H} g^h = \sum_{h=1}^{H} [M^h - x^h]. \tag{6}$$

In response to a change in tax rates, the consumers can reallocate their expenditures between the public and private goods so as to keep x^h and G constant. The equilibrium established under one tax system can then be maintained under any other.

This equivalence only holds if all consumers are contributors before and after any tax change. To see this, assume that some consumers do not contribute and choose the labelling of consumers so that $g^h = 0$ for $h = 1, \ldots, \eta$. Then

$$G = \sum_{h=1}^{\eta} T(M^h) + \sum_{h=\eta+1}^{H} M^h - \sum_{h=1}^{H} x^h + q_x \sum_{h=1}^{\eta} x^h = \sum_{h=1}^{H} [M^h - x^h], \tag{7}$$

as before. What is now different is that the consumers who do not contribute cannot maintain the constancy of x^h as the tax system changes. For $h = 1, \ldots, \eta$,

$$x^h = \frac{M^h - T(M^h)}{q_x},$$ (8)

which is determined directly by the tax system so the Bernheim equivalence result breaks down when there are non-contributors. This shows immediately that if tax policy is to affect resource allocation, there must be some non-contributors before or after the policy change.

Following these preliminaries, it is possible to analyse the question of provision. To make the issues as clear as possible, assume that all consumers have identical preferences. Now let the division between contributors and non-contributors be temporarily fixed. Using (7) and (8), the objective function of a contributor in the Nash game can be written as

$$\max_{\{x^h\}} U\left(x^{h'}, \sum_{h=1}^{H} M^h - \sum_{h=1}^{\eta} \frac{M^h - T(M^h)}{q_x} - \sum_{h=\eta+1}^{H} x^h \right).$$ (9)

The equilibrium of the game is then a set of consumption levels for the contributors given by

$$x^{h'} = x\left(\sum_{h=1}^{\eta} \frac{M^h - T(M^h)}{q_x} \right), \quad h' = \eta + 1, \ldots, H.$$ (10)

It should be noted that in equilibrium consumption levels are the same for all contributors—some further consequences of this observation are explored in Itaya, de Meza, and Myles (1997).[9]

From these calculations, it can be seen that the equilibrium is independent of q_G. In fact, with this formulation the only role for q_G is to determine the division between government and private provision with the total level of provision being independent of this division. What lies behind this is that as q_G is varied (holding q_x constant), contributors to the public good keep their expenditure upon it constant since they reason that the share of taxation in the price becomes government provision. In addition, changing q_G does not affect the set of contributors.

For the remainder of this section, attention will be focused upon linear tax systems only. A discussion of the role of non-linear taxation is given in Section 5.1. With linear taxes the argument of the function in (10) can be written

$$\frac{M^h - T(M^h)}{q_x} = \frac{M^h[1 - \tau]}{q_x} = \frac{M^h}{q'_x},$$ (11)

where τ is the tax rate on incomes and $q'_x = \frac{q_x}{1 - \tau}$. It follows from (11) that it is sufficient to focus upon taxes on the private good alone.

---

[9] In particular it is shown that utility levels are equalized despite income differences, so private provision leads to an egalitarian outcome.

Bearing this in mind, assume that the tax on the private good is denoted by t, so $q_x = 1 + t$, and that the public good is untaxed so $q_G = 1$. The decision problem of the government is to choose the tax rate, t, to maximize a utilitarian social welfare function.[10] In so doing, the government must take into account the fact that the decision of a consumer on whether or not to be a contributor is endogenously determined by the tax rate. As the tax rate changes, so does the set of contributors. To describe the solution to this optimization, the approach is taken of characterizing what happens as the tax rate is raised from zero upwards. A distinction has to be drawn between the case in which all consumers contribute when the tax rate is zero and that in which some are non-contributors at all tax rates. The analysis begins with the former.

Choose the labelling of the consumers so that $M^1 < M^2 < \ldots < M^H$.

Lemma 1. *Assume that $g^h > 0$ for all h when $t = 0$. Then there is a tax rate $t^1 > 0$ such that:*
(i) *welfare is constant for $t \in [0, t^1]$;*
(ii) *consumer 1 ceases contributing at t^1;*
(iii) *the right-derivative of social welfare (with respect to t) is positive at t^1.*

Proof. Since all consumers are contributors when the tax rate is zero, the equivalence result applies for the range of taxes up until one of the consumers becomes a non-contributor. Let the tax rate at which this happens be denoted t^1. Then it follows that social welfare is constant on the range $[0, t^1]$. It is straightforward to show that the first consumer to decide to become a non-contributor is the lowest-income consumer. To see this, note that with all contributing, the solution to the Nash game is dependent on t alone, so $x^h = x(t)$, again employing the fact that consumption levels are the same for all contributors. Non-contribution begins when $[1 + t] x(t) = M^h$, which must happen first for the lowest-income consumer.

When consumer 1 has ceased contributing, the social welfare function is

$$W = U\left(\frac{M^1}{1+t}, \frac{tM^1}{1+t} + \sum_{h=2}^{H} M^h - \sum_{h=2}^{H} x^h\right) + \sum_{h=2}^{H} U\left(x^h, \frac{tM^1}{1+t} + \sum_{h=2}^{H} M^h - \sum_{h=2}^{H} x^h\right). \tag{12}$$

Taking the derivative of (12) with respect to t, using the envelope theorem for individual choice and evaluating at t^1 gives

$$\left.\frac{\partial W}{\partial t}\right|_{t^1} = [H - 1]U_G\left[\frac{M^1}{[1+t]^2} - [H - 1]x'\right]. \tag{13}$$

The term x' can be evaluated by returning to the Nash game being played. The contributors each solve

$$\max_{\{x^h\}} U\left(x^h, \frac{tM^1}{1+t} + \sum_{h=1}^{H} M^h - \sum_{h=1}^{H} x^h\right). \tag{14}$$

[10] The assumption that the social welfare function is utilitarian is not critical.

Since the solution is symmetric between the contributors (so $x^h = x$ all h), the first-order condition can be used to calculate

$$x' = -\frac{M^1}{[1 + t]^2}\left[\frac{U_{xG} - U_{GG}}{U_{xx} - HU_{xG} + [H - 1]U_{GG}}\right]. \tag{15}$$

Substituting (15) into (13) shows that

$$\frac{\partial W}{\partial t} = \frac{[H - 1]U_G M^1}{[1 + t]^2}\left[\frac{U_{xx} - U_{xG}}{U_{xx} - HU_{xG} + [H - 1]U_{GG}}\right], \tag{16}$$

which is positive under standard assumptions on preferences. ∎

Consequently, the gradient of social welfare as a function of the tax rate is zero until t^1 and then is kinked upwards at this tax rate. The existence of this kink shows that social welfare is greater for tax rates immediately above t^1 than it is for those below. Hence it is always optimal to set a tax rate that forces the lowest income consumer to become a non-contributor. The argument of Lemma 1 can be extended to the more general conclusion of Lemma 2.

Lemma 2. *There is a kink in the welfare function at each tax rate at which an additional consumer becomes a non-contributor.*

Proof. This is a direct generalization of the calculations in the proof of Lemma 1. ∎

The consequence of Lemma 1 is that the lowest-income consumer should be forced into being a non-contributor. Lemma 2 shows that the social welfare function is kinked upward each time a critical tax rate is reached at which a further one becomes a non-contributor. However, this does not imply they should all be forced into non-contribution. The reason for this is that the gradient prior to the kink may be negative, i.e. social welfare has reached a maximum between a pair of kinks. Hence the optimum policy is to crowd out some consumers with government provision but not necessarily to crowd out all. Provision is either a mix of public and private or entirely public.

These possibilities cannot be explored fully at the level of generality used so far. Instead a numerical simulation is used below to illustrate the working of the model. Before proceeding, it is worth noting one further result. Even though incomes are fixed, the first best cannot be attained in this model. This arises because the marginal rates of substitution for those consumers crowded out cannot be manipulated by the use of a single tax instrument in a sufficient way to obtain efficiency. Looking somewhat ahead, it will be seen that this result is a product of the see-through assumption. Without this, the first best can be achieved with instrumental preferences.

Consider now the situation in which some consumers do not contribute even at a zero tax rate. There is now no range of tax rates where social welfare remains constant. Otherwise, it remains true that there is an upward kink each time a tax rate is reached at which a consumer ceases to contribute. However, a zero tax rate may be optimal. Consider a situation in which consumer 1 is the only non-contributor at a zero tax rate, then

$$
\left. \frac{\partial W}{\partial t} \right|_{t=0} = M^1[U_G(1) - U_x(1)]
$$
$$
+ \frac{[H-1]U_G M^1}{[1+t]^2} \left[\frac{U_{xx} - U_{xG}}{U_{xx} - HU_{xG} + [H-1]U_{GG}} \right]. \tag{17}
$$

The second term in (17) is positive as already noted but the first, which relates to the marginal utilities of consumer 1, is negative since consumer 1 obtains a strictly higher marginal utility from consumption of the private good. It may therefore be possible for welfare to be decreasing as the tax rate moves away from zero. A corner solution with private provision being optimal is therefore possible if income disparities are sufficiently great that there are a significant number of non-contributors in the absence of taxation. Since this result is dependent on income disparities, the role that redistributive income taxes may play is important. Discussion of this is given in Section 5.1.

This is as far as results can go using the general structure so we turn to a numerical example to obtain further insights. Consider two consumers with preferences represented by

$$
U = \log x^h + \log G. \tag{18}
$$

Letting $M^2 = \rho M^1$, $\rho > 1$, then both will contribute with zero taxes if $\rho < 3$. With only consumer 2 contributing, social welfare is

$$
W = 4 \log [1 + \rho]M^1 - \log 4 + 3 \log \frac{3}{8}, \tag{19}
$$

and, with no consumers contributing, is

$$
W = 2 \log [1 + \rho]M^1 + \log M^1 + \log \rho M^1 + 4 \log \frac{1}{2}. \tag{20}
$$

Social welfare is illustrated as a function of the tax rate in Figure 8.1a for $M^2 = 1.5M^1$ and for $M^2 = 2.5M^1$ in Figure 8.1b. These two cases illustrate the two possible outcomes. In Figure 1a, welfare is maximized when the government is the sole supplier of the public good. In this case it should raise its provision until both consumers are crowded-out from contributing. Conversely, Figure 8.1b illustrates the possibility that it may be optimal to have some private contribution. The low-income consumer, 1, is crowded out but the high-income consumer continues to contribute. Using the welfare functions given in (19) and (20), it can be seen that the break between the two cases occurs when $\rho = 2.3$. These results show that, for this specification at least, a mix of public and private contribution can be justified by sufficient income inequality. With limited income inequality, all provision should be by the government.

What is most important to be concluded from this section is how the see-through assumption supports government provision. The ability of consumers to see what the

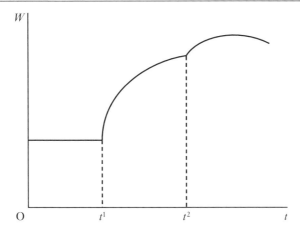

FIG. 8.1a. *Function of the tax rate for* $M^2 = 1.5M^1$

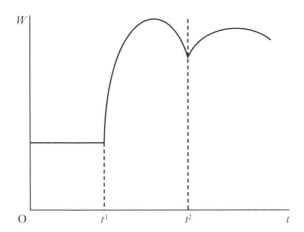

FIG. 8.1b. *Function of the tax rate for* $M^2 = 2.5M^1$

government is doing allows them to undo its endeavours but only if all are contributing. The increase in the tax rate that induces some to be non-contributors then makes it impossible for them to fully offset government behaviour and this allows the government to influence the economy. Therefore, government provision of the public good is justified. Since some crowding-out must occur, the invariance does not apply and the tax system will be distortionary. For some specifications, the optimal tax rate on the private good will be such as to crowd out all private provision. The reason that this does not occur in all cases is distributional: once a consumer is crowded out their utility falls as the tax rate is raised. Hence the optimal tax rate trades off utility loss to the low income against utility gains (through increased public good) for the higher income.

Because of the see-through assumption, the price of the public good does not affect whether contribution takes place or not. When the optimum policy is to crowd out all private provision, the price of the public good plays no role. For some income distributions public goods may be supplied by the higher-income consumers. If so, all that the price of the public good does is determine the mix between public and private contributions; total provision is independent of price.

3.2. Warm glow

The warm-glow model has received increasing attention since its introduction by Andreoni (1990). As noted in Section 2, the important property of this model is that a contribution to the public good generates a private utility benefit, in addition to any return derived from increased provision of the public good. This private benefit is motivated through feeling good about the act of contributing. The important property of the model is that it gives a reason for contribution even in a large population where the marginal effect of an individual contribution is negligible.

Two versions of the warm-glow model will be considered. The first, introduced by Andreoni, involves the donor deriving utility from the amount of public good contributed. In the second it is from the value of contribution.

3.2.1. Quantity warm-glow

Assume that the government levies taxes upon the private and the public good. Under the see-through assumption, the derivations used above show that total supply of the public good is $G = \sum_{h=1}^{H}[M^h - x^h]$ and the equilibrium of the private provision game is given by a demand for the private good of the form $x^h = x^h(q_x, q_G)$.[11] The important aspect of the warm glow is that, in contrast to the model without, non-contribution to the public good will not necessarily arise when income differentials increase. The reason for this is the warm glow is essentially a private good and which a consumer may not wish to see become zero. Although contributions could be zero, it will be assumed that they are not. A formal justification for this position would be to assume that the utility function satisfies the Inada conditions.

With quantity warm-glow and see-through, social welfare can be written as

$$W = \sum_{h=1}^{H} U\left(x^h(q_x, q_G), \sum_{h-1}^{H}[M^h - x^h(q_x, q_G)], \frac{M^h - q_x x^h(q_x, q_G)}{q_G} \right). \tag{21}$$

The nature of the policy resulting from the maximization of (21) can be derived by considering the effect of a variation in the price of the public good upon social welfare. Differentiating (21) and employing the envelope theorem,

$$\frac{dW}{dq_G} = -\sum_{h=1}^{H} U_G(h) \sum_{\substack{h'=1 \\ h' \neq h}}^{H} \frac{\partial x^{h'}}{\partial q_G} - \sum_{h=1}^{H} U_G(h) \frac{M^h - q_x x^h}{q_G^2} < 0, \tag{22}$$

---

[11] We assume that the warm glow does not extend to the public good provision financed by the taxes paid by an individual.

if $\dfrac{\partial x^{h'}}{\partial q_G} > 0$. Consequently, as long as public good provision is positive, a reduction in the consumer price of the public good always raises welfare.

The mechanism that is operating here is that a subsidy to the public good substitutes private contributions for public. This generates more of a warm glow. The resulting reduction in revenue for the government implies that it makes a smaller contribution to the public good. However, total supply of the public good actually rises since consumption of the private good falls. This result is a variant on that found in Andreoni (1990).

To incorporate the above reasoning into an optimal policy, account must be taken of the fact that the government's budget must be balanced. Clearly, since more government supply has no direct effect on welfare but only an indirect cost via the higher taxes needed to finance it, there should be no government supply of the public good. So, with quantity warm-glow and see-through, all public goods should be privately provided. The intuition behind this conclusion is that private provision generates both a private and public return whereas public provision does not provide the private return. It is therefore always best to use the tax system to encourage private provision rather than to fund public provision.

The optimal prices can be shown to satisfy

$$
q_x - q_G
$$
$$
= \frac{\displaystyle\sum_{h=1}^{H} g^h \sum_{h=1}^{H}\left[q_G U_G(h)\frac{\partial x^h}{\partial q_x} + x^h U_g(h) \right] - \sum_{h=1}^{H} x^h \sum_{h=1}^{H}\left[q_G U_G(h)\frac{\partial x^h}{\partial q_G} + g^h U_g(h) \right]}{\displaystyle\sum_{h=1}^{H} \frac{\partial x^h}{\partial q_x}\sum_{h=1}^{H}\left[q_G U_G(h)\frac{\partial x^h}{\partial q_G} + g^h U_g(h) \right] - \sum_{h=1}^{H} \frac{\partial x^h}{\partial q_G}\sum_{h=1}^{H}\left[q_G U_G(h)\frac{\partial x^h}{\partial q_x} + x^h U_g(h) \right]}.
$$

$$(23)$$

Although (23) is not particularly informative in the general case, consider what happens if there are two consumers with identical incomes. The demands, demand derivatives, and marginal utilities are then equal for both consumers and (23) reduces to

$$
q_x - q_G = \frac{U_G q_G}{U_g}. \tag{24}
$$

Using the first-order condition for consumer choice, $U_x - U_G - \dfrac{q_x}{q_G} U_g = 0$, (24) becomes

$$
U_x - U_G - 2U_g = 0, \tag{25}
$$

which is the optimality condition for this economy. Therefore, if there are no income differentials, the commodity taxes can achieve efficiency even if there is a warm glow from contributions.

3.2.2. Value warm-glow

One interpretation of the warm glow is that it reflects a feeling of self-congratulation for acting in a selfless way. Following this view, the actual level of purchases of public good made with any contribution need not be relevant; all that matters is the fact that the contribution was made. This reasoning leads into the value warm-glow model where it is the value of the contribution to the public good that enters utility. Expressed alternatively, it is the value of what is sacrificed to finance the charity rather than what is received that generates a warm glow.[12] This formulation therefore suggests that gross donations will be insensitive to their tax treatment. It will now be shown how this provides very different policy implications to the quantity warm-glow model.

Under the see-through assumption, the total quantity of the public good is again $\sum_{h=1}^{H}[M^h - x^h]$. Using the budget constraint $M^h = q_x x^h + v^h$, preferences with the value warm-glow, with the value denominated in the same units as income, can be written as

$$U(x^h, v^h, G) = U\left(x^h, M^h - q_x x^h, \sum_{h=1}^{H}[M^h - x^h]\right). \tag{26}$$

The nature of the optimal policy can be seen immediately from (26). The Nash game between the consumers will result in equilibrium choices that depend only (taking incomes as given) upon $q_x : x^h = x^h(q_x)$. This is because contributions now have unit price. Hence, of the policy variables q_x and q_G, only q_x appears in the welfare function. The price of the consumption good is therefore chosen to maximize welfare. As far as this optimization is concerned, the price of the public good is a matter of indifference. The only role it plays is to determine the division of public good provision between the public and private sector. Welfare is independent of this division. This leads to the conclusion that with value warm-glow preferences and see-through, welfare is independent of the price of the public good and the division of provision between the private and public sectors.

Maximizing social welfare, the optimal price for the private good satisfies the equation

$$-x^h \sum_{h=1}^{H} U_g(h) - \sum_{h=1}^{H} \sum_{\substack{h'=1 \\ h' \neq h}}^{H} U_G(h) \frac{\partial x^{h'}}{\partial q_x} = 0, \tag{27}$$

so that it balances the decreased private contribution that is possible as q_x rises with the increased total provision of the public good as private consumption falls.

This conclusion is worth contrasting to that for the quantity warm-glow. In that case, it was the price of the public good that was of utmost importance. Here it is the

---

[12] A further possibility would be that it is sacrifice as a proportion of income, M/r, that is the determinant of utility. This would capture a number of ancient charitable traditions but is not pursued here for reasons of space.

price of the private good that is fundamentally important with the price of the public good an irrelevance. Given such divergent findings from slight variations in the form of preferences, it becomes important to consider which is the most relevant description. More is said about this later.

4. Non-See-through

Non-see-through implies that consumers take no account of how their actions affect the government budget constraint. This may be because they are 'small' relative to the economy and non-see-through is approximately true in the way that competitive behaviour is approximately true in a large economy. Alternatively, it may hold simply through the ignorance of the consumers or because the government can run a budget deficit or surplus in the short run. Whichever is the case, the analysis remains the same.

The analysis of non-see-through bears a closer relation to the standard literature on optimal taxation than does see-through. This is not surprising since the assumption also underlies that analysis—though it is never made explicit. In any model of taxation a change in consumer behaviour that alters tax payment will affect government revenue. Only in a continuum model can the effect of a consumer be truly negligible. From this perspective, the analysis of see-through can be viewed as providing insight into the issues that would arise if that assumption were not imposed.

4.1. Instrumental preferences

With instrumental preferences, the decision problem facing a consumer is

$$\max_{\{x^h, g^h\}} U\left(x^h, \Gamma + g^h + \sum_{j=1, j \neq h}^{H} g^j\right) \text{ s.t. } M^h = q_x x^h + q_G g^h, \tag{28}$$

where Γ is taken as given. The Nash equilibrium choice of contributors is determined as

$$x = x(q_x, q_G, \Gamma). \tag{29}$$

This is common for all contributors. Non-contribution arises when

$$M^h < q_x x(q_x, q_G, \Gamma). \tag{30}$$

For the consumers for which (30) is satisfied, the level of private good demand is given by

$$x = x(q_x). \tag{31}$$

It is interesting to analyse how the contribution decision depends upon the prices. To this end, assume that demand in the contribution case (29) is independent of Γ and q_G, as for example it would be with Cobb–Douglas utility. If demand was unit elastic, the non-contribution decision would then be independent of q_x and the set of contributors would be determined by income alone and unaffected by any change in prices. Alternatively, if demand is inelastic, then a rise in q_x would make the set of contributors smaller. The converse would occur if demand were elastic. Since dependence upon q_G and Γ would allow an even broader range of outcomes, these observations show that there is no simple relationship between prices and non-contribution.

Returning to (29) the choice for a contributor is dependent upon both prices. This allows the government to exert greater control over the economy by combining taxes on both the private good and the public good.

Theorem 1. *With instrumental preferences and non-see-through, the Samuelson rule can be attained.*

Proof. Define $MRS^h \equiv \dfrac{U_G}{U_X}$. The assumptions on technology ensure that the marginal rate of transformation (MRT) between the public and private good is equal to 1. The Samuelson rule is then

$$\sum_{h=1}^{H} MRS^h = MRT = 1. \tag{32}$$

It will now be shown that this can be achieved whether or not there are any non-contributors.

Assume that there are no non-contributors. Since the optimization of each consumer involves setting $MRS^h = \dfrac{q_G}{q_x}$, choosing the price ratio so that

$$\frac{q_G}{q_x} = \frac{1}{H}, \tag{33}$$

ensures that (32) is satisfied.

If there are some non-contributors, the argument is modified as follows. Each MRS^h is a continuous function of the consumer prices of the two goods. This applies whether the consumer is a contributor or not and at the point at which non-contribution begins (although MRS^h is kinked as a function of prices at the non-contribution point). Assuming that $\lim_{x \to 0} U_x(x, G) = \infty$ and $\lim_{x \to \infty} U_x(x, G) = 0$, then $\sum_{h=1}^{H} MRS^h$ is zero as $q_x \to \infty$ and infinite as $q_x \to 0$ with q_G adjusted to maintain a given level of revenue for the government. Since $\sum_{h=1}^{H} MRS^h$ is the sum of continuous functions, it is itself continuous and there must exist a value of q_x (and an implied value of q_G) where it is equal to one. At this point the Samuelson rule is satisfied. ∎

This theorem has straightforward implications for the division of provision that can be determined as follows. Set prices as described in (33). If all consumers are contributors at these prices, then the Samuelson rule is attained with purely private provision.[13] Conversely, if some are non-contributors at these prices, the prices need to be adjusted as described in the second part of the proof. Since an increase in q_x always reduces the welfare of the non-contributors, it will never be beneficial to raise a positive level of revenue. So again all provision will be private.

4.2. Warm glow

The first modification of these assumptions is to move to warm-glow preferences. Only the quantity warm-glow will be considered. The reasoning for value warm-glow is similar but does not yield such precise conclusions.

With quantity warm-glow, the optimization problem of consumer h is

$$
\max_{\{x^h\}} U\left(x^h, \Gamma + \sum_{j=1}^{H} \frac{M^j - q_x x^j}{q_G}, \frac{M^h - q_x x^h}{q_G}\right). \tag{34}
$$

This generates, via the Nash game, a demand function for the private good and a supply of the public good with the forms

$$
x^h = x^h(q_x, q_G, \Gamma), \; g^h = g^h(q_x, q_G, \Gamma), \tag{35}
$$

and a level of social welfare

$$
W = \sum_{h=1}^{H} U\left(x^h(q_x, q_G, \Gamma), \Gamma + \sum_{j=1}^{H} g^j(q_x, q_G, \Gamma), g^h(q_x, q_G, \Gamma)\right). \tag{36}
$$

The optimal policy is determined by maximizing (36) subject to the constraints that

$$
\Gamma = [q_x - 1]\sum_{j=1}^{H} x^h + [q_G - 1]\sum_{j=1}^{H} g^h, \; \Gamma \geq 0. \tag{37}
$$

Simple economic reasoning suggests that the solution to this optimization should have $\Gamma = 0$: a reduction in government provision allows subsidization of private provision which raises the return from the warm glow. This is the same reasoning as used in Section 3.2.1. Actually establishing this for the general case is a difficult task but the following result can be proved.

Theorem 2. *Assume that the private good and contributions to the private good are gross substitutes and that the public good is normal. Then, if there are two identical consumers, there will be no public provision and the first best is attained.*

---

[13] There is one exception to this conclusion. If all consumers are identical and there is a price for the public good above which they will not contribute, then the Samuelson rule can be attained by setting the public good price above this and financing the optimal level of provision through a tax on the private good. This solution cannot apply when there are income differentials.

Proof. Using the first-order conditions for consumer choice, the necessary conditions for q_x and q_G from the optimization in (36) and (37) are

$$U_G q_x \frac{\partial g}{\partial q_G} - U_x g + \lambda \left[g + [q_G - q_x] \frac{\partial g}{\partial q_G} \right] = 0, \tag{38}$$

$$U_G q_x^2 \frac{\partial g}{\partial q_x} - U_x [M - q_G g] + \lambda \left[[M - q_G g] + q_x [q_G - q_x] \frac{\partial g}{\partial q_x} \right] = 0. \tag{39}$$

Now assume that $\Gamma = 0$. Eliminating λ between these conditions and using the budget constraint gives

$$[U_x [q_G - q_x] + U_G q_x] \left[[q_x - 1] \frac{\partial g}{q_x} + [q_G - 1] \frac{\partial g}{q_G} \right] = 0. \tag{40}$$

The gross substitutability and normality conditions imply that

$$[U_x [q_G - q_x] + U_G q_x] = 0, \tag{41}$$

or

$$q_G = q_x \left[1 - \frac{U_G}{U_x} \right]. \tag{42}$$

Substituting this into the necessary conditions gives

$$\lambda = U_x. \tag{43}$$

Using these results the necessary condition for Γ is

$$2U_G - U_x + \mu = 0. \tag{44}$$

Using the optimal prices in the consumer's first-order condition shows that

$$2U_G - U_x + U_g = 0, \tag{45}$$

which is the necessary condition for the first-best outcome. Hence $\mu = U_g > 0$ so the assumption that $\Gamma = 0$ is consistent with the Kuhn–Tucker conditions. ∎

Several points in the theorem deserve comment. Firstly, the attainment of the first best is a consequence of the assumption of fixed-income levels. If this was relaxed, the taxes would distort the labour/leisure choice and potentially disrupt this conclusion. Secondly, a similar theorem cannot be established if there are income differences. However, the proof is easily generalized to any number of identical consumers. To see this, note that the necessary condition for individual choice is

$$-U_x \frac{q_G}{q_x} + U_G + U_g = 0, \tag{46}$$

and that for the social optimum is

$$-U_x + H U_G + U_g = 0. \tag{47}$$

Equating (46) and (47) determines a price ratio

$$\frac{q_x}{q_G} = \frac{U_x - [H - 1]U_G}{U_x}, \tag{48}$$

that ensures the Samuelson rule is met with purely private provision.

5. Some Extensions

The models that have been analysed in the previous sections have been intentionally simple. This has emphasized the most important aspects of the problem without introducing issues that detract attention from these. This section briefly considers a number of potential modifications to the basic model.

5.1. Endogenous income and income taxation

Two additional issues are raised when incomes are made endogenous. Firstly, there is the interaction between the supply of labour and the tax results identified above. Secondly, endogenous income potentially makes the study of income taxation interesting. With fixed incomes, any tax would just be a lump sum. For warm-glow preferences, endogenous income does not have particularly significant consequences. The optimal characterizations of policy already given will remain valid. The incorporation of labour supply will lead to some interactions between the prices of commodities and work effort that will modify the precise expressions but will not alter the broad policy proposals. The same general comment applies to instrumental preferences under see-through.

Where labour supply is most significant is the case of non-see-through. Under the fixed-income assumption taxation can achieve an efficient Samuelson-rule equilibrium. When labour supply is endogenous this is not possible except in special cases such as Cobb–Douglas utility. Instead, what emerges is a form of Ramsey rule for setting the consumer prices. In turn, this provides a potential argument for positive provision by the government. This leads to something of a paradox: if taxes are distortionary then they should be used to finance public provision, otherwise individuals should contribute. Although this line of reasoning leads to an argument for government provision, this is perhaps the least convincing of the alternative models.

Similar comments apply when non-linear income taxes are considered. The most significant effect that income taxation, and income reallocation, can have is to affect the decision upon whether to contribute or not. The reasoning behind this statement is that the potential inefficiency of private provision is a consequence of the relative prices of the commodities and not one of income distribution. As a result, since non-contribution is not an important feature of warm-glow preferences, income taxation has little importance in this framework. It can be used to achieve some income redistribution but does not address the basic problem of public-good provision.

Now consider instrumental preferences and non-see-through. For the sake of argument, assume that preferences are linear in labour supply. Then it can be shown that income taxes and commodity taxes play two distinct roles (for details see Itaya, de Meza, and Myles 1996). Commodity taxes should be set to ensure that the Samuelson rule is achieved. The income tax is then employed to reach the most preferred income distribution. Obviously, this direct separability will break down when the linearity is absent (because of the links between labour supply and prices already identified) but the essentially different roles for the two tax instruments will still remain.

The limited role that can be played by income taxes is nicely illustrated by the following example. Take the quantity warm-glow with see-through and let there be two consumers with identical and fixed incomes. The government finances its provision of the public good through a lump-sum tax on the two consumers. For a typical consumer, the level of utility is

$$U(M - 0.5\Gamma - g, g, 2g + \Gamma). \tag{49}$$

The effect of an increase in government provision is given by

$$
\begin{aligned}
\frac{dU}{d\Gamma} &= [U_g + 2U_G - U_x]\frac{dg}{d\Gamma} + U_G - 0.5U_x \\
&= \left[1 + \frac{dg}{d\Gamma}\right]U_2 - 0.5U_3,
\end{aligned}
\tag{50}
$$

where the second equality follows from the envelope condition for individual choice. Evaluating $\frac{dg}{d\Gamma}$, it can be shown that for $\frac{dU}{d\Gamma} < 0$ it is sufficient that $U_{11} + U_{21} - U_{31} < 0$. When this condition is satisfied, the financing of public-good provision by lump-sum taxation will reduce welfare. The outcome would be even worse if distortionary income taxes were employed.

With see-through, the situation is somewhat different. If all consumers contribute, then the equivalence result still applies so that the equilibrium is independent of taxation. Once the non-contribution threshold is passed for the first consumer, social welfare is again kinked. Let z^1 denote the total income of i. Since non-contribution arises when

$$q_x x \geq z^1 - T(z^1), \tag{51}$$

the point at which non-contribution is reached can be affected by both commodity and income taxes. This observation can be used to understand the nature of the optimal policy. First note that a high price for the private good reduces the welfare of the non-contributors so that it is something to be avoided where possible. Since the optimum is achieved when all consumers are non-contributors, the income tax should be used to reduce income inequalities so that non-contribution is reached at the lowest private good price. Consequently, with a non-linear income tax all provision should be by the government.

5.2. *Government inefficiency*

The assumption that private contributions and government expenditure are equally efficient in generating public goods is one that is open to question. The economic analysis of bureaucracy suggests a number of reasons why the government may be inefficient at turning tax revenue into public goods. Accepting these, the question arises as to how such inefficiency affects the results described above.

In the case of value warm-glow and see-through in which there was previously indifference between private and public provision, there would now be a clear preference for private provision. Where private financing was previously preferred, it will be even more so with government inefficiency.

For the remaining cases, the use of government financing will always be reduced and the mix will move in favour of private financing. With instrumental and see-through, this will increase the likelihood that there will be some residual private financing.

5.3. *Public-good differentiation*

An alternative notion of government inefficiency is that it provides the wrong kind of public good. What we have in mind here is that the public good is available in a range of varieties (whether horizontally or vertically differentiated) and that the government may elect to supply a variety that is not the first choice of the consumers.

In this context, the case of vertical production differentiation seems the most relevant so that the public good is available in a range of quality levels. This opens up the possibility that consumers may choose to direct their contributions (if any) to purchases of different quality levels and public provision may be at a different quality level again. An example of this is schooling: state schools typically have higher pupil/staff ratios than private schools and poorer facilities generally.

To obtain insight into the consequences of vertical differentiation, assume that there are just two consumers. Let consumer h contribute amount g^h of quality s^h. Assume that the consumers care about the total quantity of public good provided and the (weighted) average quality and that preferences are separable. Hence

$$U^h = U\left(x^h, f\left(g^1 + g^2, \frac{g^1 s^1 + g^2 s^2}{g^1 + g^2}\right)\right). \tag{52}$$

Units of measurement are normalized so that the measure of quality, s, is also the price per unit. In the absence of taxation, the budget constraint of h is then

$$M^h = x^h + s^h g^h. \tag{53}$$

The first-order conditions for optimization are

$$-U_x(h)[g^1 + g^2] + U_G(h)f_2 = 0, \tag{54}$$

$$-U_x(h)s^h + U_G(h)f_1 + U_G(h)f_2\left[\frac{g^{\tilde{h}}[s^h - s^{\tilde{h}}]}{[g^1 + g^2]^2}\right] = 0, \quad h = 1, 2, \; h \neq \tilde{h}. \tag{55}$$

Solving these conditions, it can be seen that $s^1 = s^2$. So that if both consumers contribute, they both contribute to the same quality level.

The finding that both contribute to the same quality level is a consequence of the same factors that are responsible for the invariance and crowding-out results in the standard instrumental model. The functioning of the private provision equilibrium is therefore little different from the standard analysis without the quality differential. Moreover, it also follows that the results on taxation will also be similar in the case of see-through. Welfare will remain constant until the low-income consumer is crowded out and then it will begin to rise. Optimality will either be public provision alone or a mix of public and private. Without see-through, the important feature is that there are two dimensions of inefficiency of the private-provision equilibrium: quantity and quality. Consequently, it will not be possible to achieve efficiency using only a simple tax or subsidy on the public good. A non-linear pricing scheme that forces the correct quality to be chosen (by making the price of wrong qualities prohibitively high) could achieve efficiency.

5.4. Heterogeneous tastes and peer pressure

Not everyone enjoys a warm glow from giving and some are consumed with cold fury when others are perceived not to have contributed their 'fair' share. Evolution has bequeathed us a mix of emotions but distributed them across the population in unequal measure. Our analysis has only scratched the surface of the motivations for private contribution. A fuller account of the psychology underlying donation may well change some of our conclusions.

Peer pressure is undoubtedly important. How much one person contributes is influenced by the actions and reactions of others. A social-custom model of contribution may well be relevant here. In addition, contribution could also be motivated through the guilt associated with failing to do so. These could well provide arguments for public provision since enforced uniformity has its merits and can prevent the economy being trapped in a bad equilibrium. Indeed, it is difficult to believe that a modern society could provide a satisfactory flow of public goods just by the manipulation of prices though, as we argue, this could help. Evidence-based research in this area would be fascinating.

6. Discussion

The results derived in Sections 3 and 4 are easily summarized. With instrumental preferences and see-through, the optimum involves some government provision and possibly only government provision. The position is reversed with warm-glow preferences and see-through: entirely private provision is optimal (although the mix is irrelevant with value warm-glow). In the case of non-see through, all provision should be private with instrumental preferences. The same is true of warm-glow preferences in some cases.

It can be readily seen from this summary that the answer to the question 'Who should provide?' is highly sensitive to the specification adopted. In fact, the entire range of conclusions is possible from purely private provision being optimal through to purely government provision. Given this, the importance of determining which of these cases is valid is of significant importance.

The first point that can be addressed is the choice between the instrumental model and warm glow. The empirical and experimental evidence does not seem to support the instrumental model. But some of this evidence is inconclusive and the rejection is not complete. In fact, there may be some cases in which it is entirely appropriate. One that comes to mind is the case of federal authorities within a state contributing to a state-wide public good. The example of Bohm (1984) is worth noting in this respect. In such cases the small numbers involved suggest that the see-through assumption is also likely to be valid. This leads to the focus upon the fact that public provision should be positive and, in some cases, mixed provision may be optimal.

When considering goods benefiting large numbers of consumers, only the warm-glow model plausibly accounts for positive contributions. This as presented in the existing literature (such as Andreoni 1990) has assumed what has been here termed the quantity form. Because of the nature of the warm glow, the value version is also a reasonable structure. This is a form that has not been considered before in the literature. These two forms of preferences have very distinct implications under the see-through assumption. With quantity preferences, then it is the price of the public good that is critically important and the government should seek to minimize this. In contrast, when it is value preferences, it is the price of the private good that matters. All that the public-good price does is determine the allocation between public and private provision, and the level of welfare is independent of this division. Without see-through the outcomes are qualitatively similar with both having a mix of public and private provision.

But which form of warm glow is most appropriate? One line of argument that can give some insight into this issue is to consider contributions to charities. An important fact here is that the vast majority of individuals contribute to numerous charities. Now consider a charity with many donors so that the marginal effect of a single individual upon the total stock of public goods is negligible so the only reason for giving is some form of warm glow. The quantity warm-glow can be interpreted as a concern for the recipients of charity. Let there be many charities which can be ranked by the consumer. If each consumer has a uniquely preferred charity, then it follows that they will contribute only to that charity—since they are small relative to the economy, the marginal benefit of the recipients will not be affected by the contribution. Conversely, with value warm-glow, the concern is with the sacrifice made. This implies that the consumer is indifferent as to how the money is divided between charities—and hence to how many charities they contribute to. In fact, a natural modification when there are many charities is that the warm glow is concave in donations so there is a strict preference for diversification. This line of reasoning provides support for the value warm-glow.

An alternative way to distinguish between the two is to look for differences in response to incentives. In most tax codes contributions to charities are deductible from income taxation. With warm glow, this gives rise to the budget constraint

$$M^h = \frac{q_x}{1-t}x^h + q_G g^h. \tag{56}$$

It can be seen from (49) that changes in the tax rate cause a substitution between the private good and contributions to the public good (as well as an income effect). For value warm-glow, it can be interpreted as the total sacrifice of private consumption that is relevant for the consumer. This is given by

$$\tilde{v}^h = [1-t]M^h - q_x x^h = [1-t]v^h. \tag{57}$$

Hence the implied budget constraint is

$$M^h = \left[\frac{1}{1-t}\right][q_x x^h + \tilde{v}^h], \tag{58}$$

so that a change in the tax rate causes no substitution between the choice variables. Data on contributions to charities could be used to test this prediction.

7. Conclusions

The paper has considered the combination of government and private financing of public goods under a range of assumptions. Although the precise outcome differs between these, taken as a whole they place much greater emphasis upon the value of private contributions than expected. This is not true in every case, but the only one in which purely government provision is optimal is the least empirically justifiable. Otherwise, optimality requires either completely private financing or a mix of the two. The motivation for this conclusion is that it is less distortionary particularly when consumers enjoy giving for the government to encourage private financing than it is to simultaneously crowd out private financing and raise the revenue to provide the good itself.

The range of tax instruments has been limited to the choice of consumer prices. Our justification for this is that the inefficiency of private provision arises from pricing signals and hence these are the taxes best suited to overcome this. The role of income taxes is rather limited in this context since income distribution is not of particular significance. It can have some effects but these are minor compared to the consequences of manipulating prices. Similarly, the extensions of the analysis that were considered did not significantly affect the results. Government inefficiency due to agency problems and administrative costs gives even more emphasis to private provision.

References

Andreoni, J. (1990) 'Impure altruism and donations to public goods: a theory of warm-glow giving', *Economic Journal* 200: 464–77.

Atkinson, A. B., and Stern, N. H. (1974) 'Pigou, taxation and public goods', *Review of Economic Studies* 41: 119–28.

Bernheim, B. D. (1986) 'On the voluntary and involuntary provision of public goods', *American Economic Review* 76: 789–93.

Boadway, R., and Keen, M. (1993) 'Public goods, self-selection and optimal income taxation', *International Economic Review* 34: 463–78.

—— Pestieau, P., and Wildasin, D. (1989) 'Tax-transfer policies and the voluntary provision of public goods', *Journal of Public Economics* 39: 157–76.

Bohm, P. (1984) 'Revealing demand for an actual public good', *Journal of Public Economics* 24: 135–51.

Chamberlin, J. (1974) 'Provision of collective goods as a function of group size', *American Political Science Review* 68: 707–16.

Cornes, R. C., and Sandler, T. (1996) *The Theory of Externalities, Public Goods and Club Goods* (Cambridge: Cambridge University Press).

Diamond, P. A., and Mirrlees, J. A. (1971) 'Optimal taxation and public production 1: Production efficiency and 2: Tax rules', *American Economic Review* 61: 8–27 and 261–78.

Itaya, J., de Meza, D., and Myles, G. D. (1996) 'Optimal taxation and the private provision of public goods', *Discussion Paper 96/18*, University of Exeter.

—— —— —— (1997) 'In praise of inequality: public good provision and income distribution', *Economics Letters* **57**: 289–96.

—— —— —— (1999) 'The private provision of public goods', in S. B. Dahiya (ed.), *The Current State of Economic Science* (Rohtak: Spellbound Publications).

McGuire, M. (1974) 'Group homogeneity and aggregate provision of a pure public good under Cournot behavior', *Public Choice* 18: 107–26.

Mirrlees, J. A. (1971) 'An exploration in the theory of optimum income taxation', *Review of Economic Studies* 38: 175–208.

—— (1986) 'The Theory of Optimal Taxation', in K. J. Arrow and M. D. Intrilligator (eds.), *Handbook of Mathematical Economics* (Amsterdam: North-Holland).

Myles, G. D. (1995) *Public Economics* (Cambridge University Press: Cambridge).

—— (2000) 'Wasteful government, tax evasion, and the provision of public goods', *European Journal of Political Economy* 16: 51–74.

Samuelson, P. A. (1954) 'The pure theory of public expenditure', *Review of Economics and Statistics* 36: 387–89.

Part IV

TAX THEORY

9 An Optimal Earnings Schedule

SUDHIR ANAND

It is easy to analyse the supply of a single man's work to different opportunities of converting leisure into income that are available to him. It is much harder to establish the response of total labour to alternative earning opportunities when different members of the workforce have differing preferences as between income and leisure. That such differences in preferences should exist is entirely plausible. Many surveys (e.g. Shimmin and de la Mare 1964; Flanders 1964: Appendix E) have reported that establishments which allow regular overtime working as part of their normal work-schedules evoke wide differences in response among men in the same occupation. Some authors (see Shimmin and de la Mare) have attributed these differences to differences in family responsibility as measured by the income-tax code number. Others have correlated additional individual and social characteristics, such as age and the availability of leisure activities outside the home. The purpose here is not to examine why some groups of people prefer to work more overtime than others, but rather the consequences which follow from this fact. I will assume that the diversity of preferences can be captured by means of a single parameter.

In Shimmin and de la Mare (1964), the basic working week was fixed at forty-four hours. The first ten hours of overtime were paid at one and a quarter times the basic rate, the next six hours at one and a half times, and all subsequent hours at twice the basic rate. However, overtime rates do not always carry a premium over the basic rate. It is not uncommon to observe instances of regressive overtime structures which are effective in inducing overtime.

The traditional model of labour supply assumes the same hourly rate for all hours worked, and allows the individual to work as long as he wishes at this rate. In labour-income space this earning opportunity can be represented by a straight line (whose slope is the uniform rate) through the origin. I allow variable rates for different hours of work,[1] and call the (not necessarily continuous) curve relating wage payments to the amount of labour provided, the wage or earnings schedule.

Utility-maximizing behaviour on the part of workers enables one to predict the response of labour to various earnings schedules. When there is a single worker, it is a straightforward exercise in (two-dimensional) indifference curve geometry to find

This paper was written in June 1970 while I was a graduate student under the supervision of Jim Mirrlees, and was presented at the Second World Congress of the Econometric Society in Cambridge, England in September 1970. It is reproduced here in its original 1970 version without any changes. The paper draws on Mirrlees' path-breaking work on optimum income taxation, and I am greatly indebted to him for discussions at the time of its writing.

[1] If a given quantity of labour can be obtained using a straight wage rate, it can be obtained at lower cost through a variable wage curve. However, some requirements of aggregate labour which cannot be met by the straight wage scheme, can by the flexible scheme. This happens especially when the conventional labour supply curves are backward-bending.

how hours supplied respond to various wage schedules. One can easily see why a person might be willing to work at an overtime rate below the primary rate. Equally, the behaviour referred to in Shimmin and de la Mare (1964) can be understood by imposing particular schedules. What is not so clear is how the earnings schedule itself is to be determined.

This leads naturally to consideration of the demand side of the labour market, and some behavioural rule by the demanders of labour. In fact I shall assume there is only one employer—a monopsonist—who is keen to maximize profits. Facing him is a static labour force,[2] waiting to be employed by him. Either there aren't any other firms which demand labour of this special skill, or, if there are, they do not find it profitable to attract any of this particular labour. The firms have to cope with barriers of geographical immobility, some retraining costs, even inherent psychological immobility on the part of workers—and a host of other factors which lie outside the scope of this paper.

Restricting attention to the monopsonist, what curve should he offer a population of identical worker-consumers in order to induce total labour L at minimum cost? The representative worker is supposed to have a map of convex indifference curves between work and income. Clearly the employer will offer as the wage curve that indifference curve of the worker which goes through the origin. A correspondence is defined whereby the worker lists these alternative bundles, offering to take any one of them. The particular bundle selected by the employer is the one that maximizes profits.[3]

I have pointed out this extreme case where everyone has identical preferences. It is more interesting to explore the properties of the earnings schedule in general where people have different preferences.[4] The next section is devoted to such a search.

The optimal earnings schedule turns out to be convex in some cases, but in others it has concave regions.[5] The theme of this paper is that when preferences are distributed very skewly in the population, e.g. a large number of people valuing income relatively highly to leisure, and a small number with the opposite preferences, then the possibility of a non-convex earnings schedule emerges. I illustrate this theme with reference to the following model.

The Model

There is a single employer who faces a given population of workers with known preferences. The preference ordering of each worker can be represented by a quasi-

---

[2] In one example I permitted migration of a special sort. Workers have utility thresholds below which they are not prepared to work. This specification only affected the level of the monopsonist's optimal earnings schedule, not its shape.

[3] Actually, the earnings schedule here is a single point. The indifference curve represents all the conceivable earning opportunities the employer might offer in the face of different production conditions.

[4] I have allowed perfect discrimination only in the payment for different hours of work. If it is also possible to discriminate perfectly between men, then each man will be offered his indifference curve through the origin. And the employer will select different amounts of work from different men, so that the marginal cost of work from each man is the same.

[5] Curiously, in the cases I have examined so far, the earnings schedule is always convex for large enough amounts of work.

concave utility function $u(y, \ell)$ defined over income $y \geqslant 0$, and work ℓ, $0 \leqslant \ell \leqslant 1$. The utility function is the same for every worker except for a single parameter $t \geqslant 0$, which indicates the weight he attaches to leisure in its contribution to his utility. t is distributed in the population according to the density function $f(t)$.

Each man maximizes utility subject to his budget constraint, which is the available earnings schedule $g(\ell)$ defined for $0 \leqslant \ell \leqslant 1$. $g(\ell)$ is a curve relating wage payments (in units of output) to the amount of work performed. So t-man offers that amount $\ell(t)$ of work given as the solution to the equation

$$u_1 g'(\ell(t)) + u_2 = 0$$
$$\text{provided } 0 < \ell(t) < 1.$$
(1)

At the same time the employer is to choose $g(\ell)$ in such a way as to maximize profits. Labour is the only variable factor of production, and output is directly proportional to aggregate labour input. (Note: This is an assumption of convenience only; the analysis to come remains equally tractable with any production function.)

Units of output are measured so that

$$\text{Output} = \int \ell(t) f(t) \, dt.$$

The wage bill $= \int g(\ell(t)) f(t) \, dt$, and formally the firm is concerned to

$$\underset{g(\cdot)}{\text{Maximize}} \int [\ell(t) - g(\ell(t))] f(t) \, dt$$

subject to (1) for each t.

Equations for the general solution reveal little regarding the shape of the optimal $g(\ell)$. The properties of the optimal $g(\ell)$ will be seen to depend closely on the specific utility function, and the distribution of tastes within the population.

Rather than list several cases in which explicit solutions have been found, I shall concentrate on a single one in detail—so that the kind of solution technique used is clarified. This case also emphasizes (i) the sensitivity of the optimal earnings schedule to the distribution of tastes, and (ii) the tricky problem of choosing the endpoints of the schedule.

I take $u(y, \ell) = y^{\frac{1}{2}} + t(1 - \ell)^{\frac{1}{2}}$.

Define new variables $Y = y^{\frac{1}{2}}$
$$M = (1 - \ell)^{\frac{1}{2}}.$$

So in Y-M space, t-man's indifference curves are simply the set of parallel straight lines with slope $-t$, with ones further out representing higher utility. t may be called a 'laziness' parameter, because higher t always implies more (actually, no less) leisure chosen, whatever the earnings schedule.

As candidate for the optimum, the firm tries a $g(\ell)$, which translates into $Y = Y(M)$. $Y(\cdot)$ must be a decreasing and concave function of M, for nobody will choose points on any increasing or non-concave portions. t-man chooses the utility maximizing combination $(M(t), Y(t))$, where $M(t)$ is determined[6] as the root of the equation $Y'(M) = -t$ $(0 < M < 1)$. There is no reason at all to assume that $Y(M)$ should be differentiable, indeed even continuous. See Mirrlees (1969) for the treatment of a similar problem where no differentiability assumptions are made. I shall hope that the optimal $Y(M)$ turns out to be twice continuously differentiable.

The individual utility maximization condition can be written as

$$\dot{Y} = -t\dot{M} \tag{1a}$$

where dots denote differentiation with respect to t. In terms of these new variables, the problem is to

$$\text{Maximize}_{Y(M)} \int [1 - M(t)^2 - Y(t)^2] f(t) dt$$

subject to (1a) for each t.

In this profits integral it is certainly more convenient to think of variations in $M(t)$ (and associated variations in $Y(t)$ given from (1a)), rather than variations in $Y(M)$, as the usual calculus of variations argument does. For this to be a justifiable procedure it needs to be shown that every variation in $M(t)$ can be got from, and leads to, a variation in $Y(M)$. Given the differentiability and (strict) concavity assumptions on $Y(M)$, it is not difficult to demonstrate this proposition.

Suppose $(M(t), Y(t))$ is optimum. Introduce a Lagrange multiplier function $\lambda(t)$ to take account of the constraint (1a) for each t. One would expect the existence of such a $\lambda(t)$ from the concavity of the integrand and constraints. Then the variation of the Lagrangian

$$\int ([1 - M(t)^2 - Y(t)^2] f(t) + \lambda(t)[\dot{Y} + t\dot{M}]) dt$$

must be zero (to first order) for (first-order) variations in $M(t)$ and $Y(t)$, i.e. Euler equations for M and Y must hold. They are

$$\frac{d}{dt}\lambda(t) = -2Y(t)f(t), \text{ and } \frac{d}{dt}[t\lambda(t)] = -2M(t)f(t),$$

implying

$$\frac{d}{dt}[(M(t) - tY(t))f(t)] = Y(t)f(t). \tag{2}$$

This equation together with (1a) are a pair of linear first-order differential equations which can be solved for $M(t)$ and $Y(t)$ once $f(t)$ is specified. Hence the optimal $Y(M)$

---

[6] $M(t)$ is defined uniquely only if $Y'(M)$ is invertible, in other words, if $Y(M)$ is strictly concave. If not, there can at most be a countable number of linear segments, in which case the profits integral should be interpreted in the Lebesgue sense. I assume that no more than a finite number of linear segments occur.

is given in parametric form $(M(t), Y(t))$. I examine two functional forms for $f(t)$ where these differential equations can be solved explicitly.

(i) $f(t) = 1$: $Y(t) = \dfrac{A}{1 + t^2}$, $M(t) = A\left[\arctan t + \dfrac{t}{1 + t^2}\right] - B$,

$\therefore Y = Y(M, A, B)$.

(ii) $f(t) = \dfrac{1}{t^2}$: $Y(t) = \beta + \alpha\left[\dfrac{t}{1 + t^2} - \arctan t\right]$, $M(t) = \dfrac{\alpha t^2}{1 + t^2}$,

$\therefore Y = Y(M, \alpha, \beta)$.

A, B, α, and β are non-negative constants. The constants are to be selected (and the boundary points determined) so as to yield maximum profits. In the meanwhile, one wants to inspect the sign of $g''(\ell)$. In case (i): $g''(\ell) > 0$ for all $t > 0$, so that the optimal earnings schedule is unambiguously convex.

In case (ii): if $\beta \leqslant \alpha\pi/2$, then $g''(\ell) > 0$ all t;

if $\beta > \alpha\pi/2$, then $g''(\ell) > 0$ for $t < t_0$

and $g''(\ell) < 0$ for $t > t_0$,

where t_0 is defined by $\dfrac{t_0}{t_0^2 - 1} + \arctan t_0 = \dfrac{\beta}{\alpha}$.

In this case there is the distinct possibility of a non-convex earnings schedule, whose actual occurrence will depend on how the constants relate to each other. (Notice the possibility has emerged as a result of the distribution changing from uniform to skew.)

Consider now the manner in which the constants are to be determined. Take case (ii), and suppose it is known that $f(t) = 0$ outside the interval $[a, b]$. The extremals are a two-parameter family, each member having slope $-a$ at one end, and $-b$ at the other. The different ones can be got from each other by stretching $(M, Y) \rightarrow (\mu M, \mu Y)$ and/or by vertical subtraction/addition. Starting from a high extremal, profits are increased by pulling it down vertically (paying each man less for the same work), until b-man is indifferent between sitting tangentially at the edge and sliding off to idle at $M = 1$. Any further such (or shrinking in) move could affect profits either way. Some people's contribution is lost altogether, while the remainder are exploited more intensively. The jumping-off behaviour from the right endpoint suggests a more general formulation which allows a cluster of t-people at this endpoint. Let the offer of $Y(M)$ be cut off at a point where its slope is t_1, and suppose that people with tastes ranging from t_1 to $t_2 = \dfrac{Y(t_1)}{1 - M(t_1)}$ are bunched at this point (see Figure 9.1).

Heuristic arguments help no more. The profits expression

$$\int_a^{t_1} [1 - M(t)^2 - Y(t)^2]\frac{1}{t^2}\,dt + \int_{t_1}^{t_2} [1 - M(t_1)^2 - Y(t_1)^2]\frac{1}{t^2}\,dt$$

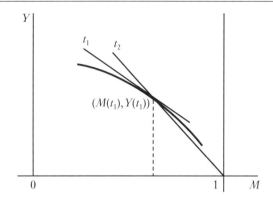

FIG. 9.1.

must be maximized with respect to the three free variables α, β, t_1. I shall not bother to write out the ugly first-order equations which give the best α, β, t_1, because they are not immediately enlightening on the question of how α and β stand in relation to each other. The configuration of the constants can go either way, depending on the population data a and b.

Conclusions

1. The model provides a technique (for other utility functions, slight variations of this technique are necessary) to write down the equations which an optimal earnings schedule must satisfy. These may or may not be soluble explicitly, but can be computed and graphed numerically.

2. Perhaps it explains in some degree the 'eight-hour day'! It shows why it may not pay the employer to have people working less than a certain minimum number of hours. With a definite cut-off in the schedule, many people will work at this minimum length of working day.

3. It points out that the optimal earnings schedule may admit situations where the marginal wage rate is lower than the average wage rate.

References

Flanders, A. (1964) *The Fawley Productivity Agreements.* (London: Faber & Faber.)

Mirrlees, J. A. (1969) 'An Exploration in the Theory of Optimum Income Taxation: Part I', Unpublished Paper (Nuffield College, Oxford).

Shimmin, S., and de la Mare, G. (1964) 'Individual Differences in Overtime Working', *Occupational Psychology*.

10 Non-linear Utility Pricing and Targeting the Poor

RAVI KANBUR, RITVA TARKIAINEN, AND MATTI TUOMALA

1. Introduction

With the accelerated move towards privatization of public utilities in developing countries, some old issues on public-utility pricing and the poor have re-emerged. Among the arguments for privatization are (a) increasing the efficiency of management by insulating it from political pressures on day operations (e.g. hiring and firing decisions) and (b) greater economic efficiency by linking pricing to costs through the profit motive. And yet there are sufficient concerns about the possible impact of untrammelled market forces in these sensitive sectors, particularly about the distributional impact of pricing decisions, that privatization under the framework of regulation and oversight is an attractive alternative to completely free markets. The sorts of regulations that might be considered are to do with broad guidelines on pricing structure, and on cross-subsidization across groups.

These concerns are not of course new. Pricing structures designed to reflect quantity used and hence underlying income or wealth of the consumer are prevalent in both developed and developing countries. In developed countries, there has been much discussion of 'lifeline rates' and other devices to give the poor lower prices for electricity (Diamopoulos 1981). In developing countries, increasing block tariffs, i.e. 'a price structure in which a commodity is priced up to a specified volume of use (block), then at a higher or several increasingly higher rates for additional blocks used', are common for water tariffs (Whittington 1992) as well as for other utilities. At the same time, differential price structures for rural versus urban areas are also found, justified on grounds of targeting predominantly poor populations.

Of course, there is a large literature on the shape of pricing schedules of regulated utilities. A recent review and exposition of non-linear pricing structures is available in Wilson (1993), which updates and extends the earlier synthesis by Brown and Sibley (1986). Earlier well-known papers include those by Meyer (1975), Berg and Roth (1976), Roberts (1979), Diamopoulos (1981), and Maskin and Riley (1984). This entire literature follows a common framework where there is a distribution of consumers differentiated by incomes or tastes who make choices on consuming the utility's output, and the utility then chooses the *single* pricing schedule to maximize some objective function —with differing weights given to distributional concerns in different studies. The literature shows that this single pricing schedule can have a range of characteristics, depending on the distribution of income, consumer tastes, and distributional concerns.

So much for single schedule analysis. And yet, in practice, it appears that there are different pricing schedules for different categories of consumers. And cross-subsidization across groups—residential versus commercial, rural versus urban, government versus private, etc.—has been a staple discussion item in the policy arena. The object of this paper is to consider the twin issues of pricing structure and cross-subsidization *jointly*, in a framework where the distributional concerns are made explicit. It will be seen that this joint analysis highlights a number of features and raises a number of concerns not present in the conventional analysis. The optimal pricing structure within a group will be seen to be intimately connected to the structure of cross-subsidization across groups, and to display surprising features.

The plan of this paper is as follows. Section 2 lays out the basic theoretical model of the optimal non-linear pricing with two distinguishable groups, and highlights the main qualitative features of the optimal pricing structures. It turns out that qualitative analysis cannot get us very far in gaining insights into the features of the optimal schedules in each of the two groups. Section 3 moves to a discussion of numerical solutions, and sets out the main results of the paper. Section 4 concludes the paper.

2. The Model

The model developed here is an adaptation of the standard model of non-linear pricing (see Wilson 1993).[1] We assume that the consumers can be divided by the utility into two mutually exclusive and exhaustive groups and that consumers are unable to switch between these groups. The groups are indexed 1 and 2. These can be thought of as rural/urban, young/old, resident/commercial, etc. Within groups consumers differ with respect to their income, denoted by real number y. This is distributed with continuous density function f_i with $f_i(y) \geq 0$, $i = 1, 2$, on closed interval $[y_0, y_t]$ where y_0 and y_t denote the lower and upper limits to the income distribution. Without loss of generality we assume that the mean of group 1's income exceeds the mean of group 2's income—we refer to group 1 as the richer group and group 2 as the poorer or 'needy' group, even though there are income overlaps between the two groups. The population share of group 1 is Θ, and that of group 2 $1 - \Theta$.

We assume that there are two goods in the economy; a composite good, x, and the good, q (subject to non-linear pricing) supplied by the utility. We assume that preferences are identical within groups but differ between them. Thus consumers who belong to group i, have identical concave utility function

$$u_i = u_i(x_i, q_i), \tag{1}$$

where $u_i \in C^2$, $\partial u_i / \partial q_i > 0$, $\partial u_i / \partial x_i > 0 \; \forall \; q_i, x_i \geq 0$. We will further assume that q is a normal good. It is typical in non-linear pricing literature to exclude income effects a priori. The usual motivation for ignoring income effects when constructing tariffs for services offered to household consumers is that their income elasticies are small and/or their residual income, x, is large in relation to their expenditures on the non-

---

[1] Much of the work in non-linear pricing literature uses techniques originally developed by Mirrlees (1971 and 1976) and Roberts (1979).

linearly priced good or services, q. These assumptions cannot always be justified and it will become clear that the properties of an optimal pricing schedule may crucially depend on income effects.

The pricing schedule is given by functions $R_i(q_i)$. If a consumer wishes to purchase an amount q_i, then he or she must pay an amount R_i to the utility. We assume that R_i is monotone and differentiable. The rate of change of total payment with respect to a change in quantity purhased $p_i(q) = dR_i(q)/dq$ is called marginal price.

A consumer with income y chooses q so as to maximize (1) subject to

$$x_i + R_i(q_i) = y. \tag{2}$$

In mathematical form this becomes the problem (P)

$$\max_{q_i, x_i} u_i(x_i, q_i) \tag{3}$$

subject to

$$q_i \geqslant 0$$
$$x_i + R_i(q_i) = y.$$
$$u_i(x_i, q_i) \geqslant u_i(y, 0).$$

The last constraint says that consumers have the option of leaving the market altogether and pay nothing to the public utility. Thus a participation constraint is required.

We assume that the utility (or the utility regulator) applies separate non-linear pricing schedules to groups 1 and 2. The objective can be described by the utilitarian social welfare function

$$W = \int_{y_0}^{y_t} [\Theta u_1 f_1(y) + (1 - \Theta)u_2 f_2(y)]dy. \tag{4}$$

The utility determines optimal schedules $R_i(q_i)$, $i = 1, 2$, by maximizing (4) subject to profit constraint

$$\int_{y_0}^{y_t} [\Theta \pi_1(q_1(y))f_1(y) + (1 - \Theta)\pi_2(q_2(y))f_2(y)]dy \geqslant 0, \tag{5}$$

where $\pi_1(\cdot) = R_1(q_1(y)) - cq_1(y) - G$, $\pi_2(\cdot) = R_2(q_2(y)) - cq_2(y) - G$, c is marginal cost (constant) and G is fixed cost. There is an additional constraint, that given the pricing schedule R_i, $i = 1, 2$, each consumer determines his or her consumption by solving problem (P).

Next we formulate the non-linear pricing problem of the public utility or government programme as an optimal control problem subject to state and control constraints. Let us define the utility of a y-consumer, when $q_i(y)$ and $x_i(y)$ are optimally chosen, as the maximum value function

$$v_i(y) = \max_{q_i, x_i}\{u_i(x_i, q_i) : x_i + R_i(q_i) - y = 0\}$$
$$= U_i(q_i(y), R_i(y), y). \tag{6}$$

By differentiating (6) with respect to y we obtain

$$dv_i/dy = [\partial U_i/\partial q_i][dq_i/dy] + [\partial U_i/\partial R_i][dR_i/dy] + \partial U_i/\partial y. \tag{7}$$

Making use of the condition, implied by consumer's utility maximization

$$[\partial U_i/\partial q_i][dq_i/dy] + [\partial U_i/\partial R_i][dR_i/dy] = 0 \tag{8}$$

we have

$$dv_i/dy = \partial u_i/\partial x_i = \partial U_i/\partial y. \tag{9}$$

This is also called a self-selection condition or incentive compatability condition.

As q is a normal good it is obvious that all consumers cannot be at a global maximum unless the following constraint holds

$$dq_i/dy \geqslant 0 \text{ for all } y \in [y_0, y_t]. \tag{10}$$

Defining the consumer's marginal rate of substitution between product and income

$$w_i(q(y), R(y), y) = -[\partial U_i/\partial q_i]/g_i(q, R, y), \tag{11}$$

where $g = -U_R$ is type y's marginal utility of income, and preferences are taken to satisfy the so called Mirrlees–Spence restriction that

$$\partial w_i/\partial y > 0. \tag{12}$$

This means that increasing y increases the marginal willingness to pay for the utility output. In fact (12) is a sufficient assumption to ensure that (6) is equivalent to (9) and q increase with income y (See Mirrlees 1976 and Roberts 1979). We assume that condition (12) holds so that we can substitute the individuals utility maximization problem by weaker condition (9).

$v_i(y)$ is continuous and strictly increasing in x_i. Thus (7) can be inverted so that $x_i(y) = h_i(v_i(y), q_i(y), y)$. Furthermore, we may eliminate $R_i(q)$ by the condition (2). Now $q_i(y)$ and $v_i(y)$ can be treated as state functions and $r_i(y) = dq_i/dy$ for all $y \in [y_0, y_t]$ as a control variable. Thus we first calculate an optimal allocation and then subsequently derive by condition (2) the marginal price schedule that implements this allocation. Now we can formulate the non-linear pricing problem as an optimal control problem as follows.

The non-linear pricing problem (Q)

$$\text{Max}_{q_i, v_i} W = \int_{y_0}^{y_t} [\Theta v_1(y)f_1(y) + (1 - \Theta)v_2(y)f_2(y)]dy \tag{13}$$

subject to state equations

$$
\begin{aligned}
&dv_1/dy = (\partial U_1/\partial y) \quad \forall y \in [y_0, y_t], \\
&dv_2/dy = (\partial U_2/\partial y) \quad \forall y \in [y_0, y_t], \\
&dq_i/dy = r_i(y), \, i = 1, 2, \forall y \in [y_0, y_t],
\end{aligned}
\tag{14}
$$

and the constraints

$$\int_{y_0}^{y_t} \{\Theta[y - h_1(v_1, q_1) - cq_1(y) - G]f_1(y)$$

$$+ (1 - \Theta)[y - h_2(v_2, q_2) - cq_2(y) - G]f_2(y)\} \mathrm{d}y \geqslant 0. \qquad (15)$$

$$v_i \geqslant u(y, 0), r_i(y) \geqslant 0.$$

Furthermore in numerical solution we use the constraints that $q_1(y) \geqslant 0$ and $q_2(y) \geqslant 0 \ \forall y \in [y_0, y_t]$.

It is self-evident that if $v_1 = v_2$ and $f_1 = f_2$, the optimal policy yields $R(q) = R_1(q) = R_2(q)$. Thus we only have an interesting situation when either preferences or distributions or both are different in different groups. It is also obvious that in general additional instruments can only improve the level of social welfare, since it is always open to the utility to set a common schedule.

Differentiating the Lagrangian of the problem (Q) with respect to $q_i(\cdot)$ and $v_i(\cdot)$ gives the first-order conditions. When consumers with different incomes are not bunched together these conditions imply a pattern of marginal prices satisfying

$$p_1(q_1) = c - \mu_1(y)[g_1(\partial w_1/\partial y)/\Theta \lambda f_1(y)]$$

$$p_2(q_2) = c - \mu_2(y)[g_2(\partial w_2/\partial y)/(1 - \Theta)\lambda f_2(y)], \qquad (16)$$

where λ is the multiplier on the profit constraint and

$$\mu_1(y) = \int_{y_0}^{y} \Theta[(\lambda/g_1) - W'][\exp - \int_{m}^{y} (\partial U_y/\partial R_1)/g_1]f_1 \mathrm{d}m$$

$$\mu_2(y) = \int_{y_0}^{y} (1 - \Theta)[(\lambda/g_2) - W'][\exp - \int_{m}^{y} (\partial U_y/\partial R_2)/g_2]f_2 \mathrm{d}m \qquad (17)$$

are the multipliers on the incentive compatibility condition from the two groups. In (16) we have used the fact that $\partial[U_y]/\partial q = gw_y$. (17) satisfies the transversality conditions

$$\mu_i(y_0) = \mu_i(y_t) = 0. \qquad (18)$$

Using (16) and (17) it can be proved that

$$\mu_i(n) < 0 \ \forall y \in [y_0, y_t]. \qquad (19)$$

We can see from (16) that the optimum distortion between marginal price and marginal cost in different groups depends upon several factors, μ, g, w_y, λ, and f. A structure of marginal prices is based on three components. The first is the marginal cost. The second term arises purely from the incentive nature of the problem. We can interpret $\mu(y)$ as measure of the social value of providing a transfer to consumers with an income above y. λ is the social value of funds to the utility.

On the basis of equations (16) to (19) we can find some general qualitative properties of schedules. It turns out that the qualitative properties of $R_i(q)$ are the same as in the single schedule model. We have the following list of properties:

(P1) $p_i \geqslant c$ for all q,
(P2) $p_i = c$ at the upper end-point of the schedule,
(P3) $p_i = c$ at the bottom end if there is no bunching at the lowest income,[2]
(P4) p_i is strictly greater than c for all q_i such that $q_i(y_0) < q_i < q_i(y_f)$.

The above well-known results provide us with a benchmark for group-specific pricing schedules but do not tell us anything in detail about the shapes of these schedules and how they depend upon parameters such as group mean incomes or group inequalities. In order to address the issues the literature and policy-makers are grappling with, we have to move to numerical simulations.

3. Numerical Simulations[3]

We can provide better understanding of the form of optimal schedules through numerical simulations. The calculations were carried out for the following utility functions

$$u_i(x_i, q_i) = (1 - \alpha_i)\ln(x_i + \epsilon) + \alpha_i \ln(q_i + \epsilon)   i = 1, 2 \tag{20}$$

$$u_i(x_i, q_i) = -[(1 - \alpha_i)/(x_i + \epsilon)] - [\alpha_i/(q_i + \epsilon)]   i = 1, 2, \tag{20'}$$

where α is the weight on q and $(1 - \alpha)$ the weight on x. ϵ is a small positive constant to ensure that (20) is well defined for all $q_i, x_i \geqslant 0$. To focus on income distribution, we assume that preferences are identical across the two groups. Incomes in different groups are taken to be distributed according to a log-normal distribution (μ_i, σ_i). The objective function of utility is the concave transformation of each consumer's utility in different groups, reflecting society's distributional preferences:

$$W = -(1/\beta)e^{-\beta v}, \tag{23}$$

where β expresses the degree of inequality aversion. The results are given for two different forms of the objective function: $\beta = 0$ (in this case we define $W = v$) corresponding to the classical utilitarian case and $\beta = 5$. The average (marginal) cost of production $c = 1$ and fixed cost is zero.

Figure 10.1 presents our base run (we set ϵ at 0.005) throughout the paper. The degree of inequality aversion β is set at zero and the expenditure share of the utility

---

[2] No consumers are excluded from the market. If there is bunching, then the consumers on the lower end do not pay marginal prices which are equal to marginal costs.
[3] The non-linear problem was solved by the FORTRAN program MISER3. This program has been developed to solve a general class of optimal control problem with constraints. The constraints are allowed to be of equality as well as inequality type. The program is based on the concept of the control parametrization technique: to transform an optimal control problem to a mathematical programming problem. The detailed usage of MISER3 is described in the User's guide (see Jennings, Fisher, Teo, and Goh 1990).

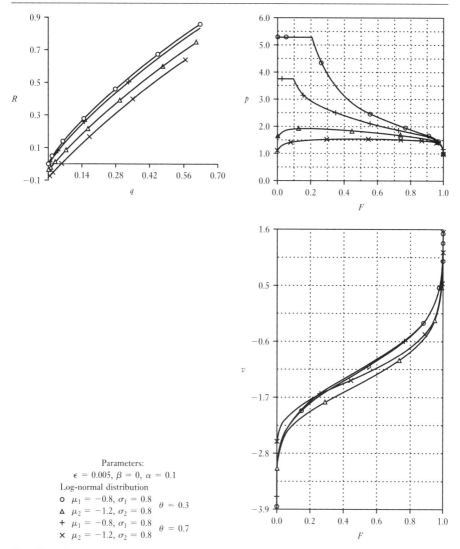

Parameters:
$\epsilon = 0.005, \beta = 0, \alpha = 0.1$
Log-normal distribution
o $\mu_1 = -0.8, \sigma_1 = 0.8$
△ $\mu_2 = -1.2, \sigma_2 = 0.8$ $\theta = 0.3$
+ $\mu_1 = -0.8, \sigma_1 = 0.8$
× $\mu_2 = -1.2, \sigma_2 = 0.8$ $\theta = 0.7$

FIG. 10.1. *Base run*

commodity, α, is set at 10 per cent. We consider two specifications of population shares, $\Theta = 0.3$ and $\Theta = 0.7$, which capture 'relatively large' and 'relatively small' numbers of the poorer group, respectively.

With $\Theta = 0.3$, Figure 10.1 demonstrates a pattern of marginal prices which decline with income over most of the range (see north-east panel). Thus, optimally, we have a quantity discount rather than an increasing block rate structure. Moreover, notice that with $\Theta = 0.7$ the structure in group 2, the poorer group, is very different. Now for most of the income range the marginal price *increases* with income (and hence quantity premium), although of course at the very top it falls to marginal cost as by the qualitative result in (P2). Thus we see *both* quantity discount (for the rich group) and increasing block rates (for the poor group).

Why does such a pattern occur? One clue is to be found in the extent of cross-subsidization. With $\Theta = 0.7$ this runs to around 60 per cent of the expenditure by the poorer group on the utility's output. Viewing this as a single group, this is a large 'negative profit requirement'. This is analogous to the revenue requirement in models of optimal income taxation, and it is argued in Immonen *et al.* (1998) that when revenue requirement is negative and large, i.e. optimality calls for large subsidy on distributional grounds, the pattern of taxation will involve a large subsidy to the poorest in the poorer group, clawed back by increasing marginal tax rates in the same group. The analog in the case of utility pricing is an increasing marginal price structure over a large portion of the income range. When the proportion of the poorer group in the population is large, the subsidy per capita is smaller and hence this effect is less likely to arise.

Some sense of the analytical basis of the numerical results can be found from (16). From it we know that the variation of the optimal marginal prices with level of purchases is a complex matter. One consideration, however, is the variation of μ_i with y. It is straightforward to show that μ_i starts and finishes with a value of zero (the transversality condition) and has a U-shape in between. Intuitively, μ_i measures the social value of giving a direct poll subsidy to a consumer with an income above y. At low level of income μ tends to decrease with y and it reaches the minimum point at which $\lambda = W'g$. When the profit requirement is low, so is λ, the social value of funds to the utility. Then a reduction in the profit requirement can be expected to shift the point at which $\mu(y)$ has a minimum to the right. Thus $\mu(y)$ will continue to decrease further into the distribution than would otherwise be the case.

Figure 10.2 shows the effect of going to the CES utility function (20′)—this is essentially the case with elasticity of substitution between the utility-produced commodity and the other good set at half rather than 1. The population share of group 1 is set at 30 per cent once again. It is seen that there is once again an increasing block rate structure in marginal prices over much of income range—it is not till almost 80 per cent of the population is crossed that the marginal price starts declining back to marginal cost, as it must. There is also an increasing marginal price phase in the pricing structure for the richer group, but this is much smaller. Figures 10.3 and 10.4 conduct sensitivity exercises with respect to inequality aversion and the mean differences between the groups. The results are as expected. Increased inequality aversion raises the marginal price schedule for the better-off group and lowers it for the poorer group, as does greater inequality *between* the two groups.

Our calculations also allow us to gauge the relative gains from using two schedules versus being restricted to only one. The gain in the base case (Figure 10.5) with $\Theta = 0.3$, is 1.5 per cent—the gain of the poorer group is 5 per cent. In the CES-case (Figure 10.6) with $\Theta = 0.3$ the gain of the poorer group is 8 per cent. Although not shown in the figures as Θ increases to 0.7, the average gain reaches 4 per cent. With $\Theta = 0.7$ and $\alpha = 0.3$, the gain rises to 15 per cent.

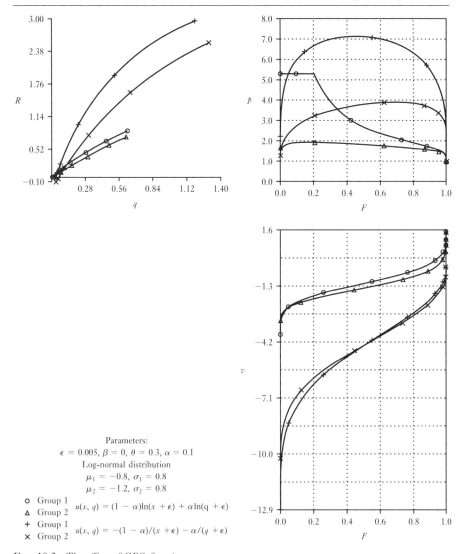

Parameters:
$\epsilon = 0.005, \beta = 0, \theta = 0.3, \alpha = 0.1$
Log-normal distribution
$\mu_1 = -0.8, \sigma_1 = 0.8$
$\mu_2 = -1.2, \sigma_2 = 0.8$

○ Group 1
△ Group 2 $u(x, q) = (1 - \alpha)\ln(x + \epsilon) + \alpha\ln(q + \epsilon)$
+ Group 1
× Group 2 $u(x, q) = -(1 - \alpha)/(x + \epsilon) - \alpha/(q + \epsilon)$

FIG. 10.2. *The effect of CES-function*

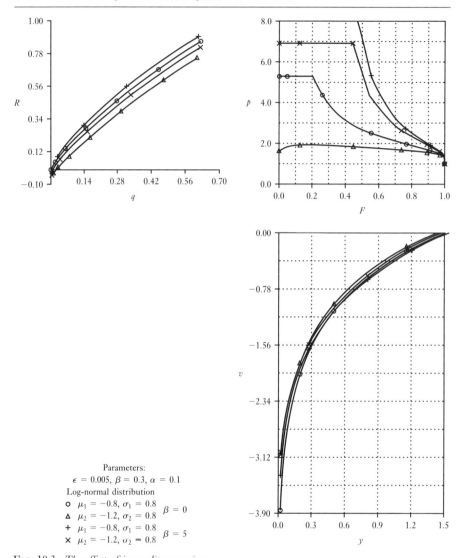

Parameters:
$\epsilon = 0.005$, $\beta = 0.3$, $\alpha = 0.1$
Log-normal distribution
o $\mu_1 = -0.8$, $\sigma_1 = 0.8$
Δ $\mu_2 = -1.2$, $\sigma_2 = 0.8$ $\beta = 0$
+ $\mu_1 = -0.8$, $\sigma_1 = 0.8$
× $\mu_2 = -1.2$, $\sigma_2 = 0.8$ $\beta = 5$

FIG. 10.3. *The effect of inequality aversion*

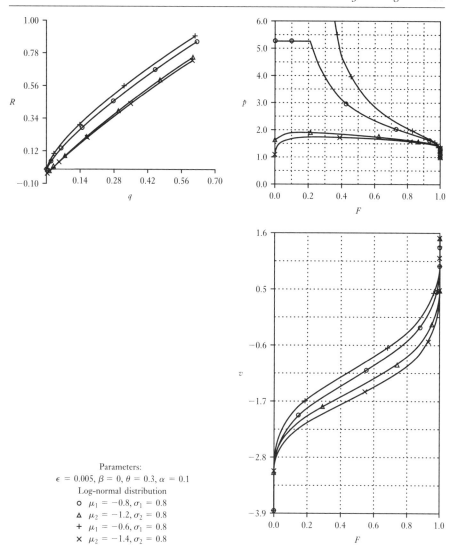

Parameters:
$\epsilon = 0.005, \beta = 0, \theta = 0.3, \alpha = 0.1$
Log-normal distribution
○ $\mu_1 = -0.8, \sigma_1 = 0.8$
△ $\mu_2 = -1.2, \sigma_2 = 0.8$
+ $\mu_1 = -0.6, \sigma_1 = 0.8$
× $\mu_2 = -1.4, \sigma_2 = 0.8$

FIG. 10.4. *The effect of mean differences*

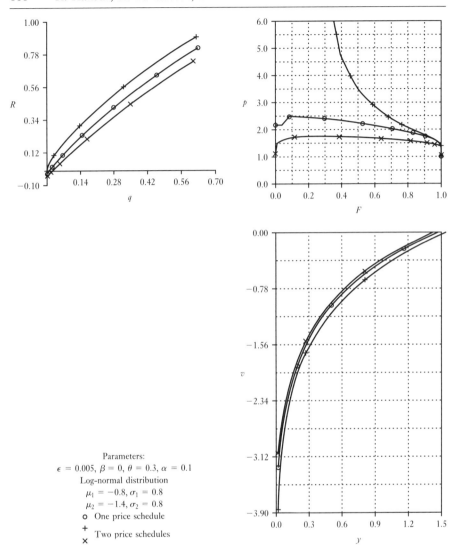

Parameters:
$\epsilon = 0.005$, $\beta = 0$, $\theta = 0.3$, $\alpha = 0.1$
Log-normal distribution
$\mu_1 = -0.8$, $\sigma_1 = 0.8$
$\mu_2 = -1.4$, $\sigma_2 = 0.8$
o   One price schedule
+
×   Two price schedules

FIG. 10.5. *One schedule vs. two schedules*

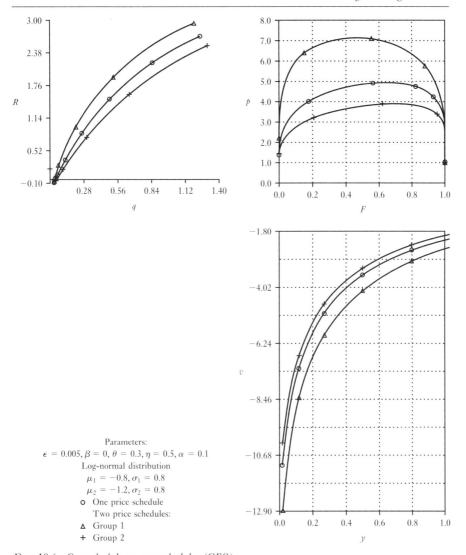

FIG. 10.6. *One schedule vs. two schedules (CES)*

4. Conclusions

We have developed a model in which the utility implements different price schedules on different groups of the population. These schemes reflect both consumers' special circumstances and incomes. The available analytical results are limited, and we have to employ numerical simulations. The simulations suggest that the gains from the appropriate use of group tariffs can be substantial. They also suggest an unexpected pattern of marginal prices, including combinations where the poorer group gets 'lifeline rates' while the richer group gets 'quantity-discount'. This indicates that the 'all-or-nothing' debate between these two structures may need to become much more nuanced in the future.

References

Berg, S., and W. Roth (1976) 'Some Remarks on Residential Electricity Consumption and Social Rate Restructuring', *Bell Journal* 7: 690–8.

Brown, S., and D. Sibley (1986) *The Theory of Public Utility Pricing*. Cambridge: Cambridge University Press.

Dimopoulos, D. (1981) 'Pricing Schemes for Regulated Enterprises and Their Welfare Implications in the Case of Electricity', *Bell Journal* 12: 185–200.

Immonen, R., R. Kanbur, M. Keen, and M. Tuomala (1998) 'Tagging or Taxing: The Optimal Use of Categorical and Income Information in Designing Tax/Transfer Schemes', *Economica* 65: 179–92.

Jennings, L. S., M. E. Fisher, K. L. Teo, and C. J. Goh (1990) MISER3, Optimal Control Software: The Theory and User Manual, EMCOSS Pty Ltd, Australia.

Maskin, E., and Riley, J. (1984) 'Monopoly Pricing with Incomplete Information, *Rand Journal of Economics* 15: 171–196.

Meyer, R. (1975) 'Monopoly Pricing and Capacity Choice under Uncertainty', *American Economic Review* 65: 326–37.

Mirrlees, J. (1971), 'An Exploration in the Theory of Optimum Income Taxation', *Review of Economic Studies* 38: 175–208.

—— (1976b), 'Optimal Tax Theory, A Synthesis', *Journal of Public Economics* 6: 327–58.

Roberts, K. (1979) 'Welfare Considerations of Nonlinear Pricing', *Economic Journal* 89: 66–83.

Whittington, D. (1992), 'Possible Adverse Effects of Increasing Water Tariffs in Developing Countries', *Economic Development and Cultural Changes* 41: 75–87.

Wilson, Robert (1993) *Nonlinear Pricing*. Oxford: Oxford University Press.

11   A Reconsideration of the Optimal Income Tax

KEVIN ROBERTS

1. Introduction

Following on from the seminal work of Mirrlees (1971), an extensive literature on the design of optimal non-linear tax schedules has developed. Whilst some of this literature (e.g. Sadka 1976) has dealt with easily understandable properties possessed by such schedules, a major drawback of the 'state-of-the-art' is that formulae used to characterize optimal schedules are defined in terms of functions that, whilst open to limited interpretation (Atkinson and Stiglitz 1979), lack the straightforwardness of direct supply elasticities, etc., that have become a commonplace of linear tax formulae.

There is no guarantee that the particular variational approach to optimization that has been adopted in the literature produces the most appealing tax formulae. Approaches that depend upon different perturbations of the tax schedule will produce formulae that can look very different. One purpose of this paper is to present an approach which is transparent and which produces tax formulae with all of the appeal of the neatest linear tax formulae (Diamond 1975; Dixit and Sandmo 1977). I consider a particular easily understandable perturbation in the tax schedule which, when broken down by a Taylor expansion, produces the optimal tax formula. As some seem to look upon non-linear tax theory as an unfathomable area, I hope that the present derivation will be found useful. Here, the aim is to present an approach to non-linear tax theory that is akin to the derivation of the Keynes–Ramsey rule in growth theory. The Appendix shows how the same formula can be derived using a control-theoretic approach using the dual approach to non-linear taxation introduced in Roberts (1979).

There has been little work looking at alternative derivations and formulae for non-linear tax schedules and the contrast with linear taxation is striking. Saez (1999) has recently looked at non-linear taxation using the idea of a perturbation of the tax schedule. The perturbation used and presentation of formulae is different to that in this paper though, as in the present analysis, he recognizes that one does not need to base formulae on the distribution in the population of some unobservable parameter like ability, as in the original Mirrlees work. Instead, the more natural distribution of income may be used. Saez derives numerical tax formulae using the actual income

This paper has had a long gestation period. The main body of this paper was circulated in October 1982 in a paper with the title 'A New Look at Optimal Income Taxation'. The appendix to this paper was contained in a paper with the title of the present paper which was circulated in August 1990. There are two principal changes made to this earlier work in the present paper. First, there is updating of references to other work. Second, an error in one of the main formulae in Section 4 is corrected and more detailed derivation of formulae is provided. The recognition of an error came to light during discussions with Emmanuel Saez and I am grateful for his interest in this work. This paper, and the papers on which it is based, incorporate suggestions from Tony Atkinson and Jim Mirrlees to whom I am grateful.

distribution derived from US tax returns and this offers a great improvement upon the numerical solutions in Mirrlees (1971) and Tuomala (1990). The other work that has investigated alternative formulae is that of Revesz (1989). He uses a calculus of variations approach based upon choosing marginal prices as in the dual approach of Roberts (1979). He derives a formula which incorporates an inverse elasticity rule as in this paper, but in other respects, it retains the structure of the original Mirrlees approach.

All previous derivations of tax formulae depend upon the seemingly innocuous assumption that the tax schedule is differentiable so that taxpayers with different preferences are not 'bunched' together at the same income level. However, the perturbation technique developed in the first part of this paper can be amended to examine the issue of whether optimal schedules are differentiable and it is shown that 'bunching' may be optimal. In earlier work (Ebert 1992; Lollivier and Rochet 1983), the existence of bunching is related to the failure of taxpayer first-order conditions to define a point of maximum utility along the tax schedule. In this paper, the differentiable tax schedules that are candidates for optimal tax schedules can possess the feature that individual taxpayers are maximizing their own utility. Our analysis uncovers some strange possibilities. For instance, it can be shown that when the income distribution is unbounded, the number of 'bunch' points may be infinite. This casts doubt on the technique of looking at limiting tax rates in such circumstances (Mirrlees 1971; Saez 1999). A second purpose of this paper is to expose these 'exotic' possibilities.

In the next section, the new formula is derived and interpreted. In Section 3, problems concerned with the marginal rate at the upper end of the tax schedule are considered. When the highest income is known at the outset, the famous (or infamous) result is obtained that the marginal tax rate should, on efficiency grounds, be zero. When this is not the case, the limiting rate may still be obtainable from a simple formula. The tax formula is derived under the assumption that the optimal tax schedule is twice differentiable. However, in Section 4, a perturbation technique is used to show that 'bunching' may be optimal. The analysis suggests that the structure of optimal tax schedules may be much more complicated than earlier analyses have suggested.

Section 5 considers how various perturbations can be put together to produce a global result like an overall increase in progressivity. When the technique is used to derive the optimal linear income tax, the 'simplified formula' of Dixit and Sandmo (1977) is reproduced. One can also obtain an insight into the structure of optimal polynomial tax schedules.

Concluding remarks are contained in Section 6.

2. The New Tax Formula

The net effect of an income taxation scheme is that post-tax income, which may be thought of as consumption,[1] is made some function of pre-tax income, the latter being

---

[1] A timeless world is being examined but consumption here could be thought of as that which is available for spending over some defined time-period, e.g. a year, and taxation is based upon yearly income. With rational agents, it would be more reasonable to relate the present value of lifetime consumption to the present value of income.

under an individual's control by varying effort, hours of work, etc. In Figure 11.1, the schedule $c(y)$ gives the consumption–income relationship implied by the *optimal* tax schedule $T^*(y)$, i.e.

$$c(y) = y - T^*(y). \tag{1}$$

For the moment, I will assume that c is twice-differentiable, which follows if and only if T^* is twice differentiable. In Section 4, the relevance of this assumption will be considered in more detail.

Different taxpayers will choose to obtain different pre-tax incomes. An advantage of the present approach is that the reasons for this difference do not need to be considered. But for simplicity, I will assume that those who choose to obtain the same income have identical tastes and are equally valued in society's objective function (a removal of this assumption does not seem to produce any unexpected changes in results). Again, in Figure 11.1, $C(y)$ shows the indifference curve of taxpayers who, under c, choose to obtain an income y^*. C is also assumed to be twice-differentiable. Taxpayers who choose to obtain different incomes will have different indifference curves that are tangential to the tax schedule. Thus, more generally, we can write $C(y, y^*)$ and this is assumed to be twice differentiable. Its properties will be investigated in more detail in Section 4.

As C is a curve of constant utility, it seems clear that its curvature is related to the compensated elasticity of supply of labour, ϵ. If w is the rate at which effort (pre-tax income) can be turned into consumption (post-tax income) then, holding utility constant, the taxpayer will choose a supply of effort y where

$$C'(y) = w \tag{2}$$

(where a prime denotes derivatives).

Now,

$$\epsilon = \frac{dy}{dw} \frac{w}{y} \tag{3}$$

so that, at y^*,

$$C''(y^*) = \frac{(1 - t)}{\epsilon y^*}, \tag{4}$$

where t is the marginal tax rate at y^*:

$$t = 1 - c'(y) = 1 - C'(y). \tag{5}$$

It may also be noted that second-order conditions of optimization give

$$C''(y^*) \geqslant c''(y^*), \tag{6}$$

which, as

$$c''(y^*) = -t', \tag{7}$$

becomes,

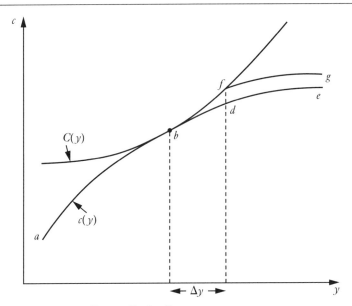

FIG. 11.1. *The Consumption/Income Trade-off*

$$\frac{(1-t)}{\epsilon y^*} \geq -t'. \tag{8}$$

This says that if the marginal tax rate falls too rapidly, taxpayers will not choose to be at that part of the income tax schedule.[2]

As c derives from the optimal tax schedule, any perturbation in the schedule must lower welfare. Some perturbations induce inefficiencies and to a first-order, cause a strict reduction in welfare. The trick that permits first-order conditions to be used to characterize optimality depends on finding perturbations that can be operated in a 'reverse' direction: if a perturbation reduces welfare to a first-order then the 'reverse' policy must raise welfare (assuming appropriate differentiability) and, as this is ruled out at the optimum, there can be no welfare change to a first-order from such perturbations.

Consider a perturbation which, in Figure 11.1, changes the consumption schedule from a, b, d, e to a, b, f, g. Up to b which occurs at some income y, the schedule is unaffected, after d the new schedule is a constant distance above the old one. The effect of such a change is that taxpayers between y and $y + \Delta y$ are encouraged to work harder, so that the disincentive effect of the tax is diminished, but this is achieved at the 'cost' of transferring resources to everybody with an income exceeding $y + \Delta y$.

To evaluate the effects of such a perturbation, it is necessary to define some more terms. First, the number of taxpayers involved is important. Let F be the cumulative

[2] In the original analyses of Mirrlees (1971) it is shown that there are no 'holes' where no taxpayers choose to locate when the schedule is optimally chosen and there is a desire for redistribution.

distribution of income *when the optimal income tax is in operation* and let f be the associated density function. Second, to evaluate the welfare effect of a change, it is necessary to posit society's trade-off between gains to some and losses to others. For this purpose, let $\alpha(y)$ be the social marginal utility of *consumption* at the optimum for taxpayers who choose to earn income y. Let λ be the marginal value of taxes to the government—this is the lowest social cost which can be incurred to raise revenue. If a pound is given to a taxpayer with income y, then the *net* gain to society, what Diamond (1975) has termed the social marginal utility of *income* $\beta(y)$, will depend upon the change in tax revenue from the taxpayer that occurs because of the labour supply response to an increase in lump-sum income. With a non-linear budget constraint, comparative static effects differ from those under linearity. If $y(w, m)$ is the pre-tax work income that somebody chooses to obtain when w is the rate at which pre-tax income can be converted into post-tax income and m is lump-sum income, then if the income y is chosen under $c(\cdot)$ it must satisfy[3]

$$y = y(c'(y), c(y) - yc'(y)). \tag{9}$$

The total effect on y of an increase in lump-sum income is given by

$$\frac{dy}{dm} = \frac{y_m}{1 - c'' \cdot (y_w - yy_m)}. \tag{10}$$

Invoking Slutksy's equation allows this to be reduced to

$$\frac{dy}{dm} = \frac{y_m}{1 + \frac{t'y\epsilon}{1-t}}. \tag{11}$$

Using λ to value the change in tax revenue, β is given by

$$\beta(y) = \alpha(y) + \frac{\lambda t y_m}{1 + \frac{t'y\epsilon}{1-t}}. \tag{12}$$

As leisure can be expected to be normal, y_m will be negative and, as the denominator of the second term in (12) is positive (see (8)), β will be less than α.

Finally, following Mirrlees (1976), we can define the social marginal utility of *transfer* γ to be the net gain of transferring one pound from the government to an individual:

$$\gamma(y) = \beta(y) - \lambda = \alpha(y) - \lambda\left(1 - \frac{ty_m}{1 + \frac{t'y\epsilon}{1-t}}\right). \tag{13}$$

As the tax schedule can be shifted both vertically upwards and vertically downwards, it is clear that with optimal taxation,

$$0 = \int_0^\infty \gamma(y)f(y)dy. \tag{14}$$

---

[3] This technique may be used to neatly follow through the comparative statics exercise for a consumer faced by a non-linear budget constraint. See Neary and Roberts (1980).

Returning to the evaluation of the perturbation, the efficiency effect which reduces the disincentive for a small number must be compared with the distributional effect for a large number. Consider the efficiency effect first. As a particular income is being discussed, let $\tilde{y}$ be used as the appropriate carrier variable. For small changes, the change in tax revenue is

$$\Delta T = \int_{y}^{y+\Delta y} (y + \Delta y - \tilde{y} - C(y + \Delta y) + c(\tilde{y}))f(\tilde{y})d\tilde{y}. \tag{15}$$

For the distributional effect, the distance between d and f in Figure 11.1 is important. This is given by $C(y + \Delta y) - c(y + \Delta y)$ and, if this is small, the effect in welfare terms is given by

$$\Delta W = \left[\int_{y+\Delta y}^{\infty} \gamma(\tilde{y})f(\tilde{y})d\tilde{y} \right] [C(y + \Delta y) - c(y + \Delta y)]. \tag{16}$$

To simplify this expression, assume that Δy is small so that (12) and (13) can be approximated by Taylor expansions. Using (5), (15) becomes

$$\Delta T = \frac{tf(y)(\Delta y)^2}{2} + o(\Delta y^2), \tag{17}$$

and using (4), (5), and (7), (16) becomes

$$\Delta W = \left[\int_{y}^{\infty} \gamma(\tilde{y})f(\tilde{y})d\tilde{y} \right] \left[\frac{1-t}{\epsilon y} + t' \right] \frac{(\Delta y)^2}{2} + o(\Delta y^2). \tag{18}$$

It may be noted that we have ignored the welfare effect of taxpayers between y and $y + \Delta y$ being made better off. This is a third-order effect and, for small Δt, is dominated by (18).[4]

The net welfare gain from the perturbation is therefore given by $\Delta W + \lambda \Delta T$. To show that this must be zero at the optimum, it is necessary to show that the 'reverse' perturbation is possible. In a symmetrical fashion, one can consider increasing the progressivity of the tax faced by taxpayers who earn income y and this is accomplished by benefiting all those who earn *lower* incomes. Using (14), one obtains the result that the welfare effect of such a perturbation is the negation of the effect that has been derived. As both changes are feasible, it must be true that the net welfare effect is zero. Thus, letting Δy tend to zero gives (using (14))

$$\lambda tf = \left(\frac{1-t}{\epsilon y} + t' \right) \Gamma(y), \tag{19}$$

where

---

[4] See Section 4 below.

$$\Gamma(y) = \int_0^y \gamma(\tilde{y}) f(\tilde{y}) d\tilde{y}. \tag{20}$$

Before considering the economic implications of (19) two points may be mentioned. First, (19) has been derived under the assumption that the tax schedule is twice-differentiable and that taxpayers' indifferences curves are smoothly tangential to the curve $c(y)$. An example of where this will not be satisfied occurs when some tax-payers choose not to work and individual optimization leads to a corner solution. The approach taken here can be amended to cope with this situation and the possible optimality of a non-differentiable schedule will be investigated in Section 4.

The second point deals with the content of (19). As it stands, it seems to define a differential equation in the marginal tax rate and its solution will depend upon some initial condition (the *level* of taxation is determined by the government revenue require-ment). However, notice that as Γ will be zero at the end-points of the income dis-tribution, if f is bounded away from zero then t will have to be zero (see (23) below). Using this, differentiation of (19) at the upper-end point $\bar{y}$, say, gives

$$t' = \left[\frac{\gamma(\bar{y})}{\lambda - \gamma(\bar{y})} \right] \frac{1}{\epsilon \bar{y}} \tag{21}$$

and this serves as a further condition to pin down the marginal tax schedule.

Looking at (19), the first point to be made is that, as promised, it provides a for-mula for the optimal non-linear income tax which is defined solely by the easily inter-pretable functions that are familiar from linear tax theory. In particular, echoing Diamond's (1975) remarks, distributional judgements are completely captured by the social marginal utilities of income (or transfer). The next remarkable feature concerns the structure of the formula. If the non-linearity feature (captured by t') is small, then (19) becomes a tax formula which incorporates an inverse elasticity rule—viewing the tax rate as a tax on general consumption, the tax rate should be inversely proportional to the compensated elasticity of labour supply.[5] Furthermore, efficiency considerations (captured by the elasticity) and distributional considerations (captured by the social marginal utilities of transfer) enter into the tax rule multiplicatively. With regard to the general shape of the tax schedule, it has already been mentioned that Γ is zero at the lowest and highest income (recall (14)). With f bounded away from zero at these end-points, (19) says that the marginal tax rate must be zero at these end-points (see Sadka (1976) for the upper-end result, Seade (1977) for the lower-end result). Furthermore, if the government would, on welfare grounds, be in favour of redistributing income from high-income taxpayers so that γ declines with y then Γ will be positive between the end-points and, using (8), the optimal marginal tax rate will be positive. Thus when the optimal schedule is differentiable and there are no corner solutions for taxpayers, the marginal tax rate starts at zero, becomes positive, and falls again to zero

---

[5] If τ is the consumption tax, then with income y, consumption c is given by $c = y/(1 + \tau)$. For this to be the equivalent to an income tax t so that $c = (1 - t)y$, τ must be given by $t/(1 - t)$.

at the top of the income distribution. This feature at the upper-end will be investigated in greater detail in the next section.

In simple cases, (19) can be used to obtain an explicit formula for the optimal tax schedule. Assume, following Phelps (1973), that the government is Rawlsian in the sense that α is non-zero only for taxpayers with the lowest income, and that there is a zero income effect of labour supply. For almost everybody γ will then be given by $-\lambda$. If one further assumes that $1 - F = k(\bar{y} - y)^\sigma$ and that everybody's compensated labour supply curve possesses the same slope s (this seems to be the simplest assumption possible), then the only feasible solution to (19) is given by

$$t = \frac{1}{(\sigma + 1)s}(\bar{y} - y), \tag{22}$$

which implies that a quadratic tax schedule with a declining marginal tax rate is optimal. But notice that if k is small, then low incomes will arise and t will exceed unity at low incomes; this will be incompatible with a smooth tangency with the tax schedule for low-income taxpayers. In this case the optimum will involve some non-differentiabilities.

3. The Limiting Tax Rate

Perhaps the strongest result to come out of optimal non-linear tax theory is that, on efficiency grounds, the taxpayer who earns the highest income should face a zero marginal tax rate (Phelps 1973; Sadka 1976). Using (19), if $\bar{y}$ is the highest income, then, close to $\bar{y}$, Γ is approximated by $\gamma(\bar{y})(y - \bar{y})f(\bar{y})$ and, locally, (19) looks like

$$t' = \frac{t}{(y - \bar{y})}\frac{\lambda}{\epsilon_y\gamma} \tag{23}$$

which solves to give $t(\bar{y}) = 0$.

The problem with this derivation is that it depends upon there being a highest income. Whilst a highest income will always exist, it is not necessarily the case that a government will have knowledge of what it will be in the *ex ante* state when the tax structure is being determined. If the government believes that the income distribution will be $f(y, r)$ with probability $g(r)$, then the maximization of expected welfare is similar to the certainty problem with income distribution h where $h(y) = \int f(y, r)g(r)dr$. Then, with a high probability, the highest income observed will fall short of the upper-bound on the support of h—the simple zero rate at the top result will not usually be applicable.[6]

---

[6] Many other arguments against the zero rate at the top can be given. For instance, assume that wages are marginal products plus an error term. Then the highest-income earner will almost certainly receive a wage greater than his marginal product and, on efficiency grounds, it will be desirable for him to face a strictly positive marginal tax rate. Of greater importance is the fact that income will be stochastic for fixed effort on the part of a taxpayer. Taxation will then have an insurance role (Varian 1980) and those with the highest incomes will be those who have had the greatest luck. In this case, the insurance aspect of taxation will be dominant.

We are thus interested in tax rates for high incomes but ones below what could, in some circumstances, be considered possible. For simplicity, assume that h has no upper bound and let us investigate the limiting marginal tax rate. If the appropriate functions tend to a limit, then (19) gives

$$lim \ t = \frac{1}{1 - \dfrac{\lambda \bar{\epsilon}(lim \frac{yf}{1 - F})}{\bar{\gamma}}}, \tag{24}$$

where $\bar{\epsilon}$ and $\bar{\gamma}$ are limiting values of ϵ and γ.

Notice that the income distribution enters through $\lim \ yf/(1 - F)$. If f is bounded below at the upper bound of its support, then the limit will be infinite and this takes us back to the zero marginal tax rate. However, $yf/(1 - F)$ is the constant Pareto parameter of the Pareto distribution so that the widely observed phenomenon that the tail of the income distribution appears to be Pareto in form is equivalent to an observation that $\mu = lim \ yf/(1 - F)$ is bounded away from zero and, being more specific, empirical work suggests that it lies between 1.5 and 3.[7] Unfortunately, as an optimal tax formula (24) has a serious defect. To uncover this, it is necessary to look more carefully at the role played by differentiability.

4. Differentiable Schedules and Optimality

The derivation of the optimal tax schedule assumed implicitly that the schedule was twice-differentiable and that taxpayers' indifference curves were tangential to the schedule at the income that they wished to earn. The possibility of a corner solution at zero income has already been mentioned. Here, the object is to see whether it is desirable for the government to introduce kinks into the tax schedule, the implication of these kinks being that taxpayers with different preferences between leisure and consumption will choose to obtain the same income.

To investigate this problem, we will take the schedule defined by (19), introduce a perturbation that produces a kink, and see what effect is produced. Figure 11.2 shows the effect of offering the consumption/income point K as well as the schedule $c(y)$. The effect of this is equivalent to introducing a small kink in the schedule at K and all taxpayers who chose to obtain income between $y - x_1$ and $y + x_2$ will now move to K. The change in tax revenue to the government is given by

$$\Delta T = \int_{y - x_1}^{y + x_2} (y - \tilde{y} - c(y) - d + c(\tilde{y})) f(\tilde{y}) d\tilde{y}. \tag{25}$$

To evaluate this, we note first that, if $C(\cdot, \tilde{y})$ is the indifference curve of a taxpayer which is tangential to $c(\cdot)$ at $\tilde{y}$, then x_1 and x_2 are defined by

$$C(y, y - x_1) = c(y) + d \tag{26a}$$

---

[7] Using tax return data, Saez (1999) estimates μ to vary between 1.8 and 2.2 over time.

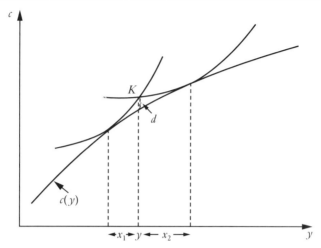

FIG. 11.2. *A Kink in the Consumption/Income Trade-off*

$$C(y, y + x_2) = c(y) + d, \tag{26b}$$

where, for all x,

$$C(y + x, y + x) = c(y + x) \tag{27}$$

and

$$C_1(y + x, y + x) = c'(y + x). \tag{28}$$

Differentiating (27) and applying (28) gives

$$C_2(y + x, y + x) = 0. \tag{29}$$

Twice-differentiation of (27) gives

$$C_{11} + 2C_{12} + C_{22} = c'' \tag{30}$$

and differentiation of this gives

$$C_{111} + 3C_{112} + 3C_{122} + C_{222} = c'''. \tag{31}$$

Multiple differentiation of (29) gives

$$C_{21} + C_{22} = 0 \tag{32}$$

and

$$C_{112} + 2C_{122} + C_{222} = 0. \tag{33}$$

Eliminating d from (26a, b) gives x_2 as a function of x_1. Because of the degeneracy induced by (29), the derivative of x_2 with respect to x_1 depends upon the second derivative of C (through l'Hôpital's rule) and we obtain

$$x_2(0) = 0$$

$$\frac{dx_2}{dx_1}(0) = 1$$

$$\frac{d^2x_2}{dx_1^2}(0) = -\frac{2}{3}\frac{C_{222}}{C_{22}} \tag{34}$$

so that, using (30) and (32) to solve for C_{22}, and (31) and (33) to solve for C_{222}, we obtain

$$\frac{d^2x_2}{dx_1} = -\left(\frac{2}{3}\right)\frac{2C_{111} + 3C_{112} - 2c'''}{C_{11} - c''}. \tag{35}$$

The denominator is related to the compensated elasticity of labour supply and the curvature of the tax function whilst the numerator is related to how an individual's elasticity changes with income, how elasticity varies across individuals, and changes to the curvature of the tax function.

Turning to (25), a Taylor expansion can be taken around $x_1 = x_2 = 0$. Differentiation with respect to x_1 with d and x_2 viewed as functions of x_1 gives

$$\frac{\partial \Delta T}{\partial x_1} = (-x_2 - c(y) - d + c(y + x_2))f(y + x_2)\frac{dx_2}{dx_1}$$

$$+ (x_1 - c(y) - d + c(y - x_1))f(y - x_1) \tag{36}$$

$$- \int_{y-x_1}^{y+x_2} d'(x_1)f(\tilde{y})d\tilde{y}.$$

$$\frac{\partial^2 \Delta T}{\partial x_1^2} = [(-1 + c'(y + x_2))f(y + x_2) + (-x_2 - c(y) - d$$

$$+ c(y + x_2))f'(y + x_2)]\left(\frac{dx_2}{dx_1}\right)^2 + [(-x_2 - c(y) - d$$

$$+ c(y + x_2))f(y + x_2)]\frac{d^2x_2}{dx_1^2} + (1 - c'(y - x_1))f(y - x_1) \tag{37}$$

$$- (x_1 - c(y) - d + c(y - x_1))f'(y - x_1) - 2d'(f(y + x_2)\frac{dx_2}{dx_1}$$

$$+ f(y + x_1)) - \int_{y-x_1}^{y+x_2} d''(x_1)f(\tilde{y})d\tilde{y}.$$

Differentiation once again and letting x_1 tend to zero gives

$$\frac{\partial^3 \Delta T}{\partial x_1^3} = 2f(y)c''(y) - 6d''(0)f(y) - (1 - c'(y))\left(4f'(y) + 3f(y)\frac{d^2x_2}{dx_1^2}\right), \tag{38}$$

where we have made use of the fact that $d(0) = d'(0) = 0$ (using (26) and (29)). Now,

$$d''(0) = C_{22} = C_{11} - c'' \qquad (39)$$

(using (30) and (32)). At $x_1 = 0$, (36) and (37) both become zero so (38) becomes the dominant effect. Using (4), (5), (38), and (39) we have ΔT as a third-order Taylor expansion in x_1

$$\Delta T = -\frac{1}{3}\left[4fi' + \frac{3f(1-t)}{\epsilon y} + 2tf' + \frac{3}{2}tf\frac{d^2x_2}{dx_1^2} \right]x_1^3 + o(x_1^3). \qquad (40)$$

This expression applies for any differentiable tax schedule. If we abstract from the change in curvature term d^2x_2/dx_1^2, as the second term in square brackets is positive, ΔT will be positive only when the proportional rise in the marginal tax rate is small relative to the proportional fall in the income distribution density. Alternatively, when the tax schedule is approximately linear so that $t' = 0$, ΔT will be positive only when the marginal tax rate is large and the density of the income distribution is falling sufficiently rapidly. This suggests that ΔT will be negative at low-income levels but may be positive at high-income levels under tax schedules observed in practice.

We now investigate whether the 'optimal' tax schedule derived in Section 2 is in fact optimal by considering the introduction of a kind. Applying (19) to (40) gives the tax effect

$$\Delta T = \frac{1}{3}\left[\frac{f}{\epsilon y} - t\left(2f' + \frac{4f^2\lambda}{\Gamma} + \frac{f}{\epsilon y} + \frac{3}{2}f\frac{d^2x_2}{dx_1^2} \right) \right]x_1^3 + o(x_1^3). \qquad (41)$$

As well as the tax revenue change, another third-order effect will be the welfare improvement brought to those with incomes between $y - x_1$ and $y + x_2$. Even if $\alpha(y) = 0$, however, (41) being positive is possible.

To investigate this further, we concentrate on the optimality of the limiting tax rates derived in the last section. If $\lim yf/(1-F) = \mu$, then $\lim yf'/f = -(\mu+1)$. Turning to the change in curvature effect, if this is small, then (41) will be positive if

$$t > \frac{1}{1 + \frac{2\epsilon}{3}(\mu+1)}. \qquad (42)$$

For instance, with a Pareto parameter μ of 2 and an elasticity of $3/4$ then (44) is satisfied if t is above $2/5$. A more reasonable assumption would be to assume that, in the limit, the compensated elasticity of a taxpayer is locally constant, and approaches a limit when viewed across taxpayers. Using (4), C will take the form

$$C_{11}(y, \tilde{y}) = \frac{C_1(y, \tilde{y})}{\epsilon y}. \qquad (43)$$

Using (43) and (35) gives

$$\frac{d^2x_2}{dx_1^2} = \left(\frac{2}{3}\right)\frac{2 + 1/\epsilon}{y}. \qquad (44)$$

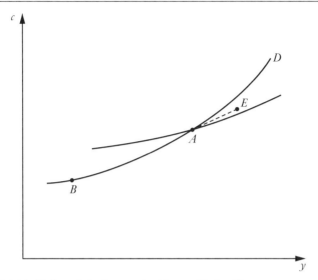

Fig. 11.3. *Multiple Kinks and the Consumption/Income Trade-off*

Equation (40) will then be positive if

$$t > \frac{3}{1 + 2\mu\epsilon}. \tag{45}$$

Taking $\mu = 2$ and $\epsilon = 3/4$, this will be satisfied if t is above $3/4$. If the limiting tax rate is set optimally, then combining (24) and (45) gives $\Delta T > 0$ if

$$\frac{1}{\mu\epsilon} < 1 + \frac{3\lambda}{2\gamma}. \tag{46}$$

When high-income earners are not given positive welfare weight ($\alpha = 0$), so that there is no direct welfare gain from the introduction of a kink, we have $-\gamma \geqslant \lambda$. If $-\gamma$ is close to λ, then (46) is never satisfied for positive μ and ϵ. But, recalling (13), if the income effect of labour supply is large, then satisfaction of (46) is made more likely.

   If all taxpayers are at kink points at the upper end of the optimal tax function, then it is not difficult to determine something of the structure of these kink points. Assume that there is an upper kink point (A in Figure 11.3) and that the taxpayer with preferences BAD and everybody with a greater preference for work (less sloped indifference curves) are bunched at A. If B is a point on the tax function that taxpayers will move to if A is withdrawn, then it is clear that the government is free to choose A anywhere on the indifference curve to the right of B without changing the composition of the bunched group or affecting everybody else in the population. As it is being assumed that $\alpha = 0$ for the bunched group, the net effect of a movement around the indifference curve is the tax change of the bunched group—clearly, taxes increase by a movement to the right whenever the slope of the indifference curve is less than unity.

Therefore, the slope of the indifference curve at the kink point must be at least unity. But now consider offering a new point E with the property that the slope between A and E is, for instance, one-half. E will be chosen in preference to A by those with the greatest preference for work and, as is obvious, the net effect will be to increase tax revenue without producing any welfare effect. Thus we have shown that there can be no upper kink point—in the optimum, there are an infinite number of kink points offered at the tail-end of the tax function.

Finally, when α is non-zero, a different picture can emerge. The direct welfare effect of the kink perturbation is approximated by

$$\Delta W = \frac{\lambda t f^2 \alpha}{3} x_1^3 \qquad (47)$$

and if this is combined with (41), then, as γ must incorporate α, the net effect of the kink perturbation is made more ambiguous. However, (47) may be combined with (41) to give a measure of the net effect of the perturbation. If α is large relative to the weight given to most taxpayers (so that λ is not correspondingly large), then (47) will dominate (41) and again the introduction of a kink can be desirable. Thus if the government weights low-income taxpayers much more highly than high-income taxpayers, then one may expect to observe a kink at the bottom of the tax schedule with a group of low-income taxpayers being bunched at the kink. In this case, the result that the optimal tax rate at the lowest income is zero (Seade 1977) will not hold.[8]

These results point to the complex nature of the non-linear taxation problem. Given the structure of the problem, one can expect to be able to provide the strongest results about taxation at the two ends of the tax schedule. The analysis of this section suggests that there can be non-differentiabilities at both ends of the schedule and results about marginal tax rates will fail to be meaningful.

5. Global Perturbations and Tax Reform

In Section 2, the fact that perturbations in a tax schedule at a particular point are permissible was used to determine a set of first-order conditions of optimality for non-linear income tax schedules and, subject to the caveat discussed in the last section, these conditions may be used to determine the optimal schedule. However, the analysis conducted is directly applicable to the situation where the tax schedule is suboptimal and one wishes to ask whether the marginal tax rate should be raised or lowered at a particular income level. Using λ, (17) and (18) may be combined to give the net welfare effect of a small perturbation. Figure 11.1 makes clear that the perturbation is, in essence, a reduction in the marginal tax rate from $1 - c'(y) = 1 - C'(y)$ to $1 - C'(y + \Delta y)$. Therefore, the change in the marginal tax rate is given by

---

[8] The possible optimality of a kink should not be too surprising. On welfare grounds it may be desirable to force those who choose to obtain higher incomes to obtain a lower income (work less). The fact that choices are decentralized through a single budget constraint implies that the best that the government can do is to bunch a group of taxpayers at a particular income.

$$\Delta t = -C'' \frac{(\Delta y)^2}{2} + o(\Delta y^2). \tag{48}$$

Thus, for small Δt, the net welfare change is given by (using (17) and (18)):

$$\Delta V = \left[\Gamma(y) \left(\frac{t'\epsilon y}{1-t} + 1 \right) - \frac{\lambda t f \epsilon y}{1-t} \right] \Delta t, \tag{49}$$

where it is here assumed that, at the margin, tax revenue is raised in a lump-sum manner.

Equation (49) can be used to compute the effect of a small perturbation in the whole schedule. Assume that the government is contemplating a change in the progressivity of the tax structure which involves the marginal tax at y, $t(y)$, changing at rate $p(y)$. The change in welfare will be given by

$$\Delta V = \int_y \left[\Gamma(y) \left(\frac{t'\epsilon y}{1-t} + 1 \right) - \frac{\lambda t f \epsilon y}{1-t} \right] p(y) dy. \tag{50}$$

As an example, assume that the tax is initially linear ($t' = 0$) and that the government is contemplating a change to a linear tax with higher rate. Then $p(y)$ would equal some constant p and (50) will become (integrating Γ by parts):

$$\Delta V = \int_y \left(\gamma - \frac{\lambda t \epsilon}{1-t} \right) y p f dy. \tag{51}$$

Equating this to zero gives the optimal *linear* tax rate:

$$\frac{t}{1-t} = \frac{\int \gamma y f dy}{\lambda \int \epsilon y f dy}, \tag{52}$$

which is exactly the 'simplified' formula of linear taxation derived by Dixit and Sandmo (1977).

Equation (50) can also be used to derive first-order conditions for optimal polynomial tax schedules, e.g.

$$T = a_o + a_1 y + \frac{a_2 y^2}{2} + \dots \frac{a_r y^r}{r}. \tag{53}$$

If a change in a_k is contemplated, then $p(y)$ is given by $a_k y^{k-1}$ and inserting this in (50) gives, on equating the result to zero, a condition for the optimal a_k.

Two final points concerning (50) are worth mentioning. First, if (50) is used to evaluate a tax reform, then the functions in the formula will be evaluated at the initial point. For instance, f will be the present observed distribution of income. Second, a particular example of (50) gives the change in tax revenue as the result of a change in tax structure. For with $\alpha = 0$, (50) becomes, apart from a multiplier λ, the change in tax revenue. Therefore, a change in the tax structure p will lead to a change in tax revenue of

$$\Delta T = -\int \left[\left(\int_y^\infty \left(1 - \frac{ty_m}{1 + \frac{t'\tilde{y}\epsilon}{1-t}} f(\tilde{y}) \right) d\tilde{y} \right) \left(\frac{t'\epsilon yf}{1-t} + 1 \right) + \frac{t\epsilon yf}{1-t} \right] p(y)dy. \tag{54}$$

Even if p is constant, (54) requires considerable calculation. However, in empirical analysis of budget changes, numerical calculation should be straightforward.

6. Concluding Remarks

The purpose of this paper has been to adopt a non-standard approach to the solution of the optimal non-linear tax problem. This approach seems to have four advantages. First, the approach itself is easily understood, being both direct and simple. Second, the formula produced for the optimal tax rate is easily interpretable as it is defined in terms of functions that are easily interpretable. This formula has close connections to formulae in linear tax theory. Third, an identical approach can be used to evaluate income tax reform and, as was shown in the last section, it is possible to evaluate different types of marginal reform that may be envisaged in a non-linear framework. Finally, it has been possible to demonstrate some of the inherent complexity of the set of problems to which the optimal income tax problem belongs. In particular, it has been shown that although a well-behaved differentiable tax function that satisfies optimality with respect to well-behaved perturbations can be found, it is sometimes the case that the problem will involve non-differentiabilities at the optimum. The problem raised by this is that it will not always be clear that well-behaved solutions are not optimal—in numerical work, the search for the optimum could be quite difficult.

APPENDIX

The purpose of this Appendix is to show how the optimal tax rule (19) can be derived using standard control methods. To do this, assume that individuals are indexed by a parameter z which determines tastes and social deservingness. The parameter z will be defined so that, *at the optimum*, the supply of effort, i.e. pre-tax income y, will be z for a z-type individual.

If $v(m, w, z)$ is the indirect utility function of a z-type individual where m is (lump-sum) income and w is the rate at which pre-tax income can be converted into post-tax income, i.e. the wage, then Roy's Identity gives

$$v_w(m, w, z) = y(m, w, z)v_m(m, w, z), \tag{A.1}$$

where $y(m, w, z)$ is the (uncompensated) supply equation ((9) in the text). When an individual chooses to be at a point on a non-linear tax schedule, he makes the same choice as he would under a linear tax schedule passing through that point with the same slope as the non-linear schedule at that point.[9] Thus a non-linear schedule

---

[9] This is discussed further in Roberts (1979).

is equivalent to a situation where individuals face linear tax schedules though the implied m and w will depend upon the tastes of the individual z. For a non-linear schedule $c(\cdot)$, $m(z)$ and $w(z)$ will be defined by

$$m(z) = c(y(z)) - c'(y(z))y(z) \tag{A.2}$$

$$w(z) = c'(y(z)), \tag{A.3}$$

where $y(z)$ is the pre-tax income choice of an individual. Differentiating (A.2) and (A.3) gives

$$\frac{dm}{dz} + y(z)\frac{dw}{dz} = 0, \tag{A.4}$$

which is the constraint imposed by the fact that $m(\cdot)$ and $w(\cdot)$ are formed from a non-linear tax schedule.

Locally around the optimum, the government's objective can be viewed as being linear in utilities:

$$W = \int_0^{\infty} \delta(z)v(m(z), w(z), z)f(z)dz, \tag{A.5}$$

where $f(z)$ is the density of z—this will, by assumption, describe the income distribution at the optimum.

Finally, there is a resource constraint faced by the government—aggregate income must be at least as great as aggregate consumption plus required government revenue R:

$$\int_0^{\infty} [y(z) - c(y(z))] f(z)dz \geqslant R \tag{A.6}$$

which, using (A.2) and (A.3), becomes

$$\int_0^{\infty} [m(z) + (w(z) - 1)y(z)] f(z)dz + R \leqslant 0. \tag{A.7}$$

Instead of choosing a tax schedule, the government may be viewed as choosing functions $m(\cdot)$ and $w(\cdot)$ to maximize (A.5) subject to (A.4), (A.7), and (A.8):

$$y(z) = y(m(z), w(z), z). \tag{A.8}$$

As λ is the value of a change in tax revenue, λ will be the multiplier associated with (A.7) in the optimization problem. Letting μ_1 and μ_2 be the multipliers associated with (A.4) and (A.8), standard control theory gives first-order conditions:

$$\delta v_m f - \lambda f - \frac{d\mu_1}{dz} - \mu_2 y_m = 0. \tag{A.9}$$

$$\delta v_w f - \lambda y f - y\frac{d\mu_1}{dz} - \mu_1 \frac{dy}{dz} - \mu_2 y_w = 0. \tag{A.10}$$

$$-\lambda(w - 1)f + \mu_1 \frac{dw}{dz} + \mu_2 = 0. \tag{A.11}$$

$$\mu_1(o) = \mu_1(\infty) = 0 \text{(transversality)}. \tag{A.12}$$

Now, by definition, $\delta v_m = \alpha$ and (A.1) gives $\delta v_w = \alpha y$. Combining (A.9) and (A.10) gives

$$\mu_1 \frac{dy}{dz} = -\mu_2(y_w - yy_m) = -\frac{\mu_2 y \epsilon}{w}, \tag{A.13}$$

the second equality following from Slutsky's equation (see (12) in the text). Now, at the optimum $dy/dz = 1$ so that solving for μ_2 from (A.11) and (A.13) and replacing μ_2 in (A.9) gives

$$\frac{d\mu_1}{dy} = \left[\alpha - \lambda + \frac{\lambda t y_m}{1 + \frac{t' y \epsilon}{(1-t)}}\right] f(y) = \gamma(y) f(y) \tag{A.14}$$

from (13) in the text ($y(z) = z$, $t = 1 - w$, $t' = -(dw/dz)$). Equation (20) therefore gives (using (A.12)):

$$\Gamma(y) = \mu_1(y). \tag{A.15}$$

Finally, (A.11), (A.13), and (A.15) give, on rearrangement

$$\lambda t f = \left(\frac{1-t}{\epsilon y} + t'\right)\Gamma(y), \tag{A.16}$$

which is the optimal tax formula in the text.

References

Atkinson, A. B., and J. E. Stiglitz (1979), *Lectures on Public Economics* (McGraw-Hill: Maidenhead).

Diamond, P. A. (1975), 'A Many-Person Ramsey Tax Rule', *Journal of Public Economics* 4: 335–42.

Dixit, A. K., and A. Sandmo (1977), 'Some Simplified Formulae for Optimal Income Taxation', *Scandinavian Journal of Economics* 79: 417–23.

Ebert, U. (1992), 'A Reexamination of the Optimal Nonlinear Income Tax', *Journal of Public Economics* 49: 47–73.

Lollivier, S., and J.-C. Rochet (1983), 'Bunching and Second-Order Conditions: A Note on Optimal Tax Theory', *Journal of Economic Theory* 31: 392–400.

Mirrlees, J. A. (1971), 'An Exploration of the Theory of the Optimum Income Tax', *Review of Economic Studies* 38: 175–208.

—— (1976), 'Optimal Tax Theory: A Synthesis', *Journal of Public Economics* 6: 327–58.

Neary, J. P., and K. W. S. Roberts (1980), 'The Theory of Household Behaviour under Rationing', *European Economic Review* 13: 25–42.

Phelps, E. S. (1973), 'The Taxation of Wage Income for Economic Justice', *Quarterly Journal of Economics* 87: 331–54.

Revesz, J. T. (1989), 'The Optimal Taxation of Labour Income', *Public Finance* 44: 453–75.

Roberts, K. W. S. (1979), 'Welfare Considerations of Nonlinear Pricing', *Economic Journal* 89: 66–83.

Sadka, E. (1976), 'On Income Distribution, Incentive Effects and Optimal Income Taxation', *Review of Economic Studies* 43: 261–8.

Saez, E. (1999), 'Using Elasticities to Derive Optimal Income Tax Rates', Massachusetts Institute of Technology, mimeo.

Seade, J. K. (1977), 'On the Shape of Optimal Tax Schedules', *Journal of Public Economics* 7: 203–36.

Tuomala, M. (1990), *Optimal Income Tax and Redistribution* (Oxford University Press: Oxford).

Varian, H. R. (1980), 'Redistribution Taxation as Social Insurance', *Journal of Public Economics* 14: 49–68.

Part V

PROJECT APPRAISAL

12 Reassessing the Diamond–Mirrlees Efficiency Theorem

PETER J. HAMMOND

1. Introduction

1.1. Old second-best theory

During the 1950s, much of the work in welfare economics had become increasingly critical of what had been accomplished during the 1930s and 1940s. It was realized that, unless all distortions in the economy could be removed, the usual first-order conditions might all become invalid. This apparently very robust negative conclusion had already been discussed in Samuelson (1947: 252–3), but it culminated in the work of Lipsey and Lancaster (1956).

Consider any distortion in the form of an enforced departure from optimality in at least one first-order condition. Then Lipsey and Lancaster claimed that, in general, every other first-order condition would also have to be violated in order to reach a constrained second-best optimum. Indeed, the irremovable presence of just one fixed distortion, it was suggested, would make it optimal to have other distortions prevail virtually throughout the whole economy.

Lipsey and Lancaster showed that this claim is indeed valid under particular assumptions concerning the nature of the distortion. It implies, of course, that marginal rates of transformation should not be equal for different producers. If so, production should be inefficient.

This negative conclusion has far-reaching implications because, if one can establish the desirability of production efficiency, there are many important corollaries such as gains from freer trade and from adopting a project whose benefits exceed its costs when these are all evaluated at suitable producer prices. All these important results risk losing their validity unless one can rely on the basic proposition that it is desirable to arrange an efficient allocation of inputs and outputs to producers.

1.2. New second-best theory

On a personal note, the academic year 1967–8 was when I began my formal study of economics. It was also Jim Mirrlees's last as a lecturer in Cambridge before he moved on to a Professorship at Nuffield College in Oxford. Thus, I was able to benefit from Jim's lectures on optimal growth, optimal taxation, and other topics in public economics. Also, early versions of Diamond and Mirrlees (1971) and of Little and Mirrlees (1968) were made available. These important publications led to a major revolution in public economics and the theory of the second-best—a revolution whose significance I have only recently begun to appreciate much more fully than I did at the time. Nor do I feel alone in my somewhat tardy recognition.

One important and practical implication of the revolution had already been set out quite clearly in Mirrlees (1969), which begins by claiming that shadow prices (or 'accounting prices') should be ' "world prices"; or more precisely and more generally, . . . prices that might be computed as a guide to particular production decisions, in the public sector and elsewhere.' Indeed, the application to project evaluation was extensively explored in Little and Mirrlees (1968, 1974). Their main message was that in a small country with no influence over border prices, projects should have their net outputs of traded goods evaluated at border prices (with other net outputs evaluated at producer shadow prices). This approach to cost–benefit analysis is in marked contrast to Dasgupta, Marglin, and Sen, as those authors readily recognize (1972: 6). It should also be noted that Little and Mirrlees advocate more complicated procedures for shadow wages and for discount rates, because of market imperfections. These important concerns go beyond the scope of this paper, however.

1.3. The argument for production efficiency

A more complete theoretical justification for this Little–Mirrlees approach to cost–benefit analysis comes, however, in a fundamental result due to Diamond and Mirrlees (1971)—see also Mirrlees (1986). In an economy without lump-sum transfers, but with linear taxes or subsidies on each commodity which can be adjusted independently, they were able to show that any second-best optimum of a Paretian social welfare function entails efficient production.

The Diamond–Mirrlees result does rely on a careful treatment of private producer profits which are distributed to consumers as dividends, as Stiglitz and Dasgupta (1971) in particular soon pointed out. Specifically, there is a need to sterilize any adverse effects on consumers' dividend incomes which arise when inefficient producers are shut down—see, for example, Mirrlees (1972), as well as Dasgupta and Stiglitz (1972). Formally, moreover, the Diamond–Mirrlees proof requires that consumers face linear budget constraints, thus excluding the non-linear taxation of income discussed by Vickrey (1945) and Mirrlees (1971). It also assumes a finite set of consumers with continuous single-valued demand functions—as is implied, for instance, if consumers' preferences are all strictly convex. Unlike in standard general equilibrium theory, for the Diamond–Mirrlees argument to hold, it is not enough that each consumer merely have an upper hemi-continuous and convex-valued demand correspondence—though actually their result does hold in this case as well, as can be shown by an argument similar to that used in proving the main theorem of this paper.

Accordingly, the principal aim here is to show how the Diamond–Mirrlees result is much more robust than has generally been recognized. This will be done by confirming its validity when several of the original assumptions have been greatly relaxed. For reasons to be explained shortly, this is much easier to do when, as in the income taxation model of Vickrey and Mirrlees, there is a continuum of consumers.

1.4. Corporate and public production

Following the example of Diamond and Mirrlees (1971), the results set out below will be derived in a formal general equilibrium framework, but allowing for an active public sector. In fact, the model used here allows for production which is undertaken by individuals, by corporations, and by the public sector. In the classical first-best setting with unrestricted lump-sum redistribution, aggregate production efficiency over the whole economy is necessary for Pareto efficiency. In a second-best setting, however, aggregate production efficiency over the whole economy may not be desirable because distortionary taxes on transactions between individuals and corporations may well be needed to redistribute real income or to finance public goods in order to reach a second-best Pareto-efficient allocation—as they are, for instance, in the Diamond and Mirrlees (1971) framework. Also, shadow prices for the public sector may differ from consumer prices. Nevertheless, the main proposition below concerns the desirability of aggregate production efficiency in the corporate and public sector together, even in the second-best setting considered here.

1.5. Incentive constraints with a continuum of consumers

The Lipsey and Lancaster theory of second best was based on *ad hoc* constraints preventing the economy from reaching a first-best allocation. Yet Vickrey (1945) and Samuelson (1947: 247–8) had already emphasized informally how private information makes it practically impossible to arrange a system of optimal lump-sum transfers of the kind that first-best theory requires. Indeed, this impossibility is clearly what motivated Diamond and Mirrlees to examine the implications of replacing lump-sum transfers by linear commodity taxation.

After the important work on incentive compatibility during the 1970s by Hurwicz, Gibbard and others—including Section 3 of Mirrlees (1986), which was originally written in 1977—it seems quite natural now to impose explicitly the incentive constraints that arise whenever some information is private. Yet the full implications of doing so are hard to analyse when the number of agents is finite—cf. Barberà and Jackson (1995) and Córdoba and Hammond (1998). The difficulty is that, when any one consumer manipulates an allocation mechanism by mimicking some different type of consumer, this affects the apparent economic environment, as described by the distribution of consumers' characteristics in the population. Thus, incentive-compatible allocations in different economic environments become inextricably linked through incentive constraints. One cannot avoid trading off good allocations in some environments against good allocations in other environments.

With a continuum of agents, on the other hand, the analysis is greatly simplified —as discussed in Hammond (1979, 1987, 1999), Guesnerie (1981, 1995), etc. Indeed, incentive compatibility with a continuum of agents is equivalent to the existence of a common budget set, independent of any private information, which decentralizes the allocation. Moreover, there are fairly obvious conditions under which incentive compatibility actually requires linear commodity taxation without lump-sum transfers

—i.e. budget constraints in the form considered by Diamond and Mirrlees. But non-linear pricing is still possible for any good which cannot be freely and anonymously exchanged among consumers. Of course, there may be welfare gains—even potential Pareto gains—from allowing non-linearities, possibly in the form of rationing, into each consumer's budget constraint. Indeed, this is clear from the work of Mirrlees (1971, 1986) himself, as well as Dasgupta and Hammond (1980), Guesnerie and Roberts (1984), Blackorby and Donaldson (1988), and others. On the other hand, there are administrative and other costs which may severely limit the use of fiscal instruments.

With these extensions and limitations in mind, this paper considers those incentive-compatible allocations which can be decentralized by budget constraints chosen from within a rather general one parameter family of 'piecewise convex' sets. Moreover, as this one parameter increases, each consumer's budget set is assumed to expand—as in one case considered by Diamond and Mirrlees themselves, where the only variable parameter is a non-negative uniform poll subsidy.

Apart from allowing a much simpler treatment of incentive constraints, having a continuum of consumers confers several additional theoretical benefits. There is no reason to restrict attention to convex preferences, to convex consumption or individual feasible sets, to convex budget sets, or even to divisible goods. In principle, the theoretical framework can include individual consumers' decisions to migrate, to make private investments involving set-up costs, to incur fixed transport costs travelling to and from work each day, etc. Allowing such features adds considerably to the practical applicability of the Diamond–Mirrlees efficiency argument. In order to ensure that mean demand is upper hemi-continuous, however, an additional 'dispersion' assumption is required, similar to those introduced by Mas-Colell (1977) and Yamazaki (1978, 1981).

1.6. Outline of paper

The main theoretical task, accordingly, is to generalize the Diamond–Mirrlees efficiency argument to a model with a continuum of consumers and individual non-convexities. Section 2 lays out the details of a formal model having these features, including indivisible goods. Then Section 3 explores how to distribute to all consumers simultaneously the additional output resulting from a gain in production efficiency in a way that generates an incentive-compatible Pareto superior allocation. These possibilities for distributing efficiency gains are assumed to be described by a one-parameter expanding family of 'piecewise convex' budget sets. Unfortunately, these specifically exclude income tax schedules whose marginal rate decreases smoothly to zero at the top of the income distribution—i.e. precisely the kind of schedule required for optimality in some economic environments, as discussed by Mirrlees (1971) and also Seade (1977). Nevertheless, though formally excluded, any such schedule can be approximated arbitrarily closely by a piecewise convex budget set, so the restriction seems not too severe.

After setting out the most substantive assumptions, Section 4 derives the continuity and unboundedness properties of the resulting individual demand correspondence.

This is followed in Section 5 by similar results for the aggregate (or mean) demand correspondence. Once these important preliminary properties have all been established, the main theorem on the desirability of enhanced production efficiency is proved in Section 6. In particular, the existence of an incentive-compatible Pareto superior allocation on the frontier of the post-reform production set will be shown. The paper concludes in Section 7, which discusses several important implications of this result when evaluating projects or analysing some other kinds of economic reform.

2. A Formal Model

2.1. Divisible and indivisible commodities

Let G denote a non-empty finite set of divisible commodities, and $\mathbb{R}^G$ the associated finite-dimensional Euclidean space. It is important for G to be non-empty so that local satiation can be avoided. Also, let H denote the (possibly empty) finite set of indivisible commodities, whose quantities must belong to $\mathbb{Z}$, the set of integers. Thus, the commodity space is $\mathbb{R}^G \times \mathbb{Z}^H$. Sometimes a vector $x \in \mathbb{R}^G \times \mathbb{Z}^H$ will be written in the partitioned form (x^G, x^H), where $x^G \in \mathbb{R}^G$ and $x^H \in \mathbb{Z}^H$.

A pair $a, b \in \mathbb{R}^G \times \mathbb{Z}^H$ may satisfy one or more of the following four vector inequalities:

$$a \geqq b \iff a_j \geqslant b_j \text{ (all } j \in G \cup H).$$
$$a > b \iff a \geqq b \text{ and } a \neq b.$$
$$a \gg b \iff a_j > b_j \text{ (all } j \in G \cup H).$$
$$a \gg^G b \iff a \geqq b \text{ and } a_j > b_j \text{ (all } j \in G).$$

Of these, the first three are standard. The last is appropriate when there is a (possibly small) increase in every divisible good, with no decrease in any indivisible good.

2.2. Consumption and domestic production

As explained in the introduction, it is assumed that there is a continuum of consumers. Suppose these are labelled by numbers ℓ that are uniformly distributed on the unit interval $[0, 1] \subset \mathbb{R}$, i.e. the distribution of their labels is described by the Lebesgue measure λ on $[0, 1]$.

Individuals can be distinguished not only by numerical labels, but also by other identifiers such as date of birth. These identifiers can in principle be used to arrange discriminatory prices or taxes and subsidies, such as state pensions paid to those born more than sixty-five years ago. It is assumed that the relevant identifiers i range over a finite set I. Numerical labels ℓ, however, are assumed to be arbitrary and so not useful as a basis for discrimination of any kind.

Furthermore, individuals have characteristics θ ranging over a specified metric space Θ with a Borel σ-field $\mathcal{J}$ of measurable sets. For obvious reasons, we restrict attention to continuous preferences. Also, so that production efficiency would be desirable in a degenerate economy where all consumers are known to be identical and have the same net demand vector, we assume both free disposal and monotone preferences, though subject to the restriction that quantities of indivisible goods must be integers.

In order to allow for domestic production, it is easier to focus on net trade vectors rather than on consumption and endowment vectors separately. Thus, each consumer is supposed to have a set of feasible net trades. Though these feasible sets may not be convex, especially if there are indivisible goods, at least they should be 'piecewise convex'—i.e. the union of a countable collection of convex sets. This is important later on when invoking the dispersion assumption which implies that the demand correspondence is upper hemi-continuous.

2.3. Consumer characteristics

Specifically, the first formal assumption is:

Assumption 1. There is a metric space Θ of possible consumer characteristics such that:

1. for each $\theta \in \Theta$, there is a closed set $X_\theta \subset \mathbb{R}^G \times \mathbb{Z}^H$ of feasible net trade vectors, which is equal to the union of a countable collection of closed convex sets $X_\theta(k)$ $(k = 1, 2, \ldots)$, each of which has the *restricted free disposal property* that, whenever $x \in X_\theta(k)$ and $x' \geqq x$ with $x' \in \mathbb{R}^G \times \mathbb{Z}^H$, then $x' \in X_\theta(k)$;
2. there exists a uniform lower bound $\underline{x} \in \mathbb{R}^G \times \mathbb{Z}^H$ such that $x \in X_\theta$ for some $\theta \in \Theta$ only if $x \geqq \underline{x}$;
3. if the sequence $\theta_n \in \Theta$ converges to θ, and if $x \in X_\theta$, then there exists a sequence satisfying $x_n \in X_{\theta_n}$ for $n = 1, 2, \ldots$ while $x_n \to x$ as $n \to \infty$;
4. for each $\theta \in \Theta$, there is a (complete, reflexive, and transitive) preference ordering $\succsim_\theta$ which is continuous on X_θ and has the *restricted monotonicity property* that, whenever $x \in X_\theta$ and $x' \geqq x$ with $x' \in \mathbb{R}^G \times \mathbb{Z}^H$, then $x' \succsim_\theta x$, and $x' >_\theta x$ if $x' \gg^G x$;
5. if the sequence of triples $(x_n, x'_n, \theta_n) \in (\mathbb{R}^G \times \mathbb{Z}^H)^2 \times \Theta$ converges to (x, x', θ) while satisfying $x_n, x'_n \in X_{\theta_n}$ and $x_n \succsim_{\theta_n} x'_n$ for $n = 1, 2, \ldots$, then $x, x' \in X_\theta$ with $x \succsim_\theta x'$.

Note that, because each component set $X_\theta(k)$ is convex, for each k there must exist a unique vector of integers $z(k) \in \mathbb{Z}^H$ such that $X_\theta(k) \subset \mathbb{R}^G \times \{z(k)\}$. But $X_\theta \cap (\mathbb{R}^G \times \{z\})$ could still fail to be convex for one or more $z \in \mathbb{Z}^H$, in which case it is assumed that $X_\theta \cap (\mathbb{R}^G \times \{z\})$ can be decomposed further into several convex components.

Because the ordering $\succsim_\theta$ is assumed to be reflexive on X_θ, note that

$$X_\theta = \{x \in \mathbb{R}^G \times \mathbb{Z}^H \mid x \succsim_\theta x\}.$$

Hence, each pair $(X_\theta, \succsim_\theta)$ $(\theta \in \Theta)$ consisting of a consumption set $X_\theta \subset \mathbb{R}^G \times \mathbb{Z}^H$ and a monotone continuous preference ordering on X_θ can be identified with the closed graph

$$\Gamma_\theta = \{(x, x') \in (\mathbb{R}^G \times \mathbb{Z}^H)^2 \mid x \succsim_\theta x'\}$$

of that ordering. Then the space of such closed graphs can be given the metrizable topology of closed convergence. After identifying each $(X_\theta, \succsim_\theta)$ with Γ_θ, the mapping $\theta \mapsto (X_\theta, \succsim_\theta)$ should be continuous. See, for example, Hildenbrand (1974: 18–19, 96–8) or Mas-Colell (1985: 10–11) for a fuller explanation and further details. In fact, one could take Θ as the whole space of graphs Γ corresponding to pairs $(X, \succsim)$ satisfying parts 1, 2, and 4 of Assumption 1, and then make $\theta \mapsto (X_\theta, \succsim_\theta)$ the identity map. Alternatively, the domain Θ of characteristics that an individual can credibly claim to possess could be a compact subset of this space. In either case, it follows from Hildenbrand that parts 3 and 5 of Assumption 1 are also satisfied. These two parts, however, respectively require only that the correspondence $\theta \twoheadrightarrow X_\theta$ should be lower hemi-continuous, while $\theta \twoheadrightarrow \Gamma_\theta$ should have a closed graph.

2.4. *Potential consumers*

Though the numerical labels $\ell \in [0, 1]$ and identifiers $i \in I$ are assumed to be publicly observable, consumer characteristics $\theta \in \Theta$ will be regarded as private information. That is, the true mapping $\theta(\ell)$ from $[0, 1]$ to Θ specifying each consumer's private characteristic θ as a function of their label ℓ is completely unknown. Feasible allocations, therefore, can only depend on θ in ways that respect incentive constraints. For this reason, it is natural to consider the entire space $A := [0, 1] \times I \times \Theta$ of *potential consumers*, specified by a known numerical label $\ell \in [0, 1]$, a known identifier $i \in I$, but an unknown characteristic $\theta \in \Theta$. The space A can be given its obvious product σ-field $\mathcal{A}$, and it will be assumed that the economy can be described by a probability measure α on $(A, \mathcal{A})$. For any $E \in \mathcal{A}$, the measure $\alpha(E)$ should be interpreted as the proportion of individuals whose label, identifier, and characteristic form a triple (ℓ, i, θ) belonging to E. It is assumed that $\alpha(V \times I \times \Theta) = \lambda(V)$ for every Borel set $V \subset [0, 1]$. That is, the marginal distribution of numerical labels is the Lebesgue measure, implying that numerical labels are indeed uniformly distributed on $[0, 1]$.

The above formulation allows the continuum economy to be interpreted as the limit of an expanding sequence of random finite economies in which there are n consumers whose triples (ℓ, i, θ) of numerical labels, identifiers, and characteristics are independently and identically drawn at random from the probability space $(A, \mathcal{A}, \alpha)$.

3. Distributing Efficiency Gains

3.1. *The* status quo

The main result below shows that, relative to a *status quo* allocation, any reform which enhances the overall efficiency of production in the combined corporate and public sector can be accompanied by a fiscal reform which will generate a strict Pareto improvement. The *status quo* allocation is not necessarily an initial allocation; rather, it is what would happen in the absence of any reform. That particular allocation is assumed to be described by some α-integrable mapping $(i, \theta) \mapsto \hat{x}_\theta^i$ from A to $\mathbb{R}^G \times \mathbb{Z}^H$ which depends only on (i, θ).

Define the set

$$\hat{S}^i := \{x \in \mathbb{R}^G \times \mathbb{Z}^H \mid \exists \theta \in \Theta : x = \hat{x}_\theta^i\}$$

as the range of the mapping $\theta \mapsto \hat{x}_\theta^i$ as θ varies over Θ, the entire domain of relevant individual characteristics.

The second formal assumption is:

Assumption 2. The range $\hat{S}^i$ is compact.

This will be true if, for instance, the domain Θ of characteristics happens to be compact and the mapping $\theta \mapsto \hat{x}_\theta^i$ is continuous.

3.2. A Decentralization

Because each consumer's characteristic $\theta \in \Theta$ is private information, it is natural to assume that the *status quo* allocation represents the outcome of a *strategyproof mechanism* in the sense that, for all $(i, \theta) \in I \times \Theta$, the *incentive constraint* $\hat{x}_\theta^i \gtrsim_\theta x$ is satisfied whenever $x \in X_\theta \cap \hat{S}^i$. That is, no potential consumer $(i, \theta) \in I \times \Theta$ is able to manipulate the mechanism determining the relevant net trade vector $\hat{x}_\theta^i$ by finding a better alternative $\hat{x}_\eta^i \in X_\theta \cap \hat{S}^i$ for some $\eta \in \Theta$. Because there is a continuum of agents, so no consumer can influence the apparent distribution α on A, note that the incentive constraints are independent of α.

Say that the set $B^i \subset \mathbb{R}^G \times \mathbb{Z}^H$ satisfies *restricted free disposal* if and only if

$$B^i \subset B^i - (\mathbb{R}^G \times \mathbb{Z}^H) = \{x \in \mathbb{R}^G \times \mathbb{Z}^H \mid \exists x' \in B^i : x \leqq x'\}.$$

Under the assumptions stated so far, the decentralization result presented in Hammond (1979) can be strengthened as follows:

Lemma 1. Any allocation $(i, \theta) \mapsto x_\theta^i$ with compact range

$$S^i := \{x \in \mathbb{R}^G \times \mathbb{Z}^H \mid \exists \theta \in \Theta : x = \hat{x}_\theta^i\}$$

is strategyproof if and only if it is *decentralizable* in the sense that, for each $i \in I$, there exists a closed *budget set* B^i satisfying restricted free disposal such that $S^i \subset B^i \subset \mathbb{R}^G \times \mathbb{Z}^H$ and also $x_\theta^i \gtrsim_\theta x$ whenever $x \in X_\theta \cap B^i$.

Proof. Because $S^i \subset B^i$, sufficiency is obvious.

Conversely, suppose that the allocation $(i, \theta) \mapsto x_\theta^i$ is strategyproof. Define $B^i := S^i - (\mathbb{R}^G \times \mathbb{Z}^H)$ as the smallest set that satisfies restricted free disposal while including S^i as a subset. Because S^i is assumed to be compact, the set B^i is easily shown to be closed.

Suppose that $x \in X_\theta \cap B^i$. Then there exists $\eta \in \Theta$ such that $x \leqq x_\eta^i$. Because $x_\eta^i \in \mathbb{R}^G \times \mathbb{Z}^H$, restricted free disposal implies that $x_\eta^i \in X_\theta$ and restricted monotonicity implies that $x_\eta^i \gtrsim_\theta x$. Because $x_\eta^i \in X_\theta$, the incentive constraints imply that $x_\theta^i \gtrsim_\theta x_\eta^i$, so $x_\theta^i \gtrsim_\theta x$ because $\gtrsim_\theta$ is transitive. ∎

Of course, this construction typically results in a non-linear budget constraint. Some significant restrictions on such a budget constraint will now be introduced.

3.3. Expanding budget sets

Define $\hat{y} := \int_A \hat{x}_\theta^i d\alpha$ as the mean net trade vector of all consumers in the *status quo* allocation. As the mean, note that $\hat{y}$ will generally not have integer components even for indivisible goods. That is, $\hat{y}$ can be a general vector in $\mathbb{R}^G \times \mathbb{R}^H$.

Consider a reform which allows the economy to reach any new mean net trade vector in some (possibly very restricted) aggregate feasible set $Y \subset \mathbb{R}^G \times \mathbb{R}^H$ describing the combined aggregate production possibilities of the corporate and public sector. It will be assumed that Y is closed and allows free disposal—i.e. if $y \in Y$ and $y' \leqq y$, then $y' \in Y$. Also, so that the reform really does enhance production efficiency, it is assumed that Y includes at least one $y \gg \hat{y}$.

In order to convert this reform into an incentive-compatible allocation which is strictly Pareto superior for consumers, the budget sets $\hat{B}^i$ that decentralize the *status quo* allocation $(i, \theta) \mapsto \hat{x}_\theta^i$ must change in order to include at least one strictly preferred net demand vector for each consumer. To make this possible, assume that for each $i \in I$ there is a one-parameter family $B^i(m)$ $(m \geqslant 0)$ of budget sets, with $B^i(0)$ as the *status quo* budget set $\hat{B}^i$. Thus, once m has been chosen, each potential consumer with identifier $i \in I$ is constrained to choosing some net trade vector x within the budget set $B^i(m)$. Assume, moreover, that each set $B^i(m)$ is closed, allows free disposal, and that there is an upper bound $\bar{x}(m)$ such that $x \leqq \bar{x}(m)$ whenever $x \in B^i(m)$ with $x \geqq \underline{x}$.

One prominent example of such a one-parameter family of budget sets appears in Diamond and Mirrlees (1971), when the set H of indivisible goods is empty. It is the family $\{x \in \mathbb{R}^G \mid qx \leqslant m\}$ of linear budget sets, for a fixed consumer price vector $q \gg 0$ and a variable non-negative 'poll' subsidy m. An obvious extension of this example is the family $B^i(m) := \{x \in \mathbb{R}^G \times \mathbb{Z}^H \mid q^i x \leqslant e^i(m)\}$ of budget sets, for fixed consumer price vectors $q^i \gg 0$ and increasing functions $e^i(\cdot)$ of m which can both depend on i. A different example is the family $B^i(m) := \{x \in \mathbb{R}^G \times \mathbb{Z}^H \mid x - u^i(m) \in B^i\}$ of possibly non-linear budget sets, for a collection of increasing vector functions $u^i : \mathbb{R}_+ \to \mathbb{R}_+^G \times \mathbb{Z}_+^H$ of m which, for all $i \in I$, satisfy $u^i(0) = 0$ and $u^i(m') \gg^G u^i(m)$ whenever $m' > m$.

Generally, then, it is assumed that:

Assumption 3. For each $i \in I$, there are closed budget sets $B^i(m)$ $(m \geqslant 0)$ allowing restricted free disposal while satisfying:

1. (expansion) If $m' > m$, then $B^i(m) \subset B^i(m')$, while for every $x \in B^i(m)$ there exists $x' \gg^G x$ such that $x' \in B^i(m')$.
2. (piecewise convexity) Each set $B^i(m)$ is equal to the union $\cup_{j=1}^\infty B^i(j, m)$ of a countable family of convex sets $B^i(j, m)$ $(j = 1, 2, \dots)$.
3. (continuity) For each $i \in I$ and each $j = 1, 2, \dots$, there exists a continuous function $\beta_j^i : \mathbb{R}^G \times \mathbb{Z}^H \to \mathbb{R}_+$ such that
$$x \in B^i(j, m) \Leftrightarrow \beta_j^i(x) \leqslant m$$

and also $\beta_j^i((1 - \lambda)x + \lambda x') < \beta_j^i(x')$ whenever $0 < \lambda < 1$ and $x, x' \in \mathbb{R}^G \times \mathbb{Z}^H$ satisfy $\beta_j^i(x) < \beta_j^i(x')$.

4. (bounded budget sets) For each $m \geqq 0$ there is an upper bound $\bar{x}(m)$ such that $x \leqq \bar{x}(m)$ whenever $x \in \cup_{i \in I} B^i(m)$ with $x \geqq \underline{x}$.

Here part 2 of Assumption 3 plays a similar role to the comparable part of Assumption 1 requiring each feasible set X_θ to be the union of a countable family of convex sets. Also, the last condition in part 3 is somewhat stronger than merely requiring each β_j^i to be quasi-convex, as already implied by the convexity of each set $B^i(j, m)$. Finally, part 4 plays an obvious role in ensuring that each potential consumer (i, θ) faces a compact constraint set $X_\theta \cap B^i(m)$.

3.4. Compact constraint sets

Next, for each $i \in I$, $\theta \in \Theta$ and $m \geqq 0$, define the collection of sets

$$H_\theta^i(j, k, m) := X_\theta(k) \cap B^i(j, m)$$

for $j, k = 1, 2, \ldots$, as well as the union

$$H_\theta^i(m) := \bigcup_{j=1}^{\infty} \bigcup_{k=1}^{\infty} H_\theta^i(j, k, m) = X_\theta \cap B^i(m)$$

Lemma 2. For each fixed $m \geqq 0$, the set $H_\theta^i(m)$ is compact and uniformly bounded, for all $i \in I$ and $\theta \in \Theta$.

Proof. By Assumption 1, if $x \in X_\theta$, then $x \geqq \underline{x}$. So the boundedness part of Assumption 3 implies that $x \leqq \bar{x}(m)$. Hence, $H_\theta^i(m)$ is uniformly bounded. Because the sets X_θ and $B^i(m)$ are assumed to be closed, so obviously is $H_\theta^i(m)$, which is therefore compact as a closed and bounded set in $\mathbb{R}^G \times \mathbb{Z}^H$. ∎

4. Continuous and Unbounded Individual Demand

4.1. Continuous compensated demand

For each $i \in I$, define the *demand correspondence* from each pair (θ, m) with $\theta \in \Theta$ and $m \geqq 0$ to the set

$$\psi_\theta^i(m) := \{x \in H_\theta^i(m) \mid x' \in H_\theta^i(m) \Rightarrow x \succsim_\theta x'\}$$

of optimal net trade vectors within the constraint set $H_\theta^i(m)$. Because $H_\theta^i(m)$ is non-empty and compact, while $\succsim_\theta$ is continuous, the demand set $\psi_\theta^i(m)$ is always non-empty.

In classical demand theory with a Walrasian budget constraint defined by a hyperplane, the compensated demand correspondence is upper hemi-continuous in many situations where the ordinary Walrasian demand correspondence may not be. A similar property applies here, with piecewise convex budget sets.

First, for each $i \in I$ and $x \in \mathbb{R}^G \times \mathbb{Z}^H$, define $\beta_*^i(x) := \inf_{j=1}^{\infty} \beta_j^i(x)$. Then, for each $i \in I$, define the *compensated demand correspondence* from each pair (θ, m) with $\theta \in \Theta$ and $m \geqslant 0$ to the set

$$\xi_\theta^i(m) := \{x \in H_\theta^i(m) \mid x' \succsim_\theta x \Rightarrow \beta_*^i(x') \geqslant m\}.$$

This implies that $\xi_\theta^i(m)$ consists of all the net trade vectors within the constraint set $H_\theta^i(m)$ which are strictly preferred to any other x' in the same set satisfying $\beta_*^i(x') < m$.

The following two lemmas show that the compensated demand correspondence has the same key properties as in the Walrasian case.

Lemma 3. For each $i \in I$, $\theta \in \Theta$, and $m \geqslant 0$, one has $\psi_\theta^i(m) \subset \xi_\theta^i(m)$.

Proof. Suppose that $x \in \psi_\theta^i(m)$. Evidently $x \in H_\theta^i(m)$.

Consider any $x' \in X_\theta$ with $x' >_\theta x$. Then there exists a sequence $x_n \in X_\theta$ with $x_n \gg^G x'$ ($n = 1, 2, \dots$) such that $x_n \to x'$ as $n \to \infty$. Because Assumption 1 implies that preferences have the restricted monotonicity property and are transitive, for each n it follows that $x_n \in X_\theta$ with $x_n >_\theta x$. Then $x \in \psi_\theta^i(m)$ implies that for each n one has $x_n \notin H_\theta^i(m) = X_\theta \cap B^i(m)$. It follows that $x_n \notin B^i(m)$ and so $\beta_j^i(x_n) > m$ for all j. Because each function β_j^i is continuous, taking the limit as $n \to \infty$ gives $\beta_j^i(x') \geqslant m$ for all j, so $\beta_*^i(x') \geqslant m$. This proves that $x \in \xi_\theta^i(m)$. ∎

Lemma 4. For each $i \in I$, the compensated demand correspondence $(\theta, m) \mapsto \xi_\theta^i(m)$ is upper hemi-continuous throughout the domain of pairs (θ, m) with $\theta \in \Theta$ and $m \geqslant 0$.

Proof. Consider any sequence of triples (θ_n, m_n, x_n) with $x_n \in \xi_{\theta_n}^i(m_n)$ ($n = 1, 2, \dots$) where $(\theta_n, m_n) \to (\theta, m)$ as $n \to \infty$. Let m^* denote $\sup_n m_n$. Then $B^i(m_n) \subset B^i(m^*)$ and so $x_n \in X_{\theta_n} \cap B^i(m^*)$ for $n = 1, 2, \dots$. By part 2 of Assumption 1, it follows that each $x_n \geqq \underline{x}$, and so $x_n \leqq \bar{x}(m^*)$ by the boundedness part 4 of Assumption 3. Thus, the sequence x_n is bounded, so has some convergent subsequence with a limit x. From now on, we restrict attention to this convergent subsequence, so $x_n \to x$ as $n \to \infty$. It remains to show that $x \in \xi_\theta^i(m)$.

Consider any $\tilde{x} \in X_\theta$ with $\tilde{x} >_\theta x$. By part 3 of Assumption 1, there exists a sequence $\tilde{x}_n \in X_{\theta_n}$ ($n = 1, 2, \dots$) such that $\tilde{x}_n \to \tilde{x}$ as $n \to \infty$. But then part 5 of Assumption 1 implies that $\tilde{x}_n >_{\theta_n} x_n$ for all large n. Otherwise there would exist an infinite subsequence of triples $(\theta_{n_r}, \tilde{x}_{n_r}, x_{n_r})$ such that $x_{n_r} \succsim_{\theta_{n_r}} \tilde{x}_{n_r}$ for $r = 1, 2, \dots$, and taking limits as $r \to \infty$ would give $x \succsim_\theta \tilde{x}$, contradicting $\tilde{x} >_\theta x$. Thus, for each large n, because each $x_n \in \xi_{\theta_n}^i(m_n)$, it follows that $\beta_*^i(\tilde{x}_n) \geqslant m_n$ and so $\beta_j^i(\tilde{x}_n) \geqslant m_n$ for all $j = 1, 2, \dots$. But β_j^i is continuous, so taking limits as $n \to \infty$ implies that $\beta_j^i(\tilde{x}) \geqslant m$ for all $j = 1, 2, \dots$.

Finally, consider any $\hat{x} \in X_\theta$ with $\hat{x} \succsim_\theta x$. Then there exists a sequence $\hat{x}_n \in X_\theta$ with $\hat{x}_n \gg^G \hat{x}$ ($n = 1, 2, \dots$) such that $\hat{x}_n \to \hat{x}$ as $n \to \infty$. Because Assumption 1 implies that preferences have the restricted monotonicity property and are transitive, for each

n it follows that $\hat{x}_n \in X_\theta$ with $\hat{x}_n >_\theta x$. The previous paragraph shows that for all $j = 1, 2, \ldots$ one has $\beta^i_j(\hat{x}_n) \geq m$ for each n. But β^i_j is continuous, so taking limits as $n \to \infty$ implies that $\beta^i_j(\hat{x}) \geq m$ for all $j = 1, 2, \ldots$. This proves that $\beta^i_*(\hat{x}) \geq m$, so $x \in \xi^i_\theta(m)$ as required. ∎

4.2. Critical parameter values

First, for each $i \in I$, $\theta \in \Theta$, and $j, k = 1, 2, \ldots$, define

$$M^i_\theta(j, k) := \{m \geq 0 \mid H^i_\theta(j, k, m) \neq \text{empty set}\}$$

as the set of parameter values allowing the potential consumer (i, θ) to reach the particular convex component $H^i_\theta(j, k, m) = X_\theta(k) \cap B^i(j, m)$ of the constraint set $H^i_\theta(m) = X_\theta \cap B^i(m)$.

Lemma 5. For each $i \in I$, $\theta \in \Theta$, and $j, k = 1, 2, \ldots$, the set $M^i_\theta(j, k)$ is closed.

Proof. Suppose that $m_n \in M^i_\theta(j, k)$ for $n = 1, 2, \ldots$ and $m_n \to m^*$ as $n \to \infty$. For each $r = 1, 2, \ldots$, define $m^*_r := \sup_{n \geq r} m_n$. Evidently $m^*_r \downarrow m^*$ as $r \to \infty$.

By definition of $M^i_\theta(j, k)$, for each $n \geq r$ there exists $x_n \in H^i_\theta(j, k, m_n) \subset H^i_\theta(j, k, m^*_r)$. In particular, $x_n \in X_\theta(k)$. It follows from Assumption 1 that $x_n \geq \underline{x}$, and then $x_n \leq \bar{x}(m^*_r)$ for all $n \geq r$ by the boundedness part of Assumption 3. So the sequence x_n is bounded, and must have a convergent subsequence with some limit point x^*. By Assumption 1, the set $X_\theta(k)$ is closed, implying that $x^* \in X_\theta(k)$. Furthermore, $\beta^i_j(x_n) \leq m^*_r$ for all $n \geq r$. Because β^i_j is continuous, taking limits as $n \to \infty$ gives $\beta^i_j(x^*) \leq m^*_r$ for $r = 1, 2, \ldots$, implying that $\beta^i_j(x^*) \leq m^*$ because $m^*_r \downarrow m^*$. It follows that $x^* \in H^i_\theta(j, k, m^*)$ and so $m^* \in M^i_\theta(j, k)$. Hence, the set $M^i_\theta(j, k)$ is closed. ∎

Next, let $m^i_\theta(j, k) := \min_m M^i_\theta(j, k)$ be the *critical parameter value* which just allows the potential consumer (i, θ) to reach the particular convex component $H^i_\theta(j, k, m)$ of the constraint set $H^i_\theta(m)$. It follows from Lemma 5 that $m^i_\theta(j, k)$ is well defined.

For each $(i, \theta) \in I \times \Theta$, let $C^i_\theta := \bigcup_{j=1}^\infty \bigcup_{k=1}^\infty \{m^i_\theta(j, k)\}$ be the set of all critical parameter values for the potential consumer (i, θ). Clearly, C^i_θ is either finite or countably infinite.

4.3. Continuous individual demand

The following lemma shows that the compensated demand $\xi^i_\theta(m)$ of each potential individual (i, θ) coincides with that individual's demand $\psi^i_\theta(m)$ away from critical parameter values $m \in C^i_\theta$.

Lemma 6. For each $i \in I$ and $\theta \in \Theta$ one has $\psi^i_\theta(m) = \xi^i_\theta(m)$ for all $m \notin C^i_\theta$.

Proof. Because of Lemma 3, it is enough to prove that $\xi^i_\theta(m) \subset \psi^i_\theta(m)$ for all $m \notin C^i_\theta$. So suppose that $x \in \xi^i_\theta(m)$, where $m \notin C^i_\theta$. Evidently $x \in H^i_\theta(m)$.

Consider any $x' \in X_\theta$ with $x' >_\theta x$. By definition of $\xi_\theta^i(m)$, one must have $\beta_j^i(x') \geq m$ for all $j = 1, 2, \ldots$. Consider any k such that $x' \in X_\theta(k)$ and then any j such that $m \geq m_\theta^i(j, k)$. The hypothesis $m \notin C_\theta^i$ implies that $m > m_\theta^i(j, k)$. So there exists $\hat{x} \in X_\theta(k) \cap B^i(j, m)$ such that $\beta_j^i(\hat{x}) < m$ and so $\beta_j^i(\hat{x}) < \beta_j^i(x')$.

Let λ_n ($n = 1, 2, \ldots$) be any sequence of positive scalars satisfying $\lambda_n < 1$ which converges to 0 as $n \to \infty$. Then let $x_n := (1 - \lambda_n)x' + \lambda_n \hat{x}$ for $n = 1, 2, \ldots$, so $x_n \to x'$. With this construction, each $x_n \in X_\theta(k)$ because $X_\theta(k)$ is a convex component of X_θ. Also, because $\beta_j^i(\hat{x}) < \beta_j^i(x')$, part 3 of Assumption 3 implies that $\beta_j^i(x_n) < \beta_j^i(x')$ for each $n = 1, 2, \ldots$. But for n sufficiently large, continuity of preferences implies that $x_n >_\theta x$. By definition of $\xi_\theta^i(m)$, one must have $\beta_*^i(x_n) \geq m$. It follows that $\beta_j^i(x') > \beta_j^i(x_n) \geq \beta_*^i(x_n) \geq m$ and so $\beta_j^i(x') > m$.

The previous two paragraphs show that $\beta_j^i(x') > m$ for all $x' >_\theta x$ and all $j = 1, 2, \ldots$. On the other hand, if $x' \in X_\theta \cap B^i(m)$, then there exists j such that $\beta_j^i(x') \leq m$, which is only possible if $x \gtrsim_\theta x'$. This proves that $x \in \psi_\theta^i(m)$. ∎

4.4. Unbounded individual demand

In the following, let $q \in \mathbb{R}_{++}^{G \cup H}$ denote any fixed strictly positive vector.

Lemma 7. Suppose the sequence m_n ($n = 1, 2, \ldots$) has the property that, for some potential consumer (i, θ), the sequence $\inf_x \{q(x - \underline{x}) \mid x \in \psi_\theta^i(m_n)\}$ remains bounded as $n \to \infty$. Then the sequence m_n itself must be bounded.

Proof. By hypothesis, there exists a bound K and, for each $n = 1, 2, \ldots$, a net trade vector $x_n \in \psi_\theta^i(m_n)$ such that $q(x_n - \underline{x}) \leq K$. Because $q \gg 0$ and because in addition $x_n \in \psi_\theta^i(m_n)$ implies that $x_n \geq \underline{x}$, the sequence x_n is bounded. So there must exist an upper bound $x^* \in \mathbb{R}^G \times \mathbb{Z}^H$ such that $x_n \ll x^*$ for all $n = 1, 2, \ldots$. Let $\hat{m} := \inf_j \{\beta_j^i(x^*) \mid j = 1, 2, \ldots \}$. For any $m > \hat{m}$, there exists j such that $\beta_j^i(x^*) < m$, so $x^* \in B^i(m)$. Because restricted monotonicity implies that $x^* >_\theta x_n$, it follows that $x_n \notin \psi_\theta^i(m)$ for all $m > \hat{m}$. Hence, $x_n \in \psi_\theta^i(m_n)$ implies, for all $n = 1, 2, \ldots$, that $m_n \leq \hat{m}$. So the sequence m_n must be bounded. ∎

5. Continuous Unbounded Mean Demand

5.1. Continuous mean compensated demand

Let $\Psi^C(m) := \int_A \xi_\theta^i(m) d\alpha$ denote the *mean compensated demand correspondence*.

Lemma 8. On the domain $\mathbb{R}_+$, the mean compensated demand correspondence $m \mapsto \Psi^C(m)$ is well defined, has non-empty convex compact values, and is also upper hemi-continuous.

Proof. By Lemma 4, for each fixed $m \geq 0$, the correspondence $\theta \mapsto \xi_\theta^i(m)$ is upper hemi-continuous. It follows that its graph is relatively closed and so measurable.

Moreover, the correspondence has uniformly bounded values because $\xi_\theta^i(m) \subset H_\theta^i(m)$, where, by Lemma 2, $H_\theta^i(m)$ is uniformly bounded. Also, the set I is finite. Arguing as in Hildenbrand (1974: 54, 61), these conditions guarantee that the mean compensated demand correspondence $m \mapsto \Psi^C(m)$ is well defined and has non-empty compact values for all $m \geqslant 0$. Also, $\Psi^C(m)$ is always convex because the measure α has no atoms.

Suppose that the sequence $m_n \geqslant 0$ ($n = 1, 2, \ldots$) converges to m as $n \to \infty$. Suppose also that the sequence $y_n \in \Psi^C(m_n)$ ($n = 1, 2, \ldots$). By definition, this means that for each $n = 1, 2, \ldots$ there exists a selection $(i, \theta) \mapsto x_{n\theta}^i$ from the correspondence $(i, \theta) \mapsto \xi_\theta^i(m_n)$ such that $y_n = \int_A x_{n\theta}^i d\alpha$. But $(i, \theta) \mapsto x_{n\theta}^i$ is a selection from the uniformly bounded and compact-valued correspondence $(i, \theta) \mapsto H_\theta^i(m_n)$, implying that y_n belongs to $\int_A H_\theta^i(m_n) d\alpha$. This in turn is a subset of the compact set $\int_A H_\theta^i(m^*) d\alpha$, where $m^* := \sup_n m_n$. It follows that the sequence y_n is bounded, so must have a subsequence converging to a limit $y^* \in \int_A H_\theta^i(m^*) d\alpha$.

Now apply Fatou's lemma for finite dimensions (Schmeidler, 1970; Hildenbrand, 1974: Lemma 3, 69) to the space $\mathbb{R}^{G \cup H}$. Because the mapping $(i, \theta) \mapsto x_{n\theta}^i$ is uniformly bounded for all n, this lemma implies the existence of an integrable function $(i, \theta) \mapsto x_\theta^i$ such that $y^* = \int_A x_\theta^i d\alpha$ and also, for α-almost every (ℓ, i, θ), some subsequence of $x_{n\theta}^i$ converges to x_θ^i. Because $x_{n\theta}^i \in \xi_\theta^i(m_n)$ and, by Lemma 4, each correspondence $m \mapsto \xi_\theta^i(m)$ is upper hemi-continuous, it follows that $x_\theta^i \in \xi_\theta^i(m)$ for all (i, θ). But then

$$y^* = \int_A x_\theta^i d\alpha \in \int_A \xi_\theta^i(m) d\alpha = \Psi^C(m)$$

confirming that $m \mapsto \Psi^C(m)$ is upper hemi-continuous. ∎

5.2. Dispersion and continuous mean demand

The demand correspondence $m \mapsto \psi_\theta^i(m)$ of each potential consumer (i, θ) may fail to be upper hemi-continuous at any critical value $m \in C_\theta^i$. To avoid these discontinuities having any significance in the aggregate, one can introduce an additional 'dispersion' assumption, motivated in part by the *dispersed needs* assumption used in Coles and Hammond (1995). Somewhat similar are Mas-Colell's (1977) assumption that the distribution of individuals' endowment vectors is absolutely continuous w.r.t. Lebesgue measure, and especially Yamazaki's (1978, 1981) *dispersed endowments* assumption.

Indeed, given any $m \geqslant 0$, define

$$C(m) := \{(i, \theta) \in I \times \Theta \mid m \in C_\theta^i\} = \cup_{i \in I} \cup_{j=1}^{\infty} \cup_{k=1}^{\infty} \{m_\theta^i(j, k)\}$$

as the set of all potential consumers (i, θ) who have m as a critical parameter value. Then assume:

Assumption 4 (dispersion). For all $m \geqslant 0$ one has $\alpha([0, 1] \times C(m)) = 0$.

Note that, for each $i \in I$ and for $j, k = 1, 2, \ldots$, the measure α on $[0, 1] \times I \times \Theta$ and the continuous function $\theta \mapsto m_\theta^i(j, k) \in \mathbb{R}_+$ together induce a measure $\sigma^i(j, k)$ defined on the Borel sets $V \subset \mathbb{R}_+$ by

$$\sigma^i(j, k)(V) := \alpha(\{(\ell, i, \theta) \in [0, 1] \times I \times \Theta \mid m^i_\theta(j, k) \in V\}).$$

This is the distribution of potential consumers' minimum wealth levels $m^i_\theta(j, k)$ that just make accessible the convex component $H^i_\theta(j, k, m)$ of $H^i_\theta(m)$. Then, as in Mas-Colell (1977), an unnecessarily strong but plausible sufficient condition for Assumption 4 to hold is that each measure $\sigma^i(j, k)$ on $\mathbb{R}_+$ should be absolutely continuous w.r.t. Lebesgue measure, i.e. there should be some integrable density function $\mu^i(j, k)(m)$ on $\mathbb{R}_+$ such that $\sigma^i(j, k)(V) = \int_V \mu^i(j, k)(m)dm$ for every Borel set $V \subset \mathbb{R}_+$.

Dispersion has the following important implication:

Lemma 9. On the domain $\mathbb{R}_+$, the mean demand correspondence $m \mapsto \Psi(m) := \int_A \psi^i_\theta(m)d\alpha$ is well defined, has non-empty convex compact values, and is also upper hemi-continuous.

Proof. Lemma 6 implies that $\xi^i_\theta(m) = \psi^i_\theta(m)$ for all $(i, \theta) \notin C(m)$. Then the dispersion Assumption 4 implies that for all $m \geq 0$ one has $\xi^i_\theta(m) = \psi^i_\theta(m)$ for α-almost all (ℓ, i, θ). So $\Psi^C(m) = \int_A \xi^i_\theta(m)d\alpha = \int_A \psi^i_\theta(m)d\alpha = \Psi(m)$ for all $m \geq 0$. The result follows immediately from Lemma 8. ∎

5.3. Unbounded mean demand

The following result confirms that $\Psi(m)$ is unbounded as $m \to \infty$.

Lemma 10. Suppose that the sequence m_n $(n = 1, 2, \dots)$ tends to ∞ as $n \to \infty$. Then, given any fixed $q \in \mathbb{R}^{GUH}_{++}$, the sequence $\min_y\{q(y - \underline{x}) \mid y \in \Psi(m_n)\}$ also tends to ∞.

Proof. For $n = 1, 2, \dots$, define $g_n := \inf_y\{q(y - \underline{x}) \mid y \in \Psi(m_n)\}$. But $\Psi(m_n) = \int_A \psi^i_\theta(m_n)d\alpha$. From Hildenbrand (1974: Prop. 6, 63), it follows that

$$g_n = \int_A \inf_{x^i_\theta}\{q(x^i_\theta - \underline{x}) \mid x^i_\theta \in \psi^i_\theta(m_n)\}d\alpha.$$

Suppose $m_n \to \infty$. Then Lemma 7 implies that the last integrand tends to ∞ as $n \to \infty$ for all pairs (i, θ), so $g_n \to \infty$. ∎

The last assumption used in the main theorem is:

Assumption 5. The set $Y(\underline{x}) := \{y \in Y \mid y \geqq \underline{x}\}$ is bounded.

This expresses the obvious requirement that, because mean net inputs must be bounded in order to satisfy $y \geqq \underline{x}$, mean net outputs must also be bounded.

Lemma 11. Suppose the sequence m_n $(n = 1, 2, \dots)$ has the property that $\Psi(m_n) \cap Y \neq \emptyset$ for all n. Then m_n must be bounded.

Proof. Suppose that $y_n \in \Psi(m_n) \cap Y$ $(n = 1, 2, \dots)$. Because of part 2 of Assumption 1, one has $y_n \geqq \underline{x}$ for all n, so $y_n \in Y(\underline{x})$. By Assumption 5, this implies that y_n is bounded. So therefore is $q(y_n - \underline{x})$, for any $q \in \mathbb{R}_{++}^{G \cup H}$. Because $y_n \in \Psi(m_n)$ for each n, the result follows from Lemma 10. ∎

6. Main Theorem

Finally, the main theorem of the paper:

Theorem. Suppose that Assumptions 1–5 all hold, and in particular, that the *status quo* allocation $(i, \theta) \mapsto \hat{x}_\theta^i$ can be decentralized by the closed and piecewise convex budget sets $\hat{B}^i = B^i(0)$ $(i \in I)$ which satisfy restricted free disposal within $\mathbb{R}^G \times \mathbb{Z}^H$. Given the *status quo* mean net trade vector $\hat{y} := \int_A \hat{x}_\theta^i d\alpha$, suppose there exists $y \in Y$ such that $y \gg \hat{y}$. Then there exists a strictly Pareto-superior allocation which, for some $m^* > 0$ such that $\Psi(m^*)$ includes a boundary point of Y, is decentralized by the closed and piecewise convex budget sets $B^i(m^*)$ $(i \in I)$ satisfying restricted free disposal.

Proof. Define $m^* := \sup \{m \in \mathbb{R}_+ \mid \Psi(m) \cap Y \neq \emptyset\}$. By Lemma 11, m^* is finite. By definition of m^*, there must exist two corresponding sequences m_n and y_n $(n = 1, 2, \dots)$ such that $y_n \in \Psi(m_n) \cap Y$ and $m_n \uparrow m^*$. By Lemma 9, the correspondence $m \mapsto \Psi(m)$ is upper hemi-continuous and compact-valued, so the sequence y_n $(n = 1, 2, \dots)$ has a subsequence which converges to some limit $y^* \in \Psi(m^*)$. Because each $y_n \in Y$ and Y is closed, it follows that $y^* \in \Psi(m^*) \cap Y$.

Next, consider any corresponding pair of sequences m_n and y_n $(n = 1, 2, \dots)$ such that $m_n > m^*$ and $y_n \in \Psi(m_n)$ for all n, while $m_n \downarrow m^*$. Then each budget set $B^i(m_n)$ $(i \in I)$ is shrinking, implying that for all $n = 1, 2, \dots$ the mean net trade vector y_n belongs to $\int_A H_\theta^i(m_1)d\alpha$. By Lemma 2, this set is bounded. Therefore, the sequence y_n has a subsequence which converges to some limit $\tilde{y}$. Because the correspondence $m \mapsto \Psi(m)$ is upper hemi-continuous, it follows that $\tilde{y} \in \Psi(m^*)$. But the definition of m^* implies that $y_n \notin Y$ for all n, so the limit $\tilde{y}$ is not an interior point of Y.

Finally, let $L := [y^*, \tilde{y}]$ denote the closed line segment whose ends are y^* and $\tilde{y}$ respectively. By Lemma 9, $\Psi(m^*)$ must be convex, so $L \subset \Psi(m^*)$. Because Y is closed, the set $Y \cap L$ is compact, and so includes a point y' which is as close as possible to $\tilde{y}$. Of course $y' \in \Psi(m^*) \cap Y$. If $\tilde{y} \in Y$, then $y' = \tilde{y}$. Otherwise $L \backslash Y$ includes a half-open line segment $(y', \tilde{y}]$. In either case, y' must be a boundary point of Y. ∎

7. Implications for Policy Reform

7.1. Potential gains from enhanced production efficiency

Diamond and Mirrlees (1971) chose to emphasize that production efficiency was necessary for a scheme of commodity taxation to maximize any given Paretian Bergson social welfare function. They themselves point out how there should then be no taxation of intermediate goods—including capital held by producers, as discussed by Judd (1999) in particular. The reason, of course, is that otherwise one would introduce unnecessary distortions which reduce efficiency in aggregate production.

Such distortions include those due to import tariffs and other policy measures which protect domestic industry. Production efficiency can only be preserved if import tariffs are restricted to goods that consumers buy directly, and if the tariffs are made equal to the usual consumer taxes on equivalent goods produced domestically. Indeed, such reasoning helps explain the results concerning second-best potential Pareto gains from free trade and from customs unions—as summarized in Hammond and Sempere (1995), for instance.

The proof used by Diamond and Mirrlees, however, actually demonstrates rather more—namely that any tax scheme leaving the economy at an interior point of the aggregate production set can be Pareto-dominated by an alternative tax scheme involving some small change in the relevant tax parameters, and so in the budget constraint facing each consumer. In fact, this process of finding Pareto improvements can continue until the resulting mean demand vector is on the boundary of the aggregate production set. This is what the main theorem above demonstrates. So production efficiency is necessary, not just for optimal taxation in the sense of Diamond and Mirrlees, but for the efficient use of any single tax instrument which generates the kind of one parameter family of budget sets satisfying Assumption 3 in Section 3.

As the argument leading to the main theorem demonstrates, this has the following general implication. Consider any reform which enhances production efficiency, so that the *status quo* mean net output vector $\hat{y}$ is an interior point of the reformed production set Y. Then the main theorem establishes that the production reform can be accompanied by a tax reform facing consumers with new budget sets $B^i(m^*)$ ($i \in I$) for some $m^* > 0$ such that the mean net demand set $\Psi(m^*)$ intersects the boundary of Y. Moreover, the result is a strict Pareto improvement.

These results are obviously in the spirit of the Kaldor–Hicks criterion for a potential Pareto improvement. Yet there is a fundamental difference. The original Kaldor–Hicks compensation tests rely on lump-sum transfers from those who gain from the policy reform to those who would otherwise lose. These transfers are generally incentive-incompatible, making it impossible to convert the theoretical potential Pareto improvement into actuality. This need to respect incentive constraints, indeed, was the basis of the vigorous disagreement between Kemp and Wan (1986) on one side, and Dixit and Norman (1986) on the other. Only in the case when the *status quo* is clearly determined by a centrally planned economic system does it seem safe to neglect these incentive constraints—a case suggested by the work of Lau, Qian, and Roland (1997) analysing reform in China.

Here, by contrast, incentive constraints have been explicitly recognized, so this kind of obstacle to finding an actual Pareto improvement cannot arise. In Hammond and Sempere (1995) we were able to adapt previous results due to Dixit and Norman (1980, 1986) and Grinols (1981) in particular to demonstrate second-best gains from freer trade. The implication is that in a small country, there should be free trade for producers, and import tariffs for consumers set equal to domestic consumption taxes. We were also able to show that similar gains can be had from customs unions, from enhanced competition between firms, and from adopting on a suitable scale any project whose benefits exceed its costs when these are all evaluated at suitable producer prices.

7.2. Project evaluation: a personal statement

At first it might seem that the efficiency result is of no relevance to project evaluation. After all, the purpose of project evaluation is presumably to identify desirable changes in production. This suggests that cost–benefit analysis should be explicitly designed for use when the economy may well remain very far from a second-best optimum, or from any kind of efficient allocation, even after any favourable project has been adopted. Then, with no presumption of production efficiency, it would seem more useful to think of demand or consumer prices rather than supply or producer prices as an aid to identifying favourable projects. That is the basic argument of Hammond (1980).

One major difficulty with this 'demand-side' approach, as Sen (1972) pointed out, is that knowing just a project's net output vector is typically insufficient. The project's effect on the economy as a whole, and so ultimately on consumer welfare, depends on other policy measures like tax reform which may be needed to re-equilibrate the economy after that project. After all, a public sector project which earns a large surplus for the government is probably favourable, but its effect on consumers depends crucially on how this surplus is used—what taxes are reduced, beneficial subsidies created, or additional public goods provided. Diewert (1983) shows how a favourable project in an open economy might benefit only foreign consumers and earn a net surplus for the domestic government, without any effect at all through price changes on domestic consumers. That prompted an investigation of how the shadow prices that should be used to evaluate projects depend on precisely what potential tax reform or other balancing policy is seen as most likely to accompany any favourable project—see Hammond (1986), for example.

Later, however, came the realization that some fairly robust results on the gains from trade do not require any kind of second-best optimality or even efficiency after trade liberalization has occurred. Such results do require, of course, that trade liberalization brings about a potential Pareto improvement which can be converted into an actual improvement through some compensation mechanism that transfers real income to those who would otherwise lose. Or better, as in the case of the Dixit and Norman (1980, 1986) scheme for freezing consumer prices, commodity taxes are required to adjust in a way that removes any possibility at all of there being any losers. Now, it turns out that the benefits from trade liberalization in the Dixit–Norman setting are entirely due to improved efficiency in the international organization of production, as countries are led to concentrate on activities where they enjoy a comparative advantage. What is more, as discussed in Hammond and Sempere (1995), the Dixit and Norman scheme allows Pareto gains to result from general reforms which enhance production efficiency, even with limits to redistribution. But really all such results are merely elaborations of the original Diamond–Mirrlees argument. Or, in somewhat more general settings, of the main theorem set out in Section 6 above.

This brings us back to project evaluation, but viewed from a different perspective. Let us readily concede that no single project which is likely ever to be submitted for evaluation will get us anywhere near what could be recognized as a second-best optimum, or even near the economy's production frontier. At best, we seem to be contemplating relatively minor alterations to the economy's projection possibility set—or rather, to a severely constrained set which allows input and outputs to be reallocated among existing firms and production activities, but which does not pretend to describe the full production possibilities taking account of all possible favourable projects.

So, suppose Y is interpreted as this severely constrained set, which must include the *status quo* net output vector $\hat{y}$. Consider a project in the form of an incremental net output vector $z \in \mathbb{R}^{G \cup H}$, with quantities of each good measured per head of population. Of course, if the *status quo* net output vector $\hat{y}$ is an interior point of Y, production efficiency can be enhanced merely by moving out to the frontier of Y, without the need for any project. So from now on assume that $\hat{y}$ is an efficient point of Y. This restriction should be regarded as indicating how constrained Y really must be.

If the project z is adopted, then the economy's production set will change from Y to $Y + \{z\}$, reflecting both the project z and the opportunities to rearrange production within the constrained set Y. Or more exactly, since one can choose whether or not to adopt the project, the new production set is $Y \cup (Y + \{z\}) = Y + \{0, z\}$. For the project z to enhance production efficiency, therefore, $\hat{y}$ should be an interior point of $Y + \{0, z\}$. That is, given that $\hat{y}$ is an efficient point of Y, there must exist some $y \in Y$ for which $y + z \gg \hat{y}$. Equivalently, one must have $z \in Z := \{\hat{y}\} + \mathbb{R}_{++}^{G \cup H} - Y$. Then the Diamond–Mirrlees efficiency argument establishes that the project z allows a potential Pareto improvement.

Viewed in this way, a cost–benefit test should be explicitly designed in order to identify efficiency enhancing projects. Then it can serve as the basis for an iterative planning procedure of accepting successive projects which pass the test. The resulting procedure will then meet some important criteria set out by Malinvaud (1967). That is, a project z should pass a cost–benefit test if and only if it is feasible and enhances production efficiency. Then, provided appropriate adjustments are made to each consumer's budget constraint, each step of the iterative procedure will produce a strict Pareto improvement. Moreover, the iterative procedure stops only when the resulting allocation is at least second-best Pareto efficient, if not a second-best welfare optimum, relative to the production set defined by combining Y with the menu of all available projects.

7.3. Evaluating small projects

Unfortunately, however, cost–benefit tests are not especially useful for identifying production efficiency gains in general. The reason is that such tests do not work well unless the project is small and the production set Y is convex or has a smooth boundary. Note that, even if Y does meet these conditions, the new production set $Y + \{0, z\} = Y \cup (Y + \{z\})$ will usually be non-convex and have a kinked boundary.

Accordingly, we shall consider instead when $\lambda z \in Z$ for all small $\lambda > 0$, so that adopting the project z on a small enough scale will produce an efficiency gain. In two obvious cases, there will be shadow price vectors $p \in \mathbb{R}^{G \cup H}$ such that cost–benefit tests of the form $pz > 0$ can be used to identify such favourable small projects.

The first case is when Y has a tangent hyperplane at $\hat{y}$.

Proposition 1. Suppose there exists a shadow price vector $p \in \mathbb{R}^{G \cup H}$ with $p > 0$ such that $py = p\hat{y}$ is the equation of the tangent hyperplane to Y at $\hat{y}$. Then $\lambda z \in Z$ for all small $\lambda > 0$ if $pz > 0$, and only if $pz \geqslant 0$.

Proof. Suppose that $pz > 0$. Because $py = p\hat{y}$ is a tangent hyperplane and Y admits free disposal, it follows that for all small $\lambda > 0$ the net output vector $\hat{y} - \lambda z$ is an interior point of Y. So for all small $\lambda > 0$, there exists $y \in Y$ with $y \gg \hat{y} - \lambda z$. It follows that $\lambda z = \hat{y} + u - y$ for some $u \geqslant 0$ and $y \in Y$, as required for λz to belong to Z.

Conversely, suppose that $\lambda z \in Z$ for all small $\lambda > 0$. Then there exist sequences of scalars $\lambda_k \downarrow 0$ and of vectors $y_k \in Y$ such that $y_k + \lambda_k z \gg \hat{y}$ $(k = 1, 2, \ldots)$. For each k one has $y_k \gg \hat{y} - \lambda_k z$, implying that $\hat{y} - \lambda_k z \in Y$ by free disposal. Because $\lambda_k \downarrow 0$ and $py = p\hat{y}$ is a tangent hyperplane, it follows that $pz \geqslant 0$. ∎

The second case is when Y is convex.

Proposition 2. Suppose that Y is a convex set. Let

$$P(\hat{y}) := \{p \in \mathbb{R}^{G \cup H} \setminus \{0\} \mid y \in Y \Rightarrow py \leqslant p\hat{y}\}$$

denote the (non-empty) set of price vectors which determine hyperplanes $py = p\hat{y}$ that support Y at the boundary point $\hat{y}$. Then $\lambda z \in Z$ for all small $\lambda > 0$ if and only if $pz > 0$ for all $p \in P(\hat{y})$.

Proof. Suppose there exists $\lambda > 0$ such that $\lambda z \in Z$. Then there exist $u \geqslant 0$ and $y \in Y$ such that $\lambda z = \hat{y} + u - y$. Consider any supporting price vector $p \in P(\hat{y})$. Clearly $p > 0$ because Y admits free disposal. So $pu > 0$. It follows that $p(\lambda z) = p(\hat{y} + u - y) > p(\hat{y} - y) \geqslant 0$, where the last inequality holds because $y \in Y$ and $p \in P(\hat{y})$. This implies that $pz > 0$. Moreover, the same is true for every $p \in P(\hat{y})$, as required.

Conversely, consider the two sets $K := \{\lambda z \mid \lambda > 0\}$ and Z. Both are non-empty and convex, with 0 as a common boundary point. If they intersect, it must be at some point $\bar{\lambda} z$ with $\bar{\lambda} > 0$. Then $\lambda z \in K \cap Z$ whenever $0 < \lambda \leqslant \bar{\lambda}$, so $\lambda z \in Z$ for all small $\lambda > 0$. On the other hand, if K and Z are disjoint, then they can be separated by a hyperplane $pz' = 0$ through the origin, with $pz' \geqslant 0$ for all $z' \in Z$, but $pz' \leqslant 0$ for all $z' \in K$, which implies that $pz \leqslant 0$. In particular, for all $u \geqslant 0$ and all $y \in Y$ one has $p(\hat{y} + u - y) \geqslant 0$, so $py \leqslant p(\hat{y} + u)$. This implies that $py \leqslant p\hat{y}$ for all $y \in Y$, so $p \in P(\hat{y})$. In other words, unless $\lambda z \in Z$ for all small $\lambda > 0$, there must exist $p \in P(\hat{y})$ such that $pz \leqslant 0$. This is the contrapositive of the desired conclusion. ∎

Note that the first part of the above proof actually demonstrates:

Corollary. If Y is convex and $z \in Z$, then $pz > 0$ for all $p \in P(\hat{y})$.

In other words, when Y is convex, then even if z is a large project, the test $pz > 0$ for all $p \in P(\hat{y})$ is necessary for z to increase production efficiency, but may not be sufficient.

A special case is when a small country can trade some commodities at fixed border prices, in which case the relevant marginal rates of substitution are equal to the ratios of these border prices. Hence, for such traded commodities, shadow prices should be set equal to border prices. That is essentially the rationale for the Little–Mirrlees approach to shadow pricing for traded goods.

7.4. Practical limitations

As was noted early on by Stiglitz and Dasgupta (1971), Dasgupta and Stiglitz (1972), as well as by Mirrlees (1972) himself, the Diamond–Mirrlees production efficiency argument faces some practical difficulties when changes in producer prices affect producer profits and so consumer incomes in ways that may be deleterious and hard to correct. Ideally, as assumed in Hammond and Sempere (1995), one would like changes in profit incomes to be sterilized in ways that freeze every consumer's after-tax income, before a uniform poll subsidy is paid to all consumers in order to distribute the benefits of a favourable reform. Presumably a government which can foresee what consumer prices would have been in the absence of any reform and can then identify and tax or subsidize any market transaction between a firm and a consumer in order to freeze consumer prices can also foresee what after-tax profits would have been in the *status quo* and freeze those also.

An important exception may come in small firms whose affairs are less subject to public scrutiny. Then profit potential in the *status quo* will often depend on private information, which therefore imposes incentive constraints on a truly feasible allocation. In this paper, however, the case when a small firm is wholly owned by just one consumer poses no problem in the main theorem because we have focused on each consumer's net trade vector. Thus, the inputs and outputs of such a small firm can be traded as if they were the personal demands and supplies of its owner. It is true that overall production efficiency may not be desirable once the production possibilities of small firms are included in the aggregate production set. But it does remain desirable for firms whose transactions with consumers and payments of profits to them can both be effectively monitored and subjected to appropriate taxes and subsidies.

A much more serious limitation is the restriction to a one parameter family of budget sets that are all independent of producer prices. Recall that in the case of linear commodity taxes, this formulation is based on the assumption that all commodity taxes can be varied in ways that sterilize all movements in producer prices, leaving consumer prices at the values they would have reached in the *status quo*. Such sterilization would seem to face at least two insuperable difficulties. Of these the first is the sheer administrative complexity, even in an age of extraordinarily powerful computers, of having what may be millions of different tax rates on different commodities. Any simplification that reduces the number of tax rates introduces the possibility that changes in some producer prices will not be fully sterilized before being passed on to consumers, some of whom may then be adversely effected. One possible remedy, suggested by the Diamond and Mirrlees (1971) discussion of Pareto improving tax changes, might be to try to 'oversterilize' price increases for goods which consumers buy in order to make sure that no consumer price rises for any such good, with the reverse holding for goods like labour which consumers sell. However, such generous tax reforms may violate the government's budget constraint even after a big increase in production efficiency. And in any case, they certainly introduce new complications which the main theorem of the paper makes no attempt at treating.

The second difficulty appears even more insuperable. This is the problem in an intertemporal economy of predicting what consumer prices would have been in the *status quo*, without any efficiency-enhancing reform. Without such predictions, freezing consumer prices at what they would have been is evidently quite impossible. Even with such predictions, disputes are likely regarding their accuracy, with some consumers claiming that their reasonable expectations have not been met.

7.5. Concluding assessment

Insuperable though these practical difficulties may be, they should be regarded as illustrating how hard it is to please everybody, and how much harder it is to make everybody admit they have been pleased. In other words, insisting on true Pareto improvements is surely excessively restrictive.

Even so, that is no excuse for disregarding the adverse effects that enhanced production efficiency can have on some consumers, such as those whose careers have become closely linked to industries, firms, and techniques of production whose continued survival is incompatible with efficiency. The Diamond–Mirrlees argument for production efficiency relied on being able to make sure that even these consumers would not be adversely effected because, for example, they could continue to supply their labour services for the same after-tax wage as in the *status quo*. If such compensation is not fully possible in the end, however, that may not by itself justify abandoning the efficiency objective. Instead, it is surely enough to have as an essential part of any efficiency-enhancing reform some reasonably generous assistance programme designed to retrain workers and to help them deal with the need to adjust their career plans. In particular, one cannot help feeling that sensitive efficiency-enhancing reform policies of this kind are likely to do much better than policies which maintain existing inefficiencies in order to placate politically powerful vested interests.

The main lesson to be drawn from the Diamond–Mirrlees efficiency theorem, therefore, may not lie in the formal details. Rather, it is a reminder that the case for enhanced production efficiency may be much more robust than had generally been recognized— certainly more robust than the prior work of Samuelson (1947) or of Lipsey and Lancaster (1956) had suggested, and possibly a little more robust than even careful readers of Diamond and Mirrlees (1971) might have supposed.

References

Barberà, S., and M. Jackson (1995) 'Strategy-Proof Exchange', *Econometrica* 63: 51–87.

Blackorby, C., and D. Donaldson (1988) 'Cash versus Kind, Self-Selection, and Efficient Transfers', *American Economic Review* 78: 691–700.

Coles, J. L., and P. J. Hammond (1995) 'Walrasian Equilibrium without Survival: Equilibrium, Efficiency, and Remedial Policy', in K. Basu, P. K. Pattanaik, and K. Suzumura (eds.), *Choice, Welfare and Development: A Festschrift in Honour of Amartya K. Sen* (Oxford: Oxford University Press): ch. 3, 32–64.

Córdoba, J., and P. J. Hammond (1998) 'Asymptotically Walrasian Strategy-Proof Exchange', *Mathematical Social Sciences* 36: 185–212.

Dasgupta, P., and P. J. Hammond (1980) 'Fully Progressive Taxation', *Journal of Public Economics* 13: 141–54.

—— S. A. Marglin, and A. K. Sen (1972) *Guidelines for Project Evaluation* (New York: United Nations).

—— and J. E. Stiglitz (1972) 'On Optimal Taxation and Public Production', *Review of Economic Studies* 39: 87–103.

Diamond, P. A., and J. A. Mirrlees (1971) 'Optimal Taxation and Public Production I: Production Efficiency' and 'II: Tax Rules', *American Economic Review* 61: 8–27 and 261–78.

Diewert, W. E. (1983) 'Cost–Benefit Analysis and Project Evaluation: A Comparison of Alternative Approaches', *Journal of Public Economics* 22: 265–302.

Dixit, A., and V. Norman (1980) *Theory of International Trade* (Welwyn, Herts.: James Nisbet).

—— and V. Norman (1986) 'Gains from Trade without Lump-Sum Compensation', *Journal of International Economics* 21: 99–110.

Grinols, E. (1981) 'An Extension of the Kemp–Wan Theorem on the Formation of Customs Unions', *Journal of International Economics* 11: 259–66.

Guesnerie, R. (1981) 'On Taxation and Incentives: Further Reflections on the Limits of Redistribution', Discussion Paper 89, Sonderforschungsbereich 21, University of Bonn; revised as ch. 1 of Guesnerie (1995).

—— (1995) *A Contribution to the Pure Theory of Taxation* (Cambridge: Cambridge University Press).

—— and K. Roberts (1984) 'Effective Policy Tools and Quantity Controls', *Econometrica* 52: 59–86.

Hammond, P. J. (1979) 'Straightforward Individual Incentive Compatibility in Large Economies', *Review of Economic Studies* 46: 263–82.

—— (1980) 'Cost–Benefit Analysis as a Planning Procedure', in D. A. Currie and W. Peters (eds.), *Contemporary Economic Analysis, ii* (Proceedings of the Conference of the Association of University Teachers of Economics, 1978) (London: Croom-Helm): ch. 8, 221–50.

—— (1986) 'Project Evaluation by Potential Tax Reform', *Journal of Public Economics* 30: 1–36.

—— (1987) 'Markets as Constraints: Multilateral Incentive Compatibility in Continuum Economies', *Review of Economic Studies* 54: 399–412.

—— (1999) 'Multilaterally Strategy-Proof Mechanisms in Random Aumann–Hildenbrand Macroeconomies', in M. Wooders (ed.), *Topics in Game Theory and Mathematical Economics: Essays in Honor of Robert J. Aumann* (Providence, RI: American Mathematical Society): 171–87.

—— and J. Sempere (1995) 'Limits to the Potential Gains from Economic Integration and Other Supply Side Policies', *Economic Journal* 105: 1180–204.

Hildenbrand, W. (1974) *Core and Equilibria of a Large Economy* (Princeton: Princeton University Press).

Judd, K. L. (1999) 'Optimal Taxation and Spending in General Competitive Growth Models', *Journal of Public Economics* 71: 1–26.

Kemp, M., and H. Wan (1986) 'Gains from Trade with and without Lump-Sum Compensation', *Journal of International Economics* 21: 111–21.

Lau, L. J., Y. Qian, and G. Roland (1997) 'Pareto-Improving Economic Reforms through Dual-Track Liberalization', *Economics Letters* 55: 285–92.

Lipsey, R. G., and K. J. Lancaster (1956) 'The General Theory of Second Best', *Review of Economic Studies* 24: 11–32.

Little, I. M. D., and J. A. Mirrlees (1968) *Manual of Industrial Project Analysis in Developing Countries, ii: Social Cost–Benefit Analysis* (Paris: OECD).

—— —— (1974) *Project Appraisal and Planning for Developing Countries* (New York: Basic Books; and London: Heinemann).

Malinvaud, E. (1967) 'Decentralized Procedures for Planning', in E. Malinvaud and M. O. L. Bacharach (eds.), *Activity Analysis in the Theory of Growth and Planning* (London: Macmillan): ch. 7, 170–208.

Mas-Colell, A. (1977) 'Indivisible Commodities and General Equilibrium Theory', *Journal of Economic Theory* 16: 443–56.

—— (1985) *The Theory of General Economic Equilibrium: A Differentiable Approach* (Cambridge: Cambridge University Press).

Mirrlees, J. A. (1969) 'The Evaluation of National Income in an Imperfect Economy', *Pakistan Development Review* 9: 1–13.

—— (1971) 'An Exploration in the Theory of Optimal Income Taxation', *Review of Economic Studies* 38: 175–208.

—— (1972) 'On Producer Taxation', *Review of Economic Studies* 39: 105–11.

—— (1986) 'The Theory of Optimal Taxation', in K. J. Arrow and M. D. Intriligator (eds.), *Handbook of Mathematical Economics, iii* (Amsterdam: North-Holland): ch. 24, 1197–249.

Samuelson, P. A. (1947) *Foundations of Economic Analysis* (Cambridge, Mass.: Harvard University Press).

Schmeidler, D. (1970) 'Fatou's Lemma in Several Dimensions', *Proceedings of the American Mathematical Society* 24: 300–6.

Seade, J. K. (1977) 'On the Shape of Optimal Tax Schedules', *Journal of Public Economics* 7: 203–35.

Sen, A. K. (1972) 'Control Areas and Accounting Prices: An Approach to Economic Evaluation', *Economic Journal* 82 (Suppl.): 486–501.

Stiglitz, J. E., and P. Dasgupta (1971) 'Differential Taxation, Public Goods and Economic Efficiency', *Review of Economic Studies* 38: 151–74.

Vickrey, W. S. (1945) 'Measuring Marginal Utility by Reactions to Risk', *Econometrica* 13: 319–33.

Yamazaki, A. (1978) 'An Equilibrium Existence Theorem without Convexity Assumptions', *Econometrica* 46: 541–55.

—— (1981) 'Diversified Consumption Characteristics and Conditionally Dispersed Endowment Distribution: Regularizing Effect and Existence of Equilibria', *Econometrica* 49: 639–45.

13 Valuing Our Future: Cost–Benefit Analysis and Sustainability

GEOFFREY HEAL

1. Introduction

Can existing patterns of human activity safely continue unaltered over the long term, or will they eventually lead to catastrophe? This central issue underlies the growing concern about sustainability.[1]

Some of the issues prompting this question are a familiar part of the daily news agenda. Consumption of carbon-based fuels and depletion of carbon-consuming forests is altering the natural carbon cycle of the planet. There is an emerging consensus that the disturbance of this cycle is increasing the global mean temperature. This leads one naturally to question whether current patterns of energy use can continue without provoking quite unacceptable outcomes: in short, whether they are sustainable.

Similar questions are prompted by the observed loss of biodiversity. We are driving species extinct at a rate unparalleled since the demise of the dinosaurs, some fifty million years ago. These are irreversible, final losses: whatever our technological sophistication, we cannot recreate species which are extinct. Biodiversity is important to humans in many different ways, so again one is led to question the sustainability of the dimensions of human activity which lead to biodiversity loss. Will they impoverish us to an unacceptable degree?

Economic decisions are driving phenomena such as global warming and biodiversity loss. The decision to use fossil rather than solar energy is economic, likewise the decision to use more rather than less energy. And the changes in habitat which lead to extinction, are also economically driven: it appears more profitable to chop down rainforests and plant coffee or other cash crops than to maintain them intact. So behind many of the offending dimensions of human activity are economic choices and calculations. We will not improve significantly the unsustainability of human activity unless we can develop an economic environment within which such choices are no longer attractive. In other words, we need to change 'the rules of the economic game' so that it becomes economically rational to pursue alternatives which are sustainable. Cost–benefit analysis is one of the most relevant rules of the game.

---

[1] This definition, although far from those common in economics, is very close to that used by Holdren, Daily, and Ehrlich (1995), who say that 'A sustainable process or condition is one that can be maintained indefinitely without progressive diminution of valued qualities inside or outside the system in which the process operates or the condition prevails.'

1.1. Outline of the study

The next section, Section 2, reviews some of the salient principles of cost–benefit analysis as it is currently practised, especially its methodological foundations in discounted utilitarianism. It notes the contrast between the implications of discounted utilitarianism with respect to the value of the future; social attitudes towards the future as revealed by policy concerns; and individual attitudes towards the future as revealed by recent economic and psychological studies. Discounted utilitarianism displays more myopia than seems consistent with either social or individual attitudes.

In Section 3 I then suggest a more future-oriented approach to cost–benefit analysis, with an emphasis on placing more weight on the long run and on the explicit valuation of environmental assets than is conventional. This draws on recent work on balancing the importance of the present and the future, and on the literature of the importance of ecosystem services to human welfare (Daily 1997).

The Appendix is devoted to a review of models of optimal development which incorporate the approach introduced in Section 3: this review is relatively technical and so is separated in the Appendix. The aim is to provide the analytical foundations of a sustainable approach to cost–benefit analysis, which is very closely related to a future-oriented approach to optimal development. The aim of the analytical framework is to see how these values can be computed, how they relate to each other, and how they relate to parameters such as discount rates, the supply conditions of environmental assets, etc. The conclusions of the Appendix are summarized in Section 4.

Section 5 sets out the implications for the foundations of cost–benefit analysis. Section 6 concludes.

2. Cost–Benefit Analysis

Cost–benefit analysis of environmental conservation operates in outline as follows. Identify the services which the environmental good will provide now and in the future, value them in money terms, reduce these to a present discounted value, and compare this with the present value of the costs of preservation. If the difference is positive, preserve the asset, and vice versa. The key problem is that this process can discriminate in subtle ways against the preservation of environmental assets, by undervaluing them. There are two central issues here.

The costs of preservation are usually in the present, whereas the benefits from preservation of many environmental assets are in the rather distant future. It is a characteristic of such assets that they provide a continuing flow of services indefinitely, so that the bulk of their contribution is *always* in the future, indeed in the distant future. For example, the Korub forest in Nigeria has provided carbon sequestration and biodiversity support services for many thousands of years, and the forests of tropical Australia have done the same for an order of magnitude longer. Given a chance, they could continue for at least as long.

In addition, the costs of preservation are frequently easily quantifiable, whereas the benefits are hard to value. Costs are typically opportunity costs associated with the restriction of industrial or commercial activity: benefits come from species diversity, water purity, aesthetic value, and a range of other contributions hard to value quantitatively but presumably nonetheless important for that. A corollary of this is that cost estimates are often relatively certain, while benefits estimates are frequently quite uncertain.

In summary, the conventional approach stacks the odds somewhat against environmental preservation in the process of valuing environmental goods and comparing the benefits from preservation with the costs. It compares benefits which are distant, hence discounted, and uncertain, against present and apparently firm costs.

There are two key steps in correcting this imbalance One is to derive a method of valuing projects which places more value on long-run benefits than does the conventional approach. The usual approach is rooted in the discounted utilitarianism of Bentham and his economic followers: we need an alternative which is as watertight logically and as practical and operational, yet reflects different values. Secondly, we need to recognize explicitly the possible values of environmental assets: we must recognize that stocks of environmental assets have value, as well as the flows of consumption which they generate.

2.1. Conclusions: a preview

My conclusions are optimistic: there are ways in which we can systematically and operationally place more value on the future than we now do, and they have several features that recommend them strongly. These approaches lead to different ways of calculating shadow prices on long-lived environmental assets, ways which produce higher prices and so more cautious use of, and more incentive to preserve, ecological assets. In particular, the approaches proposed here suggest that under certain circumstances it will be appropriate to include in the shadow prices of long-lived assets terms reflecting undiscounted the contributions that they will make in the future: these approaches sanction in a limited and partial way the idea that a zero discount rate can be appropriate for very long-lived projects.

One of the alternative approaches goes much further and indicates that ranking projects by present discounted values may be inappropriate: under some circumstances, a concept of 'sustainable net benefit' should replace that of present value. Sustainable net benefit is the flow of net benefits that a project can generate on a continuing basis:[2] in other words, the flow of net benefits it can generate sustainably. A rigorous mathematical basis is provided for all of these new results.

It is relatively straightforward also to incorporate into our analysis the notion that stocks of environmental assets are a source of value to society: this leads to a further increase in shadow prices, and emphasizes the importance of natural or ecological capital as a source of wealth and of 'sustainable income'.

The total impact of both of these changes is likely in practice to be to increase greatly the calculated economic return on conserving long-lived environmental assets, making

---

[2] It is reminiscent of the accounting concept of the profitability of a business 'as a going concern'.

a fundamental difference to the economic analysis of issues such as global warming, habitat fragmentation, and ecosystem preservation, and indicating higher returns than hitherto reported on investments in conservation of critical ecosystems. The approach to cost–benefit analysis proposed here has to be used in conjunction with results from the emerging literature on ecosystem goods and services (Daily 1997, Heal 2000). This literature details the economic contributions made by many ecosystems, some naturally quite invisible. Analysis of these contributions provides the data from which the benefits of environmental conservation can be computed.[3]

2.2. Discounted utilitarianism

The default criterion for ranking development paths and investment projects, including environmental conservation projects, is provided by the discounted utilitarian framework. Following the approach introduced by Bentham in the nineteenth century, the best path is said to be that which provides the greatest present discounted value of net benefits. Many authors have expressed reservations about the balance that this strikes between present and future. Cline (1992) and Broome (1992) have argued for the use of a zero discount rate in the context of global warming, and Ramsey and Harrod, the founders of the modern theories of dynamic economics, were scathing about the ethical dimensions of discounting in a more general context, commenting respectively that discounting the welfare of future people '*is ethically indefensible and arises merely from the weakness of the imagination*' and that it is a '*polite expression for rapacity and the conquest of reason by passion*' (see Ramsey 1928; Harrod 1948; and Heal 1993). It is ironic that a practice so roundly condemned by the founders of intertemporal economics has come to occupy so central a position in the field. It may be fair to say that discounted utilitarianism dominates our approach more for lack of convincing alternatives than because of the conviction that it inspires. It has proven particularly controversial with non-economists concerned with environmental valuations.[4]

A positive utility discount rate forces a fundamental asymmetry between the treatments of, and the implicit valuations of, present and future generations, particularly those very far into the future. This asymmetry is troubling when dealing with environmental matters such as climate change, species extinction, and disposal of nuclear waste, as many of the consequence of these may be felt only in the very long run indeed, a hundred or more years into the future. At any positive discount rate these consequences will clearly be trivialized in project evaluations. To illustrate, if one discounts present world GNP over two hundred years at 5 per cent per annum, it is worth only a few hundred thousand dollars, the price of a suburban home in an industrial country and less than the annual salaries of many business executives. Discounted at

---

[3] The valuation of these contributions in dollar terms raises a complex set of issues, which require further research: see Heal (2000).

[4] The legitimacy of discounting is in fact a most complex issue, and the comments of Ramsey and Harrod, though perceptive and pointed, do not do it justice. Discounting of future utilities is in some sense logically necessary (see Heal 1985, 1998): without it one encounters a variety of unsettling paradoxes. The distinction between discounting future utilities in the evaluation of development programmes and the discounting of future benefits in cost–benefit studies, also has to be borne in mind (Heal 1993, 1998).

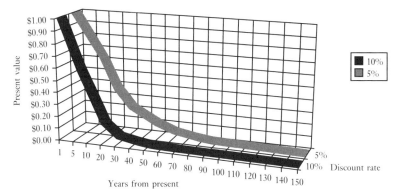

Fɪɢ. 13.1. *Present value of $1 in the future, 5 per cent and 10 per cent discount rate*

10 per cent, it is equivalent to a used car. Figure 13.1 shows the present value of $1 at various future dates, discounted at 5 and 10 per cent: clearly benefits occurring more than half a century ahead are in effect neglected, yet many of the main environmental concerns naturally require time-horizons of a century or more.

There is a mismatch between economic and scientific time-scales. To economists, twenty years is a long time: to biologists and ecologists, half a century is a relatively short time. Economic and ecological consequences unfold over different time-frames. On the basis of conventional discount rates, it is completely irrational to be concerned about global warming, nuclear waste, species extinction, and other long-run phenomena: the long-run future is irrelevant, as Figure 13.1 emphasizes! Yet societies obviously *are* worried about these issues, and are actively considering devoting very substantial resources to them. So a very real part of our collective concern about the future is clearly not captured by discounted utilitarianism. As economic institutions and procedures should capture society's values and concerns, we have to find a more satisfactory alternative. There is interesting empirical evidence, to which we shall return, that individuals making their own decisions do not in fact compare present and future by discounting the future relative to the present at a constant discount rate, as in the standard discounted utilitarian approach.

We need a framework for considering very long-time horizons which is sensitive to both present and future, and more consistent with the approach implicit in individual choices and with the valuations implicit in social concerns for the welfare of future generations. It is in part this that is driving an interest in formalizing the concept of sustainability, and the associated unease with the standard economic framework based on discounted utilitarianism.

2.3. Empirical evidence on attitudes to the future

Before reviewing a range of theoretical alternatives, consider briefly the empirical evidence on how individuals evaluate the future relative to the present. This indicates that they use a framework different in certain salient respects from the standard discounted utilitarian approach. Of course, even if we have a clear picture of how individuals form their judgements about the relative weights of present and future, this does not necessarily have normative implications: we might still feel that relative to some appropriate set of ethical standards they give too little (or too much) weight to the future, and so are an imperfect guide to social policy. However, in a democratic society, individual attitudes towards the present–future trade-off presumably have some informative value about the appropriate social trade-off and at least an element of normative significance.

There is a growing body of empirical evidence which suggests that the discount rate which people apply to future projects depends upon, and declines with, the futurity of the project. Some of this evidence is based on statistical studies of individual decisions. These include savings decisions, choices in financial markets (Lowenstein and Thaler 1989; Thaler 1981), and the valuation of public projects intended to bring present and future benefits (Cropper *et al.* 1994). This evidence is complemented and reinforced by experimental studies, carried out by economists and by psychologists: the results of the psychological research are reviewed in Lowinstein and Elster (1992). Over relatively short periods up to perhaps five years, they use discount rates which are high —in the region of 15 per cent or more. For projects extending about ten years, the implied discount rates are closer to standard rates—perhaps 10 per cent. As the horizon extends the implied discount rates drops to in the region of 5 per cent for thirty to fifty years and down to the order of 2 per cent for 100 years. It also appears from the empirical evidence that the discount rate used by individuals, and the way in which it changes over time, depends on the magnitude of the change in income involved.

2.4. *Logarithmic discounting*

This empirically identified behaviour is consistent with general results from natural sciences which find that human responses to a change in a stimulus are non-linear, and are inversely proportional to the existing level of the stimulus. For example, the human response to a change in the intensity of a sound is inversely proportional to the initial sound level: the louder the sound initially, the less we respond to a given increase. This is the Weber–Fechner law, formalized in the statement that human response to a change in a stimulus is inversely proportional to the pre-existing stimulus.[5]

The empirical results on declining discount rates cited above suggest that something similar is happening in human responses to changes in the futurity of an event: a given change in futurity (e.g. postponement by one year) leads to a smaller decrease in weighting, the further the event already is in the future. This is quite natural: postponement by one year from next year to the year after, is clearly quite a different phenomenon from postponement from fifty to fifty-one years hence. One is doubling the waiting time: the other is increasing it by 2 per cent. Although they are both postponement

---

[5] In symbols, $dr/ds = K/s$ or $r = K \log s$ where r is a response, s a stimulus, and K a constant. This relationship has been found to apply to human responses to the intensity of both light and sound signals.

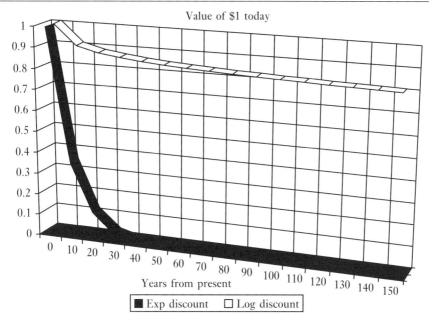

Fɪɢ. 13.2. *Logarithmic and exponential discounting*

by one year, the former represents a major change: the latter, a small one. If we assume that the reaction to postponement of a pay-off by a given period of time is indeed inversely proportional to its initial distance in the future, then the Weber–Fechner law can be applied, with the result that the discount rate is inversely proportional to distance into the future.

Another way of saying this, is that we react to *proportional* rather than *absolute* increases in the time distance. We react equally to all 10 per cent postponements, but not to all ten-year postponements.[6] This implies that we discount differently from the

---

[6] Denote the *discount factor* applied to costs or benefits in period t by $\Delta(t)$: hence a benefit B in period t is worth $B\Delta(t)$ in current terms, where $\Delta(t) < 1$. Recall that in this case the *discount rate* $q(t)$ is the rate of change of the discount factor, i.e. the rate at which the weight on the future declines over time. Hence $q(t) = -\dot{\Delta}(t)/\Delta(t)$. We can now formalize the idea that a given increase in the number of years into the future has an impact on the weight given to the event which is inversely proportional to the initial distance in the future as

$$q(t) = -\frac{1}{\Delta}\frac{d\Delta}{dt} = -\frac{K}{t} \quad \text{or} \quad \Delta(t) = e^{-K\log t} = t^{-K}$$

for K a constant.

Such a formulation has several attractive properties: the discount rate q goes to zero in the limit, the discount factor $\Delta(t)$ also goes to zero, and the integral $\int_1^\infty \Delta(t)dt = \int_1^\infty e^{-K\log t}dt = \int_1^\infty t^{-K}dt$ converges for K positive, as it always is.

Discounting where the discount rate falls to zero in the long run is called 'slow discounting' by Harvey (1994), who reviews the growing literature on non-constant discount rates. In general the phenomenon of time-varying discount rates has been referred to as 'hyperbolic discounting'. Henderson and Bateman (1995) also give an interesting review and interpretation of recent studies of non-constant discount rates.

conventional geometric or exponential model: it implies that in discounting, we measure distance into the future according to the logarithm of time. We are measuring time by equal proportional increments rather than by equal absolute increments. We shall call this 'logarithmic discounting'.[7] Logarithmic discounting at a given discount rate places very much more weight on the long-term future than does exponential discounting at the same constant rate (see Figure 13.2). It is more consistent with both individual behaviour and revealed social values than is the conventional approach.

3. Alternative Foundations for Cost–Benefit Analysis

3.1. Sustainability and valuing environmental assets

Finding a framework which allows for a comprehensive approach to the valuation of environmental assets is a central part of the agenda in defining and implementing sustainability. Unfortunately systematic research has only just begun to scratch the surface of this complex and far-reaching issue. There are several ways in which environmental assets are sources of value.[8] In this section we review these briefly and consider their implications for the choice of an analytical framework for sustainable cost–benefit analysis.

Environmental assets are valuable as sources of knowledge: this is one of the sources of value in biodiversity, the source which is tapped in biological prospecting and in the famous Merck–InBio deal.[9] The point here is that many pharmaceutically valuable products, and many agriculturally valuable crop strains, have been developed from species found in the wild. This point cannot be overemphasized: according to a report to the National Academy of Sciences of the USA, one-third by value of the pharmaceuticals sold in the USA, over $60 billion in current market value, were originally obtained from plants or insects, and many of the more robust grain species have likewise been derived from specimens found in the wild.

Environmental assets also play a profound role as life-support systems: green plants produce the oxygen without which animals die; bacteria-clean water creates and then fertilizes soil; insects pollinate plants. All of these activities are absolutely crucial in the maintenance of human life. Damage done to soil ecosystems by pollution has reduced their ability to purify water collected in reservoirs, and so increased the need for expensive water purification plants. In cases such as this, we can relatively easily asses the cost of destroying the microorganisms in the soil which purify water as it passes through. It is the cost of building and running water purification plants to provide the services once provided by the ecosystems. For the watershed of a large urban area, this can

---

[7] This is quite consistent with the approach taken in for example acoustics, where in response to the Weber–Fechner law sound intensity is measured in decibels which respond to the logarithm of the energy content of the sound waves, and not to energy content itself. In general, non-constant discount rates can be interpreted as a non-linear transformation of the time axis.

[8] For a comprehensive review of the current state of knowledge in this area, see Gretchen Daily's recent book (Daily 1997).

[9] For details of this and similar deals, see Heal (2000).

require an investment of billions of dollars.[10] This investment will have to be repeated as equipment wears out every few decades, with running costs in the interim. And even after all this expenditure, chemical purification is less satisfactory than the natural alternative.

Environmental assets, such as animals, plants, and even landscapes, also have an intrinsic value, a value in and of themselves independently of their anthropocentric value, and similarly they may have a right to exist independently of their value to humanity.[11] It is hard, if not impossible as a matter of principle, to place an economic value on such values and rights.[12]

Explicit recognition of all of the ways in which environmental assets are valuable, seems an essential step in implementing the concept of sustainability. Formally, this means that utility is derived not just from a flow of consumption that can be produced from the environment, used either as a consumption good or as an input to production: utility is also derived from the very existence of a stock, so that society's instantaneous utility at each point in time can be expressed as a function $u(c_t, s_t)$, where c_t is a flow of consumption at time t and s_t an environmental stock at that date.[13] This is the difference between valuing a forest only for the trees derived from it—in this case the utility or welfare u depends only on consumption c, and is denoted $u(c)$—and valuing the forest for this *and* as a forest in its own right, in which case welfare u depends on consumption c and on the stock of trees (or some other measure of the forest size) s, and is denoted $u(c, s)$. The stock proxies for carbon sequestration, biodiversity support, watershed functions, and many other services. Of course, to represent the values of environmental assets as just a function of a single number is a heroic oversimplification, but it does to some degree capture one of the central implications of the ecosystem services literature,[14] namely that stocks of environmental assets or natural capital affect human welfare. It is in the best traditions of growth theory, indeed economic theory in general, to take the first steps in exploring new issues by treating them in a very aggregative manner.

In many cases it is not the pure existence of a stock of an environmental asset that produces value to society: this stock has to be used in some way and its use may require complementary investments. In the case of biodiversity, the services are not a function only of the stock of biodiversity in existence. If one thinks of the provision of knowledge as discussed above, then the extent of this service depends on the stock, on the resources allocated to biological prospecting, and also on the state of our knowledge

---

[10] New York City provides a good example. It recently discovered that the cost of constructing a filtration plant to purify its water would be $6–8 billion, whereas the same result could be achieved by restoring the ecological integrity of its watershed region at the cost of $1.2 billion. The economic value of an environmental asset—a functioning watershed—is dramatically illustrated by this case. For more details, see Chichilnisky and Heal (1997) and Heal (2000).

[11] A discussion of some of these philosophical issues can be found in Kneese and Schultze (1985). A fascinating recent paper by Ng is also recommended (forthcoming).

[12] Perhaps respecting them has to be seen as a constraint on society's economic activities, and we should not seek to trade them off against other goals.

[13] As for example in Krautkraemer (1985) and in Beltratti, Chichilnisky, and Heal (1993, 1994, 1995).

[14] See Daily (1997).

of molecular biology and genetics.[15] If one thinks of the recreational services of a forest, which clearly depend inter alia on the forest stock, then these also depend on transportation possibilities and accommodation possibilities. In general, for each category of service provided by environmental assets, there will be processes by which this service is provided and complementary inputs involved in the provision of the service. Aggregative models of the type which I review here do not and are not designed to capture these details: they are intended to provide insights at a more general level about the use and conservation of environmental assets.

3.2. Sustainability and the future

Above I identified two key steps in making cost–benefit analysis more consistent with sustainability: recognizing the values of environmental assets, and valuing the future appropriately. We have discussed issues concerned with the valuation of environmental assets, and also the shortcomings of conventional cost–benefit analysis with respect to the future. What are the alternatives?

An alternative to ranking paths by the discounted sum of utilities is to rank them by some measure of their long-run pay-off. This is an approach used in game theory and dynamic programming, where in some cases the long-run average pay-off is used.[16] This is clearly closer in spirit to the concept of sustainability, and a natural generalization of this is the 'green golden rule', introduced in Beltratti, Chichilnisky, and Heal (1995). The green golden rule is the configuration of the economy which gives the maximum indefinitely maintainable benefit level (see Figure 13.7 of the Appendix for a graphical interpretation).[17] Ranking alternative strategies by their maximum sustainable utility levels is certainly placing more emphasis on the future: in fact, one can even argue that it is going too far in this respect (see Heal 1998).

There is a natural and attractive compromise between the discounted utilitarian approach, which neglects the long-run future completely, and the green golden rule or maximum sustainable utility level, which neglects the present: this is to take a mixture of the two. This approach has been clearly articulated by Chichilnisky (1995): she suggests a set of principles or axioms for ranking alternative development paths and for balancing the present and the future. She shows that these principle lead us to rank them precisely by a mixture of the utilitarian and green golden rule approaches. Chichilnisky's approach derives from a social choice perspective, in which generations are distinct members of an intertemporal society, each with its own preferences, which have to be combined into a social or representative preference representing all generations in a reasonable way. To be more precise, Chichilnisky requires that the social ordering of alternative development paths should be sensitive to changes in the paths

---

[15] I speculate that this illustrates a general point: the more our scientific knowledge advances, the more we value our environmental assets.

[16] Formally, this is defined by taking the average pay-off over an interval from period T to period T_1; and then taking the limit as T and T_1 become infinite.

[17] It is related to, and extends, the 'golden rule of economic growth' introduced by Phelps (1961), and is formalized by ranking paths according to their limiting utility values.

in the very far future (she calls this 'non-dictatorship of the present'), and also to changes in the paths in the present and near future (she calls this 'non-dictatorship of the future'). These requirements, plus some more technical mathematical requirements, lead to a unique way of ranking paths which places positive weight on the limiting properties of a path and also places positive weight on its properties in the near term.[18]

4. Sustainable Development

Beltratti, Chichilnisky, and Heal (1993, 1994, 1995) and Heal (1998) have investigated the result of studying 'optimal development' when combining a future-oriented criterion such as the green golden rule or Chichilnisky's criterion with a utility function which assigns value to environmental stocks.[19]

Any path which is optimal in either of these senses has associated with it 'shadow prices' or social valuations: they value the stocks and flows in the economy in a way which reflects fully their contributions to the objective. These are therefore the prices which we want for a more sustainable or future-oriented cost–benefit analysis and accounting: they reflect the values of various goods and services from a long-run perspective which also reflects the full range of contributions made by environmental assets. Interestingly, if one adopts either the green golden rule or Chichilnisky's criterion, it may not be the case that an optimal development schedule will maximize the present value of benefits at these prices: it may instead maximize the level of *sustainable benefits*. I shall return to this later.

We need to understand what this formalization implies for patterns of consumption, investment, and resource use over time. We also need to understand the closely related issue of what it implies for the behaviour of the shadow prices of consumption, investment, and resources, as these are the prices that should be used in cost–benefit analysis. How do these shadow prices relate to each other, to the discount rate, and to time? If we have answers to these questions, we shall know what this approach means for project evaluation. The answers to these questions can be derived from a study of the optimal development paths of economies embodying the characteristics of sustainability noted in the previous sections.[20]

[18] Chichilnisky's approach is formalized by the criterion, $\theta \int_0^\infty u(c_t, s_t) e^{-\delta t} dt + (1 - \theta) \lim_{t \to \infty} u(c_t, s_t)$.

[19] In models of optimal economic development it leads to problems which are technically more challenging than the dynamic optimization problems usual in economics. This stems from the presence of the term $\lim_{t \to \infty} u(c_t, s_t)$ in the maximand—see Heal (1998).
There are two general observations which we can make about solutions. One is that any optimal path must satisfy the 'usual' Ramsey–Hotelling first-order or local optimality conditions, reviewed at length in, for example, Heal (1973) and Dasgupta and Heal (1979). These conditions are the mathematical expression of the observation that on any path which maximizes the criterion it cannot be possible to shift consumption between two proximate dates and thereby increase the discounted integral of utilities, for if this were possible one could increase the first term in the maximand. The local behaviour of a solution over finite periods of time will therefore be quite familiar to economists from the earlier literature on optimal resource management. The second observation is that the long-run behaviour of an optimal path is influenced by the green golden rule and the path either approaches this or something close to it.

[20] This is exactly analogous to the use by Dasgupta, Marglin, and Sen (1972) and Little and Mirrlees (1974) of the neoclassical optimal growth models of the 1970s as a basis for deriving rules for project evaluation.

In the Appendix, I set out a series of models of the optimal use of an environmental asset, firstly exhaustible and then renewable. I start with the simplest such model, due to Hotelling (1931), and then move to more complex extensions of this. For each model, I investigate the optimal paths using several definitions of optimality, ranging from those which clearly are not consistent with sustainability to those which embody fully the prerequisites that we have identified for this concept, including the green golden rule. In the next section I set out the implications of these models for cost–benefit analysis: these are quite substantial.

5. Sustainability and Project Evaluation

Models of optimal development, such as those studied in the Appendix, have been used to provide an analytical framework for cost–benefit analysis.[21] They allow one to study the role of the objective function, including specifically the choice of discount rate and the degree of future-orientation, in determining shadow prices. A framework for cost–benefit analysis and project evaluation is a natural extension of this. It is obtained by using optimal development models to analyse the relationships between the shadow prices of different commodities, how these should move over time and of how they relate to exogenous parameters such as the discount rate, preferences, production functions, and resource supply conditions.

The shadow prices associated with an optimal development plan indicate the marginal contributions that increments of the associated commodities can make to the objective function. They are precisely the information needed to evaluate projects which would affect the supplies of these commodities. They are also for the same reason precisely the information needed to value the stocks of these commodities: hence their dual roles in providing frameworks for national income accounting and project evaluation. In view of this, it is important to understand the impact on shadow prices of the two features crucial to the analysis of sustainability—recognizing the value of environmental assets, and valuing the long run. We turn to this now, and see exactly how changes in the treatment of environmental assets and changes in the balance struck between present and future affect shadow prices.

5.1. Exhaustible resources

The simplest framework for exploring this issue is given by the set of models of depletion of an exhaustible resource analysed in the Appendix. There I consider four different cases, constructed to range from the conventional approach which places little or no weight on the issues which motivate our interest in sustainability, to cases which are at the other end of the spectrum and represent these concerns fully. I investigate how these alternative formulations, from less to more sustainable, affect the shadow prices, particularly of the resource. The alternative formulations considered are:

---

[21] The classic references in this latter case are Little and Mirrlees (1974) and Dasgupta, Marglin, and Sen (1972).

1. The conventional discounted utilitarian case, in which one studies optimal depletion when only the rate of use of the resource is a source of utility. This is the original Hotelling case.[22]
2. As in case 1 above, but with the flow *and the stock* as sources of utility, as indicated by Section 3 above. This is still a utilitarian formulation, but is consistent with the ecosystem services literature.[23]
3. Depletion according to the Chichilnisky criterion, still recognizing the importance of environmental capital as a source of services.[24]
4. Depletion according to the green golden rule policy, which selects the highest sustainable utility level, with utility depending on both consumption of natural resources and on their stock.[25]

These cases reflect values which are progressively more 'pro-environmental' or 'sustainable'. The first case places no weight on the long run and none on environmental assets. The second places weight on environmental assets but not on the long run: the third places weight on both, and the fourth places weight only on the long run in the time dimensions, as well as valuing environmental assets. They are summarized in Table 13.1.

The time-paths of consumption and of the resource stock which are optimal in these four cases are compared in Figure 13.3. Here the horizontal axis measures the resource stock s, and the vertical axis, the level of consumption c. The first formulation, the classical Hotelling formulation, leads to the consumption of the entire stock, as shown by the path labelled 'Hotelling path'. Adding the stock of the resource as an argument of the utility function leads to a lower consumption path, with a positive stock maintained for ever (see 'utilitarian path' in the figure). The Chichilnisky criterion leads to lower consumption and the preservation of a larger stock, as shown. Pursuing the green golden rule—the maximum sustainable utility level—leads to an extremely conservative policy, preserving the entire stock for ever.[26] Note that the initial consumption level on the optimal path is greatest on the Hotelling path, smaller on the path corresponding to valuation of the stock with the discounted utilitarian criterion, smaller again on the path optimal according to Chichilnisky's criterion, and is zero according to the green golden rule.

This gives us important information about shadow prices: shadow prices equal the marginal utility of consumption, and so are inversely related to consumption levels.[27]

---

[22] Formally, the problem is: $\max \int_0^\infty u(c_t)e^{-\delta t}dt$ s.t. $\int_0^\infty c_t dt \leq s_0$.

[23] Formally, this problem is: $\max \int_0^\infty u(c_t, s_t)e^{-\delta t}dt$ s.t. $\int_0^\infty c_t dt \leq s_0$.

[24] Now we have $\max\{\theta \int_0^\infty u(c_t, s_t)e^{-\delta t}dt + (1-\theta)\lim_{t\to\infty} u(c_t, s_t)\}$ s.t. $\int_0^\infty c_t dt \leq s_0$.

[25] $\max\limits_{c_t, s_t \forall t} \lim\limits_{t\to\infty} u(c_t, s_t)$ s.t. $u(c_t, s_t)$ constant.

[26] This depends on the assumptions that $u'_1(0) < \infty$ and $u_1(0) > -\infty$. This amounts to an assumption that consuming a flow of the resource is not essential to survival. In fact, in Heal (1998) it is shown that preserving the entire stock for ever is also optimal for the Rawlsian criterion of optimality—maximizing the welfare of the least well-off generation—and for the overtaking criterion.

[27] We know from the condition for the maximization of the Hamiltonian that the shadow price of consumption is greater than or equal to its marginal utility: hence

$$u'_1(c_0) \leq \lambda_0, = \text{ if } c_0 > 0,$$

i.e. the initial shadow price is greater than or equal to the initial marginal utility of consumption, with equality if the initial consumption level is positive.

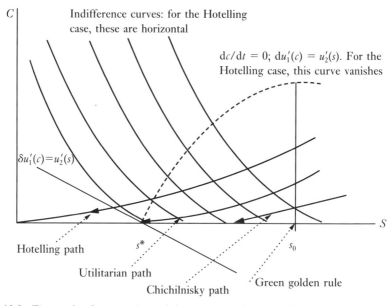

FIG. 13.3. *Time-paths of consumption and the resource stock compared*

It follows, then, that shadow prices are ranked in the opposite order in these four cases, being highest in the case of the maximization of long-run utility, less high with Chichilnisky's mixed criterion, lower again in the case of maximization of a discounted sum of utilities with the stock a source of utility, and lowest of all in the Hotelling case. In sum: *the more recognition we give to the services of environmental assets, and the more future-oriented we are, the higher is the appropriate shadow price of natural capital.*

Within each of the cases in which there is a discount rate, the initial shadow price depends on the discount rate. In these cases, *the lower is the discount rate, the higher is the initial shadow price of the resource.*[28]

So: *the effect of emphasizing considerations relevant to sustainability is to raise the shadow price of the exhaustible resource.*

Valuing the stock in a utilitarian framework raises the current (initial) shadow price above the classical Hotelling case: valuing the long run puts the shadow price up further:

---

[28] For the Hotelling problem and the discounted utilitarian case with resource stock an argument of the utility function, the proof of this is immediate. For the other case, it follows from the characterization of a stationary resource stock (see the Appendix):

$$u_2'(\hat{s}) = u_1'(0)\frac{\theta\delta}{(1-\theta)\delta + \theta}.$$

Differentiating with respect to the discount rate, we find that

$$\frac{\partial u_2'(\hat{s})}{\partial \delta} = \frac{\theta^2}{((1-\theta)\delta + \theta)^2} > 0$$

so that the steady state resource stock is decreasing in the discount rate δ.

TABLE 13.1

Case	Values *s-r*	Values *l-r*	Values assets	Initial shadow price
1	Yes	No	No	Lowest
2	Yes	No	Yes	High
3	Yes	Yes	Yes	Higher
4	No	Yes	Yes	Highest

and aiming at the maximum sustainable utility level raises the shadow price yet higher. This is not surprising: higher prices usually imply less consumption, and that is precisely the content of sustainability. Note, of course, that the value placed on the stock through its incorporation as an argument of the objective function, is reflected in the price of the flow derived from it. Table 13.1 summarizes these conclusions.

Can we be exact about the difference that the criterion function makes to the shadow prices of the resource? We can illustrate this by considering the shadow prices in the stationary states to which the solutions asymptote. In the utilitarian case the asymptotic shadow price of the resource is given by the marginal utility of the final stock, divided by the discount rate. This is the present value of a perpetual stream of benefits equal to the marginal utility of the stock.[29]

If we use the Chichilnisky criterion as a maximand, then instead the final shadow price is given by the previous expression *plus* a term reflecting undiscounted the contribution of a change in the stock to sustainable welfare.[30] In this case the shadow price is the sum of two terms: one, as before, is the present value of the stream of marginal utilities resulting from an increase in this stock. The second represents the contribution of an increase in the stock to the limiting utility level. The second term, although it represents contributions in the far distant future, *is not discounted*. Under some circumstances it could be the dominant term: this corresponds to the case when the objective places more weight on the very long run than on the more immediate future. The key point here is that if we are placing sufficient weight on the future, then the

---

[29] Formally, $\lambda_{util} = u_2'(s^*)/\delta$.

[30] In this case the economy does not reach the stationary state at which $u_2' = \delta u_1'$. The stationary state instead now satisfies:

$$\frac{u_2'(\hat{s})}{u_1'(0)} = \frac{\theta^2}{(1-\theta)\delta + \theta}.$$

Recall that at each point in time, the shadow price of the resource is equal to the marginal utility of consumption. In this case, we have that

$$-\theta u_1'(0) + \theta u_2'(\hat{s})/\delta + (1-\theta)u_2'(\hat{s}) = 0$$

or

$$\hat{\lambda} = u_2'(\hat{s})/\delta + u_2'(\hat{s})(1-\theta)/\theta,$$

where $\hat{\lambda}$ is the shadow price of the resource when the stationary state is reached. Here $u_2'(\hat{s})(1-\theta)/\theta$ measures the contribution of an increment of the stock to sustainable welfare.

shadow price for a resource may naturally contain an element representing its contribution to future benefits that is not discounted, its futurity notwithstanding. This is not equivalent to saying that a zero discount rate is appropriate: we are instead saying that the shadow price of the resource reflects its contribution to the social objective, and this is the sum of two terms, one a discounted present value and one undiscounted.

5.2. Renewable resources

Next I investigate the relationships between shadow prices, the objective, and the discount rate, in the case of renewable resources. These are rather different from the exhaustible case.[31] Consider as before four alternative objectives, placing varying degrees of emphasis on the factors defining sustainability:

1. The conventional discounted utilitarian case, in which one studies optimal depletion when only the rate of use of the resource is a source of utility.[32]
2. As in case 1 above, but with the flow *and the stock* as sources of utility, as indicated by Section 3 above. This is still a utilitarian formulation, but is consistent with the ecosystem services literature.[33]
3. Depletion according to the Chichilnisky criterion, still recognizing the importance of environmental capital as a source of services.[34]
4. Depletion according to the green golden rule policy, which selects the highest sustainable utility level, with utility depending on both consumption of natural resources and on their stock.[35]

As before, these cases reflect values which are progressively more 'pro-environmental' or 'sustainable'. The first case places no weight on the long run and none on environmental assets. The second places weight on environmental assets but not on the long run: the third places weight on both, and the fourth places weight only on the long run in the time dimensions, as well as valuing environmental assets. They are summarized in Table 13.2.

Consider first the discounted utilitarian case when the stock is not valued. In this case standard analysis[36] shows that in the long run the return on investment in the stock should equal the discount rate: this determines a stock level. In the discounted utilitarian case when the stock is valued as an argument of the utility function the stock maintained in the long run is larger than in the conventional utilitarian case. For both the Chichilnisky criterion and the green golden rule, the limiting value of the stock is greater still, and for both it is equal to the green golden rule, as shown in Figure 13.4. In this case we find that the more future-oriented or environment-oriented objectives

---

[31] The natural rate of growth of the resource case the dynamic of resource growth is: $\dot{s}_t = r(s_t) - c_t$ where as before s_t is the resource stock at date t, and c_t the consumption of the resource at t.

[32] Formally, the problem is: $\max \int_0^\infty u(c_t)e^{-\delta t}dt$ s.t. $ds_t/dt = r(s_t) - c_t$. Here $r(s_t)$ is the growth function of the resource, assumed to be increasing then decreasing as a function of the stock.

[33] Formally, this problem is: $\max \int_0^\infty u(c_t, s_t)e^{-\delta t}dt$ s.t. $ds_t/dt = r(s_t) - c_t$.

[34] Now we have $\max\{\theta \int_0^\infty u(c_t, s_t)e^{-\delta t}dt + (1-\theta)\lim_{t\to\infty} u(c_t, s_t)\}$ s.t. $ds_t dt = r(s_t) - c_t$.

[35] $\max_{c_t, s_t, \forall t} \lim_{t\to\infty} u(c_t, s_t)$ s.t. $c = r(s)$.   [36] See e.g. Dasgupta and Heal (1979).

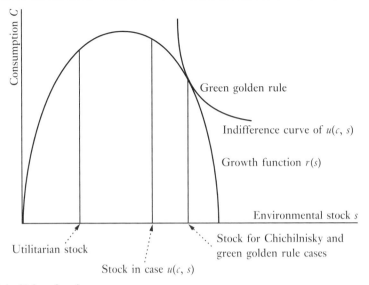

FIG. 13.4. *Value of stock*

TABLE 13.2

Case	Values s-r	Values l-r	Values assets	Long-run stock/shadow price
1	Yes	No	No	Lowest
2	Yes	No	Yes	High
3	Yes	Yes	Yes	Higher
4	No	Yes	Yes	As in 3

lead to larger resource stocks being maintained in the long run. They correspondingly place more weight on accumulation of the resource, and a higher shadow price on the resource. Table 13.2 summarizes these conclusions.

In the case of the Chichilnisky criterion, there is a new and surprising phenomenon, one which connects with our earlier discussion of individual attitudes towards the future. This is that the discount rate cannot be constant, but must fall to zero over time if there is to be a well-defined optimal path.[37] This can provide an intuitive explanation of why the optimal path according to Chichilnisky's criterion asymptotes to the green golden rule: the point is that when the discount rate is zero, then the utilitarian solution approaches the green golden rule. There is no 'impatience' to stop the system accumulating resources short of this configuration, which yields maximum sustainable utility.

---

[37] Logarithmic discounting as discussed in Section 2.4 would satisfy this requirement.

5.3. Sustainable net benefits

There is a new aspect of project evaluation which arises in the renewable resource case. Suppose that our objective is to achieve the maximum sustainable utility, the solution to which is of course to move to the green golden rule. What prices, and what private behaviour by agents in the economy, will support such an outcome? If society is so future-oriented as to wish to support the highest sustainable utility level, then we need correspondingly future-oriented behaviour on the part of agents in the economy. We need firms to seek the highest sustainable profits (i.e. the maximum value of profits that can be maintained for ever) and resource owners to manage their resources so as to yield the highest sustainable revenues from the resources. In this case, we will need a corresponding modification of the rules for project selection: the best of a set of projects will be the one which generates the largest sustainable net benefit. In other words, the rule for a small policy change (a project) to contribute positively to welfare is that it leads to a positive indefinitely maintainable (sustainable) net benefit at the prices which support (in the above sense) the highest sustainable utility level. And the best of a set of possible projects is that which makes the largest such contribution. The key point is that in this case it is not appropriate to work with present values (Heal 1998).

6. Conclusions

We have identified two of the principal areas in which cost–benefit analysis as customarily practised is deficient with respect to environmental matters. One is the valuation of the future relative to the present: the very long time-horizons of many environmental preservation projects strain the credibility of discounted utilitarianism. This approach does not seem to reflect adequately the values to which societies and individuals profess. The second area of deficiency is the valuation of environmental assets, which are important sources of welfare, providing the ecological infrastructure on which human societies operate.

In developing an approach to cost–benefit analysis in which these deficiencies are corrected, there are several stages. The first is the development of a theory of optimal economic development which is adequate in these respects, for the theory underlying cost–benefit analysis is that of optimal economic development. The analytical relationships governing the calculation and use of shadow prices are drawn from this body of theory. The second stage consists of the embedding of principles and analytical relationships from the theory of optimal development in a set of rules for evaluating benefits and costs.

In this paper I have tried to indicate that we now have the conceptual basis for beginning both of these tasks. We have a framework within which we can analyse rigorously the question: 'What is the optimal time-path of economic development in the presence of environmental resources, either exhaustible or renewable?' while respecting the need to place more weight on the future than is customary, and while attributing value to environmental stocks. Section 4 on 'Sustainable development' provided a brief outline of the way this can be done, and of the type of results which emerge. Section 5 on 'Sustainability and project evaluation' indicated how the results which emerge can be translated into statements about the valuation of stocks and flows of environmental goods and services. In this respect, several quite clear and distinctive conclusions have emerged. These include the following:

- There are conditions under which the expression for a shadow price may contain terms reflecting contributions to welfare which are completely undiscounted in spite of referring to benefits in the distant future.
- The precise shadow price to be applied to an environmental resource is a function of the relative weighting of present and future, and of the extent to which stocks are recognized as a source of value.
- It may be appropriate to use a non-constant discount rate in valuing future costs and benefits. Specifically, in the case of renewable resources, it may be appropriate to discount the future at a rate which declines over time. A concrete example is logarithmic discounting.
- In the context of a strongly future-oriented objective such as maximizing the long-run or sustainable benefit level, we seek the policy which leads to the maximum sustainable net benefit, rather than that which maximizes the present value of benefits.

Obviously, the greater part of the work in this area remains to be done. But it is clear that in principle what we want to do, can be done. It is also clear that the results which are emerging are intuitively reasonable. The next step is to make them more concrete by beginning to apply them.

APPENDIX

In this Appendix, I set out some simple formal models of optimal development of a resource-based economy under alternative specification both of the nature of the resource and of the social objective. These models, which are developed in more detail in Heal (1998), provide the framework for the analytical results on shadow prices for use in project evaluation.

A1. Sustainability and exhaustibility

First I shall look at the simplest possible model, a model of the optimal depletion of a finite stock of a non-renewable resource. This is an extension of the so-called cake-eating problem first posed and solved by Hotelling (1931). An economy is given a fixed, known initial stock s_0 of a non-renewable resource, which provides its only source of consumption. The question posed is: how fast should it use this up? What principles should determine the balance struck between present and future consumption, given that each is at the expense of the other? Hotelling, in a prescient 1931 paper that went unrecognized for many years,[38] analysed this issue when the instantaneous utility of the economy depends only on current consumption and the objective is to maximize the discounted sum of utilities:

$$\max \int_0^\infty u(c_t)e^{-\delta t}dt$$

$$\text{subject to } \int_0^\infty c_t dt \leq s_0.$$

(1)

We are in fact interested in a more complex extension of this problem, in which optimality is defined by Chichilnisky's criterion:

$$\max \left\{ \theta \int_0^\infty u(c_t, s_t)e^{-\delta t}dt + (1-\theta)\lim_{t \to \infty} u(c_t, s_t) \right\}.$$

(2)

$$0 \leq \theta \leq 1, \text{ s.t. } \int_0^\infty c_t dt \leq s_0$$

In going from the more complex criterion in (2) to the simpler one in (1), one deletes two elements of problem (2): the presence of the stock of the resource as an argument of the utility function, and the presence of the term $\lim_{t \to \infty} u(c_t, s_t)$ which places value on the limiting behaviour of the economy. I shall introduce the solution to the general problem (2) by considering the solutions of several simpler problems, of which (1) is one.

The solution of (1) is well known (see Dasgupta and Heal 1979): it involves a price p_t for the resource which rises over time at the discount rate (the 'Hotelling Rule'):

$$\frac{1}{p_t}\frac{dp_t}{dt} = \delta$$

(3)

and a consumption level for the resource which falls over time to zero according to

$$\frac{1}{c_t}\frac{dc_t}{dt} = \eta\delta,$$

(4)

where

$$\eta = c_t \frac{d^2u/dc_t^2}{du/dc_t} < 0,$$

which is known to economists as the elasticity of the marginal utility of consumption or the degree of risk-aversion and is related to what mathematicians call the Gaussian curvature of the function $u(c)$. This number is a constant for a number of widely used functional forms: I assume it to be constant. This solution involves the depletion of the entire stock of the resource, with its price rising over time exponentially.

---

[38] And was rejected by at least one major journal.

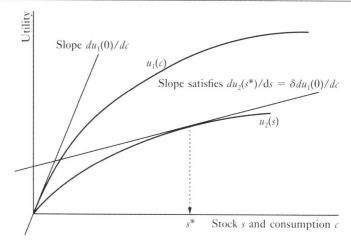

FIG. 13.5. *Determination of the stock which is preserved indefinitely. (Marginal utility of the stock equals the discount rate times that of the flow at zero)*

Consider next a variant of this problem due to Krautkraemer (1985):

$$\max \int_0^\infty u(c_t, s_t)e^{-\delta t}dt$$

$$\text{subject to } \int_0^\infty c_t dt \leq s_0 \text{ or } \frac{ds}{dt} = -c_t,$$

(5)

which differs only in the inclusion of the stock of the resource as an argument of the valuation function. Consider for simplicity the special case in which $u(c_t, s_t) = u_1(c_t) + u_2(s_t)$, with $u_1'(0) < \infty$ and $u_1(0) > -\infty$. This case is solved by Heal (1998): the solution is characterized by a stock s^* satisfying

$$\frac{du_2(s^*)/ds}{du_1(0)/dc} = \delta.$$

The optimal path is then to have consumption fall to zero, reaching zero when there is a positive remaining stock of s^*. At this stock, which is then maintained intact for ever, the marginal rate of substitution between the stock, which is s^*, and the flow,[39] which is 0, is equal to the rate of discount δ. So explicit recognition of the value of the stock may lead to permanent conservation of the stock.[40] This is a move in the direction of sustainable solutions. The determination of the stock s^* which is maintained for ever is illustrated in Figure 13.5: it is clear from this that this stock is larger, the lower is the discount rate.

---

[39] This marginal rate of substitution between stock and flow is just the slope of a contour of $u(c_t, s_t) = u(c_t) + v(s_t)$ in the $c - s$ plane.
[40] s^* is not always strictly positive: for details see Krautkraemer (1985) or Heal (1998).

The simple model embodied in (5) can be used to illustrate the 'green golden rule' concept introduced by Beltratti, Chichilnisky, and Heal (1993, 1994, 1995). This is the configuration of the economy which gives the greatest indefinitely maintainable level of utility. Make the very reasonable assumption that $u(c, s)$ is increasing in s for any c. Utility levels which can be maintained for ever are those corresponding to zero consumption levels, $u(0, s)$, as with a purely exhaustible resource zero consumption is the only consumption level which can be maintained for ever. Amongst these, the greatest is $u(0, s_0)$. The green golden rule is therefore a development path on which consumption is zero for ever and the entire initial stock is maintained completely intact for ever. This is certainly an environmentally friendly solution, possibly overly so! With renewable resources, the green golden rule is less extreme: details are given in the next section.

Finally, I review the implications of the approach to sustainability developed in the last section and based on the Chichilnisky criterion. For this we seek a solution of the problem (2) of optimal depletion with Chichilnisky's criterion, without any of the foregoing simplifications. As we are already familiar with solutions to various simplifications of (2), it is not difficult to appreciate the structure of a solution to the full problem. It is in fact a cross between a solution to the utilitarian problem with stock an argument of the utility function (5), and the green golden rule: it involves maintaining intact for ever a stock of the resource larger than would be prescribed by the solution to (5), but nevertheless smaller than the entire initial stock. This is in fact a very general property of solutions to optimal development programmes with the Chichilnisky criterion: for problems which are resource-constrained or 'dissipative' in physicists' terminology, they are typically between the solution to the utilitarian problem when the stock of the resource is valued in the utility function, and the green golden rule. They satisfy the same differential equations as the utilitarian solution, but have a different right-hand end-point and are more 'future-oriented', as one would expect. We will see in the next section an example of a problem which is not resource-constrained in the same sense, and for which the solution with the Chichilnisky criterion does not lie between the green golden rule and the utilitarian solution, but in fact unites these two solutions.

The solutions of the different problems and the relationships between them are illustrated in Figure 13.6: in all of them, consumption falls to zero, as it has to because of the finite initial stock. Differences arise with respect to how much of that stock is held intact.

A2. Sustainability with renewable resources

A more complex version of the problem just analysed arises if the resource is renewable, with its own dynamics, rather than exhaustible. Examples are natural populations of fish or animals, or of trees. Several inanimate resources also have the capacity to renew themselves: soil fertility is renewed by microbial action if the soil is not used, and the air and bodies of water have the capacity to cleanse themselves as long as

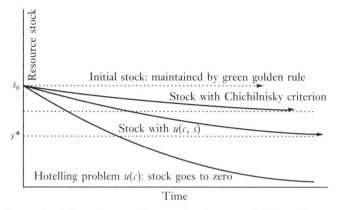

FIG. 13.6. *Time-paths of the environmental asset under alternative definitions of optimality*

pollution is below a threshold level. In all of these cases the rate of change of the stock of the resource contains a positive term reflecting the capacity of the resource to renew itself. In these cases the equivalent to problem (2) is now

$$\max\left\{\theta\int_0^\infty u(c_t, s_t)e^{-\delta t}dt + (1 - \theta)\lim_{t\to\infty} u(c_t, s_t)\right\},$$

$$0 \leqslant \theta \leqslant 1, \text{ s.t. } \frac{ds}{dt} = r(s) - c \tag{6}$$

where $r(s)$ is the rate of renewal of the resource, which is a function of the existing stock of the resource. In biological terms, it is a population growth function. We assume that it satisfies: $r(0) = 0$, $\exists \bar{s}$ s.t. $r'(s) \geqslant 0$ for $s \leqslant \bar{s}$, $r'(\bar{s}) = 0$, $r'(s) < 0$ for $s > \bar{s}$. Population growth for this resource is reduced by the rate at which it is consumed: hence the subtraction of the term c in the population growth equation.

The problem (6) is studied at length by Beltratti, Chichilnisky, and Heal (1993) and Heal (1998). The green golden rule for this model is illustrated in Figure 13.7: it is the tangency of a contour of $u(c, s)$ with the curve $r(s)$, which is often taken to be quadratic[41] and is drawn quadratic in Figure 13.7. This point of tangency gives the highest indefinitely maintainable utility level. To be more formal, it solves the problem

$$\max u(c, s) \text{ s.t. } c = r(s).$$

The condition $c = r(s)$ is a sustainability condition, requiring that consumption is at precisely the level at which the stock is maintained constant.

Beltratti, Chichilnisky, and Heal show that any path which is a solution to the utilitarian problem

---

[41] A quadratic growth function gives rise to a logistic curve for total population.

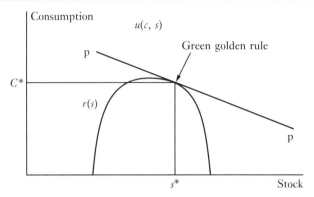

FIG. 13.7. *Green golden rule or highest sustainable utility level characterized by a tangency between an indifference curve and the set of stationary points*

$$\max\left\{\int_0^\infty u(c_t, s_t)e^{-\delta t}dt\right\}$$

(7)

$$\text{subject to } \frac{ds}{dt} = r(s) - c$$

will asymptote to a point on the locus $c = r(s)$ which is to the left of the green golden rule.[42] I show in (Heal 1998) that in general there is no solution to the problem (6): there is however a solution if the discount rate is not constant but is a function of time and goes asymptotically to zero, as discussed above. In this case the overall objective function is

$$\left\{\theta\int_0^\infty u(c_t, s_t)\Delta(t)dt + (1-\theta)\lim u(c_t, s_t)\right\},$$

(8)

where $\Delta(t)$ is the discount factor at time t which satisfies

$$\lim_{t\to\infty}\frac{1}{\Delta(t)}\frac{d\Delta(t)}{dt} = 0.$$

A particular case of this is the usual exponential discount factor with the discount rate declining to zero:

$$\exp{-\delta(t)t}, \text{ with } \lim_{t\to\infty}\delta(t) = 0$$

or logarithmic discounting with a constant discount rate, as in Section 2.4. In fact Heal (1998) shows that having the maximand of the form given in (8) with the discount

---

[42] Unless $\delta = 0$: in this case the purely utilitarian solutions have the green golden rule as their right-hand end-point. However, there may be no solution to the utilitarian problem in this case.

factor satisfying (9) is necessary and sufficient for the existence of a solution to the Chichilnisky optimization problem (6) with a renewable rather than an exhaustible resource. This indicates that there is a major qualitative difference between the behaviour of exhaustible and renewable systems with respect to this definition of sustainability.

It is rather interesting that there is a point of contact here with the experimental evidence that individuals considering intertemporal decisions display a discount rate which declines with the futurity of the event concerned, as discussed in Section 2.3. This evidence suggests behaviour with respect to the future of precisely the type needed to ensure that Chichilnisky's axioms can define optimal paths, which asymptote to the green golden rule.

References

Beltratti, Andrea, Graciela Chichilnisky, and Geoffrey M. Heal (1993) 'Sustainable Growth and the Green Golden Rule', in Ian Goldin and Alan Winters (eds.), *Approaches to Sustainable Economic Development* (Cambridge University Press for the OECD, Paris): 147–72.

—— —— (1994) 'The Environment and the Long Run: a Comparison of Different Criteria', in *Ricerche Economiche* 48: 319–40.

—— —— (1995) 'The Green Golden Rule', Working Paper, Columbia Business School 1994, *Economics Letters* 49: 175–9.

Broome, John (1992) *Counting the Cost of Global Warming* (London: White Horse Press).

—— (1996) 'What Is Sustainable Development?' Paper presented at Stanford Institute for Theoretical Economics. Published as 'An Axiomatic Approach to Sustainable Development' in *Social Choice and Welfare* 13(2): 219–48.

—— and Geoffrey Heal (1993) 'Global Environmental Risks', *Journal of Economic Perspectives* 7(4): 65–86.

—— —— (1997) 'Securitizing the Biosphere', Working paper, Columbia Business School.

Cline, William R. (1992) *The Economics of Global Warming* (Washington, DC: Institute for International Economics).

Cropper, Maureen L., Sema K. Aydede, and Paul R. Portney (1994) 'Preferences for Life-Saving Programs: How the Public Discounts Time and Age', *Journal of Risk and Uncertainty* 8: 243–65.

Daily, Gretchen (1997) *Nature's Services* (Washington, DC: Island Press).

Dasgupta, Partha S., and Geoffrey M. Heal (1974) 'The Optimal Depletion of Exhaustible Resources', *Review of Economic Studies* (symposium): 3–28.

—— —— (1979) *Economic Theory and Exhaustible Resources* (Cambridge: Cambridge University Press).

—— Steven Marglin, and Amartya K. Sen (1972) *Guidelines for Project Evaluation* (New York: United Nations).

Harrod, Roy (1948) *Towards a Dynamic Economics* (London: Macmillan).

Harvey, Charles (1994) 'The Reasonableness of Non-constant Discounting', *Journal of Public Economics* 53: 31–51.

Heal, Geoffrey M. (1973) *The Theory of Economic Planning* (Amsterdam: North-Holland).

—— (1985) 'Depletion and Discounting: A Classical Problem in Resource Economics', in R. McElvey (ed.), *Environmental and Natural Resource Mathematics* 32: 33–43, of Proceedings of Symposia in Applied Mathematics, American Mathematical Society, Providence, RI.

—— (1993) 'The Optimal Use of Exhaustible Resources', in Alan V. Kneese and James L. Sweeney (eds.), *Handbook of Natural Resource and Energy Economics* (Amsterdam: North-Holland): 855–80.

—— (1998) *Valuing the Future: Economic Theory and Sustainability* (New York: Columbia University Press).

—— (2000) Nature and the Market place: Capturing the Value of Ecosystem Services. (Washington, DC, Island Press).

Henderson, Norman, and Ian Bateman (1995) 'Empirical and Public Choice Evidence for Hyperbolic Social Discount Rates and the Implications for Intergenerational Discounting', *Environmental and Resource Economics* 5: 413–23.

Holdren, John P., Gretchen C. Daily, and Paul R. Ehrlich (1995) 'The Meaning of Sustainability: Biogeophysical Aspects', in *Defining and Measuring Sustainability: The Biogeophysical Foundations*, ed. Mohan Munasinghe and Walter Shearer, distributed for the United Nations University by the World Bank, Washington, DC: 3–17.

Hotelling, Harold (1931) 'The Economics of Exhaustible Resources', *Journal of Political Economy* 39: 137–75.

Kneese, Alan V., and William D. Schultze (1985) 'Ethics and Environmental Economics' ch. 5 of vol. i of Alan Kneese and James Sweeney (eds.), *Handbook of Natural Resource and Energy Economics* (Amsterdam: North-Holland): 191–220.

Krautkraemer, Jeffrey A. (1985) 'Optimal Growth, Resource Amenities and the Preservation of Natural Environments', *Review of Economic Studies* 153–70.

Little, Ian M. D., and James A. Mirrlees (1974) *Project Appraisal and Planning for Developing Countries* (London: Heinemann).

Lowenstein, George, and Jon Elster (eds.) (1992) *Choice over Time* (New York: Russel Sage Foundation).

—— and Richard Thaler (1989) 'Intertemporal Choice', *Journal of Economic Perspectives* 3: 181–93.

Ng, Yew-Kwang (forthcoming) 'Towards Welfare Biology: Evolutionary Economics of Animal Consciousness and Suffering', Working Paper, Monash University, Australia 3168, forthcoming in *Biology and Philosophy*.

Phelps, Edmund S. (1961) 'The Golden Rule of Accumulation: a Fable for Growthmen', *American Economic Review* 51(4): 638–43.

Ramsey, Frank (1928) 'A Mathematical Theory of Saving', *Economic Journal* 38: 543–59.

Thaler, Richard (1981) 'Some Empirical Evidence on Dynamic Inconsistency', *Economics Letters* 8: 201–7.

14 Chinese Reforms from a Comparative Perspective

ATHAR HUSSAIN, NICHOLAS STERN, AND JOSEPH STIGLITZ

1. Structural Change, Policy Reform, and James Mirrlees

We have been profoundly influenced by our intellectual interactions with James Mirrlees for more than three decades.[1] This paper, our contribution to the volume in his honour, provides an account of two decades of policy reform in China, making comparisons with the transition (in the last decade) from command towards market economies in the countries of Eastern Europe and the former Soviet Union. Thus, at first sight, it might seem a far cry from the formal analysis of highly focused policy models that many would associate with Jim. But we see it as firmly in the Mirrlees tradition.

Jim's models provide an analysis of policy choice in terms of the objectives of government, the options, instruments, and information available to the policy-maker and the reactions of agents in the economy to different kinds of incentives. Such models then provide a benchmark for the structured, but often less formal, discussion of policy in terms of how implied policy directions would be influenced if some of the assumptions on the key elements were changed. They educate our intuition, teach us to recognize policy pitfalls, and help us to identify arguments that are wrong. Understanding the logic of policy formation in simple models that are susceptible to analysis provides crucial underpinning for making policy judgements in a more complex world.

A clear example of the fruitfulness of this kind of approach is the work on cost–benefit analysis for developing countries by Little and Mirrlees of the 1960s and 1970s.[2] The approach essentially asks about the simultaneous determination of optimum policies and shadow prices where there are basic constraints on the tax and trade policies which can be selected (an important underlying theoretical framework was provided the papers by Diamond and Mirrlees of 1971).[3] This type of formulation shows how the policies and shadow prices would be changed if assumptions on the constraints on tax and trade were altered. This, in turn, leads to a challenging of some of the assumed constraints, particularly on trade. Thus an apparently technical exercise of calculating shadow prices (together with its theoretical underpinnings) was a key element of the 1960s' and 1970s' critique of the restrictive trade policies implemented by many

---

We are very grateful to Dwight Perkins for very constructive comments and to Noémi Giszpenc and Marina Wes for guidance and support.

[1] Two of us (Hussain and Stern) were graduate students of Jim Mirrlees and one of us (Stiglitz) was a close colleague for several years at Oxford.

[2] Little and Mirrlees (1969 and 1974).   [3] Diamond and Mirrlees (1971).

developing countries in the 1950s and 1960s. This work, therefore, was a key part of the, largely successful, drive for trade liberalization of the 1970s and beyond.

Jim's work has, in basic and influential ways, been about the crucial policy debates of the time. And he has always seen models as a part of a structured process of policy discussion and as a foundation for asking basic questions. We try to look at the process of change in China, contrasting it with that of the former communist countries of Europe and Central Asia, from a similar perspective. In this story, basic questioning from the perspective of the theories of policy, of information, and of organization, will be central. Key assumptions subject to scrutiny in this paper concern: responses to different kinds of policy reform; objectives of government; and available information about circumstances and reactions along the transition path. If we examine the paths of transition in China and elsewhere in this theoretical, and very Mirrlees, spirit we can learn a great deal about the process of policy reform, institutional development, and behavioural change. And, as ever, with such an approach to asking questions many are left open and further arise. The understanding of institutional and behavioural change is one of the great research challenges in the social sciences in the coming years.

2. Introduction

The transition in China began in 1979 with reforms that were simply intended to improve the performance of a command economy. Around ten years later, the transition in Central and Eastern Europe (CEE) and the former Soviet Union (FSU) began with the disintegration of the Soviet Union and the collapse of communism. Politically, both the Soviet empire and communism collapsed. The frailties of the economic system were dramatically exposed. The problems were not simply the exposure of an inefficient structure based on central planning to tests of the market. The statist approach, particularly in the FSU, had constructed, for reasons of political control as well as economic ideology, a system of extreme specialization in huge plants combined with an excessive and rigid geographical integration. The resulting structure was particularly susceptible to disruptions due to coordination failures.

China has seen twenty years of rapid growth whilst Russia and the other countries of the Commonwealth of Independent States (CIS)[4] have experienced nearly a decade of decline. At the beginning of the 1990s China's GDP was less than half that of Russia, now it is double (see Figure 14.1 and Appendix). The main argument of this paper is that China's more successful transformation has been based on a process of institutional change that preserved and built on its basic codes and practices of behaviour, or to use a term that is currently popular, its social capital.[5] This strategy facilitated

---

[4] The CIS is the former Soviet Union excluding the Baltic States of Estonia, Latvia, and Lithuania.

[5] 'Social capital' is discussed in Sections 2 and 3 in terms of acceptance of basic codes of behaviour, trust, and cooperation. We use it more broadly than some other authors who, for example, focus on networks or associations (see below and, for example, Dasgupta and Serageldin 2000). The term 'institutions', following standard English usage, covers organizations and rules. See ch. 1 of the *Transition Report 1999* for a discussion of the terms.

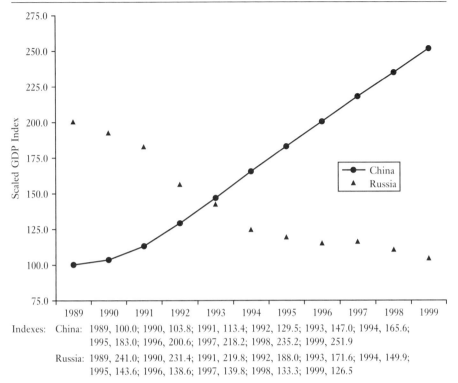

Indexes: China: 1989, 100.0; 1990, 103.8; 1991, 113.4; 1992, 129.5; 1993, 147.0; 1994, 165.6;
1995, 183.0; 1996, 200.6; 1997, 218.2; 1998, 235.2; 1999, 251.9

Russia: 1989, 241.0; 1990, 231.4; 1991, 219.8; 1992, 188.0; 1993, 171.6; 1994, 149.9;
1995, 143.6; 1996, 138.6; 1997, 139.8; 1998, 133.3; 1999, 126.5

FIG. 14.1. *Transition and GDP: China and Russia*

all three of the key processes emphasized by economists in the analysis of growth: enhanced efficiency and productivity, the accumulation of capital, and the sectoral real-location of factors. By contrast, the processes employed in Russia and the CIS led to the further deterioration of their already frail social capital and institutional structures and the weakening of incentives for innovation, investment, and structural change.

The CIS has, since 1991, witnessed the erosion of the functioning of the State, a crisis of confidence in society, and rent-seeking on a massive scale. The experience in CEE in this respect has been markedly different. It has been much less traumatic. At the outset tough macroeconomic policies to shake out inflation were implemented and a process of structural reform was initiated. Growth in CEE returned around 1993, three or four years after the process of transformation began; and for the most part, the State and society have functioned much more effectively than in the CIS.

Whilst this paper is focused mainly on China, the comparisons with the CIS, particularly with Russia, brings out strongly both the importance of the interrelation between social capital and institutional transformation, and the implications of both social capital and institutional development for economic performance. The experiences of the fifteen countries of CEE[6] and twelve countries of the CIS have differed

---

[6] All are members of the EBRD except the Former Yugoslav Republic (FYR)—the data used in the paper exclude the FYR.

strongly. These differences demonstrate that history and geography are of profound importance to economic, social, and institutional developments. But so too are economic policies. The choices made in the earlier years of transition and their implications for behaviour and institutional development have had a fundamental influence on its subsequent evolution.[7]

Such comparisons must be made with care. The countries of the CIS had experienced over seventy years of a command economy by 1991 compared with China's thirty years by 1979. They started their transformation with very different institutional and economic structures and endowments of social capital.

Thus, the paper does not argue that China's transformation was a model for that of Russia, the CIS, or CEE. The nature of the societies and economies differed fundamentally. So too did the options and challenges. But the comparison does provide basic insights into the process of economic and social transformation and points to the prospects and challenges in the next phases of transition for the two regions.

Section 2 focuses on institutional transformation in the post-1978 Chinese economy. Section 3 analyses growth experience. Section 4 looks forward to the future prospects and challenges both for the Chinese economy and for the economies of CEE and the CIS.

Given the broad sweep of the paper, generalizations are unavoidable and we do not attempt to provide comprehensive or detailed analysis of evidence or more nuanced hypotheses.[8]

3. Institutional Transformation

3.1. *The institutional and evolutionary basis for transformation and growth*

The Chinese economy presents a mixture of features of a market economy intertwined with those of a command economy. We discuss the salient *institutional elements* under three headings:

- Decentralization
- The Rural Economy
- Moving from Old to New Enterprises.

Each element is crucial to an understanding of how China was able to use its social and organizational capital to transform the economy and generate growth. Decentralization, in its many facets, allowed experimentation and change without massive dislocation. The very large rural sector provided both the source of further decentralization and productivity growth in the very early stages of China's transition and the

---

[7] For a detailed development of the arguments concerning the CEE and the CIS see the *Transition Report 1999*.

[8] Some material underpinning the arguments of the paper can be found in the *World Development Reports* of the World Bank and the *Transition Reports* of the EBRD.

source of labour for industrial growth. In turn both the decentralization and rural organizational and institutional traditions provided the basis of the new, largely collective, rural and industrial enterprises that drove China's growth from the mid-1980s. The remainder of this section is devoted to an analysis of these key elements. In Section 3 we link them to standard analyses of growth in terms of productivity changes, accumulation, and sectoral transfer.

The analysis of decentralization, the rural economy, and new enterprises provides a context and rationale for China's successful *evolutionary approach* to transition, which may be summarized in a stylized way in terms of five principles or observations.

1. The Chinese experience shows that a guided process of transition, proceeding step by step, can retain the social and organizational capital developed in previous stages of development and transform it in ways that enhance efficiency and productivity and set the stage for the next steps in a continuing reform process.

2. There are strong arguments in favour of following such an evolutionary approach which are based on information, behaviour, and understanding. First, it is not possible at one date to foresee, let alone to resolve, all the problems that will emerge at later stages. Second, behaviour and understanding of those within society have to change. The force of these arguments is enhanced when we recognize that China was engaged in a double transformation. She was moving from a less developed country with a high incidence of poverty to a more advanced economy and from a particular economic and political philosophy associated with a command economy to an economy based more on the principles of a market. At the same time the Chinese leadership was committed to ensuring that the latter transformation be conducted in ways that were consistent with an underlying social philosophy, and in a way which preserved the social fabric of society. Such profound transformations require changing mindsets, and changes in mindsets require direct experience. By making the process incremental, the Chinese leadership was trying to avoid destroying social capital and institutions based on the old order before social capital and institutions based on the new order could be created. Thus the transition embodied an evolution of institutions rather than a revolution. The arguments for the evolutionary approach were strengthened still further by the very recent, intense, and often traumatic experience of the Cultural Revolution of 1966–76. In its aftermath there was greater understanding of the importance of a more measured approach to the process of societal change.[9]

3. The reform process might not be monotonic—at some stage in the evolution it might be desirable to decentralize further, and yet at a later stage to recentralize.

4. The solutions to problems, as they arise, need not be perfect: indeed, even if perfectly fine-tuned to one stage in the transition, they would not be so perfectly matched for the next. The key is to look for *robust* solutions, i.e. solutions that work reasonably well across, or can be adapted to, a range of circumstances.

---

[9] Indeed, the 'shock therapists' or 'radical reformers' in Russia have been criticized for using the Bolshevik approach to reform, much as the communists did some sixty years earlier. They attempted to impose from above changes in society, without bringing along the populace—as evidenced by the outcomes of the 1993 elections. See e.g. Stiglitz (2000).

5. One cannot assume that good results will flow from an approach which liberalizes the economy and lets institutions develop as they may. Such a position has little theoretical[10] or, as we argue in this paper, empirical support.

We may highlight immediately a number of several specific manifestations of these principles. Each had important implications for the success of China's reforms and contrasts with the experience of Russia and the CIS more generally. They are explored in more detail below.

• Intergovernmental relations and local enterprise. The centre provided freedom—and responsibility and incentives—to local government to act to support entrepreneurship, whilst it preserved the overall stability in the functioning of the State. There were crucial implications. First, local governments were able to use localized social capital and easy observation of what was going on in local establishments to provide the necessary corporate governance. At the same time they faced clearly the consequences of overtaxing or overregulating these enterprises—officials could be held accountable for expensive rent-seeking. Second, local responsibility meant that they faced squarely the trade-offs between, on the one hand, subsidizing inefficient firms to maintain jobs and, on the other, using the scarce funds to create new establishments and new jobs. Third, they had access to savings to finance new enterprises. Fourth, local governance structures generated expectations that the funds would be well spent. Local authorities felt an obligation to create new jobs for the burgeoning population—entrepreneurship and creativity were clearly within their mandate.[11]
• Corporate governance. The new township and village enterprises (TVEs) that formed the main source of growth in the reform period of China combined ownership and management in a way that created mutual trust, a long-term view, and a willingness to invest. This kind of corporate governance structure represented an evolution of the commune governance structures that had prevailed before the reforms began.[12]
• Creation of new enterprises. The result was that strong new enterprises developed on the basis of local entrepreneurship, savings, social stability, and the positive involvement of the local authorities.

The experience in Russia has been almost diametrically opposite. On corporate governance, much of the privatization entailed insider control of existing enterprises, and has brought both resistance to change and, in many cases, plundering of the firm and asset-stripping.[13] Local authorities have often colluded with existing local firms to resist

---

[10] Indeed, there are general theorems showing that Nash equilibria in institutional arrangements are not in general efficient; there may be a socially dysfunctional institutional equilibrium. See Arnott and Stiglitz (1991).

[11] See Qian (forthcoming).

[12] There is also a long tradition of cooperation in rural irrigation systems, particularly in Southern and Eastern China where the reforms and economic performance have been strongest.

[13] See *Transition Report 1999*, Shleifer and Vishny (1998) and Wedel (1998). Stiglitz (1999a) argued that advocates of privatization were correct—it did provide strong incentives—but that the combination of a process of privatization that was widely viewed as 'illegitimate', open capital markets, and absence of appropriate legal and market structures for corporate governance provided strong incentives for asset-stripping rather than wealth creation. For other critical discussions of the role of corporate governance in the failures in transition, see Dyck (1999) and Black, Kraakman, and Tarassova (1999).

change.[14] They did not face a trade-off between preserving the old and creating the new: they saw only that shutting down old firms meant a loss of jobs and incomes. Because the enterprises were typically part of national enterprises, each community hoped to delve into what they viewed as a common pool of resources at the centre— a new version of the tragedy of the commons. The collusion between local authorities and old firms resulted in both bureaucratic obstacles to new firms and a restriction of market opportunities for their products. As a result the growth of new firms has been much weaker in Russia than in China.[15]

Poland, in contrast to Russia, has seen a much better investment climate for small firms—following a tradition of individual ownership, particularly in agriculture, even through the communist period—and there new firms have been the main drivers of economic growth. The similarities between China and Poland go deeper, however, than just an emphasis on enterprise creation. The pace and process of the privatization of old firms in Poland has been deliberate and measured.[16] Thus, the restructuring that occurred before, and as, privatization proceeded in Poland, as well as key changes in the law, meant that corporate governance problems were far less severe than in Russia.[17]

The comparison between China and Russia demonstrates not only the importance of institutional change for economic performance, but also that institutional change can be guided in a process that builds on social capital.

3.2. Decentralization

We group under 'decentralization' three features of the Chinese economy at the start of the reforms that have played a crucial role in shaping the transition in the non-farm sector. The first feature was the division, from an early stage in Chinese communism, of the economy into loosely connected and fairly self-contained geo-political segments.[18]

---

[14] New enterprises often faced obstacles from both the local authorities and the local mafia (occasionally in collusion).

[15] This was not the only problem, as noted above and in Stiglitz (1999a). For instance, privatization without restructuring left the enterprises in control of people in their fifties; the absence of well-developed capital markets meant that they were unlikely to be able to reap the benefits of any improvement in enterprise performance upon retirement (by selling shares at increased prices). Even in the case of listed shares, the vagaries in share prices meant that extracting returns from higher share prices as a result of improved corporate performance was a highly risky matter; there were far more certain returns from asset-stripping. Breaking enterprises up would have put more of them under the control of younger managers, who would have had longer time-horizons.

[16] One should not confuse 'shock therapy' in dealing with very high inflation with a blanket approach to economic reform.

[17] Even though Poland was itself a smaller country, breaking up the enterprises meant that the 'commons' problem described earlier was reduced further.

[18] In this, as in other ways, the Communist government of China built on tradition. The Qing dynasty (1644–1912) ruled through a provincial structure in which Governors played a key role. Central control weakened in the nineteenth century and broke up into the warlordism of the first quarter of the twentieth century (see e.g. Fairbank 1980). To be sure, decentralization presented risks and dangers. As late as the early 1990s, some observers worried about the fragmentation of China, as disparities between coastal and inland provinces put strains on the country. We note later that decentralization opened up the possibility of 'local protectionism', which threatened the gains from trade over a national economy. Decentralization of the banking system imposed threats to overall macrostability, as the Central government faced problems in controlling the overall growth in credit. One of Zhu Rong Ji's accomplishments—and a central part of dampening inflation—was the reassertion of central control over the banking system in the early 1990s.

This segmentation, although associated with inefficient diversification (discussed below), gave the economy resilience against disruption and provided scope for entrepreneurship using local and accessible suppliers. It also made it possible for the leadership to follow a strategy of geographically selective experimental reforms.

Second, coordination through the central plan had a limited remit. From the mid-1980s, the scope for off-plan transactions was greatly increased thereby restoring economic incentives and widening access to inputs. The two-track system sanctioned a market track in parallel with plan-mediated transactions.[19] Off-plan transactions through the intermediary of provincial or lower government tiers were common. Within fifteen years of the formal introduction of the two-track system, the plan-track has almost completely disappeared. Thus, in the dismantling of the planning system, market transactions through local governments played a key role.

Third, over the last twenty years the ownership of almost all state enterprises (including control and cash-flow rights) has become more and more dispersed among sub-central governments. These units had the discretion to undertake investment projects, including the establishment of new enterprises. This dispersion gives lower government tiers a large economic stake in the development of the local economy. The counterpart of dispersed ownership has been a decentralization of market-entry decisions that has encouraged entrepreneurship on the part of territorial governments. There has been a proliferation of new enterprises, largely public but divided into state- and collectively-owned.[20] Of particular importance amongst the new enterprises have been rural enterprises. In the process of new enterprise creation, output planning has been fading away. Government and entrepreneurship might seem strange bedfellows, but in practice over the reform period territorial governments in China have been highly entrepreneurial in the best Schumpeterian sense. They have sought out promising investment opportunities, branched into new activities and taken risks.[21] That the capital was supplied by localities may in fact have facilitated risk-taking, especially in an environment in which risk markets were underdeveloped.

---

[19] A key problem facing the country in the beginning of the transition was that it recognized that its prices were not market-based, but it also recognized that finding the market-based prices was no easy matter (entailing solving a complicated general equilibrium problem), and that large changes in prices themselves could impose huge stresses on the economy. Thus, China kept the old prices for the 'quota' production, but allowed free markets in over-the-quota production. Market prices prevailed at the margin—and thus determined incentives—but overall dislocation was kept to a minimum. Gradually, as quotas were reduced and production increased, the first track became increasingly unimportant. Conventional economists would have argued strongly against such two-tier price systems, as entailing distortions and opening up the way for corruption. These conventional discussions underestimate the real costs associated with huge redistributions. The social control systems under communism may have reduced the level of corruption from what it otherwise would have been.

[20] Collective rural enterprises are owned by lower government or quasi-government tiers such as townships or villages. They differ from state-owned enterprises in that certain rules and regulations do not apply to them. In particular these include regulations concerning terms and conditions of employment and social insurance.

[21] There has been strong competition between different localities, reminding us that competition is the key to performance and that this can function without privatization. In 1980, early in the transition, China sought the advice of American economists—but rather than turning to macroeconomists of the sort that had advocated the shock therapy that proved such a failure in Russia, they turned more to microeconomists, such as Arrow and Stiglitz, who emphasized the importance of competition over privatization.

The new state- and collectively-owned enterprises in China represent a significant departure from the old state enterprises. In this respect they resemble new firms in Poland and Hungary. But the difference is that the transition in the non-farming sector in China has been spearheaded by public enterprises and government entrepreneurship. Further, unlike in CEE and the CIS, output planning in China did not collapse but instead was made obsolete by the development of the market track. Recent years have seen both privatization and the growth of private enterprises in China. But these have followed rather than preceded the development of a market economy. Private entrepreneurship in China has grown from, and on the basis of, market development and government entrepreneurship. The emergence of private enterprises has created a set of firms with the managerial skills and capital to take over the pre-existing state enterprises, improve their management, and restructure them. Hungary accomplished the same thing by inviting in foreign firms. But Russia privatized domestically—and had neither real capital nor managerial skills to draw upon.[22]

In this respect, it is worth contrasting China's experiment in creating a socialist market economy with some of the experiments in Eastern Europe to create market socialism, *à la* Lange and Lerner.[23] After World War II, the Eastern European countries ignored the issues of control and decision-making—they assumed utopian (well-motivated, fully informed, and highly competent) central planners—but some employed market mechanisms (prices) in efforts to increase the planners' efficiency. Prices were used to convey relevant information about scarcity. Investment decisions were made centrally, presumably on the basis of forecasts concerning future prices. In contrast, in China there was more substantial decentralization, with investment decisions occurring in a myriad of townships and villages. In Lange and Lerner, the very concepts of entry and entrepreneurship were missing.

The Chinese economy presents features that resemble those observed in the loosely integrated economies such as those in the European Union. But economic reforms have spurred interregional trade and the process has accelerated with competition arising from the emergence over the last few years of buyers' markets for a wide range of commodities. The last few years have also witnessed the rise of national enterprises through a consolidation of units that previously served only local markets. This gradual integration has meant that China's growth has benefited strongly from *gains from trade* between China's regions and provinces.

The CIS on the other hand has suffered severe dislocation with the collapse of a rigid, distorted, overintegrated system. It is striking—but not surprising—how the Stalinist concept of political control through strong economic interdependence has magnified the costs of the transition, whereas Mao's decentralization and his promotion of self-sufficiency for regions provided a valuable platform for China's transition.

---

[22] The privatization typically occurred with heavily borrowed funds, and thus the 'entrepreneurs' had little to lose from mismanagement. See Stiglitz (1999*b*).

[23] See e.g. the Hungarian experiments with using prices for planning in the 1950s and 1960s, inspired by the writings of Lange and Lerner of the 1930s and 1940s, which argued that a well-run state system could mimic and match everything that markets could do. See Stiglitz (1994) for a critique of market socialism. These were, of course, not the only failures: they also failed to take into account 'political economy' concerns.

Stalin tried to design a system of mutual hostages, where it did not pay for any part of the system to pull out. Though eventually the centrifugal political forces did over-come these economic constraints, there was a high cost to be paid.

However, China's industrial structure still bears a strong imprint of the combina-tion of market segmentation and the urge on the part of territorial governments to develop local enterprises. Indeed, local government protectionism still has to be kept in check by the central government. With the exception of those industries reserved exclusively for the central government, such as oil and gas and telecommunications, many indus-tries have enterprises which are, from the perspective of economic scale, far too numer-ous for integrated output markets. This is particularly visible for consumer durables. For example, there are over ninety enterprises in the TV industry and around 120 for vehicle production and assembly. In contrast to the industrial structures of the CIS, that of China is distinctly bimodal, with the output shares split about evenly between a few large and a huge number of medium to small enterprises.[24]

With the growing integration of markets, internal competition has risen and led to two developments that are of crucial importance for the future evolution of the indus-trial structure. The first is a widening differentiation between leading and lagging enter-prises in a broad range of industries. This is surely a first step in a market selection process. The second is a sharp fall in general profitability in industry, especially in the state sector, dating from around 1995 as competition has intensified. This drop has raised the cost to territorial governments of keeping lagging enterprises in busi-ness. The third step, which is beginning, is one of consolidation, as more profitable and efficient enterprises take over the laggards. The competitive process in China is playing an ever-stronger role in promoting efficiency and innovation as integration develops.

We have argued above that Russia and the CIS have been moving away from the high level of integration that previously characterized the economy and that lower gov-ernment tiers in Russia have tightened control on local enterprises. In this respect there might appear to be a similarity between the Chinese economy at the start of the reforms and the present-day Russian economy. But there are crucial differences between the segmentation out of which the Chinese economy is growing and the one into which Russia is contracting. Chinese enterprises were well adapted to the local variant of segmentation, given the long history of a regional focus for political and economic organization. Moreover, segmentation in China has encouraged the proliferation of enterprises that have on balance played a positive role in the transition and in raising the growth rate. The Russian variant applies to enterprises that were established in a highly integrated economy with specialization and scale carried to extremes.

In Russia, except perhaps in a few urban centres, the segmentation associated with the break-up of the Soviet Union and with the regionalization of Russia itself has, as we argued above, been associated with the breakdown of a rigidly integrated production

---

[24] Leaving aside very small ones, around 7,000 large enterprises account for 44 per cent of industrial value-added and over 600,000 medium and small enterprises account for the rest (*Industrial Statistics Yearbook of China* (1998: 76–7).

system and contraction of output, without as yet any significant benefit in encouraging the growth of new enterprises. In contrast, China is now reaping the benefits of internal integration in the form of increased competition and a rationalization of industrial structure (gains from trade), albeit somewhat muddied by attempted protective policies of territorial governments. The direction of future policy and evolution for China is clear—an intensification still further of the competitive process, in part by further integration. In contrast, in Russia, the challenge is to get the competitive process and market selection moving.

Every society needs to get right the 'balance' between centralization and decentralization. China has shown enormous agility, in first decentralizing—providing enormous scope and incentives for local economic activity—and then recentralizing some aspects, such as control of the financial system. But it has continued to devolve to sub-central governments the control of small and medium-size enterprises, with the concomitant responsibility for privatization/restructuring. There is need in China for the central government to keep in check practices that impede interprovincial trade or jeopardize its membership in the WTO. It also needs to ensure that the central government has sufficient sources of revenues to keep regional imbalances within tolerable limits. Russia is on much more uncertain footing. While officially, the central government may have much more control—and while their policies of fiscal federalism effectively impose high taxes on local units, thus eviscerating incentives—in practice the local authorities seem to have considerable autonomy, and use that autonomy in ways that do not facilitate economic growth.

3.3. The rural economy

On the eve of the economic reforms, around 80 per cent of Chinese labourers were rural, most of them (around 90 per cent) engaged in farming. Some rural localities, especially in East China, had comparatively developed industry. Though the cropping pattern and remuneration were determined by collective units, in most localities households worked as a team responsible for particular tasks. The level of mechanization was low, and still is. Given that rural communes were formalized only in 1962, collective farming had been in operation for just seventeen years in 1979; household farming was an immediately feasible alternative. Indeed, during the commune period rural cadres had to struggle constantly to stop spontaneous reversion to household farming. As a result, the decollectivization of farming, once allowed, was swift and remarkably free of any major disruption. It yielded a dramatic growth in agricultural output.

It is difficult to find examples of institutional transformation that match the decollectivization of agriculture in China in depth, coverage (in terms of population and geographical expanse), and immediate benefits. The process has been both radical and rapid. In this respect China's reforms, whilst they were incremental, were not 'gradual'. The initial success of rural reforms created a huge constituency in favour of reforms that outflanked opposition to the decollectivization of agriculture and provided China's leadership with the confidence to embark on urban-industrial reforms. By raising rural incomes, they also enlarged the market for rural enterprises. These reforms provided a most powerful example of generating support for the process through creating a tangible success. Reforms in Russia, in contrast, face a crisis of confidence.

The rural economies of China and of the CIS differed not simply in terms of their relative importance but also in their organization.[25] In the latter, farming was clearly separated from non-farming activities, organized into supra-household units, and generally far more mechanized than in China. As a result, the decollectivization of agriculture in the CIS has raised issues very similar to those encountered in the privatization of industry. Indeed these are in important ways more intense given the very limited nearby alternative economic activities in a vast collective or state farm.

From the perspective of the transition, there is a further crucial feature of the Chinese economy that goes well beyond the large share of agriculture in GDP and in employment. This is the organization of the rural economy in relation to the industrial economy. In the USSR, the economies were modelled on the ideal, to use Preobrazhensky's analogy, of a big and fully integrated factory, of which agriculture was one division. Because the rural sector was looked at as a 'factory' rather than a community, the principles of specialization prevailed: it made no more sense for a rural economic unit to diversify into textiles than it did for an enterprise manufacturing cars to diversify into food production. In contrast, out of a mixture of design and the force of circumstances, China followed a hybrid model of a big factory (represented by large state enterprises) linked variously to numerous independent production units (represented by small and medium enterprises and rural communes). This hybrid character of the Chinese economy played a central role in its evolution towards a market economy.

An apparently paradoxical feature of the post-1978 rural economy in China has been that the decollectivization of farming has gone together with an explosive growth of rural collective industry. As a result, whilst farming is now largely private, rural industry, with a rising share in rural income, is predominantly collective. Thus, in industrialized rural counties the economy is no less collective than it was in 1978, although the focus of collective activity has changed. The mix between collective and private enterprises varies widely across rural localities and is rapidly changing.

Rural industry is not a post-1978 development (Perkins *et al.* 1977). Though promoted by Mao Zedong, it differed from state industry and marked a significant departure from the planned economy. For the most part, rural enterprises had to be financed from local resources and their growth depended crucially on local initiative. Compared to state industry, there has been a pronounced regional dimension to rural industry. Both before and after 1978, rural enterprises have been densely concentrated in some regions. For example, in 1998, seven out of thirty-one provinces accounted for around 55 per cent of value added of rural industry (NSB 1999*a*). While some of these, such as Jiangsu, had well-developed rural industry when the economic reforms began, some others, such as Guangdong and Zhejiang, had comparatively little. The

---

[25] Organization in CEE varied. For example, Polish agriculture in the communist period remained mostly in private hands and consisted mostly of small farms. Elsewhere in CEE there was (relatively) less private ownership than Poland, although the huge state or collective farms were essentially a feature of the former Soviet Union.

reasons for the uneven geographical distribution of rural industry lie in local factors and have little to do with government policies at higher levels.

This institutional combination of household farming and collective industry might seem anachronistic in the transition context but has in fact contributed strongly to the pace of evolution towards a market economy. In farming, the disincentive effects of collective organization of economic activity far outweighed whatever beneficial scale effect it may have had. But in industry there was, at least to begin with, no alternative to collective organization. Non-existent capital markets meant that rural households lacked capital; but they also were without the organizational capacity to undertake industrial activities beyond simple processing and handicrafts (which do not depend on long chains of coordination). Collective ownership provided an institution which could offer a partial substitute for non-existent markets, including for credit and land, and thus opened up possibilities that were not available under private owner-ship. In this sense collective ownership has served as a mechanism for overcoming a problem of collective action associated with market failure.

There is one further and important difference between collective ownership at the local level and at the national level: *competition*, both actual and 'yardstick'. The typ-ical criticism of government enterprises is that the power of taxation enables them to be inefficient: losses can simply be made up by imposing taxes on everyone else. Moreover, by closing markets to imports, a country could force consumers to sub-sidize its inefficient production. But the success of the townships and villages depended in part on attracting foreign investors, not so much for their capital, but for their technology, know-how, and access to markets. Raising new local taxes could not make up for the gaps in entrepreneurship that were opening up. Product market com-petition, though imperfect, exercised its discipline. And each township and village could see how others were doing: there was a high standard that managers in each had to attain. Thus, competition (a version of Tiebout's original hypothesis concerning col-lective action at the local level) greatly mitigated the kinds of governance problems that so often arise at the national level.

Rural townships (the lowest government tiers) and villages (quasi-governmental units) have been the midwives of township and village enterprises, or TVEs. They marshalled necessary capital and procured land for the establishment of TVEs and have also pro-vided them with a degree of insurance from market risks. Without this 'governmental entrepreneurship', rural industrialization in China would not have progressed beyond the rudimentary level. There is no developing economy, including high-performance economies in Asia, that approaches China in the scale and depth of rural industrial-ization. Further, the growth of collective rural enterprises, instead of crowding out house-hold enterprises, has facilitated their proliferation—a classic example of the effects of forward and backward linkages.

Compared to other developing economies with a large rural population, China stands out in two respects: first, in rural industrialization, and second, in having a rural gov-ernment that is not simply effective in relaying orders from the top but also has its roots in local communities and delivers local public goods. It is this combination that requires an explanation. In retrospect, the land reforms of the 1950s that transferred ownership from landlord to tenant and the subsequent rural collectivization that have been *key proximate sources of social capital formation* in rural China. Their contribution lies in eliminating gross inequalities within villages and in widening the scope of cooperative action beyond kin groups to larger units. The two are related in that large inequalities can be associated with divergence in interests that militate against cooperation beyond the level of kin.

The land reform and collectivization had their dark side, both involved violence and divided rural communities. The experience of the Great Leap and the Cultural Revolution from the late 1950s to the mid-1970s was highly traumatic. However, Chinese tradition of local organization and the experience of collective structures left a legacy of administrative capacity at the grass-roots level that, once freed from the straitjacket of collectivization and combined with economic incentives, furnished the conditions for the take-off of rural industry. It is significant that TVEs have flourished especially strongly in those localities where collective farming performed comparatively well.

The form of social cooperation that underpins TVEs consists of a web of interdependence and obligations covering the local government, the community, and enterprises. TVEs depend heavily on local governments and communities for capital, land, and also for insurance against an adverse turn of events. They are, in turn, obligated to finance local public goods and give preference to local inhabitants in labour recruitment. The distinction between 'insiders' and 'outsiders' runs deep in the TVEs and represents one of the challenges in moving China towards an efficient market economy.

In this discussion, we have emphasized the advantages that China had at the beginning of the transition in developing a rural based—but publicly owned—'market economy'. The developments were so smooth that they might seem inevitable; yet such a view ignores the numerous decisions that provided the framework for the new form of enterprises (TVEs and joint ventures) to flourish, particularly significant given the ideological basis of the economy that had prevailed over the preceding three decades.[26] On the other hand, the reformers in Russia simply did not seem to realize the magnitude of the problems they faced in the rural sector—and, given that, did not devise solutions to address them. Though much of the production in Russia was organized on the basis of large-scale farming, small plots still accounted for a large fraction of the value of output. This could have grown, some large-scale farms could have been broken up (as they were in other parts of the FSU), and even large-scale farms could have been organized on a profitable basis (cf. corporate farming elsewhere in the world); but little of this occurred. Russia failed to provide the institutional infrastructure—from the provision of capital, to marketing services for inputs and outputs—and the absence of adequate social safety-nets provided further impetus to retain old and familiar structures, as deficient as they might be. The reformers seemed to believe that the

---

[26] To be sure, Mao's emphasis on the rural sector made it natural for the political élites to focus on everything they could do to make that sector flourish; while Russia's ideological preoccupation with the urban proletariat had resulted in the weakening of the rural sector, at least in the early decades of the Soviet period.

markets for inputs and outputs would simply arise on their own, and underestimated the importance of safety-nets in facilitating change.[27]

3.4. *Moving from old to new enterprises*

The characteristics of decentralization and the rural economy, which we have just examined, have led to the emergence of the dynamic new, primarily TVE, sector in China. The success of the Chinese reforms lies not in reforming its state industrial sector but in spawning the growth of these new economic establishments in industry and in services. The transformation of the state industrial sector has been hesitant. In a marked contrast to reforms in the rural economy and to the opening of the Chinese economy to international trade and direct investment where outcomes far exceeded initial expectations, reforms in the state industrial sector have moved only slowly and delivered far less than expected.

The reform of large state enterprises in China presents problems very similar to those encountered in CEE and the CIS. Indeed, because of the continuity of the one-party State, political and ideological impediments to a transformation of state enterprises have been, in some respects, greater in China than in some post-communist States. Amongst these, of particular significance is that large and medium state enterprises in China are not only economic but also political units. For example, the party has an important say in the appointment of managers of medium and large enterprises and their selection depends not only on performance and managerial competence but also on political reliability. As a result, the depoliticization of ownership and of management has been a slower process in China than in most of the post-Communist economies of CEE and in some parts of the CIS. In both China and CEE/CIS, the transformation of the governance structure of state and privatized enterprises has turned out to be more intractable than many envisaged. The political and social obstacles to reforming large enterprises both eroded the tax base in Russia and led to a large fiscal drain in (mainly informal) subsidies.[28] The enfeebled fiscal position coupled with excessive short-term borrowing led to the financial collapse of August 1998. The big difference in China is that a strong new sector has developed. Difficult as it is proving to be, the restructuring of the old is greatly facilitated by the existence of substantial and attractive alternative sources of activity. Not only does this new source provide competition—and a role model—for the old, but in some cases ends up merging with, or taking over, the older, less efficient enterprises (when they, or at least part of them, can be salvaged).

---

[27] Microeconomists had long recognized some of these market failures under the rubric of 'coordination failures'.

[28] There is a view that privatization in fact did little to change the governance structure of corporations, except in two respects. The apparatchiks who previously were limited in the amounts of rents that they could extract from state enterprises had some of the constraints removed. They could now legally sell the assets for their own benefit. And the balance of power between central and local political authorities changed. In this view, the end of communism in Russia was not the 'revolution' that it was often portrayed to be (though there were, to be sure, marked changes in the political institutions). In Eastern Europe, there were much more dramatic changes.

The share of non-state enterprises in gross industrial output has risen from 22 per cent in 1978 to 72 per cent in 1998, and all but a small percentage of this rise is accounted for by new enterprises. The significance of new economic establishments does not lie in the creation of a substantial private sector, though that has flourished in recent years. Whilst there are many jointly held enterprises, private units, and foreign ventures, public ownership permeates most new establishments. Rural enterprises are still predominantly collective. The government (central or territorial) is the sole or the majority shareholder in most shareholding enterprises. Similarly, the government is the majority shareholder in many of the large and medium enterprises with foreign investment. In terms of ownership, new economic establishments are more mutations of public enterprises than an entirely new species.

The new enterprises are, however, different from traditional state enterprises in two important respects. First, their labour contracts are different from those of state enterprises. Compared to state enterprises, they are less constrained in choosing forms and scale of remuneration and the terms of employment. They have greater freedom to lay off employees, restrictions on which constitute a principal barrier in restructuring state enterprises. Second, their relation to the government is in various ways different from that of traditional state enterprises. They tend to face a harder budget constraint. Further there is a stronger weight on profitability in setting objectives than for the traditional state enterprises. This also holds for large state enterprises that have been transformed into corporations. It does not appear inevitable that state enterprises face soft budget constraints. (See Kornai (1986) on soft budget constraints.) Indeed, the decentralized nature of the Chinese system has served to harden budget constraints. Banks, though government owned, did not automatically lend money to state enterprises to make up for deficits; the banks were under pressure to be on a commercially sound basis, even if they were also under pressure to address 'social needs'.[29]

4. Economic Growth: Social Capital, Physical Capital, and Productivity

4.1. Social capital and the analysis of growth

In understanding institutional change and the transformation of the Chinese economy, the preceding section has laid great stress on organizational structures and existing and developing patterns of behaviour, particularly cooperative behaviour within and across institutions. In this context we have already used the term 'social capital' and in this section we shall examine this idea, and its role in growth and development, more carefully. We shall use the term social capital to cover: (i) acceptance of basic codes of behaviour, (ii) trust, and (iii) cooperative behaviour. This is a rather broader approach

---

[29] By the same token, privatization by itself may not ensure hard budget constraints not only because of direct government subsidies, but also because of 'indirect' subsidies through a state banking system—what has come to be called bank socialism in the Czech republic.

to social capital than that used by some other authors (for a helpful discussion and compendium, see Dasgupta and Serageldin 2000). We shall argue in this section that China's growth must be understood in terms of the development of productivity and of physical capital underpinned by, and in tandem with, the existence and development of social capital. In particular, China's growth has been crucially dependent on institutional and organizational arrangements and innovations that built on social capital.

The term social capital refers broadly to the set of understandings—rules, regulations, policies, norms, institutions, etc.—that govern the *relations* among individuals, allowing them to interact in ways that enhance overall productivity, i.e. the outputs that can be achieved with any given input.[30] Much (some might claim virtually all) of social capital goes beyond formal institutions, for example in legal structures. Indeed, it is apparent that there is relatively little recourse to the legal system to enforce 'good behaviour'.[31] A manifestation of the 'social capital' embedded within an organization is a corporation's typically being worth more than the value of its underlying assets. This is sometimes referred to as the firm's goodwill (which is more than the value of its reputation or its 'customer' list).

Much of the story told in this paper turns on the close relationship between policy reform, institutions, and behaviour.[32] Institutional arrangements can both foster the preservation and development of social capital and derive strength from it. Thus the development of TVEs required social capital in terms of the willingness to cooperate in local communities and the trust to take a long-term view. At the same time, the success of the TVEs reinforced social capital in terms of demonstrating the returns to the methods of work and cooperation that they embodied (see Section 3.3 below on building social capital).

---

[30] It is not clear whether social capital should, accordingly, include *organizational* and *informational* capital, the largely tacit knowledge that enables individuals to function together (who knows what, who has responsibility for doing what . . .). And large change in the organizational structure of the economy—including high levels of bankruptcy—cause a loss of this kind of capital. Stiglitz (1994), Blanchard and Kremer (1997), and others have argued that similar problems were an inevitable consequence of the breakdown of the command economy. Here, we are concerned with broader aspects of social behaviour with large economic consequences.

[31] Though this observation by itself may understate the importance of formal institutions: large penalties seldom enforced can induce good behaviour, a point emphasized in Mirrlees's early work on incentive. It is also the case that there are important interactions between formal and informal systems: the ostracism following conviction of a crime may be far more effective than any monetary penalties.

Also, while here we focus on those aspects of social capital that enhance productivity, it should be clear that the term is broader. Norms of discrimination or collusion among businessmen can be thought as part of social capital, but these decrease overall productivity. There are other instances (discussed below) where social capital may be 'negative'—indeed, norms of corruption have become prevalent in many of the CIS countries (see *World Development Report* 1997).

An aspect of 'social capital' that is hard to incorporate into standard analysis concerns 'values'. Traditionally, sociology has focused on how individuals' preferences are affected by people with whom they associate. Organizations deliberately try to change preferences. It may be 'easier' to induce desirable behaviour by changing the preferences of agents than by providing good incentives or imposing constraints on behaviour.

[32] For further discussion of definitional issues see the EBRD's *Transition Report 1999*, ch. 1. Some authors speak of the behavioural element, emphasized here in terms of 'social norms' (Elster 1989), 'values' (Fukuyama 1995), or 'informal constraints' (North's comment in Stiglitz 1989).

A few comments on the concept of social capital. While it is natural to use the term social *capital* since it typically takes time and often resources to create social capital, one should be aware that social capital is, at the same time, markedly different from other forms of capital. For instance, typically, when we use a machine, it depreciates. When we use social capital—for instance, by using the strength of community organization to enlist parental support in creating stronger schools—it actually can *enhance* social capital. In that sense, resources may not actually be required to create social capital; it can be a 'free' byproduct of other activities. And while there is a strong presumption that physical and human capital have a positive marginal productivity, many forms of social capital—such as discrimination—may actually reduce productivity. And as we shall see, social capital is probably more fragile than other forms of capital.

The use of the adjective *social* in the concept of social capital (distinguishing it from human and physical capital) serves to focus attention on the fact that this form of capital affects the *relationships* among individuals, how they cooperate together. The crucial element in our argument is that production requires individuals to work together, to cooperate, and that cooperative behaviour is determined not just by conventional monetary incentives. Thus, an analysis of growth and transformation must include an analysis of how cooperative behaviour changes over time. Earlier analyses (say, of growth in the USA) could safely ignore social capital, simply because it changed relatively slowly. But there were dramatic changes in Russia and many of the other countries in transition that had first-order effects.

This can be seen heuristically by thinking about the standard growth analysis (which will be discussed in greater detail in the next section). In Russia, at first blush, it would seem that in the process of transition, using standard production theory, a given stock of physical capital, labour, and human capital should have, through a switch from inefficient communist modes of production to (admittedly imperfect) capitalist modes, led to an enormous increase in output. The huge decrease in output can, at least in part, be 'explained' by a reduction in the level of social capital.[33]

A careful look at the *process* of transition in China and Russia (and the other CIS states) helps us see how transition in one case built on existing social capital while in the other case there was actual deterioration of social capital. In China, transition reinforced the already existing capital within the communes and enhanced trust in a government that was able both to maintain social stability and to reduce poverty. In Russia and the other CIS states, hyperinflation wiped out savings and undermined trust in the monetary system.[34] Governments claimed they had no money to pay pensions, and yet not only transferred vast amounts of state property to a few oligarchs, but allowed these oligarchs to take much of their ill-gotten wealth out of the country.

Those who had newfound (and, often, 'illegitimately gotten') wealth had little incentive to risk investing within the country when ownership rights and returns were stronger abroad and there was always a fear that at some time the basis of its ownership could

---

[33] Later, we will argue that this reduction in social capital may have, at the same time, contributed to the destruction of physical capital.

[34] Interestingly, at least one of the countries of the FSU has actually been discussing compensating those whose real value of savings was wiped out by the hyperinflation, explicitly to restore 'social capital'.

be challenged at home. This led to capital flight, asset-stripping rather than wealth creation, and an undermining of public confidence in the reform process.

Some who promoted the rapid privatization appeared to believe in a Coasean process, whereby once property rights were seemingly well established there would be incentives to create the legal foundations (and social capital) required for a vibrant market economy. But those with monopoly powers have seldom given strong endorsement to competition laws, and the new moneyed interests showed no immediate interest in creating a market economy based on social justice, competition, and the rule of law.[35] While privatization was supposed to stop the grabbing hand of the State, it became increasingly perceived that privatization provided a velvet glove which could facilitate these special interests in grabbing more, though perhaps more quietly.[36] The EBRD/World Bank 'Business Environment and Enterprise Performance Survey' (see ch. 6, *Transition Report 1999*) shows clearly that privatization is positively associated with a higher quality of governance in low-capture States but negatively associated in high-capture States. And without good governance, privatization does not contribute to growth (see Stiglitz 1999*a*). Indeed, the manner in which privatization occurred created strong political forces attempting to defend the *status quo*, thereby hindering even restructuring. By the same token, as the already weak social capital in Russia deteriorated further, it made it more difficult for new enterprises to be created. In the CIS, corruption, which can be thought of as a manifestation of an absence of adequate 'social capital', is higher than in any other region in the world (save sub-Saharan Africa). And it has been shown that high levels of corruption are significantly negatively associated with growth (see the 1997 *World Development Report*).[37]

The erosion of physical and social capital went hand in hand. While recent analyses of economic performance have emphasized the importance of social capital, too little attention has been placed on the interrelationship between physical and social capital. It is not just that social capital is a 'complement' to physical capital, in the ordinary sense of increasing its marginal productivity, but social capital is a prerequisite for the creation and preservation of physical capital. Standard economic doctrines recognize the importance of property rights, and the necessity for a legal structure to enforce those property rights. Without support for property rights, individuals and corporations will have little incentive to invest. But what has not been sufficiently recognized is that the legal system by itself is of only limited value. What stops people from stealing copper

[35] Support for stronger anti-trust laws in the USA today, for instance, does *not* come from Bill Gates and Microsoft, just as it did not come from Rockefeller at the turn of the century.

[36] There were further failures in the underlying economic logic. Many implicitly used an oversimplistic model of the firm, in which the shareholders had virtually all rights of decision-making, and simply maximized profits (or stock market value). In fact, there are many other stakeholders in firms, including workers and local governments. Privatization eliminated neither their claims nor their ability to exercise influence over the outcomes. The market structure too affected the incentives facing firm managers. Without a well-developed capital market, strategies for maximizing value (over the short-term horizon of these, often older, managers) made little sense.

[37] Working with the World Bank, the EBRD carried out a survey of over 3,000 firms in twenty transition countries and asked, *inter alia*, about the impact on their business of the sale of parliamentary legislation and presidential decrees. In Russia and Ukraine over 40 per cent reported a significant impact. See ch. 6, *Transition Report, 1999*.

telephone wires at night or panes out of a greenhouse is more than just the risk of being caught. It is a sense of moral responsibility,[38] a recognition that these are negative-sum actions. But as the already weak social fabric weakened further, and the insecurities of the future heightened, socially destructive actions became more common. Today, as one travels around some of the CIS countries, one sees a capital stock weaker than it was a decade ago. The erosion of social capital has been accompanied not just by normal depreciation of the physical capital but by its actual destruction.

In making social capital central to the comparison of China and Russia, specifically how it was a foundation for the former but weak, and weakened further in the latter, we must be careful to avoid misleading impressions on two key issues. First, we must stress that it would be ludicrous to see China's history over the last few decades as a cheerful, lyrical, and seamless passage from one successful reform step to another. The two decades of reforms of the post-1979 period were preceded by two decades marked by stress, turmoil, and catastrophic policy errors. The 'Great Leap Forward' of 1959–61 was associated with severe dislocation, famine, and the deaths of 20 or 30 million. The Cultural Revolution of 1966–76 caused turmoil and turned colleague against colleague and children against parents. Thus the period 1959–76 could not be seen as inevitably providing a foundation of harmony and trust for the reforms that followed.

On the contrary, we have argued that China's leadership drew the basic lessons from the experience of the preceding decades both concerning the dangers of overdramatic change and of the importance of market incentives. Thus they introduced their market-based reforms in a step-by-step, experimental, and evolutionary way. And in doing so, they saw the importance of building, as we have described, on the strengths that had been inherited from earlier experience.[39]

Second, we must be careful, not to jump to the conclusion that rapid privatization in Russia was necessarily a mistake. That is a matter of counterfactual history: perhaps matters would have been still worse had alternative strategies been pursued. Such a conclusion would require a careful analysis of the structure of control inherited from the perestroika and preceding periods, the political options at that time and the expectations of future political opportunities.[40]

However, the association between Poland's more gradual and structured approach to privatization and a stronger performance is strongly suggestive that alternative strategies in Russia may well have been associated with better outcomes. The potential weaknesses of voucher privatization have become evident throughout the region and were discussed at the time. For those countries not willing to sell their assets to

[38] This is what Herbert Hart has referred to as 'the inner acceptance of law'. See Hart (1972). In North's comments in Stiglitz (1989) he emphasizes that it would be impossible for complex societies to function on formal rules alone—'self-imposed standards of conduct which constrain maximization at some margins' are vital (113). 'Rule utilitarianism' could be seen as providing a partial basis for such acceptance or standards, see e.g. Smart and Williams (1973) or Sen and Williams (1982), including the piece by Mirrlees (1982).

[39] Moreover, there was, by the time of the beginning of the transition, a strong tradition of extensive dialogue on a whole variety of issues. Though the discussion may have not always been free, the dialogue may have played an important role in consensus building.

[40] In recognizing limitations on political choices we must also beware of assuming that what happened was the only feasible option. There were important examples of management buy-outs and various leasing arrangements in both Poland and Russia in the early 1990s—see Ellerman (1993).

foreigners, the question remained: who could have become meaningful owners in an economy without large wealth-holders? What we can say is that the fabric of institutions and social capital in Russia were very weak in relation to the social and institutional pressures associated with the rapid privatization. The risks were real and the outcomes not surprising.

4.2. Some growth arithmetic

We turn now to an analysis of productivity and accumulation in China, using a fairly standard growth-accounting approach. The results point fairly strongly in certain directions and suggest some clear hypotheses on the sources of growth.

In the twenty years from 1979 to 1998 China's real GNP grew by around 9.6 per cent per year, compared to the average of 5.6 per cent between 1953 and 1978.[41] Given the annual population growth rate of around 1.3 per cent over the reform period, the measured annual growth rate of per capita income comes to 8.2 per cent, implying that per capita income has almost quintupled since 1978. Chinese growth statistics suffer from problems that give grounds for suspecting an upward bias, which is likely to be higher in the pre-reform than in the reform period. But a downward adjustment to take account of such biases would be unlikely to affect two conclusions:

1. The average growth rate over the reform period has been substantially higher than that preceding 1978.
2. The growth rate compares favourably with the pre-1997 average in 'high-performance Asian economies'.

Rapid growth in China has persisted too long to be explained away in terms of a conjunction of favourable but incidental circumstances.

Given that the growth rate between 1952 and 1978 averaged 5.6 per cent per year, an immediate question is whether the post-1978 growth is qualitatively different from that pre-1979?

A part of the acceleration in the growth since 1978 is due to higher growth of factor inputs. The labour force has grown marginally more rapidly—2.8 per cent in 1979–98 compared to 2.6 per cent per year in 1953–78—and the (fixed) investment ratio has been substantially higher, 30.7 per cent in 1979–98 compared to 22.6 per cent in 1953–78. How much of the acceleration of the growth rate since 1978 is due to higher productivity?

The 'decomposition' of reported growth into growth of factor inputs and that of factor productivity would lead to two conclusions.

• Almost all of growth pre-1978 is attributable to growth in total factor inputs (TFI).
• In contrast, growth of TFI explains no more than 72 per cent of growth since 1979.

The total factor productivity growth rate comes to around 2.7 per cent per year, which compares favourably with the productivity growth rates from similar calculations for

---

[41] For the details of data sources and calculations see the Appendix.

countries in East and South-East Asia. Thus a broad, and probably fairly robust, conclusion is that the reforms in China have substantially raised productivity, and that economic growth since 1979 is qualitatively different from the growth until then.

A number of factors can be cited to explain the qualitative difference between the pre- and post-1978 economic growth. These include the opening of the Chinese economy to trade and direct investment, which have extended the range of available techniques—both physical and managerial—and the reintroduction of economic incentives. Rather than cover all possibilities, we focus on just two interrelated factors:

- In a developing economy such as that of China a central strand of economic growth is the transfer of labour from farming to non-farming activities as described, for example, in some dual-economy models of growth.
- In the reform period, it is the rural economy that has been the major locus of institutional transformations in the form of the decollectivization of farming and an explosive growth of rural industry.

Related to these, there are two important observations for speculation on prospects for growth, looking forward:

- Output per head in farming is currently marginally less than a quarter (23 per cent) of that in the non-farming sector. This gap has varied over time but has always been substantial.
- The reform period since 1979 has witnessed a marked acceleration in the rate of transfer of labour from farming to non-farming activities. Whereas in the twenty-six years from 1952 to 1978 the percentage share of farm labour in the total labour force dropped by 13 percentage points (from 84 per cent in 1952), the share has fallen by as much as 21 percentage points in twenty years from 1979 to 1998. Non-farming activities in rural areas now employ around a third of the rural labour force.

The transfer of labour out of farming acquires a special significance in explaining the growth rate when non-farming activities (in particular manufacturing) are subject to increasing returns to scale, an argument to which Kaldor attached great significance.[42]

The mechanisms through which the transformations in the rural economy since 1979 have affected this labour transfer from farm to non-farm activities have been described in Section 2. They may be summarized in growth terms as follows. First, the decollectivization of farming has shifted decisions about labour deployment from cadres to households or individuals, thus reducing a key impediment to the transfer of labour out of farming. Second, the growth of rural enterprises (both collective and household) has enhanced investment opportunities in non-farming activities.

---

[42] See Kaldor and Mirrlees (1962) for a formal presentation of some Kaldorian hypotheses. However, Kaldor focused on large-scale enterprises (such as steel); much of the manufacturing that developed in China in the last twenty years has been small scale, and so it is difficult to ascertain the importance of returns to scale. It is plausible, however, that there may exist Marshallian returns to scale—externalities outside the firm, e.g. associated with the provision of intermediate inputs.

As long as non-farming activities were largely confined to the urban state sector, investments in these activities reflected the institutional bias towards manufacturing and the capital-intensive end of the technical spectrum and against services and processing. As a result, the investment needed to transfer a person out of farming was comparatively high.[43] With the emergence of new organizations such as TVEs and household enterprises, which have a limited access to credit, considerations determining investment choices have changed. The result is a reduction in investment associated with the transfer of a person out of farming. Thus the institutional transformation has opened up possibilities that were previously closed off by the earlier institutional structure.

We have seen, therefore, that at one level a story of capital accumulation plus labour transfer à la Ricardo/Marx/Lewis/Kaldor, together with efficiency and technological gains from trade and integration both within and outside China, would seem to provide a coherent account of growth in China. But we have also seen that it is important to go beyond this slightly technical story and to ask how the labour transfers, productivity change, and capital accumulation were actually determined and shaped. It is here that we have to introduce the role of social capital and institutional development if we are to provide a convincing account of growth in China.[44]

Before leaving the growth arithmetic, we should ask why investment and saving have been so high in China, particularly in contrast to CEE and the CIS. Following the downfall of the command economy and the one-party State in CEE and the CIS, investment contracted even more sharply than output. The investment ratio stabilized with macroeconomic stabilization and has begun to rise in some economies. Generally, however, the rise in investment has not been matched by a rise in domestic savings, which still remain precariously low (thus there have been big balance of payments deficits in many CEE and CIS countries—see *Transition Reports*). In contrast, the investment ratio in the post-1978 Chinese economy has been higher than in the pre-reform period and is among the highest in the world (currently around 40 per cent). And domestic savings have also been high. In fact, given that during much of the 1990s, China has run a balance of payments surplus, domestic savings have generally exceeded investment.

Why has China's saving rate been so high? In the growth context the relevant notion of saving is 'national saving' (the sum of government, enterprise, and household saving). The determinants of non-household and household savings are different. In particular, with limited capital markets, non-household savings[45] are, arguably, driven by investment opportunities. The same also holds for rural and urban households with their own enterprises. The counterpart of the urge to invest and to establish new enterprises on the part of lower government tiers is higher savings on their part.[46]

---

[43] Moreover, the transfer of an individual from the rural to the urban sector required heavy investment in housing and infrastructure; these investments too were reduced by the rural development strategy.

[44] There are other elements too which contributed to the success: the competition among the many TVEs spurred efficiency. Such competition was largely absent in Russia.

[45] We have seen that government and enterprise decisions in China have been closely intertwined.

[46] From this perspective, the savings may be driven more by bureaucratic imperatives than by 'rational' choice considerations; that is, local government officials' 'power' was affected by their control of resources, and this in turn was enhanced by successful investments. There is little evidence, however, of a large incongruence between the actions of the local officials and what individuals might have chosen for themselves.

We can understand the development of household savings in China in terms of liquidity, insurance against future contingencies (the precautionary motive), as well as the changing demographic structure. The need for savings for liquidity for households in China arises from the absence or the rudimentary level of commercial consumer credit. The argument goes as follows. With the start of reforms household incomes increased sharply and the range of available consumer goods widened. With price controls on necessities, much of the extra household income went towards consumer durables. Given the absence of commercial credit, households had to accumulate in advance of purchasing the desired item. This type of savings, driven by financing constraints, may continue for a while because of rising household incomes, a high marginal propensity to spend on consumer durables, and the arrival of new consumer durables. These savings would, however, be undermined by the development of consumer credit markets. Most recently, many Chinese households have been saving because of a desire to buy cars and housing.[47]

Turning to the precautionary motive, the general argument is that with the transition to a market economy uncertainty rises. The sources of heightened uncertainty include the replacement of free service provision such as healthcare and education with a partial or full user-fee system and the prospect of unemployment. The former is equivalent to the replacement of full insurance with partial or no insurance and its implications for households are magnified by a rise in the relative cost of various services. Unemployment, which was previously low and confined to new entrants, has risen sharply and applies to all age groups. The new enterprises do not have the same obligation to 'look after' their employees and even those in state enterprises must be less confident of medium-term support for sickness and health benefits and for pensions.

Finally, the changing demographic structure and the one-child policy, in the context of the traditional norm of depending on male children for old-age support, is likely to have a strong effect on saving, particularly for couples without a son. From one perspective its effect is the same as that of the replacement of a pay-as-you-go pension system with a fully funded system. The effects are likely to be particularly strong in rural areas where there are no old-age pensions.[48]

4.3. Creating social capital

Given that social capital has played a prominent role in our understanding of China's growth and its contrast with the experience of the CIS, it is natural to ask how social capital can be created, bearing in mind that social capital can also be eroded or destroyed.

---

[47] This is known in the savings literature as 'target savings'. Savings rates in China are only marginally higher than in the rest of East Asia, and so it is worthwhile looking at *common* factors. Another hypothesis (in addition to those already put forward) is that consumption lags income, so that when the growth rate is increased, the savings rate increases. There has been a demographic shift throughout East Asia, though not everywhere as dramatic as in China. In some countries, there has actually been a reduction in unemployment and a more secure overall economic environment, suggesting that the 'precautionary' explanation may not be as important as the other explanations.

[48] Although, following similar reasoning, the one-child policy has been less rigid in these areas.

We focus first on its creation. The subject of the factors that might influence the development of codes of behaviour, trust, and cooperation is potentially vast and complex. We cannot pretend to provide a serious analysis in a short subsection. We can offer here only a few suggested ideas and examples focusing on aspects that might be influenced by economic or social policy and political action. The issues involved are of great importance for the understanding of the processes of transformation and growth and are priorities for further research.

If we focus on social capital in terms of behaviour associated with cooperation and trust, we can point to five types of factors that may favour its creation: (i) the production process, (ii) the physical environment, (iii) education, (iv) legislation and social control, and (v) external threats. The factors may interact and complement each other.

As an example of the first, one can argue that the irrigation techniques, particularly for rice, in southern and eastern China have generated a deep recognition of the importance of collaboration in agriculture. This is in contrast to the different technologies for wheat in northern China.

The physical environment, particularly in cities, can nurture, or undermine, a sense of community, belonging, and mutual support. Thus shaping cities to become liveable and dynamic could make a major contribution to social capital, particularly where they are growing rapidly with movements out of rural areas and agriculture.[49]

Education systems and practice can place more or less emphasis on codes of behaviour and building social and community values. For example, the integration of the school system in the southern states of the USA has played a part in breaking down societal barriers.

Legislation and social control can also have a powerful influence. Examples include legislation against discrimination in the USA and Europe. Stronger policing in the 1990s in New York City has contributed to a greater sense of participation and civic pride in city life.

Some have argued that World War II in the UK, with its powerful external threat, generated a transformation in terms of cooperative behaviour and an understanding of common interest and mutual support. This underpinned the election by a landslide of a Labour Government in 1945 and social transformations of the post-war welfare state, including the National Health Service.[50]

There may be special circumstances or moments in history that are particularly favourable to the creation of social capital. Balcerowicz (1995) has argued that the early years of the transition in CEE represented a period of 'extraordinary politics' where the community was ready to accept radical change, make common sacrifices, and begin to create new institutions. These special circumstances also create special responsibilities, since decisions made in those formative years can establish very powerful vested interests further down the road.

The President of Uzbekistan (whose GDP today relative to that a decade ago surpasses that of any of the other CIS states) has emphasized the creation of social

---

[49] See Stiglitz (1999*c*).

[50] The generation of fear of an external threat has been a common and unattractive ploy by politicians faced with internal dissent. See also Putzel (1997) on the 'dark side' of social capital.

capital in his writings and policies. He has tried to build social unity, for instance, by re-emphasizing the country's history and lauding the country's writers. He has also supported local participation, through the recreation of a system of local communal-based welfare.

Social capital can be eroded or destroyed more easily than it can be created. Many argue that standards of honesty and mutual support have eroded rapidly in Russia over the last ten years. 'Grabbing', often unethical and sometimes brutal, has become pervasive (Shleifer and Vishny 1998). It must be recognized, however, that such behaviour was also commonplace under the old regime—'beating the system' was a way of life. Nevertheless, the dramatic rise in poverty and inequality in the last ten years in Russia must have taken its toll on the sense of community and mutual responsibility. Critical in maintaining social capital is abiding by the implicit social contract and maintaining a broad sense of equity. In Russia, the reformers paid little attention to the social contract and turned a blind eye to growing inequalities.

Economics has paid little attention to social capital, preferring to focus on the 'more tangible' or measurable. The process of transition, however, is one of profound social change where the role of social capital in the growth and development of living standards can be fundamental. And one should also recognize, although it is not our main subject here, that social capital is not only an input into the process of production, but can contribute directly to the well-being of individuals. Societies where basic codes of behaviour are observed, and where there is a sense of trust and community, are more pleasant places to live.

5. Prospects and Challenges

5.1. *Prospects for growth in China*

Having identified factors that might promote or hinder growth in China and CEE and the CIS, it is natural to ask about prospects and challenges in terms of the likely strength of these factors in the future. We remain optimistic about China's future growth prospects, based on the following considerations:

- *Sectoral transfer*: the fraction of the labour force in agriculture is still as high as 47 per cent and its productivity is still well below that of activities elsewhere. Thus the process of sectoral transfer still has some way to go.
- *Technological advance/catch-up*: on average China's technology is still substantially below that of middle-income developing countries in East Asia.
- *Resource allocation*: as markets develop there are likely to be improvements in efficiency. Joining the WTO will further enhance competition and lead to greater integration of the economy as a whole. It may force the elimination of some implicit subsidies, putting strains on the economy.
- *High savings*: as rates of return to investment fall and credit markets develop, enterprise and household savings rates may fall.

- *The role of TVEs*: as markets and enterprises develop the specific institutional structure of TVEs is likely to come under pressure. They will compete with other organizations and different shareholder structures. They will increasingly raise capital from
outside.

- China will belatedly face the problems addressed (so unsuccessfully) by so many of
the other economies in transition—restructuring the state-owned enterprises
(SOEs). But it starts that process on a much firmer basis, with a large number of
vibrant enterprises, some of which may take over those SOEs that, with restructuring,
can remain viable, and with a large non-SOE sector able to absorb the labour freed
from the SOEs as they restructure.

- China will restructure its society, becoming more urban, reflecting the agglomeration economies that have driven the urbanization process elsewhere. That the government is, at the same time, aware of the problems posed by urbanization means
that the country may be able to avoid the pitfalls of unplanned urban growth that
have marred so many other developing (and developed) countries.

- As China's economy has grown, it no longer can rely to the same extent as it did in
the past on export-led growth; it will have to develop its domestic markets. Reforms
already under way, for instance, in financial and housing markets, have laid the foundations for this.

- China recognizes the importance of maintaining and strengthening its social
capital. The process of creating a national 'safety-net' (e.g. a nationwide system of
old-age pensions), divorcing the 'social' functions from the 'production functions'
of enterprises, will continue, as will efforts at ensuring that disparities between the
wealthiest and poorest provinces are kept in bounds.

Taking the likely development of these factors together, it would seem to be reasonable to predict a gradual slowdown in China's growth. But the processes of sectoral
transfer, catch-up, and the development of entrepreneurial market responses are likely
to remain strong. Whilst fragilities, particularly in a developing financial sector, cannot be ruled out, there is no reason why China's human and social capital together
with its willingness to save and its stage of development should not imply per capita
growth rates on the order of 5 to 6 per cent per annum over the coming decade.

5.2. Prospects for growth in Russia and the CIS

For Russia and the CIS on the other hand, the forces for growth are not yet established. One challenge is to rebuild social capital after the traumatic experience of the
last decade. No one should predict that this will be easy, especially bearing in mind
that social capital is much more easily destroyed than created. And in the country today
there is a widespread sense that the market reforms have served to benefit the few at
the expense of the many. The nature of the challenge is reflected in the statement that
the country must make it attractive for the capital that has gone abroad to return. But
think what that means: it means that the wealth of the oligarchs would be protected,

that the inequalities that have been created be preserved. Even if there were some way of making such commitments, what would this imply for the nature of their society? The fact is that there is no way that such commitments can be made, at least within a democratic society.

The two key short-term policy challenges are to restructure, strengthen, and regulate the banking system and to maintain macroeconomic stability. The reining in of expenditure plus some growth in tax revenues, associated in part with rising oil and gas prices, have, together with moderate monetary policies, prevented inflation in Russia from spiralling out of control in the last year or so. The erosion of real incomes of state workers and pensioners will put real pressures on expenditure. Whilst there is no doubt that there is waste and inefficiency on the expenditure side of the budget, it is preferable that the bulk of fiscal strengthening should be on the revenue side.

So far, Russia has shown little willingness to collect even the taxes that could easily be collected, e.g. on oil and gas. The increasing reliance of the economy on natural resources—reflecting the decline of manufacturing—means the country is increasingly dependent on the vagaries of international commodity prices. While the surge in oil prices in 1999 and early 2000 have been of enormous benefit—just as the decline somewhat earlier had contributed to its travails—the country has not used the opportunity of high oil and gas prices to build up a budget surplus and foreign exchange reserves. Instead, capital flight proceeded at a rapid pace throughout 1999. This implies that if oil prices fall dramatically, as predicted, in the future, Russia's plight may indeed worsen.

The devaluation of August 1998 has generated some growth in import-substituting industries. But it has led to little increase in manufacturing exports. In short, this recovery will not be sustained unless the longer-term and more fundamental problems of Russia are addressed. For Russia and the CIS this means, above all, creating the environment for the growth of new firms and the restructuring of old firms. In China the growth of TVEs and the private sector meant that much restructuring could effectively be postponed until alternative opportunities had grown. Russia and the CIS do not have this luxury. Unless the structural problems in industry are addressed macroeconomic stability will be threatened and the prospects for investment and growth will be limited.

For Russia and the CIS industrial reform must involve the promotion of the forces of competition by reducing barriers to entry (particularly barriers such as organized crime and bureaucratic interference) and facilitating restructuring and exit. Restructuring will be much less difficult if realistic alternative activities develop, for example through the creation of small and medium enterprises. For those workers who cannot find alternatives some form of social support would be necessary. Without such alternative activities or support, political and social obstacles to restructuring are likely to remain strong.[51]

---

[51] For further discussion of economic prospects in CEE and the CIS, investment climate issues, and the growth of SMEs, see the *Transition Report 1999*.

5.3. Prospects for growth in CEE

There was a time, around two to three years ago, when some saw the CIS as following a similar path to that of CEE, but with a two- or three-year lag, taking account of the later start (1991–2 as opposed to 1989–90). This was when it looked as though growth in the CIS, just turning positive in 1997, would become firmly established. We can now see that this was unrealistic. The institutional foundations in CEE and its social capital are much stronger than in the CIS. And the prospect of joining the EU offers a powerful incentive for stable institutional development. The enterprises of CEE have shown their ability to compete on world markets. The growth prospects for CEE seem much more secure than those of the CIS.

5.4. China's challenges in the coming years

In institutional terms China's transformation seems now to be entering a new period. The era of growth driven by a rapid growth of TVEs seems to be coming to an end. They were a brilliantly successful institutional innovation that overcame many problems associated with weaknesses or failures in capital and labour markets. Their rapid growth took a lot of pressure off the large SOEs. The growth of the new and the transformation of the old are both key elements in the transition process—and they are complementary. The transformation of the old can create new firms and new opportunities through spin-offs and reduction of overintegration. And the growth of the new eases the transformation of the old by creating opportunities for displaced labour. Whilst much of the talk in China in the last twenty years was about 'SOE reform', the real driving force behind growth was the TVEs.

China is now moving into a different era. It is now that the creation of strong legal and financial institutions to foster sound market development should move to the top of the agenda. Standing still is not an option for China. The market and private enterprise system in China is growing rapidly. But if structured institutions to support the market system do not develop, then problems of vested interests, monopolistic positions, corporate governance, and corruption could corrode the economy and society. Further, it should be clear that any attempt to step back to the rigidity of the plan is no longer realistic.

The experience of the last twenty years in China carries strong lessons for the role of government. It must be active in the promotion of transition. But it must focus on the right issues at the right time. China has had dramatic success with first focusing on the household responsibility system in agriculture, and then allowing an environment that fostered the growth of TVEs. Now the challenge is to create the environment, particularly the institutional environment, for the sustained and healthy growth of the private sector.

A special challenge in this process will be to preserve and foster social cohesion. A key achievement of the TVEs is that whilst they were much less rigid than the SOEs, they both maintained and built on the strength of the local community. A growing market economy will see not only a growing division of labour, but also a growing

division of social functions. The firm or enterprise will no longer have indefinite responsibility for the housing, employment, or pensions of its workers. The State, separable
from the firm, must accept responsibility for some aspects of social support. It must
also foster effective markets for housing and for labour. These are central challenges
for all governments in making market economies work well wherever they are.
Governments must also exercise responsibility for the 'rules of the game', particularly
concerning competition, hard budget constraints, and corporate governance.

The outstanding challenge for China now is to build institutions and a role for
redefining the role of the State in a market economy. Building on social capital and
maintaining social cohesion are vital to the economic success of the next stage of transition. China will need to draw still further on the strong reserves of creativity and
commitment that generated the great successes of the last twenty years.

APPENDIX

The figures for China in the paper are from National Bureau of Statistics (1999*a*, *b*).[52]
The figures for Russia are from the European Bank of Reconstruction and
Development.

Growth rates are presented in Tables 14.1 and 14.2 for China, CEE, and the CIS.
For the purpose of constructing Figure 14.1 we have taken Russia's 1989 real GDP
at around US$1,000bn and China's at around $500bn. Thus we have styled the comparative graph at index levels of 200 for Russia and 100 for China. Given the problems of constructing and comparing indices for these countries in this period, one should
not attempt great precision on levels of GDP. However, the levels suggested for the

TABLE 14.1. *GDP indexes: 1989 = 100. China, Russia, CEE, and Poland*

	China	Russia	CEE	Poland
1989	100.0	100.0	100.0	100.0
1990	103.8	96.0	93.3	88.4
1991	113.4	91.2	83.2	82.2
1992	129.5	78.0	80.1	84.3
1993	147.0	71.2	80.6	87.6
1994	165.6	62.2	83.8	92.1
1995	183.0	59.6	88.5	98.6
1996	200.6	57.5	92.2	104.6
1997	218.2	58.0	96.2	111.8
1998	235.2	55.3	98.5	117.1
1999	251.9	52.5	100.6	121.2

[52] The GDP 1989 figure for China is converted at the then-prevailing exchange rate of $1 = Rmb 3.77.

TABLE 14.2(a). *GDP indexes: 1989 = 100. Central and Eastern Europe*

	1989	1990	1991	1992	1993	1994	1995	1996	1997	1998	1999
Albania	100.0	90.0	65.1	60.4	66.2	72.4	78.8	86.0	80.0	86.4	90.7
Bulgaria	100.0	90.9	80.3	74.4	73.3	74.6	76.2	67.9	63.2	65.4	66.1
Croatia	100.0	92.9	73.3	64.7	59.5	63.1	67.3	71.4	76.0	78.1	78.1
Czech Republic	100.0	98.8	87.5	84.6	85.1	87.8	93.4	97.0	98.0	95.3	95.3
Estonia	100.0	91.9	79.4	68.1	62.0	60.8	63.4	65.9	73.4	76.4	78.6
FYR Macedonia	100.0	90.1	79.2	62.5	56.8	55.8	55.1	55.5	56.4	58.0	55.7
Hungary	100.0	96.5	85.0	82.4	81.9	84.3	85.5	86.6	90.6	95.2	99.0
Latvia	100.0	102.9	92.2	60.0	51.1	51.5	51.0	52.7	56.2	58.2	59.7
Lithuania	100.0	95.0	89.6	70.5	59.1	53.3	55.1	57.6	61.2	63.8	65.4
Poland	100.0	88.4	82.2	84.3	87.6	92.1	98.6	104.6	111.8	117.1	121.2
Romania	100.0	94.4	82.2	75.0	76.1	79.1	84.7	88.2	82.3	76.3	74.0
Slovak Republic	100.0	97.5	83.3	77.9	75.0	78.6	84.1	89.6	95.4	99.6	100.1
Slovenia	100.0	95.3	86.8	82.0	84.3	88.8	92.5	95.5	99.1	103.1	105.7
CEE	100.0	93.3	83.2	80.1	80.6	83.8	88.5	92.2	96.2	98.5	100.6

TABLE 14.2(b). *GDP indexes: 1989 = 100. CIS States*

	1989	1990	1991	1992	1993	1994	1995	1996	1997	1998	1999	2000
Armenia	100	92.6	76.8	36.4	31.0	32.7	34.9	37.0	38.2	41.0	42.6	44.9
Azerbaijan	100	88.3	87.7	67.9	52.2	41.9	37.0	37.4	39.6	43.6	46.8	49.1
Belarus	100	97	95.8	86.6	80.1	70.0	62.7	64.4	71.8	77.7	80.1	81.7
Georgia	100	87.6	69.6	38.4	28.6	25.4	26.0	28.7	31.9	32.8	33.8	35.1
Kazakhstan	100	99.6	86.7	84.1	76.4	66.8	61.3	61.6	62.7	61.5	62.2	63.9
Kyrgyzstan	100	103	97.9	79.3	66.6	53.2	50.3	53.9	59.2	60.5	61.8	63.1
Moldova	100	97.6	80.5	57.1	56.4	38.8	38.3	35.3	35.7	32.7	31.0	31.3
Russia	100	96	91.2	78.0	71.2	62.2	59.6	57.5	58.0	55.3	56.4	57.5
Tajikistan	100	98.4	91.4	64.9	57.8	46.8	41.0	39.2	39.9	42.0	43.5	44.8
Turkmenistan	100	102	97.2	92.1	82.8	68.5	63.6	59.3	52.6	55.3	64.6	72.4
Ukraine	100	96.6	85.4	73.7	63.2	48.7	42.7	38.5	37.2	36.6	36.4	36.8
Uzbekistan	100	101.6	101.1	89.9	87.8	84.1	83.4	84.7	86.8	90.6	94.3	95.3
CIS	100	96.4	89.9	76.7	69.3	59.5	56.1	54.3	54.9	53.6	54.7	55.8
CIS without Russia	100	97.0	87.8	74.7	66.1	55.1	50.5	49.0	49.9	50.8	51.9	53.1
Russia	100	96.0	91.2	78.0	71.2	62.2	59.6	57.5	58.0	55.3	56.4	57.5

TABLE 14.3.

	Observed average annual growth rate (%)		Estimated share coefficient (%)	Estimated contribution to average annual growth rate (% of the output growth rate)	
	1953–78	1979–98		1953–78	1979–98
GDP	5.6	9.6			
Capital	7.39	9.89	0.5824	4.30	5.76
				(76.8)	(59.4)
Labour	2.6	2.8	0.4176	1.09	1.17
				(19.5)	(12.5)
Productivity				0.21	2.67
				(3.8)	(28.1)

Note: Observed GDP and labour force growth rate figures are from National Statistics Bureau and the capital growth rate figures are from Chow and Li (2000).

two countries are in a fairly standard 'ball park' for estimates of GDP per capita for the two countries at that time—something over $6,000 for Russia and $400–500 for China.

Turning to the TFP growth rate in China, there is now a large literature on the subject (Chow 1993; Kraay 1996; Chow and Li 2000). Our principal concern here is with the difference in the TFP growth rate in the planning (1952–78) and the reform period (1979–98), not with the absolute figures. The estimation of TFP growth rate for China is severely constrained by deficiencies in available data. The capital stock series has to be constructed by successive additions of real net investment to the estimated capital stock at the end of 1952 (see Chow 1993). This is complicated by the absence of a reliable capital goods price index series and meaningful depreciation figures. Labour input has to be measured in terms of the size of the labour force, unadjusted for the hours of work. The estimation of the TFP growth rate for China has to make do with factor input growth rates measured with a significant margin of error.

There are two options for obtaining weights on factor input growth rates, both of which raise particular problems. The first is to use the factor share estimates from functional distribution data, such as those for the formal employment sector in China (Hu and Khan 1996). The second is to use the estimated coefficients from a regression of output growth rates on factor input growth rates either for a pooled cross-section of economies (Manikw *et al.* 1992) or just for China (Chow 1993; Chow and Li 2000; Kraay 1996). Using the regression estimates for the Chinese data in Chow and Li (2000), the observed GDP growth rate divides as follows into that due to growth in factor inputs and that to productivity growth.

Though TFP growth rates vary with the estimated production function and the data on factor input growth rate (especially the growth rate of the capital stock), the following conclusions always hold (Chow 1993; Hu and Khan 1996; Kraay 1996; Chow and Li 2000): (i) the TFP growth rate was negligible in the planning period (1952–78) but substantial in the reform period (1979–98); (ii) the TFP growth rate for China since 1979 compares favourably with those for East and South-East Asian economies (see in particular Kraay 1996).

References

Arnott, R., and J. Stiglitz (1991). 'Moral Hazard and Non-Market Institutions: Dysfunctional Crowding Out or Peer Monitoring', *American Economic Review* 81(1): 179–90.

Balcerowicz, Leszek (1995). *Socialism, Capitalism, Transformation* (Budapest and New York: Central European University Press).

Black, B., R. Kraakman, and A. Tarassova (1999). 'Russian Privatization and Corporate Governance: What Went Wrong?', mimeo.

Blanchard, Olivier, and Michael Kremer (1997). 'Disorganization', *Quarterly Journal of Economics* 112(4): 1091–126.

Chow, Gregory C. (1993). 'Capital Formation and Economic Growth in China', *Quarterly Journal of Economics* 107 (Aug.): 809–42.

—— and Li Kui-Wai (2000). 'Accounting for China's Growth: 1952–1998', mimeo.

Diamond, Peter, and James Mirrlees (1971). 'Optimal Taxation and Public Production', *American Economic Review* 61: 8–27 and 261–78.

Dasgupta, Partha, and Ismail Serageldin (eds.) (2000). *Social Capital: A Multifaceted Perspective* (Washington, DC: IBRD).

Dyck, A. (1999). 'Privatization and Corporate Governance: Principles, Evidence and Future Challenges', Harvard Business School, mimeo.

Ellerman, David (ed.) (1993). *Management and Employee Buy-Outs as a Technique of Privatization* (Ljubljana: Central and Eastern European Privatization Network).

Elster, Jon (1989). 'Social Norm and Economic Theory', *Journal of Economic Perspectives* 3(4): 99–117.

European Bank for Reconstruction and Development (EBRD). *Transition Report*. Yearly publication since 1995, with yearly updates (London: EBRD).

Fairbank, John K. (1986). *The Great Chinese Revolution 1800–1985* (New York: Harper & Row).

Fukuyama, Francis (1995). *Trust: The Social Virtues and the Creation of Property* (New York: Free Press).

Hart, Herbert (1972). *The Concept of Law* (New York: Oxford University Press).

Hu, F. Zuliu, and Mohsin S. Khan (1996). 'Why is China Growing So Fast?', IMF, mimeo.

Kaldor, Nicholas, and James Mirrlees (1962). 'A New Model of Economic Growth', *Review of Economic Studies* 29 (June): 174–92.

Kornai, Janos (1986). 'The Soft Budget Constraint', *Kyklos* 39(1): 1–30.

Kraay, Aart (1996). 'A Resilient Residual: Growth Performance in Light of the Asian Miracle' (Policy Research Department, World Bank), mimeo.

Little, Ian, and James Mirrlees (1969). *Manual of Industrial Project Analysis in Developing Countries: Social Cost Benefit Analysis* (Paris: OECD).

—— —— (1974). *Project Appraisal and Planning for Developing Countries* (London: Heinemann).

Manikw, Gregory, David Romer, and David Weil (1992). 'A Contribution to the Empirics of Economic Growth', *Quarterly Journal of Economics* 106: 407–37.

Mirrlees, James (1982). 'The Economic Uses of Utilitarianism', in Amartya Sen and Bernard Williams (1982): 63–84.

National Bureau of Statistics of PRC (1999*a*). *Statistical Yearbook of China 1999* (Beijing: China Statistics Press).

—— (1999*b*). *Comprehensive Statistical Data and Materials on 50 Years of New China* (Beijing: China Statistics Press).

Perkins, Dwight H. *et al.* (1977). *Rural Small Industry in the PRC* (Berkeley and Los Angeles: University of California Press).

Qian, Yingi (forthcoming). 'The Institutional Foundations of China's Market Transition', Paper presented to 1999 Annual Bank Conference on Development Economics.

Putzel, James (1997). 'Accounting for the "Dark Side" of Social Capital: Reading Robert Putnam on Democracy', *Journal of International Development* 9(7): 939–49.

Sen, Amartya, and Bernard Williams (1982). *Utilitarianism and Beyond* (Cambridge: Cambridge University Press): 63–84.

Shleifer, Andrei, and Robert Vishny (1998). *The Grabbing Hand* (Cambridge, Mass.: Harvard University Press).

Smart, J. J. C., and Bernard Williams (1973). *Utilitarianism: For and Against* (Cambridge: Cambridge University Press).

Stiglitz, Joseph E. (1989). *The Economic Role of the State* (Oxford: Blackwell).

—— (1994). *Whither Socialism?* (Cambridge, Mass.: MIT Press).

—— (1999*a*). 'Quis Custodiet Ipsos Custodes? (Who is to Guard the Guards Themselves?) Corporate Governance Failures in the Transition', *Challenge* 42(6): 26–67.

—— (1999*b*). 'Reflections on Lessons from Transition', Paper presented to the Fifth Nobel Symposium in Economics, Stockholm, 11 Sept.

Stiglitz, Joseph E. (1999*c*). 'China: Forging a Third Generation of Reforms', Speech presented at Beijing University, 23 July.

Wedel, Janine R. (1998). *Collision and Collusion: The Strange Case of Western Aid to Eastern Europe 1989–1998* (New York: St Martin's Press).

World Bank (1978–1999/2000). *World Development Reports.* Yearly publication, includes selected World Development Indicators (New York: Oxford University Press).

Part VI

INDUSTRIAL ORGANIZATION

15 Capital Structure and Imperfect Competition in Product Markets

FRANKLIN ALLEN

1. Introduction

It is often acknowledged that the question of how firms choose their capital structure has not been satisfactorily answered yet: current theories seem to be unable to explain the financing decisions firms actually make. The debate has mainly centred around two apparent empirical regularities. First, many firms paying corporate taxes use only a small amount of debt. Debt ratios are typically of the order of 20 to 30 per cent (see e.g. Wald 1999). Second, similar firms in the same industry often have significantly different capital structures (see e.g. Myers 1984).

The most widely taught theory of capital structure is still Modigliani and Miller (1958) extended to include corporate taxes and bankruptcy costs. Firms trade off the corporate tax advantage of debt arising from interest being tax deductible, against the costs of bankruptcy. Given the first regularity, these costs must be large for the theory to be plausible. In a number of early papers, such as Scott (1976) and Kim (1978), liquidation costs, which are potentially large, are the main costs the authors seem to have in mind. A possible reason is that bankruptcy is often followed by liquidation. However, as Haugen and Senbet (1978) stress liquidation is a capital budgeting decision whereas bankruptcy is a transfer of assets. Standard models do not explain why bankruptcy should cause liquidation. Given this, the trade-off theory is difficult to reconcile with the first observation since the other costs appear to be small. As Myers (1984) argues, it also seems inconsistent with the second since it suggests similar firms should have similar capital structures. In fact there are significant differences between similar firms.

These and other difficulties have led to alternative theories being developed. One approach is to include personal as well as corporate taxes (see e.g. Stiglitz 1973; King 1974; Miller 1977; and De Angelo and Masulis 1980). By retaining earnings and in various other ways, firms can help their shareholders avoid the personal tax on equity income. To the extent that firms do this, the corporate tax advantage to debt is mitigated by a personal tax advantage to equity. Provided most personal taxes on equity income are avoided, these theories do not require bankruptcy costs to be large to be consistent with the first observation. The problem is that the empirical evidence on dividends suggests that only a limited amount of personal tax on equity income is avoided

I would like to thank R. Heinkel, P. Knez, A. Postlewaite, C. Spatt, and J. Williams, participants at a number of seminars and particularly M. Roe for many helpful comments and suggestions. Financial support from the NSF is gratefully acknowledged.

(see e.g. Peterson, Peterson, and Ang 1985). Moreover, the predictions of the theory are again difficult to reconcile with the second observation.

Other approaches are concerned with asymmetric information and with contracting difficulties (see e.g. Jensen and Meckling 1976; Leland and Pyle 1977; Myers and Majluf 1984; Titman 1984; and Leland 1998). These theories provide plausible explanations of phenomena at a detailed level. However, it can be argued that the severity of these problems is not sufficient for them to be the primary explanation for the observations mentioned above. Many of these theories abstract from taxes. If these were included, the apparent magnitude of tax shields suggests that direct solutions such as more acquisition of information might be better than having a low debt ratio.

A theory of capital structure is presented below where bankruptcy causes partial or complete liquidation. It is based on imperfections in firms' product markets. Most corporations, particularly large ones, operate in product markets with only a few firms. For simplicity, a linear duopoly model with a Cournot market structure is analysed. In addition, it is assumed that because of the way the bankruptcy laws operate, which is described below, the effect of bankruptcy is to delay investment decisions. This delay is not costly in itself. However, given the imperfectly competitive product market, it means the bankrupt firm is at a strategic disadvantage and is forced to contract if fixed costs are small or liquidate if they are large. Thus when choosing the amount of debt to use, firms trade off the corporate tax advantage against these liquidation costs. The nature of equilibrium also depends on the fixed costs of capacity. If these are small, the equilibrium is symmetric so both firms adopt the same strategy. If they are large the equilibrium is asymmetric. One firm goes for the tax advantage of debt and the other goes for the strategic advantage of equity. Thus, even though the firms are similar, they can have different capital structures.

A number of other papers also consider models of investment and financing in a duopolistic industry. Brander and Lewis (1986) and Maksimovic (1988) show how debt acts as a pre-commitment device and this leads to more aggressive product market behaviour. These papers explain why firms find the use of debt advantageous but the puzzle has been why it is not used more. In the current paper, greater debt increases the probability of bankruptcy and liquidation which is costly. Thus more debt will be associated with less aggressive product market behaviour subsequently. The theory is consistent with the observation that firms use little debt despite its apparent tax advantages. Fudenberg and Tirole (1986) and Bolton and Scharfstein (1990) develop theories where an agency problem between the firm and providers of finance leads to financial constraints and these may encourage product market competitors to engage in predatory pricing. Higher debt leads a firm to engage in less aggressive product market behaviour because access to capital is decreased. Rotemberg and Scharfstein (1990) consider a model where investors are not as well informed as firms about future profitability. The firms choose their product market actions to manipulate investors' beliefs and maximize the firm's stock market value. This can lead to either more or less aggressive product market strategies depending on the nature of inferences drawn by investors from the performance of different firms in the industry. In contrast, the model presented below does not rely on asymmetric information. More importantly,

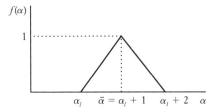

FIG. 15.1. *The density function for* α

the trade-off considered is between the tax benefit of debt and costs of liquidation rather than between the manager–shareholder agency problem and the predatory behaviour of competitors. Glazer (1994) focuses on the role of long-term debt and shows that the accumulated profit is important in determining product market behaviour in this case. Here the focus is on short-term debt and accumulated profits do not play any role.

The paper proceeds as follows. Section 2 outlines the model. In Section 3 equilibrium is analysed. Section 4 discusses the relationship between the results and empirical evidence. Finally, Section 5 contains concluding remarks.

2. The Model

There are two identical firms denoted j and k. The market structure is Cournot. Each period the firms produce quantities q_j and q_k, place them on the market and together these determine the market clearing price p.

Demand for the industry is stochastic. The demand curve has the form

$$p = \alpha - \beta(q_j + q_k), \tag{1}$$

where the intercept α is a random variable and the slope β is a constant. The density function of α is linear:

$$f(\alpha) = \alpha - \alpha_l \text{ for } \alpha_l \leqslant \alpha \leqslant \bar{\alpha} \tag{2}$$

$$= \alpha_l + 2 - \alpha \text{ for } \bar{\alpha} \leqslant \alpha \leqslant \alpha_l + 2, \tag{3}$$

where $\bar{\alpha} = \alpha_l + 1$.

This density function is illustrated in Figure 15.1. It is assumed that α_l is sufficiently large that in equilibrium $p > 0$ for all possible realizations of α. The realizations of α in each period are independently and identically distributed.

A firm's output is equal to its capacity which is determined by its initial investment I_j. The cost of capacity is a linear function

$$I_j = 0 \text{ for } q_j = 0$$

$$= \phi + \mu q_j \text{ for } q_j > 0,$$

where ϕ is the fixed cost and μ is the constant marginal cost.

There are two periods with period 1 starting at date 0 and finishing at date 1 and period 2 starting at date 1 and finishing at date 2. The sequence of events in each period is the following:

1. Initially firms make their investment decisions and determine their capacities. At the same time they make their financing decisions. The capital markets meet, the firms issue the securities corresponding to their decisions, and use the proceeds to pay the costs of their investments. All this is done before α is realized.

2. Output is produced; α is realized.

3. The two firms' quantities q_j and q_k, together with α, determine the price. Revenues pq_j and pq_k are received. These are used to pay the corporate income tax and make payments on the securities issued at stage 1.

Capital markets are perfectly competitive and frictionless. Investors are risk-neutral and securities sell for their expected value. The interest rate is zero.

Firms have two financing instruments, debt and equity. Debt is a promise to repay D_j at the end of the period or the firm goes bankrupt and the bondholders acquire it. Equity receives the profits (if any) remaining at the end of the period after taxes and payments to debtholders.

At the start of each period, before firms make their investment and financing decisions, they are entirely owned by equity holders. When firms finance their investment they issue debt with par value D_j. If the debt is risky, its market value D_j^M will be less than D_j. The remainder required to finance the investment, $I_j - D_j^M$, is raised by issuing equity. Since the capital markets are perfect, the original shareholders' total expected pay-off is the expected value of the firm. Hence their objective when they make the investment and financing decisions is to maximize this.

The corporate tax rate is τ. Investment costs are tax deductible. Nominal debt D_j is also deductible so that there is a tax bias in favour of debt finance. The taxes paid by a firm are

$$T_j = \tau[pq_j - (\phi + \mu q_j) - D_j]. \tag{4}$$

Taxes are paid when the tax base is positive and subsidies are received when it is negative. To prevent firms from issuing an infinite amount of debt D_j, and claiming the infinite subsidy this would give rise to, there is an upper bound on the amount of debt that is tax deductible

$$D_j \leq D_u. \tag{5}$$

This corresponds to the limited loss carry-over provisions in the actual code.

For simplicity, there are no personal taxes on either debt or equity income or equivalently the marginal personal rate on equity income is the same as the marginal personal rate on debt income.

Bankruptcy occurs when the total receipts at the end of the period from selling the goods less any tax payments (or plus any subsidies) are insufficient to repay the debt

$$pq_j - T_j \leq D_j. \tag{6}$$

This condition assumes that equity holders do not have the opportunity to raise funds against future profits and use them to repay the debt and possibly prevent bankruptcy. This is the simplest case to consider. If future profits were included in the bankruptcy condition, there would still be a determinate bankruptcy point and a similar analysis to that below would be possible.

The condition also assumes that the equity holders cannot repurchase the debt at its current market value just before bankruptcy as suggested by Haugen and Senbet (1978, 1988). The justification for this is that it will be difficult for a firm to repurchase its debt securities when it is near bankruptcy if they are held by more than one person. This is because, similarly to Grossman and Hart (1980), there is a free-rider problem. Given some people accept the firm's repurchase offer, anybody who holds out and refuses it can expect the value of their securities to increase. If the firm were to go bankrupt, its assets would be divided between fewer bonds and so the pay-off on each would be increased. If bankruptcy is avoided, each bond owner has an incentive to hold out for the entire savings in bankruptcy costs. Roe (1987) terms this the 'buoying up effect'. The end-result of it is that standard debt cannot be repurchased when it is widely held.

It is not possible to use non-standard forms of debt contract which eliminate the free-rider problem and permit bankruptcy to be avoided. The reason is the restrictions placed on bond contracts by the Trust Indenture Act of 1939. Roe (1987) points out the purpose of these restrictions is to precipitate bankruptcy. The proponents of the law suggested that to prevent minority bondholders being cheated, it is necessary to ensure that any change in a bond's terms occur in bankruptcy under the supervision of the court rather than before bankruptcy. Without such protection it was argued that equity holders could, for example, obtain a majority of a firm's bonds and vote to expropriate the minority bondholders. In fact for this and other reasons (see Roe (1987) for a complete account) it was standard practice prior to 1939 to issue bonds which did not allow bankruptcy to be avoided. Thus not only is debt of this type not observed currently, it was rare historically.

The crucial assumption of the model is that the effect of bankruptcy is to cause a delay in the bankrupt firm's investment decision. The basis for this is the operation of the bankruptcy laws. Under Chapter 11 of the current code a plan of reorganization must be agreed upon after bankruptcy occurs. This outlines a new financial structure for the firm and any necessary investments or sales of assets. The plan must be approved by two-thirds of each class of claimant. If it is rejected, an amended plan is produced and the process repeated until one is approved. Once the plan is agreed upon the judge must also give her consent to it. The firm can then emerge from bankruptcy and continue operations normally. Although it is possible for those in control of the firm to sell assets or raise money outside of the plan, the approval of the judge must be obtained and this is only given in special cases. Moreover, even if this is obtained it can be challenged by the security holders of the firm. If any claimants' bargaining power is reduced by the change they will have an incentive to do this. (See Baird and Jackson (1985) for a full description of the operation of Chapter 11.)

The bankruptcy process is protracted and usually takes between two and three years to complete (see e.g. Eberhart, Moore, and Roenfeldt 1990 and Franks and Torous 1989, 1994). It is this lengthy procedure and the restrictions placed on the firm while it is going through it that is the basis for the assumption that the investment decisions of the bankrupt and solvent firm are not simultaneous.

When a firm's debt is not widely held, then attempts to recapitalize and avoid bankruptcy may be successful. However, the negotiations to achieve such work-outs can be complex and drawn out because they involve bargaining over the division of the firm between security holders. To the extent that these negotiations delay investment the theory below remains valid when financial distress occurs even if actual bankruptcy is avoided.

Thus in the model, the effect of bankruptcy (or financial distress) at the end of a period is to delay the investment decision at the start of the next period. If both firms are in the same position at the end of period 1 so they are either both solvent or both bankrupt, they make their decisions simultaneously at the start of period 2, and so play a Nash game. However, if one firm is solvent and the other is bankrupt so its investment decision is delayed, they play a Stackelberg game with the solvent firm as leader and the bankrupt one as follower. Hence if one firm is bankrupt, it is at a strategic disadvantage.

3. Equilibrium

A perfect Nash equilibrium concept is used. The solution procedure involves solving backwards by first looking at the possibilities in period 2 and then analysing the decisions for period 1 given that the firms play equilibrium strategies in the period 2 subgames. The equilibrium of the model depends crucially on the level of the fixed cost of capacity ϕ. This determines the outcome of the Stackelberg subgame the firms play in period 2 if one of them goes bankrupt at the end of period 1. If there is no fixed cost, it is always profitable for the follower to remain in business at a reduced size. However, if the fixed cost is sufficiently large, it is optimal for the leader to expand and make the profits of the follower fall below the level of the fixed cost. This causes the follower to liquidate and the leader becomes a monopolist. The magnitude of the fixed cost therefore determines the marginal cost of bankruptcy and hence the form of equilibrium.

In Section 3.1 the case with no fixed costs is analysed. The opposite extreme where the fixed costs are large is considered in Section 3.2. Section 3.3 deals with the intermediate case. Finally, Section 3.4 contains a brief summary.

3.1. No fixed cost of capacity

In this subsection it is assumed

$$\phi = 0 \tag{7}$$

so there is only a marginal cost of capacity.

First, consider decisions for period 2, which are made at $t = 1$. Since the only effect of bankruptcy is to delay investment decisions in the subsequent period, it follows that bankruptcy in period 2 has no effect so that firms will always use as much debt as possible. To save having to repeatedly write a lump-sum subsidy component, τD_u, in profit expressions, it is simplest to assume that in period 2, $D = D_u = 0$. At $t = 1$ the only decision firms are then concerned with is the level of investment I or equivalently their period 2 capacity q_2.

There are two possibilities at $t = 1$. Either both firms are solvent or both are bankrupt in which case they play a Nash game. Alternatively, one firm is solvent and the other is bankrupt in which case they play a Stackelberg game. Consider the Nash game first. Each firm chooses its second-period capacity to maximize expected profits given the other firm's capacity:

$$\text{Max}_{q_{2j}}(1 - \tau)[\bar{\alpha} - \beta(q_{2j} + q_{2k}) - \mu]q_{2j}$$

taking q_{2k} as given.

The first-order condition implies

$$q_{2j} = \frac{\bar{\alpha} - u}{2\beta} - \frac{q_{2k}}{2}.$$

Similarly for q_{2k}. Solving these simultaneously gives the standard results

$$q_{2j} = \frac{\bar{\alpha} - \mu}{3\beta} \tag{8}$$

$$E\pi_{2j} = (1 - \tau)\frac{Z}{9}, \tag{9}$$

where $E\pi_{2j}$ is the expected profit of j in period 2 and

$$Z = \frac{(\bar{\alpha} - \mu)^2}{\beta}.$$

The other possibility is that one firm, say k, is solvent and the other, j, is bankrupt. Firm k acts as leader and makes its investment decision while j is tied up in bankruptcy court. When j finally makes its investment decision it takes k's as given. Firm k takes this into account when it makes its decision initially in the usual Stackelberg way. Firm j's decision as follower is

$$\text{Max}_{q_{2j}}(1 - \tau)[\bar{\alpha} - \beta(q_{2j} + q_{2k}) - \mu]q_{2j} \tag{10}$$

taking q_{2k} as given. Hence

$$q_{2j} = \frac{\bar{\alpha} - u}{2\beta} - \frac{q_{2k}}{2}. \tag{11}$$

Then firm k's decision as leader is

$$\underset{q_{2k}}{\text{Max}}\,(1 - \tau)\left[\bar{\alpha} - \beta\left(q_{2k} + \frac{\bar{\alpha} - \mu}{2\beta} - \frac{q_{2k}}{2}\right) - \mu\right]q_{2k}.$$

It follows

$$q_{2k} = \frac{\bar{\alpha} - \mu}{2\beta} \tag{12}$$

$$E\pi_{2k} = (1 - \tau)\frac{Z}{8} \tag{13}$$

$$q_{2j} = \frac{\bar{\alpha} - \mu}{4\beta} \tag{14}$$

$$E\pi_{2j} = (1 - \tau)\frac{Z}{16}. \tag{15}$$

The effect of a single firm going bankrupt can be seen by comparing (8) and (9) with (12)–(15). The leader expands its capacity above that in the Nash case. The follower is at a strategic disadvantage, and as a result has a lower capacity than before. The bankrupt firm is worse off since its profits are reduced from $(1 - \tau)Z/9$ to $(1 - \tau)Z/16$. The solvent firm is made better off since its profits are increased from $(1 - \tau)Z/9$ to $(1 - \tau)Z/8$. Hence the delay in a firm's investment decision, although not costly in itself, means bankruptcy is undesirable.

Next consider the decisions of the firms at $t = 0$. In period 1 it is assumed that $D_u > 0$. The analysis will be concerned with interior solutions such that (5) does not bind.

In period 1 firm j's expected profits are

$$E\pi_{1j} = (1 - \tau)[\bar{\alpha} - \beta(q_j + q_k) - \mu]q_j + \tau D_j, \tag{16}$$

where q_j and q_k are the firms' period 1 capacities and D_j is j's period 1 debt.

The realization of the demand parameter α at the end of period 1 determines whether or not the firms go bankrupt and hence the type of game played and the expected profits in period 2. In order to derive an expression for j's expected profits in period 2 evaluated at $t = 0$, it is necessary to define the level of demand, α_j^*, such that firm j goes bankrupt at the end of period 1. Using (1), (4), (6) with an equality, and (7),

$$\alpha_j^* = \frac{D_j}{q_j} + \beta(q_j + q_k) - \frac{\tau}{1 - \tau}\mu. \tag{17}$$

For values of α above α_j^*, firm j is solvent; for values below it is bankrupt. Similarly for k. If $\alpha_j^* \geq \alpha_k^*$ then

$$E\pi_{2j} = (1 - \tau)\left[\int_{\alpha_l}^{\alpha_k^*}\frac{Z}{9}f(\alpha)d\alpha + \int_{\alpha_k^*}^{\alpha_j^*}\frac{Z}{16}f(\alpha)d\alpha + \int_{\alpha_j^*}^{\alpha_l + 2}\frac{Z}{9}f(\alpha)d\alpha\right]. \tag{18}$$

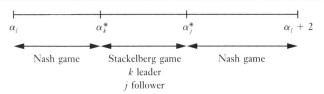

FIG. 15.2. *Relationship between the realization of α at date l and the second-period game*

As illustrated in Figure 15.2, for α between α_l and α_k^* both firms go bankrupt and in period 2 they play a Nash game so j's expected profits are $(1 - \tau)Z/9$. From α_k^* to α_j^* firm j is bankrupt but k is not. They play a Stackelberg game with j as a follower so its expected profits are $(1 - \tau)Z/16$. For α above α_j^* they again play a Nash game. For $\alpha_j^* \leqslant \alpha_k^*$,

$$E\pi_{2j} = (1 - \tau)\left[\int_{\alpha_l}^{\alpha_j^*} \frac{Z}{9} f(\alpha)d\alpha + \int_{\alpha_j^*}^{\alpha_k^*} \frac{Z}{8} f(\alpha)d\alpha + \int_{\alpha_k^*}^{\alpha_l+2} \frac{Z}{9} f(\alpha)d\alpha\right]. \qquad (19)$$

This is the same as when $\alpha_j^* \geqslant \alpha_k^*$ except that between α_j^* and α_k^*, j is the leader so its expected profits are $(1 - \tau)Z/8$.

Since the objective of the initial shareholders is to maximize the total value of the firm as explained in Section 2, firm j's decision problem at $t = 0$ for choosing its period 1 capacity and debt is

$$\underset{q_j, D_j}{\text{Max }} E\pi_j = E\pi_{1j} + E\pi_{2j}$$

taking q_k and D_k as given.

The equilibria of interest are those where firms are at interior optima and so attention is restricted to these. Two types are possible. The first is symmetric with $\alpha_j^* = \alpha_k^*$ so both have the same capacity and debt. In the other $\alpha_j^* > \alpha_k^*$ (say) so that the equilibrium is asymmetric. One firm goes for the tax advantage of debt and the other goes for the equity advantage of being leader if demand is low.

In a symmetric equilibrium, each firm has the same level of debt and capacity. For an equilibrium to exist each firm must perceive that if it increases or reduces its debt or capacity, taking those of the other firm as given, then its profits will fall.

First consider firm j's debt decision. Differentiating (17) gives:

$$\frac{\partial \alpha_j^*}{\partial D_j} = \frac{1}{q_j}$$

$$\frac{\partial \alpha_k^*}{\partial D_j} = 0.$$

Hence if j increases its debt a small amount then $\alpha_j^* > \alpha_k^*$ and so (18) is the relevant expression for period 2's profits. Thus

$$\frac{\partial E\pi_j^+}{\partial D_j} = \tau - m_F f(\alpha_j^*)\frac{\partial \alpha_j^*}{\partial D_j} = \tau - m_F \frac{(\alpha_j^* - \alpha_l)}{q_j}, \tag{20}$$

where $m_F = (1-\tau)\dfrac{Z}{9} - (1-\tau)\dfrac{Z}{16} = (1-\tau)\dfrac{7}{144}Z.$ (21)

The first term, τ, in (20) is the tax benefit in period 1 from increasing debt. The second term is the loss in expected profits in period 2 arising from the fact that firm j will go bankrupt in more states. Instead of having expected profits of $(1-\tau)Z/9$ when playing a Nash game, j only expects $(1-\tau)Z/16$ as a Stackelberg follower and the difference between them is $(1-\tau)(7/144)Z$.

In contrast if j reduces its debt then $\alpha_j^* < \alpha_k^*$ and (19) is the relevant expression for period 2 profits. Thus

$$\frac{\partial E\pi_j^-}{\partial D_j} = \tau - m_L\frac{(\alpha_j^* - \alpha_l)}{q_j}, \tag{22}$$

where $m_L = (1-\tau)\dfrac{2}{144}Z.$ (23)

In this case the change in expected profits resulting from bankruptcy, m_L, is the difference between those from being a Stackelberg leader, $(1-\tau)Z/8$, and those in the Nash game, $(1-\tau)Z/9$.

It can be seen

$$m_F > m_L \tag{24}$$

and

$$\frac{\partial E\pi_j^+}{\partial D_j} - \frac{\partial E\pi_j^-}{\partial D_j} = (m_L - m_F)\frac{(\alpha_j^* - \alpha_l)}{q_j} < 0 \tag{25}$$

so that $E\pi_j$ is kinked at $\alpha_j^* = \alpha_k^*$. Moreover, the kink is concave so that it can correspond to a maximum.

Changes in capacity can be similarly analysed. Since these affect the levels of demand the two firms go bankrupt at, there is again a kink. An increase results in a smaller absolute effect on profits than a reduction. This means the kink is concave so that it can correspond to a maximum. These changes of capacity and the other features of the symmetric equilibria of the model are considered in detail in the Appendix.

The second type of equilibrium that could exist is asymmetric with $\alpha_j^* \neq \alpha_k^*$. This possibility is considered in detail in the Appendix. It is shown formally there that an asymmetric equilibrium cannot exist when $m_F > m_L$. To see why this is, suppose for the sake of discussion $\alpha_j^* > \alpha_k^*$. In such an equilibrium firm j goes bankrupt in states that k doesn't. Consider firm j's debt decision. If the firm increases its debt, α_j^* rises and its pay-off in the marginal states switches from the Nash level of $(1-\tau)Z/9$ to the Stackelberg follower level of $(1-\tau)Z/16$. A small reduction in debt leads to the opposite, namely a switch from the Nash level to the Stackelberg follower level. Thus

$$\frac{\partial E\pi_j^+}{\partial D_j} = \frac{\partial E\pi_j^-}{\partial D_j} = \frac{\partial E\pi_j}{\partial D_j} = \tau - m_F\frac{(\alpha_j^* - \alpha_l)}{q_j} = 0. \tag{26}$$

In contrast to the symmetric case, the right- and left-hand derivatives are equal and there is no kink. Similarly for firm k. As it alters its debt level, the change is from the Nash to the Stackelberg leader outcome.

$$\frac{\partial E\pi_k^+}{\partial D_k} = \frac{\partial E\pi_k^-}{\partial D_k} = \frac{\partial E\pi_k}{\partial D_k} = \tau - m_L\frac{(\alpha_k^* - \alpha_l)}{q_k} = 0. \tag{27}$$

For an interior equilibrium to exist, the marginal costs of bankruptcy for the two firms must be equal

$$m_F\frac{(\alpha_j^* - \alpha_l)}{q_j} = m_L\frac{(\alpha_k^* - \alpha_l)}{q_k}. \tag{28}$$

Now $m_F > m_L$ and $\alpha_j^* > \alpha_k^*$. The only possibility if there is to be an equilibrium is that q_j is sufficiently larger than q_k. It is shown in the Appendix that this is not possible.

The basic problem is that firm j not only has a high cost of bankruptcy m_F, it also has a high marginal probability of going bankrupt, $(\alpha_j^* - \alpha_l)$. In contrast, k has both a low cost of bankruptcy, m_L, and a low marginal probability of bankruptcy, $(\alpha_k^* - \alpha_l)$. Firm j's marginal bankruptcy cost of debt is therefore higher than k's. However, in equilibrium they must be equal since both firms receive the same marginal benefit from the tax shield provided by debt. Thus no asymmetric equilibrium can exist.

The results of this section are summarized by the following proposition.

Proposition 1. *When $\phi = 0$ the only type of equilibrium that exists is symmetric with $\alpha_j^* = \alpha_k^*$. At each firm optimum profits are a non-differentiable function of capacity and debt.*

3.2. High fixed costs of capacity

In this subsection the fixed cost of capacity is such that

$$\frac{Z}{16} \leq \phi \leq \frac{Z}{9}. \tag{29}$$

The right-hand inequality is necessary to ensure that both firms are viable in a Nash equilibrium. The significance of the left-hand inequality will be seen below.

As before, in order to find the equilibrium it is necessary to first consider investment decisions at $t = 1$. If both are solvent or both are bankrupt, the firms play a Nash game similarly to (10) except with the inclusion of ϕ. Each firm's optimal capacity is again as in (8) and their expected profits are

$$E\pi_{2j} = (1 - \tau)\left(\frac{Z}{9} - \phi\right).$$

When one firm, say k, is solvent and the other, j, is bankrupt they play a Stackelberg game with k as leader and j as follower. In this case if k sets $q_{2k} = (\bar{\alpha} - \mu)/2\beta$ as in (12) then it follows that the highest profits j can obtain with a positive output are

$$E\pi_{2j} = (1 - \tau)\left(\frac{Z}{16} - \phi\right).$$

The left hand inequality of (29) implies $E\pi_{2j} \leq 0$ and j's optimal strategy in this case is to liquidate so that

$$q_{2j} = 0; \ E\pi_{2j} = 0.$$

The q_{2k} in (12) was derived on the assumption that $q_{2j} = (\bar{\alpha} - \mu)/4\beta$. However, it turns out that even if $q_{2j} = 0$ firm k can do no better than $q_{2k} = (\bar{\alpha} - \mu)/2\beta$. This can easily be seen from the first-order condition for k's problem as a monopolist. Thus k's profits when it is the Stackelberg leader are

$$E\pi_{2k} = (1 - \tau)\left(\frac{Z}{4} - \phi\right).$$

The analysis of decisions at $t = 0$ is then similar to that in Section 3.1. Expected profits in the first period are as in (16) except for the inclusion of the fixed cost ϕ. If $\alpha_j^* \geq \alpha_k^*$, expected profits in the second period are

$$E\pi_{2j} = (1 - \tau)\left(\frac{Z}{9} - \phi\right)\left[\int_{\alpha_l}^{\alpha_k^*} f(\alpha)d\alpha + \int_{\alpha_j^*}^{\alpha_l+2} f(\alpha)d\alpha\right].$$

Profits are of this form since for α between α_k^* and α_j^*, j is forced to liquidate and receives nothing in the second period. If $\alpha_j^* \leq \alpha_k^*$, j is the leader between α_j^* and α_k^* and receives $(1 - \tau)(Z/4 - \phi)$ so

$$E\pi_{2j} = (1 - \tau)\left[\left(\frac{Z}{9} - \phi\right)\left(\int_{\alpha_l}^{\alpha_j^*} f(\alpha)d\alpha + \int_{\alpha_k^*}^{\alpha_l+2} f(\alpha)d\alpha\right)\right.$$
$$\left. + \left(\frac{Z}{4} - \phi\right)\int_{\alpha_j^*}^{\alpha_k^*} f(\alpha)d\alpha\right].$$

For symmetric equilibria the partial derivatives of $E\pi_j$ with respect to D_j are the same as in (25) and (27) except now

$$m_F = (1 - \tau)\left(\frac{4}{36}Z - \phi\right) \tag{30}$$

$$m_L = (1 - \tau)\frac{5}{36}Z. \tag{31}$$

In contrast to (24),

$m_F < m_L$.

There cannot be any symmetric equilibria since from (25) the kinks at firms' optima are now convex and correspond to minima rather than maxima.

Next consider the possibility of an asymmetric equilibrium. The analysis is similar to that in Section 3.1 except now m_F and m_L are given by (30) and (31), respectively. Since it is possible for (28) to be satisfied an asymmetric equilibrium can exist. This is shown formally in the Appendix. The basic reason is that firm j which has a high marginal probability of bankruptcy now has a low marginal cost of bankruptcy; firm k, which has a low marginal probability, has a high cost. It is therefore possible for both firms to have a marginal bankruptcy cost of debt equal to the marginal tax benefit.

The results of this subsection are summarized by the following proposition.

Proposition 2. *If $Z/16 \le \phi \le Z/9$ the only type of equilibrium that exists is asymmetric. If $\alpha_j^* > \alpha_k^*$ (say), then for realizations of α in period 1 such that $\alpha_k^* < \alpha < \alpha_j^*$, the bankrupt firm j liquidates at $t = 1$ and k becomes a monopolist in period 2.*

3.3. Intermediate fixed costs of capacity

This subsection considers the case where

$$0 < \phi < \frac{Z}{16}. \tag{32}$$

With no fixed costs of capacity, a bankrupt firm acting as follower chooses a smaller capacity in the equilibrium at $t = 1$ than it would if it were not bankrupt. With a high fixed cost, a bankrupt firm acting as follower liquidates. With intermediate fixed costs, it is shown both of these are possible. Below a certain level ϕ_1^* the follower stays in the market; above it, the firm leaves. Similarly, the equilibrium is symmetric for ϕ below a certain level $\phi_2^* > \phi_1^*$ and asymmetric above.

Consider the decision of a bankrupt firm, say j, at $t = 1$ given that the solvent firm k has already chosen capacity q_{2k}. It can either set $q_{2k} = 0$, or it can set it so that (11) is satisfied and profits are maximized given a positive capacity. Its profits in the latter case are

$$E\pi_{2j} = (1 - \tau) \left[\beta \left(\frac{\bar{\alpha} - \mu}{2\beta} - \frac{q_{2k}}{2} \right)^2 - \phi \right].$$

Hence if

$$\left(\frac{\bar{\alpha} - \mu}{\beta} - q_{2k} \right)^2 \le \frac{4\phi}{\beta} \tag{33}$$

the firm liquidates; otherwise it stays in the market.

In Section 3.2 it was shown that if $\phi > Z/16$ and k chooses the monopoly capacity of $(\bar{\alpha} - \mu)/2\beta$, the follower liquidates. If $\phi = 0$, k's optimal strategy is also to choose a capacity of $(\bar{\alpha} - \mu)/2\beta$ but now j remains in the market. For intermediate ϕ, k has two possible courses of action. First, it could set q_k so that (33) is satisfied. This pushes j out of the market and k becomes a monopolist. Alternatively, it could allow j to remain in the market. In order to determine which of these it should do, it is necessary to find the profitability of each.

If k is a monopolist its profits are

$$E\pi_{2k} = (1 - \tau)[(\bar{\alpha} - \mu - \beta q_{2k})q_{2k} - \phi].$$

For k to be able to make a positive profit $q_{2k} < (\bar{\alpha} - \mu)/\beta$. Given this, (33) is satisfied if

$$q_{2k} \geq \frac{\bar{\alpha} - \mu}{\beta} - 2\left(\frac{\phi}{\beta}\right)^{1/2}. \tag{34}$$

When $\phi < Z/16$ the right-hand side of this inequality is greater than $(\bar{\alpha} - \mu)/2\beta$. For such q_{2k}, k's profits as a monopolist are a decreasing function of capacity. Hence if k wants to force j to liquidate it should choose q_{2k} so that (34) is satisfied with an equality. Its expected profits are then

$$E\pi_{2k}^0 = (1 - \tau)\left[2\left(\frac{\phi}{\beta}\right)^{1/2}(\bar{\alpha} - \mu) - 5\phi\right].$$

If k allows j to remain in the market, it can be shown similarly to the case where $\phi = 0$ that its optimal capacity is again $(\bar{\alpha} - \mu)/2\beta$ and its expected profits are

$$E\pi_{2j}^+ = (1 - \tau)\left(\frac{Z}{8} - \phi\right).$$

It follows from these that for ϕ satisfying (32)

$$E\pi_{2k}^0 = \gtrless E\pi_{2j}^+ \text{ as } \phi = \gtrless \phi_1^*$$

where $\phi_1^* = \frac{1}{4}\left(\frac{1}{2} - \frac{1}{8^{1/2}}\right)^2 Z = 0.0054Z$.

All this implies the following proposition.

Proposition 3. *In the Stackelberg equilibrium at $t = 1$, if $0 \leq \phi \leq \phi_1^*$ the solvent firm chooses a capacity of $(\bar{\alpha} - \mu)/2\beta$ and the bankrupt firm stays in the market at a reduced size. For $\phi_1^* < \phi < Z/16$ it is optimal for the solvent firm to expand capacity above $(\bar{\alpha} - \mu)/2\beta$ and force the bankrupt firm to liquidate.*

The other question of interest concerns whether equilibrium at $t = 0$ in this intermediate case is symmetric or asymmetric. It can be seen from the analyses of the previous subsections that this is determined by whether m_F is above or below m_L. If $m_F > m_L$, the equilibrium is symmetric; if $m_F < m_L$, it is asymmetric.

For $\phi \leq \phi_1^*$, m_F and m_L are as in (21) and (23) and the equilibria are symmetric. For $\phi > \phi_1^*$,

$$m_F = (1 - \tau)\left(\frac{Z}{9} - \phi\right)$$

$$m_L = (1 - \tau)\left[2\left(\frac{\phi}{\beta}\right)^{1/2}(\bar{\alpha} - \mu) - \frac{Z}{9} - 4\phi\right].$$

Hence

$$m_F = \gtrless m_L \text{ as } \phi = \lessgtr \phi_2^*,$$

where ϕ_2^* is the value of ϕ such that $m_F = m_L$ or

$$2\left(\frac{\phi_2^*}{\beta}\right)^{1/2}(\bar{\alpha} - \mu) - 2\frac{Z}{9} - 3\phi_2^* = 0$$

and

$$\phi_2^* = 0.0198Z.$$

This gives the following.

Proposition 4. *For $0 \leqslant \phi \leqslant \phi_2^*$ the equilibrium at $t = 0$ is symmetric and for $\phi_2^* < \phi < Z/16$ it is asymmetric.*

3.4. Summary

The results of this section are summarized diagrammatically in Figure 15.3. The crucial determinant of the form of equilibrium is the fixed cost of capacity. For $0 \leqslant \phi \leqslant \phi_1^*$ a solvent firm acting as a Stackelberg leader at $t = 1$ chooses a capacity of $(\bar{\alpha} - \mu)/2\beta$. The bankrupt firm acting as follower is forced to reduce its size

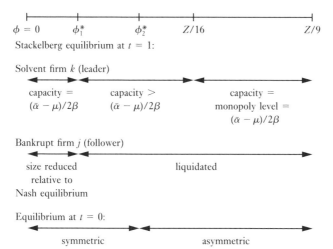

FIG. 15.3. *The relationship between fixed costs and equilibrium*

relative to the equilibrium if it were not bankrupt, but still remains in the market. For $\phi_1^* < \phi < Z/16$ the solvent firm expands its capacity above $(\bar{a} - \mu)/2\beta$ in order to force the bankrupt firm to liquidate. For $Z/16 \leq \phi \leq Z/9$ the solvent firm produces the monopoly output which is again $(\bar{a} - \mu)/2\beta$ and the bankrupt firm's best response is to liquidate.

As far as the equilibrium at $t = 0$ is concerned, it is symmetric so that firms have the same capacity, use the same amount of debt, and so on if $0 \leq \phi \leq \phi_2^*$. It is asymmetric if $\phi_2^* < \phi < Z/9$. One firm goes for the tax advantage of debt and the other goes for the equity advantage of being able to force the levered firm out of the market if demand turns out to be low.

4. Relationship to Empirical Evidence

The model developed above involves a number of simplifying assumptions such as there being two periods, linear demand, and density functions and so on. These are designed to allow theoretical results to be derived. Their disadvantage is that, as it stands, the model is an unsuitable basis for an empirical investigation. However, it is possible to demonstrate that the theory is broadly consistent with the two regularities mentioned initially. It is also consistent with a number of recent studies on product and capital market interactions.

The first observation was that most tax-paying firms use predominantly equity finance, debt ratios are typically around 20 to 30 per cent. In the model, firms making their capital structure decision in the first period, take into account that an increase in their debt level will cause them to go bankrupt in more states and as a result they will be forced to either partially or completely liquidate. Since liquidation costs can be significant, this implies the marginal bankruptcy costs of debt can be large. Even at low debt ratios the model therefore provides a rationale for why marginal bankruptcy costs might be large enough to offset the tax advantage of debt.

The second observation was that similar firms in the same industry often have different capital structures. In asymmetric equilibria of the model the two firms can have capital structures that differ significantly, which is consistent with this.

There have been a number of empirical studies considering the relationship between product markets and financial markets. Opler and Titman (1994) find that highly levered firms lose significant market share to their less levered rivals during economic downturns. This is consistent with the model above when firms are in bankruptcy and also if they delay investments when they are in financial distress. Chevalier (1995) and Phillips (1995) find that firms that have dramatically increased debt invest less than competitors with lower debt. Kovenock and Phillips (1997) find that after debt recapitalizations firms in highly concentrated industries are more likely to close plants and reduce investment while rival firms with less debt are less likely to do these things. Khanna and Tice (1998) discover that higher leverage makes firms less aggressive. These studies are thus broadly consistent with the results of the model presented here which suggests that more levered firms are less aggressive.

5. Concluding Remarks

This paper models bankruptcy as causing a delay in investment which in itself is cost-less. If the product market is imperfectly competitive, this delay puts a bankrupt firm at a strategic disadvantage. In particular, the bankrupt firm is either partially or completely pushed out of the market and forced to liquidate by the solvent one. In such cases the total costs of bankruptcy include these costs of liquidation. In equilibrium firms determine their optimal capital structure by weighing the tax advantages of debt against its bankruptcy and liquidation costs.

For many years the most widely taught theories of capital structure have involved a trade-off of one sort or another. In essence the model presented above is also a trade-off theory. It is more complex than traditional theories in that it suggests firms take account of their strategic position within an industry. The effect of this is that bankruptcy leads to liquidation. As a result the theory provides a rationale for why liquidation costs should be included in bankruptcy costs and hence why these may be large. It is also consistent with the fact that similar firms in the same industry often have such different capital structures.

APPENDIX

A1. Symmetric equilibria

In this subsection symmetric equilibria of the model where firms are at interior optima are analysed. It is shown that such equilibria can only exist when $m_F > m_L$.

The effect of changes in debt on profits are given in (20) and (22). Next consider changes in capacity. Now,

$$\frac{\partial \alpha_j^*}{\partial q_j} = -\frac{D_j}{q_j^2} + \beta < \frac{\partial \alpha_k^*}{\partial q_j} = \beta.$$

For increases in capacity (19) is therefore the relevant expression for $E\pi_{2j}$.

Using the fact that in symmetric equilibria $\alpha_j^* = \alpha_k^*$ it can be shown

$$\frac{\partial E\pi_j^+}{\partial q_j} = (1 - \tau)[\bar{\alpha} - \mu - \beta(2q_j + q_k)] + m_L(\alpha_j^* - \alpha_l)\frac{D_j}{q_j^2}.$$

For reductions in capacity (18) is relevant, so

$$\frac{\partial E\pi_j^-}{\partial q_j} = (1 - \tau)[\bar{\alpha} - \mu - \beta(2q_j + q_k)] + m_F(\alpha_j^* - \alpha_l)\frac{D_j}{q_j^2}. \qquad (35)$$

Hence

$$\frac{\partial E\pi_j^+}{\partial q_j} - \frac{\partial E\pi_j^-}{\partial q_j} = (m_L - m_F)(\alpha_j^* - \alpha_l)\frac{D_j}{q_j^2}. \qquad (36)$$

Similarly for firm k. There is again a kink that can correspond to a maximum if it is concave.

It follows from (25) and (36) that an equilibrium can only exist if $m_F > m_L$. Otherwise the left-hand derivatives are less than the right-hand ones and the point could not be a maximum.

When firm j increases its debt it goes bankrupt in more states than k and becomes the follower in these. When it decreases its capacity firm j also goes bankrupt in more states than k. Hence one equilibrium is where $\partial E\pi_j^+/\partial D_j$ and $\partial E\pi_j^-/\partial q_j$ are both zero. Solving (20) and (35) simultaneously and using the definition of α_j^* in (17) it can be shown

$$\alpha_j^* - \alpha_l = \frac{\tau[(1-\tau)(\bar\alpha - \mu) + \tau\alpha_l + \tau^2\mu/(1-\tau)]}{(3-\tau)\beta m_F - \tau^2} \tag{37}$$

$$q_j = \frac{m_F(\alpha_j^* - \alpha_l)}{\tau} \tag{38}$$

$$D_j = [\alpha_j^* - 2\beta q_j + \tau\mu/(1-\tau)]q_j. \tag{39}$$

The other possibility involves $\partial E\pi_j^-/\partial D_j$ and $\partial E\pi_j^+/\partial q_j$ both equal to zero. The equilibrium is as in (37)–(39) except m_F is replaced by m_L.

It can be seen that there always exist solutions to (37)–(39). However, these only correspond to an interior equilibrium if

$$0 \leq \alpha_j^* - \alpha_l \leq 1.$$

Otherwise equilibrium involves corner solutions to the firms' debt or capacity choice problems.

A2. Asymmetric equilibria

In this subsection it is shown that asymmetric equilibria where firms are at interior optima can only exist when $m_F < m_L$. As in the text the case considered is $\alpha_j^* > \alpha_k^*$.

Consider first the case in Section 3.1 where $m_F > m_L$. The first-order conditions corresponding to debt choices are given by (26) and (27). For capacity choices they are

$$\frac{\partial E\pi_j}{\partial q_j} = (1-\tau)[\bar\alpha - \mu - \beta(2q_j + q_k)] + \beta m_F(\alpha_k^* - \alpha_j^*) + \left(\frac{D_j}{q_j^2}\right)m_F(\alpha_j^* - \alpha_l)$$
$$= 0$$

$$\frac{\partial E\pi_k}{\partial q_k} = (1-\tau)[\bar\alpha - \mu - \beta(q_j + 2q_k)] + \beta m_L(\alpha_j^* - \alpha_k^*) + \left(\frac{D_k}{q_k^2}\right)m_L(\alpha_k^* - \alpha_l)$$
$$= 0. \tag{40}$$

Solving all of these simultaneously and using the definitions of α_j^* and α_k^* it can be shown

$$\alpha_j^* - \alpha_l = C\left(\beta m_F + \frac{\beta m_L}{\tau} - \tau\right) \tag{41}$$

$$\alpha_k^* - \alpha_l = C\left(\beta m_L + \frac{\beta m_F}{\tau} - \tau\right) \tag{42}$$

$$q_j = m_F \frac{(\alpha_j^* - \alpha_l)}{\tau}$$

$$q_k = m_L \frac{(\alpha_k^* - \alpha_l)}{\tau}$$

$$D_j = [\alpha_j^* - \beta(q_j + q_k) + \tau\mu/(1-\tau)]q_j$$
$$D_k = [\alpha_k^* - \beta(q_j + q_k) + \tau\mu/(1-\tau)]q_k,$$

where

$$C = \frac{(1-\tau)\bar{\alpha} - [1 - \tau - \tau^2/(1-\tau)]\mu + \tau\alpha_l}{(\tau - 2\beta m_F/\tau)(\tau - 2\beta m_L/\tau) - \beta^2(m_F - m_L/\tau)(m_L - m_F/\tau)}.$$

If $C < 0$ then it can be shown only corner solutions are possible. This follows from the fact that given (2) and $\alpha_j^* > \alpha_k^*$ it is necessary for an interior solution that

$$0 \leqslant \alpha_k^* - \alpha_l < \alpha_j^* - \alpha_l \leqslant 1. \tag{43}$$

This along with (41) and (42) implies that if $C < 0$, then

$$\tau^2 > \beta m_F + \tau\beta m_L$$

so

$$\tau > (\beta m_F)^{1/2}. \tag{44}$$

Similarly

$$\tau > (\beta m_L)^{1/2}. \tag{45}$$

Also (26), (27), and (43) imply

$$q_j \leqslant \frac{m_F}{\tau} \tag{46}$$

$$q_k \leqslant \frac{m_L}{\tau}. \tag{47}$$

Using (44)–(47) and the definitions of m_F, m_L, and Z it follows

$$\bar{\alpha} - \mu - \beta(q_j + 2q_k) > 0.$$

This and $\alpha_j^* > \alpha_k^*$ mean that (40) cannot be satisfied since all the terms on the left-hand side are positive. Hence for interior asymmetric solutions it is necessary that

$$C > 0. \tag{48}$$

From (41) and (42)

$$\alpha_j^* - \alpha_k^* = -C\left(\frac{1}{\tau} - 1\right)(m_F - m_L). \tag{49}$$

Using (48) $0 < \tau \leqslant 1$ it follows that if $m_F > m_L$, this cannot be satisfied and no asymmetric equilibrium can exist.

Next consider the case in Section 3.2 where $m_F < m_L$. Here (49) means that an interior asymmetric equilibrium can exist provided τ is sufficiently small so that $C > 0$ and $\tau \leqslant \beta(m_L + m_F/\tau)$. For large τ either one or both firms set $D_j = D_u$ in equilibrium and are at a corner solution to their optimization problems.

References

Baird, D., and T. Jackson (1985). *Cases, Problems and Materials on Bankruptcy*. (Boston, Mass.: Little Brown & Co.).

Bolton, P., and D. Scharfstein (1990). 'A Theory of Predation Based on Agency Problems in Financial Contracting', *American Economic Review* 80: 93–106.

Brander, J., and T. Lewis (1986). 'Oligopoly and Financial Structure: The Limited Liability Effect', *American Economic Review* 76: 956–70.

Chevalier, J. (1995). 'Capital Structure and Product Market Competition: Empirical Evidence from the Supermarket Industry', *American Economic Review* 85: 415–35.

DeAngelo, H., and R. Masulis (1980). 'Optimal Capital Structure under Corporate and Personal Taxation', *Journal of Financial Economics* 8: 3–29.

Eberhart, A., W. Moore, and R. Roenfeldt (1990). 'Security Pricing and Deviations from the Absolute Priority Rule in Bankruptcy Proceedings', *Journal of Finance* 45: 1457–69.

Franks, J., and W. Torous (1989). 'An Empirical Investigation of US Firms in Reorganization', *Journal of Finance* 44: 747–69.

—— (1994). 'A Comparison of Financial Recontracting in Distressed Exchanges and Chapter 11 Reorganizations', *Journal of Financial Economics* 35: 349–70.

Fudenberg, D., and J. Tirole (1986). 'A "Signal-Jamming" Theory of Predation', *RAND Journal of Economics* 17: 366–76.

Glazer, J. (1994). 'The Strategic Effects of Long-Term Debt in Imperfect Competition', *Journal of Economic Theory* 62: 428–43.

Grossman, S., and O. Hart (1980). 'Takeover Bids, the Free-Rider Problem and the Theory of the Corporation', *Bell Journal of Economics* 11: 42–64.

Haugen, R., and L. Senbet (1978). 'The Insignificance of Bankruptcy Costs to the Theory of Optimal Capital Structure', *Journal of Finance* 23: 383–93.

—— (1988). 'Bankruptcy and Agency Costs: Their Significance to the Theory of Optimal Capital Structure', *Journal of Financial and Quantitative Analysis* 23: 27–38.

Jensen, M., and W. Meckling (1976). 'Theory of the Firm: Managerial Behavior, Agency Costs and Ownership Structure', *Journal of Financial Economics* 3: 305–60.

Khanna, N., and S. Tice (1998). 'Strategic Responses of Incumbents to New Entry: The Effect of Ownership Structure, Capital Structure and Focus', Working Paper, Michigan State University.

Kim, E. (1978). 'A Mean-Variance Theory of Optimal Capital Structure and Corporate Debt Capacity', *Journal of Finance* 33: 45–63.

King, M. (1974). 'Taxation and the Cost of Capital', *Review of Economic Studies* 41: 21–35.

Kovenock, D., and G. Phillips (1997). 'Capital Structure and Product Market Behavior: An Examination of Plant Exit and Investment Decisions', *Review of Financial Studies* 10: 767–803.

Leland, H. (1998). 'Agency Costs, Risk Management, and Capital Structure', *Journal of Finance* 53: 1213–43.

—— and D. Pyle (1977). 'Information Asymmetries, Financial Structure and Financial Intermediation', *Journal of Finance* 32: 371–87.

Maksimovic, V. (1988). 'Capital Structure in Repeated Oligopolies', *RAND Journal of Economics* 19: 389–407.

Miller, M. (1977). 'Debt and Taxes', *Journal of Finance* 32: 261–75.

Modigliani, F., and M. Miller (1958). 'The Cost of Capital, Corporation Finance and the Theory of Investment', *American Economic Review* 48: 152–97.

Myers, S. (1984). 'The Capital Structure Puzzle', *Journal of Finance* 39: 575–92.

—— and N. Majluf (1984). 'Corporate Financing and Investment Decisions when Firms have Information Investors do not have', *Journal of Financial Economics* 13: 187–221.

Opler, T., and S. Titman (1994). 'Financial Distress and Corporate Performance', *Journal of Finance* 49: 1015–40.

Peterson, P., D. Peterson, and J. Ang. (1985). 'Direct Evidence on the Marginal Rate of Taxation on Dividend Income', *Journal of Financial Economics* 14: 267–82.

Phillips, G. (1995). 'Increased Debt and Industry Product Markets: An Empirical Analysis', *Journal of Financial Economics* 37: 189–238.

Roe, M. (1987). 'The Voting Prohibition in Bond Work-outs', *Yale Law Journal* 97: 232–79.

Rotemberg, J., and D. Scharfstein (1990). 'Shareholder-Value Maximization and Product Market Competition', *Review of Financial Studies* 3: 367–91.

Scott, J. (1976). 'A Theory of Optimal Capital Structure', *Bell Journal of Economics* 7: 33–54.

Stiglitz, J. (1973). 'Taxation, Corporate Financial Policy and the Cost of Capital', *Journal of Public Economics* 2: 1–34.

Titman, S. (1984). 'The Effect of Capital Structure on a Firm's Liquidation Decision', *Journal of Financial Economics* 13: 137–51.

Wald, J. (1999). 'How Firm Characteristics Affect Capital Structure: An International Comparison', *Journal of Financial Research* 22: 161–87.

16 Renegotiation In Repeated Oligopoly Interaction

JOSEPH FARRELL

1. Introduction

What determines whether an oligopoly can sustain prices above competitive levels, and if so how much above?[1] Modern oligopoly theory offers two general answers to this question. First, there are static models in which price competition is muted because of product differentiation or because firms compete in dimensions less cut-throat than price; the main examples are Cournot oligopoly theory and models of spatial product differentiation. But these models ignore the often obvious dynamic features of oligopoly markets: in particular, firms' actions are based on predictions about competitors' reactions.

Second, there are dynamic models in which price competition can be muted through the prospect of such reactions. These dynamic models are analysed using the theory of infinitely repeated games, usually with the solution known as subgame-perfection. The folk theorem states that generically almost any outcome—in particular, many outcomes involving joint monopoly pricing—can arise as the subgame-perfect equilibrium path of a repeated game, provided only that there is sufficiently little discounting. Thus, the model can explain the persistence of pricing substantially above cost on the part of a small or moderate number of firms, even when products are undifferentiated, total capacity greatly exceeds demand, and firms choose prices simultaneously within each period.

But (with plausible ancillary assumptions) these models also claim that even with many firms, monopoly pricing is possible. For instance, in repeated n-firm Bertrand oligopoly with constant marginal costs, shared monopoly is sustainable in subgame-perfect equilibrium provided that the per-period discount factor δ is at least $1 - (1/n)$. With $\delta = 0.99$, representing a plausible interest rate if the detection and response lag is a month,[2] this means that 100 firms can sustain the monopoly price. And Shapiro (1989: 365–6) calculates that (with the same assumptions, plus linear demand) a

I thank Luis Cabral, Dennis Carlton, Andrew Dick, Richard Gilbert, Matthew Rabin, and Carl Shapiro for their helpful comments, Rene Kamita for research assistance, and the National Science Foundation for early financial support (Grant SES-9111095).

[1] A theoretical sharpening of this question is why competition among the few does not drive prices all the way down to costs. Tirole (1988: 209) calls this the 'Bertrand Paradox'.

[2] This assumes that ordinary discounting is the primary component of the discount factor δ. If there is uncertainty (of the right kind) about whether a firm will remain in the market, or the market will survive, then δ might plausibly be considerably lower, even if firms do not know when it is their last active period. If firms do know when it is their last period, and if they can and will then cut price and take a large share, then cooperation breaks down whenever *any* firm is moribund. This may make cooperation predictably short-lived—and thus hard to sustain even if in fact all firms are flourishing—with relatively modest numbers of firms and levels of 'ordinary' discounting.

symmetric Cournot industry can sustain a shared monopoly with up to 400 firms, even if punishment consists of Cournot reversion rather than the harsher minimax punishments allowed by the folk theorem. Still more dramatic numbers emerge if we look at Cournot competition with minimax punishments.[3]

These theories therefore suggest that we should be concerned about coordinated pricing even in markets with fifty or 100 equal-sized firms.[4] Yet in practice there is what I will call a *structural consensus* that coordinated pricing is normally unlikely to be a major problem even in markets considerably more concentrated than that. Thus, the 1992 *Horizontal Merger Guidelines* of the US Department of Justice and Federal Trade Commission indicate that there will usually be little competitive concern about a merger that leaves a market 'unconcentrated', in the sense of having a Herfindahl concentration index (HHI) of 1000 or less (the equivalent of at least ten equal competitors).[5] And there is perhaps some evidence that if changes in industry competitive behaviour can be systematically associated with concentration levels, the cut-off point may often be at about four-firm concentration ratios of 0.5 to 0.6,[6] which would correspond to six to eight equal-sized firms. Summarizing what he describes as numerous case studies, Potter (1991: 12) claims that 'hostility', by which he seems to mean the tendency towards competitive pricing when there is excess capacity, will often stop 'when the industry has consolidated down to three or four key players'.

The theory that purports to explain cases of collusion therefore explains too much: the structural consensus contrasts sharply with the game theory models, and implies that the standard subgame-perfection condition is not generally the *binding* constraint on collusion.

Focusing attention on a constraint that is not binding is a serious problem. Not only will it wrongly estimate the extent of collusion, but it also risks suggesting wrong lessons about comparative statics and policy. That is, a structural or legal change that tightens the subgame-perfection constraint will appear pro-competitive if analysed as

---

[3] In order to sustain monopoly pricing with n firms in the linear-demand ($p = 2 - X$) zero-cost Cournot case, for example, δ must be at least equal to $1 - 4n/(n + 1)^2$; this follows from the fact that (by the Folk Theorem) the worst subgame-perfect punishment for either player is zero. In the Bertrand case this is straightforward, since charging $p = 0$ forever is obviously a subgame-perfect equilibrium. In the Cournot case the minimax punishment is more complicated, since the innocent firm must produce 2 per period if the guilty is to be held down to zero, and if this were meant to be kept up forever then the innocent firm would want to cheat by producing less in any period. But for large enough values of the discount factor a firm can be punished with an 'almost' zero continuation value. Note that I am following fairly standard economics practice by describing a defector from coordinated pricing as the 'guilty' firm and non-defectors as 'innocent'; this language fits well with the general idea of cooperation as desirable and thus fits rather awkwardly with the oligopoly problem.

[4] The role of 'size' is really that, in the models, any firm could readily take the whole market.

[5] 1992 *Horizontal Merger Guidelines*, 2 April 1992, section 1.51(a). Schmalensee (1987: 50) describes the 1984 version of this provision as 'clearly warranted: mergers that leave markets atomistic almost never increase the likelihood of collusion noticeably.' Strictly, these statements concern the *incremental* competitive concern from a merger, and do not address the *level* of coordinated pricing to be expected in such an industry. However, I think that most informed observers would justify the statements by saying that even after such a merger there is little threat of coordinated supercompetitive pricing—not (for instance) by saying, in contrast, that coordinated monopoly pricing is to be expected in the absence of the merger, so the merger would make little difference.

[6] See e.g. White (1987) and references therein.

if subgame-perfection were the binding constraint. Yet logically it may simultaneously weaken the actually binding constraint, and thus in fact be anti-competitive. Thus it is important to try to find the *binding* constraint.

What, then, is the binding constraint? Why is coordinated high pricing much harder— if the structural consensus rather than the textbook theory is correct—than the repeated-interaction models predict? In this paper I explore one possible candidate: the punishments for deviation specified in the folk theorem (or under Nash reversion), although subgame-perfect, are not really credible if the firms can renegotiate. I explore the extent to which oligopolists can sustain above-cost pricing in equilibria that are not only subgame-perfect but 'renegotiation-proof'. Using an apparently reasonable definition of renegotiation-proofness (when renegotiation is perfect), I show that collusion is severely limited by the number of firms, *even in the limit* as discounting becomes very unimportant ($\delta \to 1$). These results seem appealingly consistent with the structural consensus.

In most of this paper, following economists' sometimes casual usage, I use the term 'collusion' and its cognates to denote oligopoly pricing (far) above cost. Such pricing may be achieved by explicit collusion, or might occur through other means ('conscious parallelism').[7] To the extent that they differ, the paper's analysis, which assumes a communication-rich environment, would be primarily about explicit collusion and thus perhaps only loosely linked to the structural consensus, which is arguably much more about parallelism. For this reason, as I discuss in the Conclusion, I am not convinced how much weight to put on the results' similarities to the structural consensus. I therefore offer the paper mainly in the hope of provoking more exploration.

2. Renegotiation as a Constraint on Collusion

The textbook theory of repeated games implicitly assumes that players can coordinate on any of the enormous range of subgame-perfect equilibria in the repeated game. This approach may seem reasonable if the players have ample opportunities for communication. But this very assumption also subverts the standard subgame-perfect analysis. If, indeed, players can efficiently coordinate on an equilibrium, what would really happen after (out of equilibrium) one player cheated? If the prespecified punishment would hurt the innocent as well as the guilty, then we might well expect *renegotiation*, perhaps in the simple form of an agreement to ignore the transgression 'this time'. Such undiscriminating punishments may therefore lack credibility, even if they are subgame-perfect. This suggests that credible punishments must be renegotiation-proof, at least in the sense that not all players are hurt by them. Levenstein (1997), for instance, argues that the bromine cartel before World War I was unable to use Abreu, Pearce, and Stacchetti (1986) punishments because they were not renegotiation-proof.

---

[7] I am grateful to Richard Gilbert for encouraging me to pursue this distinction. The issue of how these differ has been recognized in principle for a long time: see e.g. Asch and Seneca (1976)—but not adequately studied.

This line of thought led Bernheim and Ray (1989) and Farrell and Maskin (1989) to develop a theory of 'weak renegotiation-proofness' in repeated games.[8] As the name suggests, weak renegotiation-proofness (WRP) is best conceived as a *necessary* condition for credibility of an equilibrium in a repeated game when (re)negotiation is completely smooth. Attempts to develop sufficient conditions have been less successful, but this paper focuses on necessary conditions and shows that collusion among scores or hundreds of firms, which can be consistent with subgame-perfection as discussed above, is not even weakly renegotiation-proof. Specifically, I show that with more than three symmetrically placed firms in Bertrand oligopoly, full collusion (or anything close to it) is inconsistent with what might seem a reasonable form of renegotiation-proofness, even if the discount factor δ is arbitrarily close to 1. I also show that in Cournot oligopoly, full collusion is unsustainable (in the same sense) among more than nine firms with linear demand.

I shall repeatedly use the result (and the method of proof) of a characterization theorem for WRP equilibrium in two-player games, derived by Farrell and Maskin (1989). Their Theorem 1 states that in a two-player game a necessary condition for a pair of average pay-offs,[9] $v \equiv (v_1, v_2)$, to be weakly renegotiation-proof (WRP) for large enough values of the discount factor δ is that there exist (possibly mixed) punishment-phase action-pairs $a^1 \equiv (a_1^1, a_2^1)$ and $a^2 \equiv (a_1^2, a_2^2)$, to punish players 1 and 2 respectively. These must be such that the punishment for each player is sufficiently severe, yet the 'innocent' player is not tempted to renegotiate. Formally, for instance, the punishment action-pair a^2 must be such that, in the stage-game while player 2 is being punished, player 2 cannot (even by cheating) get a payoff of more than v_2 when player 1 plays a_1^2, and must be such that player 1's payoff $g_1(a_1^2, a_2^2)$ from (a_1^2, a_2^2) is at least v_1. (In a useful notation, we require that $c_2(a_1^2) \equiv \max_a g_2(a_1^2, a) \leqslant v_2$, and that $g_1(a_1^2, a_2^2) \geqslant v_1$.) Of course a similar condition must hold for the action-pair a^1 that is used to punish player 1. Intuitively, the action-pair a^2 is used for a suitably chosen number of periods after player 2 deviates from prescribed behaviour; then normal play resumes. Farrell and Maskin also showed that this condition (with strict inequalities replacing weak) is sufficient for v to be WRP for large enough δ.

It is important to note that although the innocent player's action during the punishment phase might hold the guilty player perhaps only slightly below his normal-phase payoff (that is, he could perhaps get almost his normal-phase payoff in a punishment period if he cheated on his punishment), he may get much less than that according to the prescribed actions in a punishment period. In the simple oligopoly context, it is easy to specify actions that hold down the guilty player's *intended*

---

[8] I use the Farrell–Maskin terminology: Bernheim and Ray called the same concept 'partial Pareto perfection'. Both of these papers also developed further, stronger renegotiation-proofness conditions, but those are unsatisfactory in various ways. Pearce (1987) and Rabin (1991) have also developed different theories of renegotiation in infinitely repeated games. Benoit and Krishna (1993) develop a theory for finitely repeated games, but (like the subgame-perfection theory) it predicts no collusion at all in finitely repeated versions of the simple oligopoly games we consider.

[9] In a repeated game with discount factor δ, a player who gets payoff x_t in period t has a discounted payoff of $D \equiv \sum_0^\infty \delta^t x_t$, and an 'average' payoff of $(1 - \delta)D$; the term makes sense because, for instance, if $x_t = x$ for all t then the average payoff is also x.

punishment-phase payoff, by telling him to stay out of the market; this also helps to make the innocent player unwilling to renegotiate. As we will see, it is a lot harder to hold down the guilty player's payoff from cheating during the punishment phase (without also hurting the innocent player).

3. Repeated Bertrand Oligopoly

Consider n identical price-setting firms selling undifferentiated products, each with constant marginal costs c and no capacity constraints. The demand side is represented by a demand curve $X = D(p)$, where X is total industry quantity and p is the price that consumers face (i.e. the lowest price set by any firm). Let $\pi(p) \equiv (p - c)D(p)$ be industry profits when consumers must pay price p. We assume for simplicity that the function $\pi(\cdot)$ is strictly increasing in the range (c, p^m), where of course p^m is the monopoly price, i.e. the price that maximizes $\pi(p)$. Write $\pi^m \equiv \pi(p^m)$.

In each of infinitely many periods, each firm i chooses its price p_i (all firms choose simultaneously within a period). Firm i's within-period payoff is $\pi(p_i) \equiv (p_i - c)D(p_i)$ if p_i is uniquely the lowest price, $\pi(p_i)/m$ if it is one of m equal lowest prices, and zero otherwise. Each firm's action becomes common knowledge before the beginning of the next period; thus, firms' actions can depend on what others have done in the past. The firms share a common and constant discount factor $\delta \in (0, 1)$. We shall be concerned with equilibrium (average) payoffs as $\delta \to 1$.

Following Farrell and Maskin (1989), we ask to what extent innocent firms can hold down the best-response payoff of a guilty firm in punishment periods, while simultaneously getting a good payoff themselves. Farrell and Maskin addressed this issue with the following duopoly result for the linear-demand case. We prove it here for a general demand curve, and then extend it to oligopoly with more than two firms.

Lemma 1. *In symmetric Bertrand duopoly with constant costs and no capacity constraints, the following results characterize an innocent firm's ability to minimize its guilty rival's best-response expected payoff v while maximizing its own expected payoff u. (a) If the innocent firm is restricted to pure strategies (that is, its price is known to its rival), then it cannot hold its rival's best-response payoff strictly below its own intended payoff: thus $u \leq v$. (b) If the innocent firm can commit to randomizing its price (in such a way that the distribution of its price, but not the price itself, is observable by its rival before the latter chooses its own price), then it can hold its rival's best-response expected payoff down to any $v \in (0, \pi^m)$, while itself earning an expected payoff of $u = v(1 + \log(\pi^m/v)) > v$.*

Proof. First, note that in choosing strategies a^2 to satisfy conditions of the form $g_1(a^2) \geq v_1$ and $c_2(a^2) \leq v_2$, we can assume without loss of generality that firm 2 plays only prices $p > p^m$ in a_2^2. That is, it is meant to set prices high enough that it gets no business while firm 1 sets prices $p \in [c, p^m]$. Of course this implies that $g_2(a^2) = 0$, but it is important to understand that a punishment strategy must limit $c_2(a^2) \equiv \max_a g_2(a_1^2, a)$, not (only) $g_2(a^2)$.

First consider pure strategies on the part of the innocent firm, firm 1. If it charges $a_1^2 = p$, its intended stage-game payoff $g_1(a^2) = u$ cannot exceed $\pi(p)$ (and any $a_2^2 > p^m$ will lead to that value of u). For any $\epsilon > 0$, the guilty firm can undercut p by a small enough amount to get a payoff that exceeds $u - \epsilon$. Thus it cannot be held to any best-response punishment-phase payoff strictly less than u. Except for an uninteresting open-ness problem, we have $c_2(a_1^2) \geqslant g_1(a^2)$ (with equality for $c \leqslant a_1^2 = p \leqslant p^m$). This proves part (a).[10]

Now consider mixed-price strategies a_1^2 for the innocent firm. To hold its rival's best-response expected payoff $c_2(a_1^2)$ down to v, the innocent firm must ensure, for every p, that if the guilty firm sets price p, then it will have no more than a $v/\pi(p)$ chance of getting the whole market (we deal with ties below). Thus, if $F(\cdot)$ is the distribution function of the innocent firm's price, we require that for all p such that $\pi(p) > v$,

$$F(p) \geqslant 1 - \frac{v}{\pi(p)}. \tag{1}$$

Since the punishment-design task is to maximize the innocent firm's payoff (with the guilty firm out of the market) while holding the guilty firm's best-response payoff down to v, and since $\pi(\cdot)$ is increasing in the relevant range, we can assume without loss that condition (1) holds with equality for $p \in (p(v), p^m)$, where $p(v)$ is defined by $\pi(p(v)) \equiv v$, and the remaining mass of v/π^m is at p^m.

By construction, this implies that firm 2 cannot achieve an expected payoff strictly above v by setting any price other than the monopoly price. To show that the mixed strategy a^2 in question truly holds firm 2 down to an expected payoff of v, we need only check that its expected payoff from $p = p^m$ is no more than v. But this expected payoff is equal to v even if all ties are resolved in firm 2's favour. Under this strategy, moreover, when firm 2 sets prices above p^m, firm 1's profits are

$$u(v) = \int_{p(v)}^{p^m} \pi(p) dF(p) + \frac{v}{\pi^m} \pi^m.$$

Substituting for dF from (1), integrating by parts, and changing variable from p to π, we find that the innocent firm's expected profits are

$$u(v) = v\left(1 + \log \frac{\pi^m}{v}\right).$$

This proves part (b) of the Lemma. ∎

---

[10] The reader may ask: if the innocent firm chooses a pure strategy p that would yield strictly positive $u > 0$, why can't the guilty firm undercut p infinitesimally and thus get almost u but give the innocent firm zero? But we are not comparing payoffs of a Stackelberg equilibrium. Rather, the question is, if (say) firm 1 chooses an intended punishment action-pair a^2 that involves an unmixed a_1^2, then how do $g_1(a^2)$ and $c_2(a_1^2)$ compare? The same clarification addresses a question a number of readers have asked: if v is nearly π^m, doesn't the Lemma claim that each firm can get the full monopoly profit? No: the Lemma says (in that case trivially) that firm 1 can get π^m (if firm 2 stays out of the market) using a pricing strategy under which firm 2's *cheating best response* wouldn't get it more than π^m.

Lemma 1 implies the following result, which was shown by Farrell and Maskin (1989: 339–441) for the linear-demand case:

Proposition 2. *In the simplest repeated Bertrand duopoly, symmetric collusion is possible in WRP equilibrium for large enough discount factors; so is asymmetric collusion provided that it is not too asymmetric.*

Since all the relevant calculations are in profit space, the calculation of how asymmetric the profit shares can be is no different from that in Farrell and Maskin: each firm must get no less than a fraction z of the shared monopoly profits, where $z(2 - \log z) = 1$, or $z \approx 0.32$. As we will see, it is important that this number is less than a third but more than a quarter.

4. Beyond Duopoly: Asymmetric and Quasi-Symmetric Punishments

With two players, it is natural to suppose that renegotiation is blocked if the innocent party would benefit from implementing the agreed-upon punishment. With more than two players, we have to ask who can block renegotiation—equivalently, how many of the innocent would have to join the guilty party in order to push renegotiation through.

Obviously, a wide variety of answers would be possible. One candidate would be that any player can block renegotiation: with this assumption, weak renegotiation-proofness means that no continuation equilibrium of the equilibrium can Pareto-dominate any other. This is perhaps the most obvious generalization of the two-player definition. It turns out to imply that firms 'should' use highly asymmetric punishments and that by doing so they can sustain a great deal of collusion.

Indeed, with this assumption, punishments can be designed as follows: if firm i has cheated, nominate some other firm $j \neq i$ to be the renegotiation-blocker, and (during the punishment phase) concentrate all production in firm j, specifying that firm i and all firms $k \neq j$ produce nothing. This makes weakly renegotiation-proof (in this sense) collusion very easy. Formally, a simple extension of the two-firm analysis implies the following:

Proposition 3. *Consider repeated Bertrand oligopoly and assume that asymmetric punishments are allowed and that any one firm can block renegotiation. Then, the average payoffs $(\pi_1, \ldots, \pi_n)$ are WRP for large enough δ if for every i there is a $j \neq i$ such that*

$$\pi_j < \pi_i \left(1 + \log \frac{\pi^m}{\pi_i}\right).$$ *In particular, symmetric division of the monopoly profit among n symmetric firms is WRP (with large enough δ) for all n.*

Proof. Lemma 1 tells us that a Bertrand duopolist can hold its rival to a maximum expected payoff of v (where $v < \pi^m$ is given) while itself earning up to $v(1 + \log[\pi^m/v])$ if the rival keeps out of the market (as we can assume it is meant to do during punishment). Hence, for firm i to be effectively punished without hurting firm j requires that we can find v such that $v(1 + \log[\pi^m/v]) \geq \pi_j$ while $v < \pi_i$. This condition ensures that punishment is possible and that firm j would block renegotiation. We have in effect reduced the problem to a duopoly problem by telling all firms other than j—including both the 'guilty' firm i and all 'third' firms—to stay out of the market during i's punishment phase.

We must also consider the incentives of firms other than i to cheat during i's punishment. We can specify that if any firm cheats during another's punishment, then the original punishment is cancelled and the most recent cheater is punished. With this (standard) assumption, firm j will not cheat during i's punishment if it would not cheat during the normal phase, since it is getting more payoff without cheating and yet it would be punished just as severely for cheating. Other firms $k \neq i, j$ are at worst being asked to remain out of the market, as if they were being punished themselves, and so if no firm would cheat on its own punishment, then none will cheat on another's.

The claim then follows on substituting $\pi_i = \pi^m/n$ for all i. ∎

Clearly, unrestricted asymmetric treatment of the innocent firms is a very powerful tool for blocking unanimous renegotiation. Indeed, Horniacek (1996) has applied similar arguments, exploiting asymmetries of treatment among innocent players after a deviation, to argue that a version of WRP, and even a weakened version of strong perfect equilibrium (Rubinstein 1980), is little constraint on cooperation when there are three or more players.

In symmetric oligopoly games, however, one might expect that the innocent firms will all be treated alike in the punishment of a guilty firm. In that case, and in some cases even where not all are treated exactly alike, either all the innocent firms gain from that punishment (so that renegotiation will plausibly be blocked), or all lose (making renegotiation likely). Following that idea, we extend the two–player definition of a weakly renegotiation-proof equilibrium to the many-player case as follows:

Definition. *A subgame-perfect equilibrium is quasi-symmetrically weakly renegotiation-proof (QSWRP) if, evaluated at the beginning of the period after player i alone deviates from prescribed play, every other player's continuation payoff (weakly) exceeds what it would have been had player i not just deviated. Thus no innocent player would want to forget and forgive.*

In the remainder of the paper I will show that symmetric oligopolies with more than a handful of firms cannot sustain full—or, indeed, much—collusion in QSWRP repeated Bertrand equilibrium, even for discount factors very near 1, and even if we allow for verifiable randomizations in punishment periods.

5. Full Collusion in Repeated Bertrand Competition

We begin by revisiting the textbook repeated-Bertrand oligopoly model and asking again whether or not full collusion can be sustained when the discount factor is high. Our answer stands in stark contrast to the subgame-perfect theory.

Proposition 4. *In repeated Bertrand competition, full collusion is impossible in QSWRP equilibrium if n > 3, even for discount factors very close to 1.*

Proof. Again we use the result of Lemma 1. Suppose that full collusion is a QSWRP equilibrium with n firms. Without loss of generality, there is at least one firm, firm 1, say, whose normal-phase payoff is no greater than π^m/n; let $\pi_1 \leqslant \pi^m/n$ be its normal-phase average payoff.

Since the claim is that for $n > 3$ collusion is impossible, let us tactically suppose that the innocent firms can correlate their strategies and are not constrained by issues of distribution of profits among themselves. This reduces their problem to choosing a distribution of the lowest price quoted by any of the innocent firms: call this lowest price p_0. They must choose the distribution of p_0 so as to give themselves expected profits of at least $\pi^m - \pi_1$ while holding down an opportunistic Bertrand rival to expected profits of less than π_1. The problem is that making it impossible for the guilty firm to make high expected profits even by 'cheating on its punishment' requires that with high probability p_0 must be small: but this conflicts with the need (so as to avoid the temptation to renegotiate) to make profits for themselves.

By assuming that the innocent firms can correlate their strategies, we reduce the problem analytically to that of a single innocent firm who must make a profit of $\pi^m - \pi_1$ while holding a guilty firm down to π_1. Thus, by Proposition 1, a necessary condition is that

$$\pi^m - \pi_1 \leqslant \pi_1 \left(1 + \log \frac{\pi^m}{\pi_1} \right).$$

Since $\pi_1 \leqslant \pi^m/n$, this implies that

$$\frac{n-1}{n} \pi^m \leqslant \frac{\pi^m}{n} (1 + \log\ n),$$

which reduces to $n - \log\ n \leqslant 2$, or (in integer terms) $n \leqslant 3$.

Thus $n \leqslant 3$ is a necessary condition for QSWRP full collusion (symmetric or not) in infinitely repeated Bertrand oligopoly, however large the discount factor δ, and even if the innocent firms can correlate their strategies, and their randomizations are observable, in a punishment phase. ■

The proof essentially notes that each firm must get at least a critical share of the shared monopoly profits. This is just as in the duopoly case, and the same calculation (as in Farrell and Maskin) implies that this critical share is slightly less than a third: four firms or more cannot all get this much. Three can, so we might expect that three can collude according to this criterion.

If the innocent firms cannot correlate their strategies in the punishment phase, then the distribution of p_0 must be the minimum-value distribution of $n - 1$ independently distributed prices, and each innocent firm must have a sufficient chance of winning, at a sufficiently high price, that it would not prefer to renegotiate back to the *status quo* as if the deviation had not happened.

To see whether symmetric collusion is sustainable in this way, we need only consider the case $n = 3$, since we have shown that such collusion is impossible anyway for $n > 3$ and Proposition 2 showed that it is possible with $n = 2$. Here, we show that correlation of strategies in the punishment period is not essential for collusion with $n = 3$, but that observability of randomization is.

Proposition 5. *Two or three firms can symmetrically collude in QSWRP equilibrium in repeated Bertrand oligopoly for high enough discount factors even if the innocent firms cannot correlate their punishment randomizations.*

Proof. Consider a guilty firm that must be held to a maximum (cheating-on-its-punishment) payoff of v, while the other two (who cannot now correlate their randomized prices) try to do as well as they can subject to inflicting this punishment. Suppose that each randomizes with distribution function $F(\cdot)$ on $[p(v), p^m]$—there is no need to charge prices less than $p(v)$ and it is foolish to charge prices greater than p^m. Define $G(p) \equiv 1 - F(p)$. Then the firm being punished can get, in the short run, $\max_p \pi(p)G(p)^2$. The innocent firms want to choose $G(\cdot)$ to keep this down to v and, subject to that, to maximize their expected profits. Since $\pi(\cdot)$ is monotonic, the innocent firms want to charge high prices as much as possible. Therefore $G(\cdot)$ will satisfy

$$G(p) = \sqrt{\left(\frac{v}{\pi(p)}\right)}, \; p(v) \leqslant p < p^m,$$

and the remaining $\sqrt{(v/\pi^m)}$ weight is an atom at price p^m.

Now consider the expected profit of each of the innocent firms. An innocent firm that bids $p < p^m$ wins the market with probability $G(p)$; if it bids $p = p^m$, there is a positive probability of a tie, which I assume leads to equally divided profits. Thus an innocent firm's expected profit (within a punishment-phase period) is

$$\int_{p(v)}^{p^m} \pi(p)G(p)\mathrm{d}F(p) + \sqrt{(v/\pi^m)}(1 - \tfrac{1}{2}\sqrt{(v/\pi^m)})\pi^m.$$

We can rewrite this in terms of the variable π as

$$\int_v^{\pi^m} \pi\sqrt{(v/\pi)}\tfrac{1}{2}\sqrt{(v/\pi^3)}\mathrm{d}\pi + \sqrt{(v/\pi^m)}(1 - \tfrac{1}{2}\sqrt{(v/\pi^m)})\pi^m,$$

which is

$$\tfrac{1}{2}v\log\frac{\pi^m}{v} + \sqrt{(v\pi^m)} - \tfrac{1}{2}v. \tag{2}$$

When $v = (1/3)\pi^m$, (2) is approximately $0.59\pi^m > (1/3)\pi^m$, so each innocent firm can get more than $\pi^m/3$ while holding a guilty firm strictly below $\pi^m/3$ during a punishment period. Consequently, symmetric Bertrand collusion with three firms is QSWRP for large enough δ even if the innocent firms cannot correlate their punishment strategies. ∎

Note that this is *not* a mixed-strategy equilibrium in the sense that each of the innocent firms expects an equal payoff from each of the prices over which it randomizes. On the contrary: an innocent firm that sets price $p < p^m$ gets an expected this-period profit of $\pi(p)G(p) = \sqrt{(v\pi(p))}$, which is strictly increasing in p (for $p < p^m$). Thus, innocent firms are tempted (in the short-run sense) to deviate from their specified punishment strategy during punishment.

If randomizations are unobservable, collusion is not sustainable at all. For, in order to punish effectively, the innocent firm(s) must randomize with support going all the way down to $p(v)$, or else the guilty firm can get more than v by undercutting. But if the innocent firms were playing a mixed-strategy equilibrium in the sense that their short-run payoffs were equal across realizations of the randomization, this would mean that they (jointly) were not expecting more than v. That is, the innocent firms' *joint* payoff during a punishment phase cannot exceed the guilty firm's best-response payoff during that punishment phase. In turn, this latter must be strictly less than the guilty firm's (per-period) normal-phase payoff, unless the guilty firm is playing a best response during the normal phase. Applying these observations to the firm with the lowest normal-phase payoff, we see that no collusion is sustainable. ■

6. Partial Collusion in Repeated Bertrand Oligopoly

If full collusion is impossible, can the firms collude on a price between c and p^m? One of the unsatisfactory predictions of the subgame-perfect theory is that it answers no: either full collusion is subgame-perfect, or no collusion is.[11] Here, by contrast, firms who are too numerous to collude fully may be able to collude partially, i.e. on a price greater than c but less than p^m.[12] However, in numerical terms, I find that the efficiency consequences (deadweight losses) due to this partial collusion are small, even if δ is close to 1 and even if n is as small as five.[13]

The function $v(1 + \log[\pi^m/v])$, which gives the profits the innocent firms together can achieve while effectively punishing the guilty firm by holding its payoff below v, has an infinitely steep slope for small v. Thus, for any n,

$$(n - 1)v < v\left(1 + \log\frac{\pi^m}{v}\right)$$

for small enough v. Since this is the condition for a payoff of v per firm to be sustainable in QSWRP equilibrium for large enough discount factors δ, it follows that,

[11] The reason is that for firms to collude in symmetric subgame-perfect equilibrium on a price p that yields industry profits of $\pi(p)$ requires precisely that the present value of one-nth of a perpetual stream of $\pi(p)$ be at least equal to $\pi(p)$. Clearly, $\pi(p)$ and p drop out of this comparison and all that matters is n versus δ.

[12] For parameter values for which the renegotiation-proof theory predicts partial collusion, the subgame-perfect theory predicts full collusion, not none. This follows from the fact that every WRP equilibrium is a subgame-perfect equilibrium.

[13] Even if $n = 4$ the losses are not large. A previous version of the paper haltingly explored a different efficiency issue: the extent to which QSWRP equilibrium must give substantial market shares even to high-cost firms.

TABLE 16.1. *Comparison of mark-up and deadweight loss ratios under partial collusion in repeated Bertrand oligopoly and monopoly (constant elasticity demand with c = 0.5, n = 4, 5, 6)*

Elasticity	n = 4		n = 5		n = 6	
	Mark-up ratio	DWL ratio	Mark-up ratio	DWL ratio	Mark-up ratio	DWL ratio
1.1	0.069	0.087	0.022	0.014	0.009	0.003
1.5	0.157	0.102	0.056	0.017	0.023	0.003
2.0	0.192	0.104	0.071	0.018	0.029	0.003
3.0	0.219	0.105	0.083	0.018	0.034	0.003
5.0	0.236	0.106	0.091	0.018	0.038	0.003

Note: The mark-up ratio is calculated as $(p^b - c)/(p^m - c)$. p^b is the price which corresponds to maximum sustainable partial collusion under repeated Bertrand oligopoly. p^m corresponds to the monopoly price. The deadweight loss ratio (DWL ratio) is the ratio between the deadweight loss from maximum sustainable partial collusion under repeated Bertrand oligopoly (DWL(p^b)) and the deadweight loss from monopoly (DWL (p^m)).

for every n, *some* collusion is possible in QSWRP equilibrium for large enough δ. But even for $n \approx 5$, the condition implies a small value of nv/π^m (little collusion), as we now show.

Suppose the firms can collude on a price p that yields industry profits $\pi(p)$. By the same argument as before, for this to be sustainable in QSWRP equilibrium requires that

$$(n - 1)\frac{\pi(p)}{n} \leqslant \frac{\pi(p)}{n}\left(1 + \log\frac{\pi^m}{\pi(p)/n}\right),$$

which reduces to $\pi(p)/\pi^m \leqslant ne^{2-n}$.

For example, if $n = 4$ (the smallest number of firms that cannot fully collude), they can collude only on prices p such that $\pi(p)/\pi^m \leqslant 4e^{-2} \approx 0.54$.[14] A price that yields roughly half of the monopoly profit implies only a smaller fraction of the monopoly mark-up and a smaller fraction still of the deadweight loss. For instance, with constant-elasticity demand, Table 16.1 shows that the maximum sustainable partial collusion leads to mark-ups well below monopoly mark-ups and to a deadweight loss of no more than an eighth of the monopoly deadweight loss for four firms facing a wide range of demand elasticities.[15]

[14] Numerical calculations also indicate that for $\delta = 0.99$, the four firms can capture only a fraction 0.51, rather than 0.54, of the potential monopoly profits.
[15] Because we relate outcomes to the monopoly outcome, the demand elasticity must exceed 1. A similar calculation assumes linear demand $X = 2 - p$ and zero marginal costs; then the monopoly price is 1. A collusive profit of 0.54 corresponds to a collusive price of approximately 0.33, a third of the monopoly mark-up, and hence a ninth of the monopoly deadweight loss (since loss is proportional to the square of the mark-up).

TABLE 16.2. *Comparison of mark-up ratios under partial collusion in repeated Bertrand and one-shot Cournot oligopoly (constant elasticity demand with c = 0.5, n = 4, 5, 6)*

	n = 4		n = 5		n = 6	
Elasticity	Bertrand partial collusion	One-shot Cournot	Bertrand partial collusion	One-shot Cournot	Bertrand partial collusion	One-shot Cournot
1.1	0.069	0.029	0.022	0.022	0.009	0.018
1.5	0.157	0.100	0.056	0.077	0.023	0.063
2.0	0.192	0.143	0.071	0.111	0.029	0.091
3.0	0.219	0.182	0.083	0.143	0.034	0.118
5.0	0.236	0.211	0.091	0.167	0.038	0.138

Note: The mark-up ratio under partial collusion in repeated Bertrand oligopoly is calculated as $(p^b - c)/(p^m - c)$. Similarly, the mark-up ratio for one-shot Cournot oligopoly is calculated as $(p^{nc} - c)/(p^m - c)$, where p^{nc} corresponds to the one-shot Cournot price.

For $n = 5$, the condition is that $\pi(p)/\pi^m \leqslant 5e^{-3} \approx 0.25$. Again, results for constant-elasticity demand are shown in Table 16.1, suggesting a deadweight loss of no more than 2 per cent of the monopoly deadweight loss for elasticities between 1.1 and 5.[16] For $n = 6$, $\pi(p)/\pi^m \leqslant 6e^{-4} \approx 0.11$, which corresponds to still smaller mark-ups and deadweight losses.[17] For $n \geqslant 7$, $\pi(p)/\pi^m \leqslant ne^{2-n} \leqslant 7e^{-5} \approx 0.05$.

These prices are quite low by the standards of conventional oligopoly models. For $n \geqslant 5$, calculations suggest that the imperfectly collusive prices in this model are significantly less than those in a one-shot Cournot model (see Table 16.2). Moreover, since deadweight loss is of second order in the mark-up, these fairly small mark-ups— even for $n = 4$ or $n = 5$—have small welfare consequences, and for larger values of n the maximum deadweight loss declines dramatically.

7. Repeated Cournot Competition

I now consider the repeated Cournot case. As above, I first derive conditions on n for shared monopoly to be QSWRP (for discount factors very close to 1); I then ask how much firms can collude if those conditions fail. In this section I work with linear demand $p = 2 - X$: neither the general demand case nor the constant-elasticity case has proven tractable. To keep the notation simple I assume zero marginal costs; this is a mere normalization once one assumes constant and equal marginal costs.

[16] In the linear case the maximum collusive mark-up with five firms is approximately $p \approx 0.15$, with deadweight loss of $(1/2)(0.15)^2$ or about 2 per cent of the monopoly deadweight loss.

[17] For our linear-demand example this corresponds to a mark-up of less than 6 per cent of the monopoly mark-up, and a deadweight loss of less than 0.4 per cent of the potential monopoly deadweight loss. For our constant-elasticity cases shown in Table 16.1, it produces a deadweight loss of about 0.3 per cent of the monopoly deadweight loss.

Full collusion

Proposition 6. *In repeated Cournot oligopoly, full collusion is not QSWRP with more than nine firms, even for δ very close to 1.*

Proof. If the innocent firms each produce y during the punishment phase, then (since we can assume without loss of generality that the firm being punished produces nothing) each innocent firm gets a per-period payoff during the punishment phase of $\pi^I = y(2 - (n - 1)y)$. Meanwhile, by cheating during a punishment period, the guilty firm could achieve a single-period payoff of $\chi \equiv \max_z z(2 - (n - 1)y - z) = (1/4)(2 - (n - 1)y)^2$. Thus Theorem 1 of Farrell and Maskin (1989) requires that it must be possible to choose y so that π^I is at least as large as the normal-phase (collusive) per-period payoff, which is $1/n$, while $\chi < 1/n$. This amounts to requiring that y satisfy $y(2 - (n - 1)y) \geqslant 1/n$ and $(1/4)(2 - (n - 1)y)^2 < 1/n$. These two conditions on y can hold simultaneously if and only if $n < 9$. To see this, write $a \equiv 2 - (n - 1)y$, so that the conditions are $a(2 - a) \geqslant (n - 1)/n$ and $a^2 < 4/n$. These can both be made to hold if and only if the first can be made to hold strictly with the second one holding with equality, so we can substitute $a = 2/\sqrt{n}$ in the first condition to yield $(\sqrt{n} - 2)^2 < 1$, or $n < 9$. ∎

As a technical observation, note that the case $n = 9$ is right on the boundary: the conditions can be made to hold weakly but not strictly. This means that the necessary condition for WRP equilibrium holds, but the sufficient condition does not: we must remain agnostic about the possibility. As we will see next (and as is not surprising given the calculations above), nine firms can all but fully collude in QSWRP equilibrium in repeated Cournot play with our cost and demand assumptions, if δ is close to 1.

Partial collusion

Now we put a bound on the amount of profit (and welfare loss) that can stem from QSWRP partial collusion in Cournot oligopolies with $n \geqslant 9$ firms, in which (as we have seen) complete symmetrical collusion is not a QSWRP equilibrium.

Proposition 7. *If $n > 9$, the firms can symmetrically divide in QSWRP equilibrium a total profit of less than $16n/(n + 3)^2$, corresponding to a price of less than*

$$p = 1 - \frac{\sqrt{((n - 9)(n - 1))}}{n + 3}.$$

Proof. To sustain a per-firm profit of π, there must be punishment actions satisfying the now-familiar conditions. Let Y be the aggregate output of the $n - 1$ innocent firms in a punishment period; then we require that $Y(2 - Y) \geqslant (n - 1)\pi$ and $(1/4)(2 - Y)^2 \leqslant \pi$. Writing $q \equiv \pi^{1/2}$, we require $Y(2 - Y) \geqslant (n - 1)q^2$ and $2 - Y \leqslant 2q$; hence, $q \leqslant 4/(n + 3)$, and the Proposition follows when we set $\pi = p(2 - p)/n$. ∎

For comparison, under one-shot Cournot equilibrium, the price is $2/(n + 1)$ and total profit is $4n/(n + 1)^2$; and of course price and total profit is 1 under full collusion.

For large n, therefore, roughly four times more profit is sustainable in QSWRP equilibrium than without collusion, but vanishingly less than under full collusion, even as $\delta \to 1$.

8. Efficient Punishments

The results above show that frictionless renegotiation would make self-enforcing collusion impossible for even moderate numbers of firms. It would also be interesting to derive results in the other direction, suggesting when collusion *is* possible. Unfortunately, since weak renegotiation-proofness is not a convincing sufficient condition for credibility, the analysis above cannot help very much with that. But if collusion can be sustained by means of punishments that themselves divide monopoly profit among the innocent firms, then full collusion will be a 'strong perfect equilibrium' (Rubinstein 1980).

This can never happen in repeated Bertrand competition, even with $n = 2$, as Farrell and Maskin (1989) noted. The problem is that an effective punishment must involve randomization by the innocent firm(s), which is inconsistent with their collecting the full monopoly profit during a punishment phase.

Turning to repeated Cournot oligopoly (with our linear demand and zero-cost assumptions), when can full collusion be sustained with efficient punishments? In a punishment phase, the $n - 1$ innocent firms divide the monopoly output (i.e. 1) among them. By cheating in this phase, the guilty firm can achieve a per-period payoff of $\max_y y(2 - 1 - y) = 1/4$. Hence, each firm must get *strictly* more than this per period in the normal phase; if a firm got 1/4 or less in the normal phase then it should cheat for a period and could not be effectively punished, given that only Pareto-efficient punishments are being considered. To give each firm strictly more than 1/4 in the normal phase requires $n \leqslant 3$. At the same time, it is clear that with $n \leqslant 3$ this punishment (suitably repeated) works to sustain collusion for δ close enough to 1. Thus we have:

Proposition 8. *There is a strong perfect equilibrium (in which both the equilibrium path and punishments involve the monopoly price) in infinitely repeated Cournot competition with linear demand and with sufficiently little discounting, if and only if $n \leqslant 3$. No such equilibrium is possible in repeated Bertrand competition.*

9. Rebuttal and/or Conclusion

In this somewhat inconclusive concluding section, I try to distinguish more carefully between explicit collusion and conscious parallelism—a distinction that most game theory ignores—and in the process raise some doubts about the interpretation of the results above.

A priori, we surely should analyse renegotiation as well as negotiation of collusive agreements. If one likes its details (in particular the QSWRP assumption), the model above therefore seems appealing on the input side. On the output side, the model says that a few firms can sustain significantly supercompetitive prices, but only a few. It also says that oligopolies can sustain somewhat supercompetitive prices when they cannot sustain a monopoly price, but only to a (rapidly) decreasing extent as the number of firms grows. These predictions resonate appealingly with the structural consensus. Dare one thus hope that this is broadly the 'right' theory of self-enforcing collusion in oligopoly?

Unfortunately, I am sceptical. To discuss why, let us become more careful in our language: *collusion* is explicit agreement or communication to raise prices; *coordination* is raising prices with or without such communication. The theory above predicts that (in unconcentrated industries) it is hard to coordinate on high prices when there is (and will always be) explicit collusion, whereas the structural consensus is that (in such industries) it is hard to coordinate on high prices if explicit collusion is *not* possible. Since collusion surely affects firms' ability to coordinate, these are not directly comparable predictions.[18] The discussion below is not very deep, but it took me some time to clarify to this point, so I hope it will be helpful to others.

It is helpful to distinguish three negotiation environments for oligopoly pricing. The first is the purely theoretical benchmark of *perfect negotiation*. This is plainly assumed above, and also by at least the more advanced forms of the textbook 'subgame-perfect' theory: both equilibrium pricing and punishments can be negotiated in a sophisticated way, and everyone understands what is going on, sometimes even down to coordination of random pricing.[19] As this paper assumes, in this environment one might also expect perfect renegotiation.

In the second environment, there is *imperfect negotiation*. Imperfections arise for many reasons, often including asymmetries among firms, imperfect information about one another's costs and about demand, and perhaps also the need to keep negotiations (collusion) secret. Nevertheless, explicit negotiation does take place in this environment: firms explicitly agree on prices and quite possibly on what will happen if deviations are detected. Any renegotiation will presumably also be imperfect. This environment represents the case in which firms collude.

In the third environment, *no explicit negotiation* takes place. Firms recognize their interdependence, and may engage in some relatively costly and clumsy signalling of intentions, but signalling bandwidth is quite limited.

---

[18] Of course, in cross-section, explicit collusion (where it's illegal) will tend to occur where other factors make non-collusive coordination at least somewhat difficult (otherwise why risk prison terms?). Thus, in principle, collusion might even be negatively correlated with success at raising price. One should not confuse this correlation with the effect of collusion. I thank Dennis Carlton for this observation. See also Werden and Baumann (1986).

[19] In the literature, the oldest papers assumed reversion to one-shot Nash behaviour, while more recent work (including this paper) tends to construct optimal punishments, which can be quite complex. Researchers of course recognize informally that the latter impose heavier demands on negotiation, and thus more thoroughly assume perfect collusion, but there does not seem to be analysis following up on this point.

In this framework, the model above, and the textbook models, clearly concern the perfect-negotiation environment. The structural consensus, however, concerns the observed mix of the imperfect-negotiation and the no-negotiation environments. Thus, to make much of the assonance between my results and the structural consensus would require (something like) that the three negotiation environments do not differ very much in terms of the prevalence of successful price coordination. That is not something one would want to assume. Although there is some academic debate on the point, I think it is natural to believe that the laws against collusion matter, which means that the imperfect-negotiation and no-negotiation environments differ substantially. Let me call this natural hypothesis the *concern over collusion*. It does not contradict the structural consensus if the observed regime is one in which prohibitions on collusion are often obeyed. Then it just says, very plausibly, that coordinated high pricing can become much easier with explicit negotiation, whether this is when explicit collusion is legal (see Dick 1996 on Webb–Pomerene cartels and Suslow 1991 on international cartels) or when prohibitions are violated (see Fraas and Greer 1977 on price-fixing prosecutions).[20]

Is coordination monotonic in coordination costs?

Absent renegotiation, one can (and most people do) take a simple monotone view of the role of the three negotiation environments. Coordinated pricing would be rather easy in the theoretical perfect-negotiation environment (the textbook models), is harder with imperfect negotiation (how much harder depending on how imperfect), and is harder still (especially if more than a handful of firms are involved) with no explicit negotiation. This view seems consistent with (a) the calculations discussed in the Introduction about how many firms can collude if negotiation is perfect, (b) limited evidence on the extent of successful collusion with imperfect negotiation, and (c) the structural consensus if the legal prohibitions on explicit collusion are mostly obeyed (at least outside the most concentrated industries). The great gulf between the textbook calculations and the structural consensus, which I presented in the Introduction as a problem or puzzle, is then viewed just as a big difference between the perfect-negotiation regime and the observed regime. Anti-trust enthusiasts might attribute more of the difference to the difference between imperfect negotiation and the observed regime; anti-trust cynics might attribute more of it to the difference between perfect and imperfect negotiation.

Thinking about renegotiation complicates this picture considerably. As McCutcheon (1997) has stressed, when obstacles to negotiation also obstruct renegotiation (more precisely when they are expected to do so), it is not so obvious that

---

[20] Very briefly, some kinds of evidence: (a) there continue to be convictions and confessions in *per se* price-fixing cases, indicating that executives are sometimes willing to risk prison in order to collude; (b) where collusion is legal, cartels of substantial size seem to spring up: see for instance Dick (1996) and Suslow (1991); (c) the structural consensus strongly suggests that it would be rare for cartels of comparable size to arise absent collusion; (d) both lawmakers and business people seem to believe that the laws matter.

more obstacles will always lead to more competitive pricing. In a moderately un-concentrated industry, the model above says that successful collusion will be rare in the perfect-negotiation environment, while the concern over collusion says that it will be more common in the imperfect-negotiation environment than in the no-negotiation environment.

This view implies that when renegotiation is possible, the extent of supercompetitive pricing is *not everywhere monotonic* in the ease of negotiation. Because of this non-monotonicity, it is hard to regard the model above as 'the right explanation' for the structural consensus, even if they give similar predictions.

This non-monotonicity is also superficially consonant with McCutcheon's concern that anti-collusion policy might be counterproductive. However, here, the implied paradoxical effect (in which banning smoke-filled meetings leads to higher prices) occurs between the perfect-negotiation environment and the imperfect-negotiation environment. This is not where anti-collusion policy operates: recall that perfect negotiation is only a theoretical benchmark. Legal prohibitions on explicit collusion, to the extent that they are respected, shift us from the regime of imperfect negotiation to the regime of no explicit negotiation; to the extent that they are covertly violated, they leave us in the second regime but presumably make negotiation harder, sketchier, and more imperfect.

All of this makes it seem important to distinguish, as does the law, between explicit collusion and coordination without collusion. Game-theoretic models typically gloss over this difference: by staying firmly within the perfect-negotiation environment, they do not address the difference in outcomes between the imperfect-negotiation and no-negotiation environments. Game theory generally proceeds by asking whether or not *there is* an equilibrium with certain (as for instance collusive) properties. For the most part, it does not address whether such an equilibrium can readily be *attained*.[21]

The 1984 *Guidelines* made a very explicit distinction on these lines. In section 3.11(a), they stated of markets with HHI below 1000 that 'implicit coordination among firms is likely to be difficult and . . . the prohibitions of section 1 of the Sherman Act [forbidding collusion] are usually an adequate response to any explicit collusion that might occur.' There was no claim that explicit collusion would be prohibitively difficult (if attempted) simply because of the moderately large number of firms in such a market.[22] Thus they incorporated the *concern over collusion* in their discussion of the *structural consensus*.

Having now put my model in its place (I think), what is the bottom line? Clearly, neither negotiation nor renegotiation is perfect in reality. The model does show that taking account of the prospects for renegotiation can affect *ex ante* incentives very greatly.

---

[21] Parts of the literature on 'cheap talk' (see e.g. Farrell and Rabin 1996: esp. 114) address this point, but so far it has probably conferred intellectual respectability on the question more than it has provided answers. Obviously analysis of talk is particularly relevant to collusion. Other refinement concepts might, generously, be seen as addressing the question in the form of 'which equilibrium will happen?'

[22] It is not part of the argument here, but I would note my own scepticism at the 1984 suggestion that merger policy should not be used simply because explicit collusion is already illegal. Presumably nobody in the non-Anti-trust divisions of the Justice Department was claiming that locks were unnecessary because burglary was illegal.

The dramatic difference between the renegotiation-proof and the subgame-perfect predictions (in the perfect-negotiation environment where they live) may suggest that neither one is a reliable policy guide in its precise predictions, although studying both will surely help one to assess real-world threats of collusion. Comparison of the model with what we believe is true in practice (which presumably reflects the possibility of imperfect renegotiation or its no-negotiation analogue)[23] further suggests that the interaction with the negotiation environment is quite subtle.

Finally (within its world, but in contrast to the textbook models) the model says that, it is difficult to sustain collusion using only threats of price retaliation. This difficulty might suggest a strong private incentive to develop richer cartel institutions that would hamper deviations, ease the punisher's pain (or exacerbate the punished firm's), or retard renegotiation.[24]

References

Abreu, Dilip, David Pearce, and Ennio Stacchetti (1986) 'Optimal Cartel Equilibria with Imperfect Monitoring', *Journal of Economic Theory* 39: 251–69.

Asch, Peter, and Seneca, J. J. (1976) 'Is Collusion Profitable?', *Review of Economics and Statistics* 58: 1–12.

Benoit, Jean-Pierre, and Vijay Krishna (1993) 'Renegotiation in Finitely Repeated Games', *Econometrica* 61: 303–24.

Bernheim, B. Douglas, and Debraj Ray (1989) 'Collective Dynamic Consistency in Repeated Games', *Games and Economic Behavior* 1: 295–326.

Dick, Andrew (1996) 'When Are Cartels Stable Contracts?', *Journal of Law and Economics* 39: 241–83.

Farrell, Joseph, and Eric Maskin (1989) 'Renegotiation in Repeated Games', *Games and Economic Behavior* 1: 327–60.

—— and Matthew Rabin (1996) 'Cheap Talk', *Journal of Economic Perspectives* 10: 103–18.

Fraas, Arthur, and Douglas Greer (1977) 'Market Structure and Price Collusion: An Empirical Analysis', *Journal of Industrial Economics* 26: 21–44.

Horniacek, Milan (1996) 'The approximation of a strong perfect equilibrium in a discounted supergame', *Journal of Mathematical Economics* 25: 85–107.

Levenstein, Margaret (1997) 'Price Wars and the Stability of Collusion: A Study of the Pre-World War I Bromine Industry', *Journal of Industrial Economics* 45: 117–37.

McCutcheon, Barbara (1997) 'Do Meetings in Smoke-Filled Rooms Facilitate Collusion?', *Journal of Political Economy* 105: 330–50.

Pearce, David (1987) 'Renegotiation-Proof Equilibria: Collective Rationality and Intertemporal Cooperation', Yale mimeo.

Potter, Donald V. (1991) 'Success Under Fire: Policies to Prosper in Hostile Times', *California Management Review* 33: 1–15.

---

[23] Dick (1996) studies attempts at 'reorganization' of (legal) cartels after a breakdown of discipline. This might be a promising source of information on renegotiation, with the usual caveat that the observed cases represent *actual* defections, while the theory concerns how the prospect of defection and renegotiation affects how cartels might be designed so as to eliminate defections.

[24] I thank Dennis Carlton for this point.

Rabin, Matthew (1991) 'Reneging and Renegotiation', Working Paper, University of California, Berkeley and Los Angeles.

—— (1994) 'A Model of Pre-Game Communication', *Journal of Economic Theory* 63: 370–91.

Rubinstein, Ariel (1980) 'Strong Perfect Equilibrium in Supergames', *International Journal of Game Theory* 9: 1–12.

Schmalensee, Richard (1987) 'Horizontal Merger Policy: Problems and Changes', *Journal of Economic Perspectives* 1: 41–54.

Shapiro, Carl (1989) 'Theories of Oligopoly Behavior', in R. Schmalensee and R. Willig (eds.), *Handbook of Industrial Organization* (Amsterdam: North-Holland).

Suslow, Valerie (1991) 'Cartel Contract Duration: Empirical Evidence from International Cartels', Working Paper, University of Michigan Business School.

Tirole, Jean (1988) *The Theory of Industrial Organization* (Cambridge, Mass.: MIT Press).

US Department of Justice and Federal Trade Commission (1984, 1992) 'Horizontal Merger Guidelines', available at ftc.gov and usdoj.gov/atr websites.

Werden, Gregory J., and Michael G. Baumann (1986) 'A Simple Model of Imperfect Competition in which Four are Few but Three are Not', *Journal of Industrial Economics* 34: 331–5.

White, Lawrence J. (1987) 'Antitrust and Merger Policy: A Review and Critique', *Journal of Economic Perspectives* 1: 13–22.

17 Competing against Bundles

BARRY NALEBUFF

1. Introduction

One of the distinguishing features of our modern economy is the competitive success achieved by product bundles, Microsoft Office being the case in point. It has achieved a commanding market share over previously dominant firms selling individual software applications, such as WordPerfect, Quattro or Lotus, Adobe PageMill, and Harvard Graphics. While no one single factor explains Microsoft's success, one part of the explanation can be found in the writings of Cournot (1838).[1] But this is not the classic Cournot oligopoly model that has become the textbook standard. Instead, it is Cournot's dual.

The classic Cournot oligopoly model has a limited number of commodity sellers each putting a quantity out in the market. With linear demand, price is determined by

$$p = A - b * (q_1 + q_2 + \ldots + q_n). \tag{1}$$

Although the standard textbook model is Cournot quantity competition, there are few real markets—perhaps the Fulton fish market—which satisfy this characterization. It is rare to find a firm that simply dispenses some quantity of goods on the market and then accepts the market price.[2] Instead, firms set prices, taking into account the expected prices set by other firms and the anticipated demand at those prices.

As Cournot himself realized, it is entirely possible to flip the ps and qs. In this case, the goods are complements rather than substitutes and the strategic variable becomes price, not quantity:

$$q = A - b * (p_1 + p_2 + \ldots + p_n). \tag{2}$$

In this interpretation, consumers are interested in buying a collection of n complementary products, for example, hardware and software. Each of the products is sold separately at price p_i. When determining whether or not to purchase this bundle, the

One of the many things I learned from Professor Mirrlees in the Nuffield College classrooms was the value of taking the dual perspective. As for how well these lessons were learned, the pudding will be in the proofs. My heartfelt thanks go Adam Brandenburger, Erik Brynjolfsson, Jeremy Bulow, Richard Zeckhauser, and seminar participants at Stanford and UCLA whose perceptive comments led me to tackle this problem.

[1] Other explanations include Novell and other's delay in updating their products to be compatible with Windows in its migration from DOS.

[2] Kreps and Scheinkman (1983) provide an elegant defence of the Cournot model. They demonstrate that Cournot quantity competition is equivalent to Bertrand price competition in a two-stage game where firms first pick capacity levels and then choose quantities in a capacity-constrained second period. This greatly expands the applicability of the Cournot model. However, in an economy increasingly dominated by knowledge goods and where increasing returns to scale are the order of the day, firms rarely face capacity constraints.

consumer takes into account the aggregate cost. Thus a computer-user examines the cost of hardware and software. A student looks at the cost of tuition, room, and board. A skier considers the price of lodging, transportation, lift tickets, equipment, and lessons.

In Cournot's own words:

> We imagine two commodities, (a) and (b), which have no other use beyond that of being jointly consumed in the production of the composite commodity (ab). . . . Simply for convenience of expression we can take for examples copper, zinc, and brass under the fictitious hypothesis that copper and zinc have no other use than that of being jointly used to form brass by their alloy. (1838: ch. ix)

In Cournot's analysis, each component that goes into the bundle is unique—one type of hardware and one type of software. There is a monopoly in each component. How then will the components be priced? Cournot shows that if the two monopolists get together they would price the bundle of their goods *lower* than they would acting individually.

The two-firm case illustrates the general result. One firm sets the price of good 1 and the other sets the price of good 2. The equilibrium has each firm setting a price of $1/3$. The bundle price is then $2/3$ and total sales are then $1/3$. This result should seem familiar. As Sonnenschein (1968) observed, the mathematics are exactly the same as with the standard Cournot–Nash equilibrium, only here we have switched prices for quantities and complements for substitutes. Consider what happens if the two firms get together and coordinate their pricing decision. Now they would choose $p_1 + p_2 = 0.5$ and joint profits would rise from 0.22 to 0.25.

While it is not surprising that coordinated pricing leads to higher profits, what might be surprising is that coordinated pricing leads to a reduction in prices. Both consumers and firms are better off.[3] The reason is that in the case of complementors, when one firm lowers its price, the other firm's sales increase, an externality that is not taken into account with uncoordinated pricing. Thus there is an advantage to bundling when two firms each have market power, but each is missing one of the complementary products.[4]

In this paper, we take the next step in this dual to the Cournot model. We examine what happens when there is imperfect competition between the component products that go into the bundle. There are three cases to consider, component against component, bundle against bundle, and bundle against components.

In the first case, each component is sold separately—hardware against hardware and software against software. The second scenario considers bundle against bundle—a

---

[3] The fact that coordination leads to higher profits suggests that a company that sells two complementary products will have a higher incentive to innovate than when the products are sold separately, see Heeb (1998).

[4] It is interesting to note that Posner (1979) looked at the case for bundling pure complements. He concluded that as consumers care only about the price of the bundle, there would be no point in trying to leverage a monopoly in A to B so as to raise the price of B above its otherwise competitive level. Raising the price of A would do just as well. The surprise is that this argument no longer holds when B is sold by an oligopoly. Because its price lies above the competitive level, the A monopoly wants to use its leverage to *lower* the price of B.

hardware-software package competes against a rival package.[5] The third case presents bundle against uncoordinated component sellers. Here we have a hardware-software package competing against independent sellers of hardware and software.

Our interest is in the third case, bundle against components. We use the first two scenarios to form our basis for comparison. This allows us to better understand what happens when a player in the market aggregates a collection of complements and sells them as a bundle while the competition remains independent or uncoordinated.

Following the intuition of Cournot, it will not be a surprise that the bundler does better than the collection of independent competitors. But the scale of the advantage is remarkable. Once there are four or more items to the bundle, the bundle aggregator does better than the sum of its previous parts. And this outcome is stable as the disadvantaged independent sellers do not have an incentive to form a rival bundle. This is because the resulting 'ruinous' competition of bundle against bundle would leave the independent sellers even worse off than their present disadvantaged position.

Thus the results of this paper suggest that a firm who creates or simply aggregates a bundle of complementary software applications would have a substantial pricing advantage over its rivals and thereby achieve a leadership position in the market. This is especially true as the bundle grows in scale. Thus Microsoft's taking the lead in creating a software application bundle—putting together word-processing, spreadsheet, presentation, HTML editing, and e-mail applications—may help explain the stunning market success of Microsoft Office suite.

This paper also contributes to an explanation of how Freeserve gained the lead over AOL as the dominant Internet service provider in the UK. Consumers in this market pay a metered charge for local telephone service. In this case, the model suggests that Freeserve's success was in part due to the fact that Freeserve provided a bundle of internet connectivity and phone service while AOL customers paid separately for phone connection and Internet connection.

2. The Model

Our model of imperfect competition is duopoly. We assume that for each component there are two competing alternatives in the market, A and B. The A and B components are only imperfect substitutes. We imagine that the 'A' components are all located at 0 while the 'B' components are all located at 1.

We further assume that the consumer only gets the value of the products if all the components are purchased. Thus, in the case of a two-good bundle, each consumer will buy one of (A_1, A_2), (A_1, B_2), (B_1, A_2), or (B_1, B_2). The value of the package is

---

[5] The first two scenarios are closely related to the work of Matutes and Regibeau (1989, 1992). Their papers ask the question whether competing firms would make their products compatible or not and whether or not it would be advantageous to sell them in bundles or not. After we have presented the model and our results, we return to explain the relationship between our papers.

sufficiently large (relative to the equilibrium prices charged) so that all consumers will purchase one or the other bundle. Each consumer is interested in exactly one unit of the bundle.

Consumers assemble the package that best suits their preferences. Each consumer purchases the bundle with the smallest total cost, where total cost is comprised of price plus a linear transportation cost. The cost of component i to consumer of type α is $-\alpha_i - p_{A_i}$ for the A_i product and $-(1 - \alpha_i) - p_{B_i}$ for the B_i product. We assume that α is uniformly distributed over the unit hypercube.

We further assume that production cost is zero, although with constant marginal costs everything perfectly translates into mark-up over cost.

In a series of models we will examine the pricing equilibrium that results for various bundle sizes and market structures. We begin with the simplest case, two firms each selling a one-component product. A one-product bundle is the limiting case of a bundle.

For firm A, demand and profits are:

$$D_A = 0.5 + 0.5 * (p_B - p_A).$$
$$\Pi_A = p_A * D_A. \tag{3}$$

For firm B, the functions are symmetric. This leads to the following first-order conditions

$$D_A - (0.5) * p_A = 0;$$
$$D_B - (0.5) * p_B = 0. \tag{4}$$

In equilibrium, prices equal 1 and the market is evenly split between firms A and B.

$$p_A = p_B; \quad D_A = D_B = 1/2; \quad p_A = p_B = 1. \tag{5}$$

More generally, this result holds true for any number of components. The only subtlety is how to interpret the nature of the competition when there are multiple components. For example, assume that there are two A components (A_1, A_2) and two B components (B_1, B_2). In this case there would be four firms, two A firms, each selling one of the A components and two B firms, each selling one of the B components.

Each consumer will purchase two components (A_1 or B_1, A_2 or B_2). He evaluates how far he is from each of the items on a component-by-component basis. For example, a customer located at $\alpha = (0.1, 0.5)$ has a strong preference for A_1 and is indifferent between A_2 and B_2. Customers are allowed to mix-and-match in forming their own bundles. Consequently, consumers optimize their purchase decision component-by-component. With a uniform distribution of α (on the unit hypercube) this leads us back to the one-component product case:

$$P_{A1} = P_{A2} = P_{B1} = P_{B2} = 1. \quad \Pi_{A1} = \Pi_{A2} = \Pi_{B1} = \Pi_{B2} = 1/2.$$

This case is the baseline from which we can evaluate the impact of coordinated pricing decisions. In this baseline case, consumers mix-and-match their preferred components and pay a price of n for their n-good customized bundle.

3. Bundle against Bundle

Next we consider the case where all the A firms coordinate their pricing and sell their product as a bundle against the B firms, who have also coordinated their pricing decisions. We assume that consumers buy only one of the two bundles.[6]

Let bundle A sell for an amount $P_A = P_{A1} + P_{A2} + \ldots + P_{An}$, and bundle B sell for P_B defined similarly. We assign Δ to represent the price premium of bundle B over bundle A, $\Delta = P_B - P_A$.

A consumer of type α will prefer to purchase the A bundle over the B bundle if

$$\alpha \cdot 1 \leqslant \frac{n + \Delta}{2}. \tag{6}$$

Recall that our consumers are uniformly distributed over the unit hypercube. With n goods in the bundle and a price difference of Δ, the demand for bundle A is thus

$$D(\Delta, n) = \frac{1}{n!} \sum_{k=0}^{n} (-1)^k \binom{n}{k} \max[0, (n + \Delta)/2 - k]^n. \tag{7}$$

For the two-good case, $n = 2$, and demand simplifies to

$$D(\Delta, 2) = (1/2)[(1 + \Delta/2)^2 - 2 \max(0, \Delta/2)^2]. \tag{7'}$$

As expected at $\Delta = 0$, demand is 0.5. At $\Delta = 2$ even the consumer located at $(1, 1)$ is just willing to 'travel' the extra distance of 2 to purchase the A bundle at $(0, 0)$ in order to save an extra \$2 in price; thus all of the consumers will go to A and demand for bundle A will be 1.

We now proceed to calculate the symmetric duopoly equilibrium.[7] Firm A maximizes Π_A:

$$\Pi_A = P_A * D(\Delta, n), \quad \Delta = P_B - P_A. \tag{8}$$

The first-order conditions are

$$D(\Delta, n) + P_A D'(\Delta, n) = 0. \tag{8'}$$

---

[6] Even if the two technologies are compatible, equilibrium prices are too high to justify buying both bundles until $n \geqslant 4$. At $n = 4$, some consumers would buy both bundles in order to mix-and-match. In the $n = 4$ equilibrium we calculate below, bundle prices are 1.5; thus, the consumer of type $\alpha = (0, 0, 1, 1)$ would buy both bundles in order to consume A_1, A_2, B_3, B_4. We simplify our analysis by assuming that the A and B products are incompatible so that consumers must buy only one or the other.

[7] We would normally call this a Bertrand complements duopoly. Although Cournot was the first to consider a pricing game among complementary products, calling this a Cournot equilibrium would be too confusing.

At the symmetric equilibrium, $\Delta = 0$ and $D(0, n) = 1/2$. Thus, $P_A = P_B = -1/2D'(0, n)$ where

$$D'(0, n) = -(1/2) * \left[\frac{1}{(n-1)!} \sum_{k=0}^{n} (-1)^k \binom{n}{k} \max[0, n/2 - k]^{n-1} \right] = 0. \qquad (9)$$

For $n = 2$, this simplifies to

$$D'(0.2) = -1/2, \quad \Rightarrow \quad P_A = 1, \quad \Pi_A = 1/2. \qquad (10)$$

Profits fall by 50 per cent. We repeat, profits fall by 50 per cent. Profits fall by 50 per cent because the aggregate bundle price has fallen by 50 per cent. The price of the entire bundle is reduced to the prior price of each of the single components. In hindsight, the intuition is relatively straightforward. Cutting price brings the same number of incremental customers as when selling individual components. So the bundle price must equal the individual price in a symmetric equilibrium.

As the number of elements in the bundle increases, the equilibrium price rises, but slowly.

$$n = 2 \Rightarrow P_A = P_B = 1.00, \quad \Pi_A = \Pi_B = 0.50.$$
$$n = 3 \Rightarrow P_A = P_B = 1.33, \quad \Pi_A = \Pi_B = 0.66.$$
$$n = 4 \Rightarrow P_A = P_B = 1.50, \quad \Pi_A = \Pi_B = 0.75.$$
$$n = 5 \Rightarrow P_A = P_B = 1.67, \quad \Pi_A = \Pi_B = 0.83.$$
$$n = 6 \Rightarrow P_A = P_B = 1.82, \quad \Pi_A = \Pi_B = 0.91.$$
$$n = 7 \Rightarrow P_A = P_B = 1.95, \quad \Pi_A = \Pi_B = 0.97.$$

Bundle against bundle is ferocious competition. To put this in perspective, in the seven-good case, if each of the goods were sold separately the price would add up to 7, rather than 1.95, and industry profits would be 3.5 times bigger. From the firms' perspective, the problem with bundle-versus-bundle competition is that the stakes are too high. Lowering the price of any one component increases the sale of all n components. The result is that the component prices fall down to such a low level that those incremental sales, all combined, are just enough to offset the loss in margin.

We can use the normal approximation to calculate the limiting result as n gets large. We know that the sum of any number of independent distributions approaches the normal. In this case, the value of each component has a uniform distribution over $[0, 1]$ with mean $1/2$ and variance $1/12$. Thus the density approaches a normal with mean $n/2$ and variance $n/12$. The density at the mean $f(\mu) = 1/\sqrt{(2\pi\sigma^2)} = 1/\sqrt{(2\pi(n/12))} = \sqrt{(6/\pi n)}$.

At the symmetric equilibrium, price is simply $1/f(\mu)$, which implies

$$P_A(n) = P_B(n) \approx \sqrt{(\pi n/6)}. \qquad (11)$$

The equilibrium bundle price rises with the square root of n when competition is over bundles, while the bundle price rises with n when components are sold individually.

4. Bundle against Components

We are now ready to consider the case of interest, bundle against components. The pricing externality suggests that the bundler will have an advantage over the component sellers. But the results of the previous section suggest that this gain may be offset by an increase in competition induced by the A firms only selling their products as bundle. Which effect dominates?

We start with the case where the A and B components are incompatible. This simplifies the analysis as consumers must choose between buying the A bundle or buying all the B components and thereby assembling a B bundle. In the Appendix, we allow a consumer to buy B components along with the A bundle (since A components are not sold individually, the reverse case isn't applicable).

Just as before, a consumer of type α will prefer to purchase the A bundle over the B bundle if

$$\alpha \cdot 1 \leq \frac{n + \Delta}{2}. \tag{12}$$

With n goods in the bundle and a price difference of Δ, again the demand for bundle A is

$$D(\Delta, n) = \frac{1}{n!} \sum_{k=0}^{n} (-1)^k \binom{n}{k} \max[0, (n + \Delta)/2 - k]^n. \tag{13}$$

The mathematics of bundle against components is very similar to bundle against bundle. The significant difference from the previous section is that there is no one firm B making a coordinated pricing decision. Instead, each of the B component firms sets its own price. Hence there is no longer a symmetric equilibrium. The first-order conditions for firm A and the n firm Bs are:

$$P_A D' = -D,$$
$$P_{B_i} D' = -(1 - D), \quad \{i = [1, n]\}. \tag{14}$$

This implies:

$$\Delta = [D(\Delta, n) - n(1 - D(\Delta, n))]/D'(\Delta, n). \tag{15}$$

Where $D(\Delta, n)$ is defined in (13) and

$$D'(\Delta, n) = -1/2 \left[\frac{1}{(n-1)!} \sum_{k=0}^{n} (-1)^k \binom{n}{k} \max[0, (n + \Delta)/2 - k]^{n-1} \right]. \tag{16}$$

The Δ that solves (15) is the equilibrium price gap between the A bundle and the B bundle. Plugging this back into (14) reveals the equilibrium values of P_A and P_{B_i}.

In general, (15) is best solved via computer. But when $n = 2$ the solution can be found directly.[8]

---

[8] Note, in calculating the solution below, we assume that $\Delta \leq 2$ and show this assumption is justified.

$$\Delta = [D - 2(1 - D)]/D'$$
$$= [3D - 2]/D', \tag{17}$$

$$D(\Delta, 2) = 1/2\left[\left(1 + \frac{\Delta}{2}\right)^2 - 2\left(\frac{\Delta}{2}\right)^2\right]$$
$$= 1/2[1 + \Delta - \Delta^2/4], \tag{18}$$

$$D'(\Delta, 2) = -1/2\left[\left(1 - \frac{\Delta}{2}\right)\right]. \tag{19}$$

$$\Delta = [1 - 3\Delta + 3\Delta^2/4]/[1 - \Delta/2] \Rightarrow$$
$$0 = 1 - 4\Delta + 5\Delta^2/4 \Rightarrow$$
$$\Delta = [4 \pm \sqrt{(16 - 5)}]/(5/2)$$
$$= [8 - 2\sqrt{(11)}]/5 = 0.273. \tag{20}$$

$$P_A = 2 * P_{B_i} - \Delta = 1.45,$$
$$P_{B_i} = 1 - \Delta/2 = 0.86. \tag{21}$$

Although the solution is harder to calculate for larger n, computer simulation is quite tractable. The results for $n = [2, 8]$ are reported in the table below:

$n = 2 \Rightarrow P_A = 1.45,\ P_{B_i} = 0.86,\ \Pi_A = 0.91,\ \Pi_{B_i} = 0.32.$

$n = 3 \Rightarrow P_A = 2.09,\ P_{B_i} = 0.88,\ \Pi_A = 1.47,\ \Pi_{B_i} = 0.26.$

$n = 4 \Rightarrow P_A = 2.84,\ P_{B_i} = 0.92,\ \Pi_A = 2.15,\ \Pi_{B_i} = 0.22.$

$n = 5 \Rightarrow P_A = 3.63,\ P_{B_i} = 0.94,\ \Pi_A = 2.88,\ \Pi_{B_i} = 0.19.$

$n = 6 \Rightarrow P_A = 4.48,\ P_{B_i} = 0.96,\ \Pi_A = 3.69,\ \Pi_{B_i} = 0.17.$

$n = 7 \Rightarrow P_A = 5.40,\ P_{B_i} = 0.99,\ \Pi_A = 4.56,\ \Pi_{B_i} = 0.15.$

$n = 8 \Rightarrow P_A = 6.36,\ P_{B_i} = 1.02,\ \Pi_A = 5.48,\ \Pi_{B_i} = 0.14.$

There are several interesting things to note. First, as expected, the bundler does much better that the sum of the uncoordinated B firms. When the bundles are small ($n = 2, 3$) the bundler does a bit worse than the first baseline case where each component is sold in an uncoordinated fashion.[9] The explanation is that the success of the bundle takes away so much market share from the B firms that their resulting equilibrium prices are so low that the A firm is worse off. But this setback is only temporary. By the time the bundle has four or more items, the bundler is doing better than previously. The gap in prices continues to grow and consequently, so does the bundler's market share.[10]

---

[9] The $n = 3$ case is a very close call. The bundling firm has a profit of 1.47 compared to an aggregate profit of 1.5 in the component-versus-component baseline case.

[10] We note that once the bundle has eight or more items the price of the B items begins to exceed 1. Hence consumers will not find it worthwhile to engage in mixed bundling.

It is also interesting that this game is not a prisoner's dilemma. While it is true that the profits of the *B* firms are very seriously depressed, they would not improve their lot by getting together and forming a rival bundle. This is because the intensity of the bundle-against-bundle competition so much reduces profits that the *B* firms are better off accepting what they get as individual players in the above equilibrium.

This suggests that the first firm to create a bundle wins. It wins in terms of profits, once the bundle has four or more items. It always wins in terms of market share. And, the victory is long-lasting. The rival firms will only hurt themselves more by forming a competitive bundle.[11]

5. Literature Review and Conclusions

Firms have many incentives to bundle, even absent competition. Bundling can help a multi-product monopolist achieve better price discrimination (Adams and Yellen 1976; McAfee, McMillan, and Whinston 1989; Bakos and Brynjolfsson 1999).[12] It can also help lower costs and lead to superior products (Salinger 1995).

Bundling can also be used as an entry-deterrence device, as first recognized by Whinston (1990). The ability to leverage a monopoly had previously been in doubt as there is little gain from bundling a monopolized good along with one sold in a competitive market.[13] The gain arises when the incumbent has market power in two (or more) goods. In Whinston's model and in related work by Aron and Wildman (1998), a monopolist's commitment to bundling makes it a tougher competitor to a one-good entrant. By committing to a bundle, the firm uses its surplus in good *A* to cross-subsidize good *B*, the one under attack. This denies market share to the entrant, often enough to deter it from entering. One qualification to these results is that if entry does occur, bundling ends up hurting the incumbent and thus there must exist some way to credibly commit to a bundling strategy.

A companion work to this paper (Nalebuff 1999) re-examines bundling as an entry deterrent using a Stackelberg pricing game. Here, too, an incumbent firm with a monopoly in several components can help protect these multi-monopolies from entry by bundling them together. This is because a one-product entrant faces a very restricted market compounded by a low incumbent price all of which makes entry much less profitable. And now credibility is not an issue as the incumbent does better using a bundle against an entrant compared to losing a head-to-head competition on one of the components.

---

[11] This, of course, doesn't take into account the fact that forming a competing bundle would also destroy the rival *A* firm's profits. Misery loves company. Or, more to the point, firms may prefer not to be in such an asymmetric position relative to a rival when there are issues of R&D financing or similar dynamic issues in a repeated game.

[12] Note that bundling as a price discrimination device works best when the items have a negative correlation in value. If the items are highly complementary and hence always bought as a package, then there is no gain from superior price discrimination.

[13] Some limited gains are possible when consumers purchase variable quantities of the two goods.

These models leave open the issue of multi-product entry (or sequential entry by independent firms). This paper helps us better to understand how bundling can change the nature of competition, post-entry. Of course it is difficult to come up with two or more products so as to have simultaneous entry. But having done so, there are much lower profits available to an entrant if the incumbent has a bundle in the market. If the challenger comes in with a bundle, everyone's profits are very depressed. If two firms come in at the same time (or there is one latent firm who becomes active with the second firm's entry), here, too, the entrants' profits are greatly reduced compared to when the incumbent sells its product as components or the incumbent is in fact two separate monopolies, each selling its one component.

The results of this paper are perhaps closest to the work of Matutes and Regibeau (1989, 1992). They consider a model with two firms each selling two goods. They ask whether these two firms would choose to make their products compatible or not and whether the firms would prefer to sell their products as a bundle or not. In our first two baseline cases the two approaches essentially converge. Consider first component-versus-component competition. If all the components are compatible, then there is no externality created by lowering the price of one. Hence there is no gain from getting the two *A* firms (or the two *B* firms) to coordinate their pricing.[14] Thus our four-firm oligopoly and their two-firm duopoly yield the same outcome. In the case of bundle-versus-bundle competition, compatibility is irrelevant as consumers cannot mix and match. The bundle-versus-bundle competition reduces the number of firms from four to two and thus is a model of duopoly. We, too, observe that bundle-versus-bundle competition leads to the lowest profits—and the result only gets worse as the bundle size grows beyond two goods.

Our third scenario, the model of a bundler versus component sellers, is where the two approaches truly diverge. We are able to focus on the coordination problem of component sellers against a bundler.[15] This is the imperfect competition extension to Cournot's multi-product monopoly model. We also see that the results from two-good bundles may turn around as the bundle grows in scope. The disadvantage of creating a two-good bundle essentially disappears when there are three goods and even becomes an advantage once there are four or more items together.

Putting all of these results together a fuller picture of bundling emerges. As power-ful as bundling is to a monopolist, the advantages are even larger in the face of actual competition or potential competition. Selling products as a bundle can raise profits absent entry, raise profits even against established but uncoordinated firms, all the

---

[14] Matutes and Regibeau do not assume that valuations are all sufficiently high so that every consumer makes a purchase. When the market is not all served, there would be a small advantage as lower prices expand the market. Because the whole market may not be served, their paper also is better designed to examine consumer welfare implications. In our case, component selling is unambiguously the best since all consumers, by mixing and matching, will end up with their most preferred package. The bundle-versus-bundle option restricts choice and therefore reduces social welfare. The bundle versus components is even worse for social welfare. This is because prices are no longer symmetric. Consequently, consumers who should naturally prefer the *B* firm products are induced to travel inefficiently far in order to get the lower price on the *A* bundle.

[15] This coordination problem doesn't arise in Matutes and Regibeau's duopoly model.

while lowering profits of existing or potential entrants, and putting these rivals in the no-win position of not wanting to form a competing bundle. The only real disadvantage of bundling is the potential cost of inefficiently including items consumers don't desire. This is less important when the items are complementary and when the marginal cost is essentially zero, as with information goods. Thus we can expect bundling to be one of the more powerful and prevalent tools, perhaps we should say weapons, in our information economy.

APPENDIX: BUNDLE AGAINST COMPONENTS

Mixed Bundles

In this Appendix we extend the results in Section 4 to consider the slightly more complicated equilibrium when consumers can purchase B items along with their A bundle. For example, a customer who is particularly well matched with WordPerfect might buy this product along with the Office bundle. (Note that in our model it is not possible to mix the other way. Since the A products are only sold as part of a bundle, any customer who wants any of the A components must buy all of them.)

Consider the choice of a consumer who is already buying the A bundle. It is worth purchasing a B component in addition to the bundle if

$$1 - \alpha_i + P_{B_i} \leq \alpha_i \Leftrightarrow \alpha_i \geq (1 + P_{B_i})/2. \qquad (A1)$$

Conversely, consider the case of a consumer who plans to purchase B_1 because he who prefers B_1 to A_1. It is still worthwhile to buy the A bundle and throw away A_1 provided

$$\alpha_2 + P_A \leq (1 - \alpha_2) + P_{B_2} \quad \alpha_2 \leq (1 + P_{B_2} - P_A)/2. \qquad (A2)$$

These two regions are depicted in Figure 17.1.

In this environment, demand adds up to more than one. For example, B_2 gets an extra demand from the upper-left-corner trapezoid (from people who buy B_2 along with the bundle) but loses a smaller triangle in the lower right from people who choose to buy B_1 along with an A bundle rather than consume B_1 along with B_2.

We calculate the equilibrium for $n = 2$. The result is quite similar to the previous case. This is not surprising as the component prices are relatively close to 1 and hence few consumers are interested in buying a bundle plus components. (Once n reaches 8 the equilibria are identical as the individual components are priced at above 1 so that none are bought in addition to a bundle.)

Since the two demands don't add up to 1, we need to calculate each separately. The notation is a bit simpler if we define $L = 1 - \Delta/2$. For the B_1 firm,

$$D_{B_1} = (1/2)L^2 + (1/8)[1 + 2 * P_{B_2} + P_{B_1} - 2P_A](1 - P_{B_1}) - (1/8)(1 - P_{B_2}). \quad (A3)$$

The equation for B_2 is symmetric. For the bundle provider

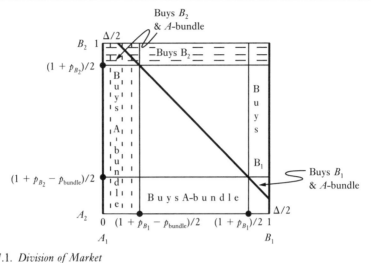

FIG. 17.1. *Division of Market*

$$D_A = 1 - 1/2L^2 + 1/8[(1 - P_{B_1})^2 + (1 - P_{B_2})^2]. \tag{A4}$$

One simplification in all this is that it turns out that D' is very simple for both types of firms

$$D'_{B_i} = -1/2$$
$$D'_A = L/2. \tag{A5}$$

In equilibrium, $P_{B_1} = P_{B_2}$ so that

$$D_{B_i} = (1/2)L^2 + (1/4)(1 - P_B)\Delta. \tag{A6}$$
$$D_A = 1 - (1/2)L^2 + (1/4)[(1 - P_B)^2].$$

The first-order conditions then reduce to

$$P_A * L/2 = 1 - L^2 + (1/4)(1 - P_A^2).$$
$$P_B/2 = L^2/2 + \Delta/4 * (1 - P_B). \tag{A7}$$

Note that now both P_A and P_{B_i} are functions only of L, which in turn is a function of Δ. And since $\Delta = 2P_{B_i} - P_A$ we have an implicit equation for Δ, the solution to which is

$$\Delta = 0.23, \quad P_A = 1.39, \quad P_{B_i} = 0.81.$$
$$D_A = 0.616, \quad D_{B_i} = 0.404.$$
$$\Pi_A = 0.856, \quad \Pi_{B_i} = 0.327. \tag{A8}$$

Once again the bundler dominates the individual component sellers. Prices for both firms are a little lower (1.39 versus 1.45 for firm A and 0.81 versus 0.86 for the B firms) as each firm can now expand the market with lower prices. The lower prices are almost exactly offset by the increase in total demand so that profits are almost unchanged. Thus, although the mathematics are more complicated, the intuition and the results are very similar to those in Section 4.

References

Adams, William J., and Yellen, Janet L. (1976). 'Commodity Bundling and the Burden of Monopoly', *Quarterly Journal of Economics* 90 (Aug.): 475–98.

Aron, Debra, and Wildman, Steven (1998). 'Effecting a Price Squeeze through Bundled Pricing', Working Paper, Northwestern University.

Bakos, Yannis, and Brynjolfsson, Eric (1999). 'Bundling Information Goods: Pricing, Profits, and Efficiency', *Management Science* (forthcoming).

Cournot, Augustin (1838). *Recherches sur les principes mathématiques de la théorie des richesses* (Paris: Hachette). English trans.: (N. Bacon, trans.), *Research into the Mathematical Principles of the Theory of Wealth* (James & Gordon, Mountain Center: Calif. 1995).

Heeb, Randal (1998). 'Innovation and Vertical Integration in Complementary Software Markets', University of Chicago Ph.D. thesis.

Kreps, David, and Scheinkman, Jose (1983). 'Quantity Precommitment and Bertrand Competition Yield Cournot Outcomes', *Bell Journal of Economics* 14(2): 326–37.

McAfee, R. Preston, McMillan, John, and Whinston, Michael D. (1989). 'Multiproduct Monopoly, Commodity Bundling, and Correlation of Values', *Quarterly Journal of Economics* 104 (May): 371–84.

Matutes, Carmen, and Regibeau, Pierre (1989). 'Standardization across Markets and Entry', *Journal of Industrial Economics* 37: 359–72.

—— —— (1992). 'Compatibility and Bundling of Complementary Goods in a Duopoly', *Journal of Industrial Economics* 40(1): 37–54.

Nalebuff, Barry (1999). 'Bundling', Working Paper available at http://papers.ssrn.com/paper.taf?abstract_id=185193.

Posner, Richard (1979). 'The Chicago School of Antitrust Analysis', *University of Pennsylvania Law Review* 127: 925.

Salinger, Michael A. (1995). 'A Graphical Analysis of Bundling', *Journal of Business* 68 (Jan.): 85–98.

Sonnenschein, Hugo (1968). 'The Dual of Duopoly Is Complementary Monopoly: or, Two of Cournot's Theories Are One', *Journal of Political Economy* 76(2): 316–18.

Whinston, M. D. (1990). 'Tying Foreclosure, and Exclusion', *American Economic Review* 80 (Sept.): 837–59.

18 On the Optimal Location of Capital

ANTHONY J. VENABLES

1. Introduction

In his paper 'The Optimum Town', Mirrlees (1972) posed the question, what is the optimal spatial organization of individuals around a town centre in which they work? He characterized the optimal consumption level and residential area to be given to individuals at different distances from the centre and pointed out that, in general, inequality of income distribution was part of the social optimum, even if all individuals are identical.

The present paper also addresses the spatial organization of activity, but whereas Mirrlees's context was urban (a town centre and surrounding residential area), this paper's is international. Mirrlees postulated the existence of a town centre surrounded by a continuum of other locations; benefits are derived from being close to the centre, but fixed land supplies mean that consumer/workers have to locate at varying distances from it. In our international context the centre is a country (or group of countries) with established manufacturing activity, and the surrounding locations are countries that trade with the centre. Our concern is not with the location of individuals—which we assume to be fixed by national boundaries—but rather with the location of industrial capital and production. There are advantages to locating close to the centre, but supplies of immobile factors mean that some industries will be located far away from it. What is the equilibrium pattern of industrial location, how does this determine the distribution of income across locations, and how might a socially optimal allocation differ from the equilibrium?

We look first at the spatial organization of production activities. The location of industry is generally determined by the interaction of industry characteristics with country characteristics. Thus, in factor endowment-based trade theory, factor intensities of goods interact with factor endowments of countries to determine the pattern of specialization, and in spatial models the transport intensity of goods interacts with the geographical position of locations (in the tradition of von Thunen 1826). In this paper we combine these elements, to show how both factor intensities'/factor endowments and transport intensities/distance from the centre jointly determine the structure of production and pattern of trade.[1] Associated with this, we show how factor prices and income levels vary across the economic space. Countries remote from the centre have lower real incomes, so our model provides an analysis of the geographical disadvantage borne by remote regions.

---

[1] This paper is complementary to Venables and Limao (1999) in which these issues are addressed in a Heckscher–Ohlin–von Thunen framework. In the present paper we have sector-specific factors and investigate factor mobility.

The second question we address is, where does industrial capital locate? If capital becomes internationally mobile, then it will be drawn into some locations at the expense of others. It may be drawn into central locations, in which case capital mobility depresses the income of poorer countries, while raising incomes in richer countries that are located close to the centre. We show that although this is perhaps the most likely outcome, it is not the only possible one. For some parameter configurations capital will move towards remote locations; capital mobility then provides a force for convergence of international income levels.

An alternative way of investigating the location of capital is to suppose that, while existing stocks of capital remain immobile, some additional capital becomes available. Where does this capital locate? Typically it goes to just a subset of regions, usually, but not necessarily, those close to the centre. Raising the supply of capital increases the set of countries receiving investment, and further benefits countries that are already recipients. However, many countries remain unaffected. The model therefore suggests that foreign direct investment will bring an uneven process of development, raising income in some countries while others are left behind. This is consistent with the observation that, in the period 1993–7, two-thirds of all foreign direct investment flows to developing countries went to just ten countries.[2]

Finally, we turn to welfare economics, and investigate the optimal location of capital. Although our model is one with no market imperfections, cross-country variations in prices and income levels create arguments for locating capital differently from the equilibrium allocation.[3] We investigate how the optimal inflow is influenced both by countries' locations and by their factor endowments.

Ingredients of the model are kept very simple—there are constant returns to scale and perfect competition in all the production activities. This means that we abstract from most of the concerns of the recent 'new economic geography' literature on the spatial location of activity.[4] In this literature the focus is on the location decisions of firms that operate under increasing returns to scale, and on the implications of positive externalities (pecuniary or technological) between firms. These externalities create a tendency for firms to cluster together, giving rise to outcomes with agglomeration of economic activity, multiple equilibria (since the location, and possibly also the size and form of the agglomeration are not uniquely determined), together with spatial lock-in of activity and locational hysteresis.

This paper has none of these elements. Quite a rich structure of results emerges, nevertheless. The main message of the paper is that capital mobility may be good for some countries, but is likely to be damaging for others. Development led by capital flows from central regions will raise incomes in some countries, but leave others unaffected. Global welfare maximization will typically put more capital in countries that are remote or that have low capital endowments than does the equilibrium.

---

[2] See Shatz and Venables (2000).

[3] There is perfect competition and no externalities of any kind. However, there are incomplete markets, insofar as factors of production are not internationally tradable.

[4] See Fujita, Krugman, and Venables (1999) for development of this approach.

2. The Model

In this section we outline the model, and in the next we analyse the equilibrium for given levels of each country's factor endowments. In Sections 4 and 5 we turn to the equilibrium and the socially optimal location of capital.

In the tradition of von Thunen (1826), our approach takes as given a central location in which there is a concentration of certain economic activities. The central location has the defining properties that: (a) there is one good (or composite of goods) that is produced only in the centre, (b) the centre imports all other tradable goods, and (c) all other locations can be arranged on a line going through the centre. Assumptions (a) and (b) are restrictive, but in line with the context of this paper. We think of the central location as the established industrial countries that export a range of high-technology products (or services) for use both in final consumption and as intermediates in production. The reason for the centre's trade pattern is not modelled, although this could easily be done by giving it the appropriate factor endowment, or some Ricardian advantage, or by modelling agglomeration forces binding production of certain goods to the centre. Assumption (c) restricts the geography of the world to be one-dimensional. We doubt that the generalization to two dimensions would change qualitative results.

Countries away from the centre are endowed with three factors of production: labour, land, and capital. They produce two goods, agriculture and manufactures, each using as inputs intermediate goods (supplied by the centre), labour, and a specific factor— land for agriculture and capital for manufactures. Both agriculture and manufactures are distinct products from the good produced by the centre.[5] Their labelling as agriculture and manufactures derives significance only insofar as we shall let capital—the specific factor in manufactures—become internationally mobile, while factors used in agriculture remain internationally immobile.

The geography of the model is provided by the fact that all goods are subject to trade costs which depend on the distance shipped. These trade costs create price functions over the space which, in equilibrium, are lined up with production costs, determining factor prices, techniques of production, and hence—together with factor endowments—the structure of production.

Turning to a more formal model description, let us assume that the three tradable goods are subscripted 0, m, and a. Good 0 is the composite produced by the centre, and goods m and a are manufactures and agriculture. The geographical space is the unit interval, points on which are labelled $z \in [0, 1]$ so, for example, $p_i(z)$ and $x_i(z)$ denote the price and production of good i at location z. We take point 0 as the central location, and look only at points to the right of the centre ($z > 0$), since the concentration of activities at 0 means that there is no interaction between economies on either side of this point.

---

[5] Thus, the manufactures may be lower-technology goods, or perhaps final products assembled using parts imported from the centre.

The central location has a predetermined pattern of trade, exporting good 0 and importing goods m and a.[6] The central prices of all goods are fixed, and are denoted $p_i(0)$.[7] Goods are subject to iceberg trade costs, so to deliver one unit of good i from location r to location z, $\tau_i(r, z) \geqslant 1$ units have to be shipped. We assume that these costs are exponential in distance, so $\tau_i(r, z) = \exp[t_i \, | \, r - z \, |]$. This means that the prices of goods at location z which are bought from the centre (good 0) or sold to it (goods m and a) are given by:

$$p_0(z) = p_0(0)\exp(t_0 z), \quad p_m(z) = p_m(0)\exp(-t_m z), \quad p_a(z) = p_a(0)\exp(-t_a z). \quad (1)$$

The consumer price of good 0 therefore increases exponentially at more remote locations, while prices of goods m and a decline, as the net export receipts from selling these goods to the centre falls. These equations define prices unless a remote country or set of countries become detached from the central price system, as would occur if they ceased to trade a good with the centre. In this paper we rule out this possibility, so all countries trade all goods with the centre and have prices determined by equation (1).[8]

Locations away from the centre, $z > 0$, are endowed with three factors, labour, capital, and land, denoted L, $K(z)$, and $N(z)$. We assume that all locations up to the edge of the economy have the same endowment of labour, set at unity, $L = 1$; stocks of capital and land may vary across space.[9] Prices of labour, capital, and land are $w(z)$, $r(z)$, and $v(z)$, creating income levels

$$y(z) = w(z) + r(z)K(z) + v(z)N(z). \quad (2)$$

Consumers at each location consume all three goods. Their preferences are described by a homothetic expenditure function, so the equality of income to expenditure is

$$y(z) = e(p_0(z), p_m(z), p_a(z))u(z), \quad (3)$$

where $u(z)$ is total utility at location z.

Each location can produce goods m and a using imported intermediates (good 0), labour, and a sector specific factor—capital for manufacturing and land for agriculture. Unit costs are expressed as $b_m(w(z), r(z), p_0(z))$ and $b_a(w(z), v(z), p_0(z))$, and equal prices, so[10]

$$p_m(z) = b_m(w(z), r(z), p_0(z)), \quad p_a(z) = b_a(w(z), v(z), p_0(z)). \quad (4)$$

Factor market clearing at each location is given by

---

[6] These goods can also be produced in the centre, although the centre is a net importer.

[7] In many of the experiments we conduct supplies to and demands from the centre will change. We assume that the centre is large enough for these changes to have no effect on prices.

[8] The price of good a (resp m) is set as in equation (1) at each location, z^*, providing locations $z \geqslant z^*$ are, collectively, exporters of good a (resp m) to the centre. We assume that endowments and preferences are such that this holds. A more general structure in which zones with different trade patterns form is investigated in Venables and Limao (1999).

[9] The assumption that labour is uniformly distributed is of no consequence, since there are constant returns to scale in all activities and goods prices are fixed.

[10] The presence of sector-specific factors ensures that all locations produce both goods.

$$1 = x_m(z) \frac{\partial b_m(w, r, p_0)}{\partial w} + x_a(z) \frac{\partial b_a(w, v, p_0)}{\partial w},$$

$$K(z) = x_m(z) \frac{\partial b_m(w, r, p_0)}{\partial r},$$

$$N(z) = x_a(z) \frac{\partial b_a(w, v, p_0)}{\partial v}. \tag{5}$$

Given product prices, equilibrium factor prices and production are determined directly from (4) and (5).

3. The Spatial Organization of Production

Each country's structure of production and trade is determined by its factor endowment and by its location. The clearest way to see the interaction of these elements is to show how the equilibrium production structure varies across countries, which we do by totally differentiating the equilibrium with respect to location, z; the proportionate changes in variables with respect to z are denoted by $\hat{\ }$. Moving to more remote locations increases the price of good 0 at rate t_0, and decreases those of a and m at rate t_i, i.e. $\hat{p}_0 = t_0$, $\hat{p}_i = -t_i$, $i = a, m$ (see equation (1)). Since prices equal unit costs, factor price changes are related to goods price changes according to $\hat{p}_m = \alpha_m \hat{w} + \beta_m \hat{r} + \gamma_m \hat{p}_0$ and $\hat{p}_a = \alpha_a \hat{w} + \beta_a \hat{v} + \gamma_a \hat{p}_0$, where α_i, β_i, γ_i denote the shares of labour, the specific factor (capital or land), and intermediates in the costs of each industry ($\alpha_i + \beta_i + \gamma_i = 1$). Combining these ingredients, gives the following expression for spatial variations in the wage in each sector

$$\hat{w}_m = \frac{(\hat{K} - \hat{L}_m)\beta_m/\sigma_m - (t_m + \gamma_m t_0)}{\alpha_m + \beta_m}, \quad \hat{w}_a = \frac{(\hat{N} - \hat{L}_a)\beta_a/\sigma_a - (t_a + \gamma_a t_0)}{\alpha_a + \beta_a}, \tag{6}$$

where full employment of the specific factors is assumed, σ_i is the elasticity of substitution,[11] L_i is employment in the sector, and w_i the sectoral wage. Since labour is intersectorally mobile wages in the two sectors are equal, so we equate these expressions and use labour market clearing to derive the following expression for the change in the share of employment in manufacturing:

$$\frac{\hat{\mu}}{1 + \mu} \left[\frac{\beta_m}{(\alpha_m + \beta_m)\sigma_m} + \frac{\mu\beta_a}{(\alpha_a + \beta_a)\sigma_a} \right]$$

$$= \frac{\beta_m \hat{K}}{(\alpha_m + \beta_m)\sigma_m} - \frac{\beta_a \hat{N}}{(\alpha_a + \beta_a)\sigma_a} + \left[\frac{t_a + \gamma_a t_0}{\alpha_a + \beta_a} - \frac{t_m + \gamma_m t_0}{\alpha_m + \beta_m} \right], \tag{7}$$

---

[11] We assume that capital and labour are separable from the intermediate input, so elasticities of substitution are implicitly defined by $(\hat{L}_m - \hat{K}) = \sigma_m(\hat{r} - \hat{w})$, $(\hat{L}_a - \hat{N}) = \sigma_a(\hat{v} - \hat{w})$.

where μ is the ratio of manufacturing to agricultural employment, $\mu(z) \equiv L_m(z)/L_a(z)$.

This expression tells us how manufacturing employment—and hence the structure of production and trade—changes as we move to locations further from the centre. It depends both on distance, as captured by the terms in transport costs, and on variation in the endowments of specific factors, as given by the terms in $\hat{K}$ and $\hat{N}$. Factor endowment variations enter as would be expected—more capital abundant locations have a higher share of employment in manufacturing. The effects of factor endowment variations are larger the greater the share of specific factors in production (β_m and β_a), and the smaller the elasticities of substitution between factors (σ_m and σ_a).

Transport costs are contained in the final term in square brackets on the right-hand side. We call the two terms in these brackets the 'transport intensities' of the goods, and say that agriculture is more transport intensive than manufactures if,

$$\textit{agriculture relatively transport intensive:} \quad \frac{t_a + \gamma_a t_0}{\alpha_a + \beta_a} > \frac{t_m + \gamma_m t_0}{\alpha_m + \beta_m}. \tag{8}$$

These expressions contain the costs of shipping the final good and imported intermediate inputs (input share weighted), expressed relative to the share of immobile inputs in production (the denominators). The effect of distance from the centre on the structure of production is given by the difference in the transport intensities of the two sectors (equation (7)). As would be expected, the more transport-intensive sector is located closer to the centre, so if manufacturing is transport unintensive and there is no variation in endowments, then $\hat{\mu} > 0$.

This analysis generalizes von Thunen's zones of specialization. In his model there is a single immobile factor, land, so that each location becomes fully specialized. Here there are three immobile factors, ensuring that locations are not fully specialized, but instead the production mix varies smoothly with more remote locations having a higher share of employment in the less transport-intensive sector, unless offset by variations in factor endowments. If endowments do vary, then equation (7) tells us how factor endowments and locational effects combine to determine production.

We can also see how factor prices vary across locations. Expressions for the wage are given in equation (6) and analogous equations for returns to specific factors take the form,

$$\hat{r} = \frac{(\hat{L}_m - \hat{K})\alpha_m/\sigma_m - (t_m + \gamma_m t_0)}{\alpha_m + \beta_m}, \quad \hat{v} = \frac{(\hat{L}_a - \hat{N})\alpha_a/\sigma_a - (t_a + \gamma_a t_0)}{\alpha_a + \beta_a}. \tag{9}$$

Holding endowments of specific factors uniform it is apparent that variations in these prices depend just on transport intensities. If manufacturing is less transport intensive (so $\hat{\mu} > 0$), then:

$$\hat{v} < -\frac{t_a + \gamma_a t_0}{\alpha_a + \beta_a} < \hat{w} < -\frac{t_m + \gamma_m t_0}{\alpha_m + \beta_m} < \hat{r}. \tag{10}$$

These inequalities are as would be expected from a specific-factors model. Changes in the wage lie between changes in goods prices (as captured by transport-intensity measures), while changes in the prices of the sector-specific factors lie outside them.[12] Notice that the nominal wage and return to land are certainly falling, although the return to capital (or generally, the specific factor in the transport-unintensive sector) could increase with distance.

The analysis of capital mobility to which we turn in the next section depends on the behaviour of $\hat{r}$, and in particular whether r is higher or lower at more remote locations. From equation (9) with (7) we can establish that $\hat{r} > 0$ if and only if

$$\frac{\beta_a}{(\alpha_a + \beta_a)\sigma_a}\left[\hat{N} + \mu\left(\hat{K} + \frac{(t_m + \gamma_m t_0)\sigma_m}{\alpha_m}\right)\right] + \frac{t_m + \gamma_m t_0}{\alpha_m} < \frac{t_a + \gamma_a t_0}{\alpha_a + \beta_a}. \quad (11)$$

This can be written more informatively if endowments of capital and land are uniform. We can then delineate two cases, which we refer to as case I and case II. In case I the return to capital is lower at more remote locations;

$$\text{Case I:} \quad \hat{r} < 0 \text{ if } \frac{t_m + \gamma_m t_0}{\alpha_m}\left(1 + \frac{\sigma_m \mu \beta_a}{\sigma_a(\alpha_a + \beta_a)}\right) > \frac{t_a + \gamma_a t_0}{\alpha_a + \beta_a}. \quad (12)$$

In case II, although the wage is declining, the return to capital is increasing, so:

$$\text{Case II:} \quad \hat{r} > 0 \text{ if } \frac{t_m + \gamma_m t_0}{\alpha_m}\left(1 + \frac{\sigma_m \mu \beta_a}{\sigma_a(\alpha_a + \beta_a)}\right) < \frac{t_a + \gamma_a t_0}{\alpha_m + \beta_m}. \quad (13)$$

A necessary, but not sufficient condition for case II is that manufacturing is less transport intensive than agriculture. Being less transport intensive implies a higher share of employment at more distant locations, raising demand for capital. But the inherent transport cost penalty of remoteness depresses all factor prices, so only if demand for capital increases sharply enough will r increase.

Figures 18.1 and 18.2 illustrate equilibria in each case. They are constructed with manufacturing relatively transport unintensive and with the same factor endowments everywhere. (This and subsequent figures come from simulation of the model; details are given in the Appendix.) In case I the difference in transport intensities of the two goods is quite small, so that all factor prices decline with remoteness. In case II the transport intensity of agriculture is higher, so it contracts more rapidly, raising demand for capital and the rate of return. The dashed lines in the figures are the paths of value added in each sector, the gradients of which are given by the transport intensities.

The inequalities which define cases I and II contain endogenous variables—factor shares, and employment in manufacturing relative to agriculture, $\mu(z)$. It is possible, therefore, that $r(z)$ is not monotonic, and that the economy switches between case I and case II at different locations. Thus, if technology is Cobb–Douglas (so factor shares are constant) and manufacturing is transport unintensive (so $\mu(z)$ is increasing, increasing the left-hand sides of inequalities (12) and (13)), the economy may switch

---

[12] See Dixit and Norman (1980).

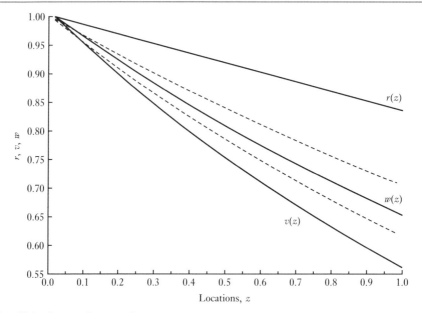

FIG. 18.1. *Factor prices, case I*

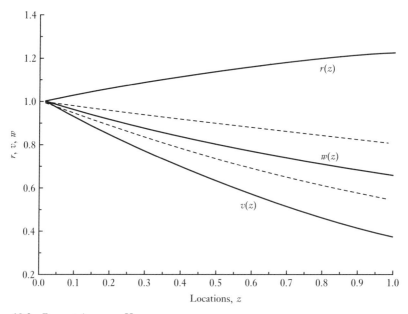

FIG. 18.2. *Factor prices, case II*

from case II to case I. The function $r(z)$ then attains a maximum in the interior of the economy.[13]

These figures and discussion refer to nominal factor prices, but the cost of living also varies across locations, tending to increase insofar as there is consumption of imports from the centre, and to decrease because of consumption of goods *a* and *m*. However, if all locations have the same endowments then utility declines monotonically with distance from the centre. The terms of trade deteriorate, as import prices rise and unit export receipts fall.

4. The Location of Capital

With this as background, we now turn to the location of capital. If capital is allowed to be internationally mobile, then where will it locate? And how does international mobility of capital change the structure of production, factor prices, and international income inequalities?

Capital internationally mobile. Our first experiment is simply to let all existing stocks of capital become mobile. We assume that capital bears no 'transport costs' of any type and that recipients of capital income are immobile, in which case capital mobility equalizes the rate of return in all countries, so $\hat{r} = 0$. Inequality (11) defines the dividing line between $\hat{r} > 0$ and $\hat{r} < 0$, so making this hold with equality characterizes the equilibrium location of capital. In the case when land is uniformly distributed ($\hat{N} = 0$) we have,

$$\frac{\mu \beta_a \hat{K}}{(\alpha_a + \beta_a)\sigma_a} = \frac{t_a + \gamma_a t_0}{\alpha_a + \beta_a} - \frac{t_m + \gamma_m t_0}{\alpha_m}\left[1 + \frac{\sigma_m \mu \beta_a}{(\alpha_a + \beta_a)\sigma_a}\right]. \tag{14}$$

Outcomes depend on whether case I or case II applies. In case I, $\hat{K} < 0$, so capital is drawn from remote regions into more central ones. Consequently manufacturing activity increases in regions close to the centre, while more remote regions become more dependent on agriculture. Conversely, in case II, manufacturing's transport intensity is very low (relative to agriculture's) and remote regions are relatively specialized in manufactures. Capital moves from central locations to remote ones, the intuitive reason being that the high transport intensity of agriculture causes low wages, raising the return to capital.

The two cases have quite different implications for international income distribution. As capital is added to a location so the wage is increased and returns to both capital and land decreased. Case I therefore reduces wages in remote areas, widening wage inequalities. In case II the reverse happens.

Results are summarized in Table 18.1. The top section of the table relates the share of manufacturing employment, μ, to transport intensity, under conditions of fixed (and uniform) location of capital; whether remote locations are more or less specialized in

---

[13] This is driving the concavity of $r(z)$ which is apparent in Figure 18.2.

TABLE 18.1. *Transport intensities, the structure of production, and the location of capital:* $(\hat{N} = 0)$

Capital immobile: $(\hat{K} = 0)$	$\dfrac{t_m + \gamma_m t_0}{\alpha_m + \beta_m} > \dfrac{t_a + \gamma_a t_0}{\alpha_a + \beta_a}$ $\hat{\mu} < 0$		$\dfrac{t_m + \gamma_m t_0}{\alpha_m + \beta_m} < \dfrac{t_a + \gamma_a t_0}{\alpha_a + \beta_a}$ $\hat{\mu} > 0$	
Capital mobile:	$\dfrac{t_m + \gamma_m t_0}{\alpha_m} > \dfrac{t_a + \gamma_a t_0}{\alpha_a + \beta_a}$ $\hat{\mu} < 0$		$\dfrac{t_m + \gamma_m t_0}{\alpha_m} < \dfrac{t_a + \gamma_a t_0}{\alpha_a + \beta_a}$ $\hat{\mu} > 0$	
	Case I $\dfrac{t_m + \gamma_m t_0}{\alpha_m}\left(1 + \dfrac{\sigma_m \mu \beta_a}{\sigma_a(\alpha_a + \beta_a)}\right)$ $> \dfrac{t_a + \gamma_a t_0}{\alpha_a + \beta_a}$ $\hat{K} < 0$		*Case II* $\dfrac{t_m + \gamma_m t_0}{\alpha_m}\left(1 + \dfrac{\sigma_m \mu \beta_a}{\sigma_a(\alpha_a + \beta_a)}\right)$ $< \dfrac{t_a + \gamma_a t_0}{\alpha_a + \beta_a}$ $\hat{K} > 0$	

Agriculture more t-int: $(t_a + \gamma_a t_0)/(t_m + \gamma_m t_0)$ larger $\rightarrow$

manufacturing depends on relative transport intensities of products, as discussed in Section 3. The bottom section gives the condition for mobile capital to be drawn into either central or remote locations, as derived from equation (14). The middle section reports what happens to manufacturing employment when capital is mobile (derived from (7) and (9)); it indicates that the share of employment in manufacturing depends on transport intensities, as is the case when capital is immobile. However, the manufacturing transport intensity now has α_m rather than $\alpha_m + \beta_m$ in the denominator, since it measures the share of the immobile factor in production.

The relationship between the conditions is given by the position of the vertical lines in each section of the table, and movements to the right across the table are associated with more transport-intensive agriculture (higher values of $(t_a + \gamma_a t_0)/(t_m + \gamma_m t_0)$). Thus, if parameters are such that $\hat{\mu} = 0$ under capital immobility (top section), then mobile capital will be drawn into central regions ($\hat{K} < 0$, bottom section), and as a consequence central regions will come to have more manufacturing employment than remote ones ($\hat{\mu} < 0$, middle section).

The location of new capital. A second way of approaching the effect of international capital mobility is to suppose that initial endowments of industrial capital are fixed, but some additional capital becomes available. Where will it locate? Figures 18.3 and 18.4 are analogous to Figures 18.1 and 18.2, but now give factor prices after an additional amount of capital (equal to 20 per cent of the initial level) has become available, and has been allocated to countries with the highest return; solid lines are the new equilibrium factor prices, and the dotted lines are the initial factor prices (identical to those illustrated on Figures 18.1 and 18.2).

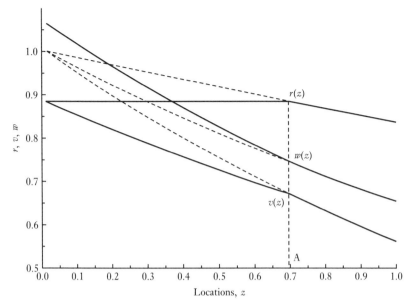

FIG. 18.3. *Extra capital, case I*

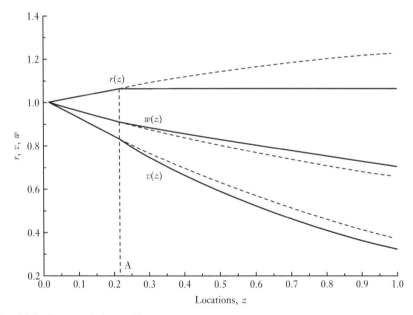

FIG. 18.4. *Extra capital, case II*

In case I (Figure 18.3), capital goes to locations close to the centre, those to the left of point A; the wage in these locations is bid up and the rate of return falls, as does the return to land, $v(z)$. The interesting point to note from the figure is that making capital mobile only affects some locations—more remote locations beyond A are left untouched. Letting more capital become available (or equivalently, reducing the supply price at which it becomes available) shifts point A to the right, so a further set of locations become affected, while points to the left of A experience a further capital inflow and wage increase. The message is that development driven by capital mobility does not benefit all countries, but instead favours locations that are close to existing centres of economic activity.

It is worth recalling that we have assumed that goods prices are fixed. However, the extra capital increases production of manufacturing, reduces production of agriculture, and increases demand for the intermediate, good 0. If prices were flexible these quantity changes would also create terms-of-trade effects that might benefit remote locations specialized in agricultural production.

Case II (Figure 18.4) is the converse. In the initial situation r is high in the remote locations, and as a consequence capital flows first to these locations, bidding up the wage. It therefore narrows international wage differences. Increasing the volume of capital flows expands the set of capital-importing regions (shifting point A to the left) and further raises wages in capital importing regions.

Finally, recall that the initial $r(z)$ is not necessarily monotonic. As discussed in Section 3 there is a set of parameters for which $r(z)$ has an interior maximum in which case capital will go first to a zone of intermediate locations, the width of which increases the more capital is made available.

Concluding this section, there are several main points. Foreign investment flows will not generally go to all countries, but instead will tend to concentrate in just a subset. Which countries receive capital depends on the transport intensity of sectors that use internationally mobile capital relative to the transport intensity of other sectors, but it is likely to be locations that are close to the centre rather than remote locations that benefit.

5. The Optimal Location of Capital

The equilibrium allocation of capital is Pareto efficient but, as we have seen, may well result in outcomes that magnify inequalities in world income. Why might a utilitarian social-welfare-maximizing allocation differ from the equilibrium? Although the value of the extra output produced by capital is simply $r(z)$, adding capital changes factor prices and real incomes, and these income changes may have different values in different locations. For example, the cost of living varies across locations; other things being equal, it is better to raise income in a location with a low cost-of-living index. And if the marginal social valuation of income is decreasing in income, then it is better to raise income in low-income countries. Furthermore, these arguments may be magnified by cross-location differences in endowments and preferences.

To formulate the welfare-maximizing problem we need to be more explicit about who receives income flows; the model contains three sources of factor income flows, and these must be assigned to individuals. We do this by assuming that a representative individual in location z receives all the income in the economy, minus payments on imports of industrial capital, denoted $\tilde{K}(z) \geqslant 0$. The individual's income is therefore $y(z) - r(z)\tilde{K}(z)$, national rather than domestic income. Notice that this means that the locally owned *endowment* is now defined as the total amount used in production minus capital imports, $K(z) - \tilde{K}(z)$. We shall assume that all capital imports are supplied by individuals located in the centre, who therefore receive flow of income from country z of $r(z)\tilde{K}(z)$.

We take as welfare criterion

$$W = \int_0^1 \left[\varphi\left(\frac{y(z) - r(z)\tilde{K}(z)}{e(z)} \right) + r(z)\tilde{K}(z) \right] dz. \tag{15}$$

The first term inside the square brackets is location z national income deflated by the cost of living index (the unit expenditure function from equation (3)) within a strictly increasing welfare function $\phi(\ )$. The second term is the return to the centrally located holders of mobile industrial capital, for whom the marginal social value of income is unity.

The task is now to allocate a fixed amount of capital, $\int_0^1 \tilde{K}(z)dz$, across locations z to maximize this objective, with $\tilde{K}(z) \geqslant 0$. A necessary condition for optimality is that the marginal value of capital inflow, λ, should be the same in all countries that receive some inflow, and less than or equal to this value in locations that receive no inflow. Differentiating (15) the marginal value of capital inflow is,

$$\lambda(z) = \frac{\varphi'(z)}{e(z)} \left[\frac{\partial y(z)}{\partial K(z)} - r(z) \right] + r(z) + \left[1 - \frac{\varphi'(z)}{e(z)} \right] \tilde{K}(z) \frac{\partial r(z)}{\partial K(z)}. \tag{16}$$

This is interpreted as follows. The first term is zero, since the rate of return equals the marginal contribution of capital to domestic income. The second term, $r(z)$, is the value of the extra output produced by adding a unit of capital to country z. In addition, in the third term, adding industrial capital to a country reduces the rate of return, $\partial r(z)/\partial K(z) < 0$. This is a terms of trade change, the value of which depends on the total amount of foreign investment, $\tilde{K}(z)$. A reduction in $r(z)$ is a benefit to recipients of capital inflow and a loss to the central suppliers of capital, the net value of which depends on marginal valuations of income in the centre and the recipient. The former is unity, and the latter $\varphi'(z)/e(z)$. This will be greater than unity insofar as the cost-of-living index is decreasing with remoteness, or if income is falling and the welfare function ϕ is strictly concave.

Figure 18.5 illustrates factor prices for the optimal allocation (for case I, with ϕ strictly concave, and details given in the Appendix). The optimum is given by the solid lines, and the dashed lines give the equilibrium, when the same amount of capital is allocated to equalize the return to capital across countries.[14] As expected, the optimum allocates

---

[14] Enough capital is being supplied for all locations to have some capital inflow in the equilibrium.

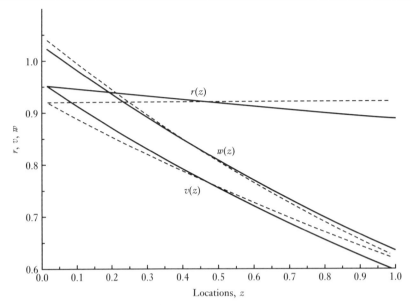

FIG. 18.5. *Optimal location of capital*

relatively more capital to remote locations than central ones. This shows up in the fact that $r(z)$ is declining (as compared to the equilibrium, where it is flat), and the wage is declining less rapidly than in the equilibrium. Qualitatively, the same picture holds if ϕ is linear in which case differences between the equilibrium and the optimum are driven just by cost-of-living differences.

Case II is qualitatively similar. Although the equilibrium now puts more capital in remote regions, it is still the case that both the cost of living and real income are lower in these regions. This direction of bias is therefore as in case I, so the optimum supplies more capital to remote regions than does the equilibrium.

What happens if countries differ not just in location, but in other respects, such as their endowment? Figure 18.6 looks at the optimum in a case where a set of intermediate countries own no capital, so $K(z) - \tilde{K}(z) = 0$; dashed lines are equilibrium factor prices with full international capital mobility, and solid ones mark factor prices when capital is optimally allocated. We see that once capital is optimally allocated the wage in these locations is higher (and rate of return lower) than elsewhere, meaning that these locations are receiving a particularly large amount of capital inflow. There are two reasons for this: one is that they are poor, so curvature of the $\phi(\ )$ function increases the value of capital. The second, and quantitatively more important reason, can be seen from inspection of the expression for the marginal value of capital imports (equation (16)). The terms-of-trade effect is more important the larger are capital imports; giving a country a low initial endowment will tend to make imported capital a larger share of the overall capital stock, enabling the country to benefit more from the terms-of-trade gain. Putting the same point differently, the capital inflow reduces returns to

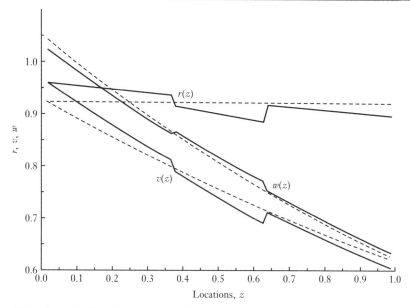

F<small>IG</small>. 18.6. *Optimal allocation of capital with varying endowments*

specific factors and raises the wage; the smaller the amount of specific factors owned by a country, the larger will be its overall income gain.

6. Concluding Comments

The location of production has a direct bearing on manufacturing wages and real income levels in all countries of the world. In this paper a simple geographical structure has been developed in which this locational issue can be addressed. In the structure remote countries have systematically lower wages and per capita income levels than do countries close to an established economic centre, and have a pattern of specialization depending on both their location and their factor endowment.

Does capital mobility benefit or hurt these low-income countries? A precise condition is found to determine which way it goes, and the likelihood is that capital is drawn to countries that are close to the centre, so are already relatively rich. This may take the form of capital moving from remote countries to more central ones, causing wages in remote countries to fall. Alternatively, if there is an increase in the overall supply of capital, then this additional capital will locate in countries close to the centre, benefiting them and leaving remote regions unaffected—a finding consistent with observed flows of foreign direct investment. This equilibrium outcome contrasts with a socially optimal outcome in which the poorest economies are allocated greater capital stocks.

APPENDIX

All figures are constructed with Cobb–Douglas preferences with 20 per cent of expenditure going to good 0 and 40 per cent to each of goods m and a. Each location is endowed with 1 unit of labour, 1 unit of land, and 0.5 units of industrial capital, unless otherwise stated. Technologies are Cobb–Douglas with labour share in costs of $\alpha_i = 0.5$, specific factor share of $\beta_i = 0.25$, and intermediate input share of $\gamma_i = 0.25$.

Transport costs are: Case I: $t_0 = 0.25$, $t_m = 0.2$, $t_a = 0.3$; Case II: $t_0 = 0.25$, $t_m = 0.1$, $t_a = 0.4$.

The economy is 1 unit distance from centre to edge, so to deliver 1 unit of good 0 from centre to edge requires that 1.284 ($= \exp(0.25)$) units be shipped.

In Figures 18.3 and 18.4 an amount of capital equal to 20 per cent of the initial stock is made available and allocated to countries with the highest return.

In Figure 18.5 individuals in each country own 0.15 units of industrial capital, assumed immobile. The remaining capital stock is allocated to maximize W (equation (15)), in which the function ϕ is iso-elastic, with elasticity 0.25, and level scaled such that the marginal utility of income at the location closest to the centre is unity. Figure 18.6 is similar, except that for an intermediate set of location individuals own 0 units of industrial capital; correspondingly more is optimally allocated by a central agent.

References

Dixit, A. K., and V. Norman (1980), *The Theory of International Trade* (Cambridge: CUP).

Fujita, M., P. Krugman, and A. J. Venables (1999), *The Spatial Economy; Cities, Regions and International Trade* (Cambridge, Mass.: MIT Press).

Leamer, E., and J. Levinsohn (1995), 'International Trade Theory; the Evidence', in G. Grossman and K. Rogoff (eds.), *Handbook of International Economics*, iii (Amsterdam: Elsevier).

Limao, N., and A. J. Venables (1999), 'Infrastructure, Geographical Disadvantage and Transport Costs' *Policy research working paper* no 2257, World Bank, Washington, DC.

Mirrlees, J. (1972), 'The Optimum Town', *Swedish Journal of Economics* 74: 114–36.

Samuelson, P. A. (1983), 'Thünen at Two Hundred', *Journal of Economic Literature* 21: 1468–88.

Shatz, H., and A. J. Venables (2000), 'The Geography of International Investment', in G. L. Clark and M. Feldman (eds.), *The Oxford Handbook of Economic Geography*, forthcoming (Oxford: OUP).

Venables, A. J., and N. Limao (1999), 'Geographical Disadvantage: a Heckscher–Ohlin–von Thunen Model of International Specialisation', CEPR dp no. 2305.

Von Thünen, J. H. (1826), '*Der Isolierte Staaat in Beziehung auf Landtschaft und Nationalokonomie*, Hamburg. (English trans. by C. M. Wartenburg, *Von Thünen's Isolated State* (Oxford: Pergamon Press).

NAME INDEX

SUBJECT INDEX